THE *unofficial* GUIDE® TO New Orleans

6TH EDITION

ALSO AVAILABLE FROM JOHN WILEY & SONS, INC.:

Beyond Disney: The Unofficial Guide to Universal, SeaWorld, and the Best of Central Florida

Mini-Mickey: The Pocket-Sized Unofficial Guide to Walt Disney World

The Unofficial Guide to Adventure Travel in Alaska

The Unofficial Guide to California with Kids

The Unofficial Guide to Central Italy: Florence, Rome, Tuscany, and Umbria

The Unofficial Guide to Chicago

The Unofficial Guide to Cruises

The Unofficial Guide to Disneyland

The Unofficial Guide to England

The Unofficial Guide to Hawaii

The Unofficial Guide to Ireland

The Unofficial Guide to Las Vegas

The Unofficial Guide to London

The Unofficial Guide to Maui

The Unofficial Guide to Mexico's Best Beach Resorts

The Unofficial Guide to New York City

The Unofficial Guide to Paris

The Unofficial Guide to San Francisco

The Unofficial Guide to Walt Disney World

The Unofficial Guide to Walt Disney World for Grown-Ups

The Unofficial Guide to Walt Disney World with Kids

The Unofficial Guide to Washington, D.C.

THE *unofficial* GUIDE® TO New Orleans

6TH EDITION

EVE ZIBART *with* TOM FITZMORRIS
and WILL COVIELLO

Please note that prices fluctuate in the course of time and that travel information changes under the impact of many factors that influence the travel industry. We therefore suggest that you write or call ahead for confirmation when making your travel plans. Every effort has been made to ensure the accuracy of information throughout this book, and the contents of this publication are believed to be correct at the time of printing. Nevertheless, the publishers cannot accept responsibility for errors or omissions, for changes in details given in this guide, or for the consequences of any reliance on the information provided by the same. Assessments of attractions and so forth are based upon the authors' own experiences; therefore, descriptions given in this guide necessarily contain an element of subjective opinion, which may not reflect the publisher's opinion or dictate a reader's own experience on another occasion. Readers are invited to write the publisher with ideas, comments, and suggestions for future editions.

Published by:
John Wiley & Sons, Inc.
111 River Street
Hoboken, NJ 07030-5774

Produced by Menasha Ridge Press

Cover design by Michael J. Freeland

Interior design by Vertigo Design

ISBN 978-0-470-38001-7

Manufactured in the United States of America

5 4 3 2 1

CONTENTS

LIST *of* MAPS

ABOUT *the* AUTHOR *and Contributors*

EVE ZIBART is a native of Nashville who began her career as a reporter at age 17 at *The Tennessean* in Nashville. She moved to Washington, and the *Washington Post,* in 1977 and served as critic, editor, and columnist at various times for the newspaper's "Style," "Weekend," "TV," "Metro," and "Magazine" sections. For the past decade, she has roamed Washington's restaurants, carryouts, bars, and nightclubs, with the occasional foray into museums and legitimate theater, first for the *Post* and now for *Washingtonian* magazine. In addition to her *Post* columns, Eve has written or cowritten eight books and regularly appears in a variety of lifestyle magazines. In spite of God's repeated physical admonishments, Eve continues to play a variety of sports, split her own firewood, and haul rocks into what she hopes will become a Japanese garden within her lifetime.

TOM FITZMORRIS has written a weekly restaurant review column in New Orleans for more than 30 years. He is also the host of the daily three-hour *Food Show* on WSMB radio, and he publishes the *New Orleans Menu Daily* at **www.nomenu.com.** He has written 20 dining guides and cookbooks about the New Orleans food scene. Tom was born on Mardi Gras.

WILL COVIELLO is the arts and entertainment editor for *Gambit Weekly* in New Orleans. He has covered entertainment, arts, culture, and news for various local and national publications. He came to New Orleans for Mardi Gras in 1992 and never left.

ACKNOWLEDGMENTS

SCORES OF NEW ORLEANIANS were gracious enough to talk about their city, both on and off the record, and I thank them all, especially Lea Sinclair, Diane and Charlie Genre, and Macon and Hill Riddle.

Everybody needs a place to hang out: thanks to Jeanine, Julie and Kim, Lisa, Paul, Tiffany, Michael, Simone, Marc, Karen, Amy, Sean, Rudy, Chris, Marco, Shannon, and Char.

Very special thanks to tour guide and amateur historian Noah Robert for more good stories than I could fit in; to Grace Rogers for taking on the chauffeuring duty; and to Tom Fitzmorris and Will Coviello for their contributions.

My love as always to my brother, Michael (Pimm's and kisses), Margaret, Dodger, and Terry. Thanks to Bob, Molly, Holly, Marie, Steve, Annie, Lady Vowell Smith, and Jan Carroll for pushing forward and reading behind.

And—always and everywhere—Margi Smith and Joe Hemingway, the best dinner companions any traveler could ever ask for. Hold the table, darlings.

—*Eve Zibart*

INTRODUCTION

LET *the* GOOD TIMES ROLL

A FINE SPRING EVENING IN JACKSON SQUARE. As the sun gradually lowers, the shadows of St. Louis Cathedral and the Cabildo stretch across the flagstones, brushing the tables of the tarot readers; young couples with souvenir hurricane cups stand around a man playing saxophone, its case open in front of him.

And there it is, the mystique of New Orleans in a single vignette: empire, religion, music, voodoo, and alcohol. *Laissez les bons temps rouler*—let the good times roll.

And yet there are fewer and fewer artists or even mule-drawn carriages gathered in the square. Many residents say that what passes for "good times" is rolling too long and too strong these days—especially among college students and young workers. Post-Katrina rebuilding in the French Quarter, particularly along Bourbon Street, has increased the "touristy" factor—strip joints, rude- and perverse-T-shirt shops, two-for-one or even three-for-one drink offers—at the expense of mom-and-pop establishments. And although many visitors assume money spent there "trickles down" to the rest of the city, most of it goes to keeping the beer resupplied and the strippers in stockings. There is a battle raging for the heart of New Orleans, laid bare throughout the North Ward, Lakeview, and elsewhere; and for its soul, most visibly in and around the French Quarter. And while it is not a contest between good and evil, at least not in the classical sense, it will, in the next few years, determine whether the character of this unique city is lost, restored, or permanently altered.

That the character of the Vieux Carré has already changed is clear from a few hours' acquaintance. An odd confluence of factors—renovation of some older houses into upscale condominiums and the gradual decline of others; a much-publicized increase in street crime; and heavy investment by outside commercial interests in redevelopment, frequently uprooting smaller local businesses—has reduced the number of the French Quarter's permanent residents from about 15,000 a generation ago to fewer than 3,300 today (and that was before the hurricane sisters' unwelcome visits). City officials have made impressive efforts to relocate the homeless and the handout-seekers, but the near-empty streets and parks are just as telling to veteran visitors.

A high tide of cheap-souvenir and T-shirt shops has swamped Bourbon Street, and glossy, private club-style strip joints, several bankrolled from out of town, are squeezing out the older, more authentic burlesque houses. At the same time, the number of bars offering heavily amplified rock and blues music, their doors open and competing for volume dominance, makes the retreat of jazz and Dixieland more obvious. Sit-down bars that specialized in classic New Orleans cocktails such as hurricanes and Sazeracs, touristy though they may have seemed before, now appear almost quaintly sophisticated when you compare them to the carryout frozen margarita and daiquiri counters with crayon-colored mixes spinning in laundromat-like rows.

Yes, souvenir shops are brighter than bars, but they certainly have less character. Sure, live blues is great, but it's more Texan than Louisianan—and increasingly it's classic rock you hear, not blues or even the canned zydeco of a few years ago. There's even a bull-riding country-and-western music hall next to a barbecue joint from North Carolina (and around the corner from a "Brazilian" steak house). Mardi Gras, once the most elegant and elaborate of festivities, has become the world's largest frat party, its traditions degraded, its legends distorted, and its principal actors, the Grand Krewes, overshadowed by the mobs of drinking and disrobing "spectators." Several of the oldest and most prestigious krewes have withdrawn from the celebration, and travel agents say that as many residents flee New Orleans during Carnival as tourists come in.

Altogether, New Orleans is teetering on the verge of becoming a parody of itself, a simulacrum à la Epcot or Busch Gardens Williamsburg. Nowadays the Mississippi riverfront is a microcosm of the city's spirit (for good or for ill), combining franchised entertainment, name-brand boutiques and music clubs, huge international tankers and simulated steamboats, "real" Civil War coffee with chicory, reinvented Cajun cuisine, 18th-century voodoo, and 21st-century vampires. They *laissez les bons temps rouler,* all right; they just make sure it's your money roll behind the good-timing. The posters and prints feature wrought-iron fences, but the real courtyards are gated and locked tight. Steamboats play recorded music intentionally out of tune—"old-fashioned" in the hokiest sense. Self-appointed tour guides mix all their legends together: the statue in St. Anthony's Garden behind St. Louis Cathedral, memorializing French sailors who volunteered as nurses during a yellow fever epidemic, has even been explained as "the Mardi Gras Jesus" because the statue's outstretched hands are supposedly reaching for throws!

And yet for all the tawdriness and commercialization, one cannot help falling under the city's spell. New Orleans is a foreign country within American borders, not merely a multilingual hodgepodge like Miami or New York, but a true Creole society blended through centuries. It is Old South in style, New South in ambition. It has a natural beauty that refutes even the most frivolous of franchised structures, a tradition of craftsmanship and even luxury that demands aesthetic scrutiny and surrender, and a flair for almost-exquisite silliness—like those Jackson Square fortune-tellers with their Pier 1 Imports turbans—that keeps all New Orleanians young. Fine arts, fine cuisine, voodoo, vampires, and Mardi Gras. It's all muddled up, sometimes enchanting, sometimes infuriating. And it needs your affection more than ever before—as much as it needs financial and charitable support.

We hope to help you find the real New Orleans, the old and gracious one, that is just now in the shadow of the Big Too-Easy. We want to open your heart, not your wallet. We think you should leave Bourbon Street behind and visit City Park, one of the finest and most wide-ranging public facilities in the United States. We want you to see Longue Vue House as well as St. Louis Cemetery. We'd like you to admire not only the town houses of Royal Street and the mansions of St. Charles but the lofts and row houses of the Warehouse District, the combined Greenwich Village and TriBeCa of New Orleans. We hope you'll walk Chartres Street in the evening shade, watch the mighty Mississippi churn contemptuously past the man-made barriers, and smell the chicory, whiskey, and pungent swamp water all mixed together the way that Andy Jackson and Jean Lafitte might have the night before the great battle.

So get ready, get set, go. *Laissez les bons temps rouler!*

ABOUT *this* GUIDE

HOW COME "UNOFFICIAL"?

MOST GUIDES TO NEW ORLEANS tout the well-known sights, promote the local restaurants and hotels indiscriminately, and leave out a lot of good stuff. This one is different.

Instead of pandering to the tourist industry, we'll tell you if the food is bad at a well-known restaurant, we'll complain loudly about high prices, and we'll guide you away from the crowds and traffic for a break now and then.

Visiting New Orleans requires wily strategies not unlike those used in the sacking of Troy. We've sent in a team of evaluators who toured each site, ate in the city's best restaurants, performed critical evaluations of its hotels, and visited New Orleans's wide variety of nightclubs. If a museum is boring or standing in line for two hours to view a famous attraction is a waste of time, we say so—and, in the process, make your visit more fun, efficient, and economical.

CREATING A GUIDEBOOK

WE GOT INTO THE GUIDEBOOK BUSINESS because we were unhappy with the way travel guides make the reader work to get any usable information. Wouldn't it be nice, we thought, if we were to make guides that are easy to use?

Most guidebooks are compilations of lists. This is true regardless of whether the information is presented in list form or artfully distributed through pages of prose. There is insufficient detail in a list, and prose can present tedious helpings of nonessential or marginally useful information. Not enough wheat, so to speak, for nourishment in one instance, and too much chaff in the other. Either way, these types of guides provide little more than departure points from which readers initiate their own quests.

Many guides are readable and well researched, but they tend to be difficult to use. To select a hotel, for example, a reader must study several pages of descriptions with only the boldfaced hotel names breaking up large blocks of text. Because each description essentially deals with the same variables, it is difficult to recall what was said concerning a particular hotel. Readers generally must work through all the write-ups before beginning to narrow their choices. The presentation of restaurants, nightclubs, and attractions is similar except that even more reading is usually required. To use such a guide is to undertake an exhaustive research process that requires examining nearly as many options and possibilities as starting from scratch. Recommendations, if any, lack depth and conviction. These guides compound rather than solve problems by failing to narrow travelers' choices down to a thoughtfully considered, well-distilled, and manageable few.

HOW *UNOFFICIAL GUIDES* ARE DIFFERENT

READERS CARE ABOUT THE AUTHORS' OPINIONS. The authors, after all, are supposed to know what they are talking about. This, coupled with the fact that the traveler wants quick answers (as opposed to endless alternatives), dictates that authors should be explicit, prescriptive, and, above all, direct. The authors of the *Unofficial Guides* try to be just that. They spell out alternatives and recommend specific courses of action. They simplify complicated destinations and attractions and allow the traveler to feel in control in the most unfamiliar environments. The objective of the *Unofficial Guide* authors is not to give the most information or all of the information, but to offer the most useful information.

An *Unofficial Guide* is a critical reference work; it focuses on a travel destination that appears to be especially complex. Our authors and research team are completely independent from the attractions, restaurants, and hotels we describe. The *Unofficial Guide* to New Orleans is designed for individuals and families traveling for the fun of it, as well as for business travelers and conventioneers, especially those visiting the Crescent City for the first time. The guide is directed at value-conscious, consumer-oriented adults who seek a cost-effective, though not spartan, travel style.

Special Features

The *Unofficial Guide* offers the following special features:

- Friendly introductions to New Orleans's most fascinating neighborhoods and districts.
- "Best of" listings giving our well-qualified opinions on things ranging from raw oysters to blackened snapper, four-star hotels to 12-story views.
- Listings that are keyed to your interests, so you can pick and choose.
- Advice to sightseers on how to avoid the worst of the crowds, and advice to business travelers on how to avoid traffic and excessive costs.
- Recommendations for lesser-known sights that are away from the French Quarter but no less worthwhile.
- Maps that make it easy to find places you want to go to and avoid places you don't.
- Expert advice on avoiding New Orleans's notorious street crime.
- A hotel chart that helps you narrow down your choices fast, according to your needs.
- Shorter listings that include only those restaurants, clubs, and hotels we think are worth considering.
- A table of contents and detailed index to help you find things quickly.
- Insider advice on the French Quarter, Mardi Gras, Jazz Fest, best times of day (or night) to go places, and our secret weapon—New Orleans's streetcar system.

What You *Won't* Get:

- Long, useless lists where everything looks the same.
- Information that gets you to your destination at the worst possible time.
- Information without advice on how to use it

HOW THIS GUIDE WAS RESEARCHED AND WRITTEN

ALTHOUGH MANY GUIDEBOOKS have been written about New Orleans, very few have been evaluative. Some guides come close to regurgitating the hotels' and tourist office's own promotional material. In preparing this work, nothing was taken for granted. Each hotel, restaurant, shop, and attraction was visited by a team of trained observers who conducted detailed evaluations and rated each according to formal criteria. Team members conducted interviews with tourists of all ages to determine what they enjoyed most and least during their New Orleans visit.

Our observers are independent and impartial, and while they may have special expertise or at least more travel experience, they visited New Orleans just as you would, as tourists or business travelers, noting their satisfaction or dissatisfaction.

The primary difference between the average tourist and the trained evaluator is the evaluator's skills in organization, preparation, and observation. The trained evaluator is responsible for much more than simply observing and cataloging. Observer teams use detailed checklists to analyze hotel rooms, restaurants, nightclubs, and attractions. Finally, evaluator ratings and observations are integrated with tourist reactions and the opinions of patrons for a comprehensive quality profile of each feature and service.

In compiling this guide, we recognize that a tourist's age, background, and interests will strongly influence his or her taste in New Orleans's wide array of attractions and will account for a preference for one sight or museum over another. Our sole objective is to provide the reader with sufficient description, critical evaluation, and pertinent data to make knowledgeable decisions according to individual tastes.

LETTERS, COMMENTS, AND QUESTIONS FROM READERS

WE EXPECT TO LEARN FROM OUR MISTAKES, as well as from the input of our readers, and to improve with each new book and edition. Many of those who use the *Unofficial Guides* write to us asking questions, making comments, or sharing their own discoveries or lessons learned in New Orleans. We appreciate all such input, both positive and critical, and encourage our readers to continue writing. Readers' comments and observations will be frequently incorporated in revised editions of the *Unofficial Guide*, and will contribute immeasurably to its improvement.

How to Write the Author:

Eve Zibart
The Unofficial Guide to New Orleans
P.O. Box 43673
Birmingham, AL 35243
unofficialguides@menasharidge.com

When you write by mail, be sure to put your return address on your letter as well as on the envelope—sometimes envelopes and letters get separated. And remember, our work takes us out of the office for long periods of time, so forgive us if our response is delayed.

Reader Survey

At the back of the guide you will find a short questionnaire that you can use to express opinions about your New Orleans visit. Clip the questionnaire out along the dotted line and mail it to the above address.

The *Unofficial Guide* Web Site

The Web site of the *Unofficial Guide* Travel and Lifestyle Series, providing in-depth information on all *Unofficial Guides* in print, is at **www.theunofficialguides.com.**

"INSIDE" NEW ORLEANS *for* OUTSIDERS

IT'S A FUNNY THING ABOUT NEW ORLEANS TRAVEL GUIDES: most of them tell you too much, and a few tell you too little. That's because New Orleans is such a complex city, so ornate and enveloping and layered with history and happenstance, that it's hard to stop acquiring good stories and passing them on.

But statistics show that the majority of visitors to New Orleans stay only three or four days—and all too frequently that includes spending part of the time in seminars or conventions. How much can you squeeze into a long weekend? How much do you want to see? Walking tours of the French Quarter and Garden District often point to buildings with obscure claims to fame and with only partial facades to their name (and no admission offered in any case). Walking tours of the farther reaches are often redundant; even the keenest architecture critic will probably lose heart trying to cover the third or fourth neighborhood in 48 hours. Some tour books either stint on shopping or endorse every dealer in town; some forget any fine-arts or theater productions at all, as if Bourbon Street bars were the sole form of nightlife available in the city. Some are too uncritical, some too "insider." Some have all the right stuff but are poorly organized; others are easy to read but boring.

So, hard as it is to limit this book, we have—sort of. We have tried to make the do-it-yourself walking tours short enough that they won't exhaust you, but full enough of sights and stories to give you the city's true flavor. (And if you want to do more, we'll tell you how.) We've tried to take things easy, but we don't forgive exploitation or boost unworthy distractions. If it isn't fun, informative, or accurate, we don't want you to go. If there's a better alternative, we want you to know. We don't make purely philosophical judgments—some people believe in the supernatural, some don't—but we do try to evaluate in a dispassionate fashion what you get for your money. We hope to keep the quality of your visit high, the irritation quotient low.

We've also divided the attractions up in various ways, often overlapping, so you can pick out the ones you'd most enjoy: in Part Two, Planning Your Visit, we suggest attractions by type—family-style, musical, festive, spooky, and so on. The neighborhood profiles in Part One, Understanding the City, are more strictly geographical descriptions to help you get your bearings and focus your interests, while the maps are designed to help you with the logistics of arranging accommodations and sightseeing. More-elaborate walking tours are laid out for you in Part Seven, Sightseeing, Tours, and Attractions, and particular museums and exhibits in each area are explored in more detail and rated for interest by age group. And for those who don't wish to do-it-themselves at all, we have listed a number of commercial and customized tours tailored to almost any interest.

In addition, even granting that your time will be tight, we have included a list of opportunities to exercise or play. That's partly because we at the *Unofficial Guides* try to keep up with our workouts when we're on the road, and also because you may be visiting old friends, old teammates, and tennis players. Beyond that, although you may not think you'll want to make time for a run or ride, experience has taught us that sightseeing and shopping can be exhausting, make you stiff, and make you long for the outdoors—and New Orleans has some of the prettiest outdoors you'll ever see.

Finally, for visitors lucky enough to have more than a couple of days to spend, or who are returning for a second or third go-round, we have sketched out a few excursions outside the city.

Please do remember that prices and hours change constantly, especially post-Katrina. We have listed the most up-to-date information we can get, but it never hurts to double-check times in particular (if prices of attractions change, it is generally not by much). And although usually a day or so is all the advance notice you need to get into any attraction in New Orleans, you might try calling ahead if your party is large.

HOW INFORMATION IS ORGANIZED: BY SUBJECT AND BY GEOGRAPHIC AREA

TO GIVE YOU FAST ACCESS TO INFORMATION about the best of New Orleans, we've organized the material in several formats.

HOTELS Since most people visiting New Orleans stay in one hotel for the duration of their trip, we have summarized our coverage of hotels in charts, maps, ratings, and rankings that allow you to focus quickly your decision-making process. We do not go on for page after page, describing lobbies and rooms that, in the final analysis, sound much the same. Instead, we concentrate on the specific variables that differentiate one hotel from another: location, size, room quality, services, amenities, and cost.

RESTAURANTS We provide plenty of detail when it comes to restaurants. Since you will probably eat a dozen or more restaurant meals during your stay, and since not even you can predict what you might be in the mood for on Saturday night, we provide detailed profiles of the city's best places to eat in Part Eight, Dining in New Orleans.

ENTERTAINMENT AND NIGHTLIFE Visitors frequently try several different clubs or nightspots during their stay. Because clubs and nightspots, like restaurants, are usually selected spontaneously after arriving in New Orleans, we believe detailed descriptions are warranted. The best nightspots, clubs, and lounges in New Orleans are profiled in Part Eleven, Entertainment and Nightlife.

GEOGRAPHIC AREAS Once you've decided where you're going, getting there becomes the issue. To help you do that, we have divided the city into geographic areas:

French Quarter
Central Business District
Faubourg Marigny
Mid-City–Esplanade
Uptown and the Garden District

All profiles of attractions, restaurants, and nightspots include area names. If you've just visited Madame John's Legacy, for example, and are interested in Creole restaurants within walking distance, scanning the dining profiles for restaurants in the French Quarter will provide you with the best choices.

greater new orleans

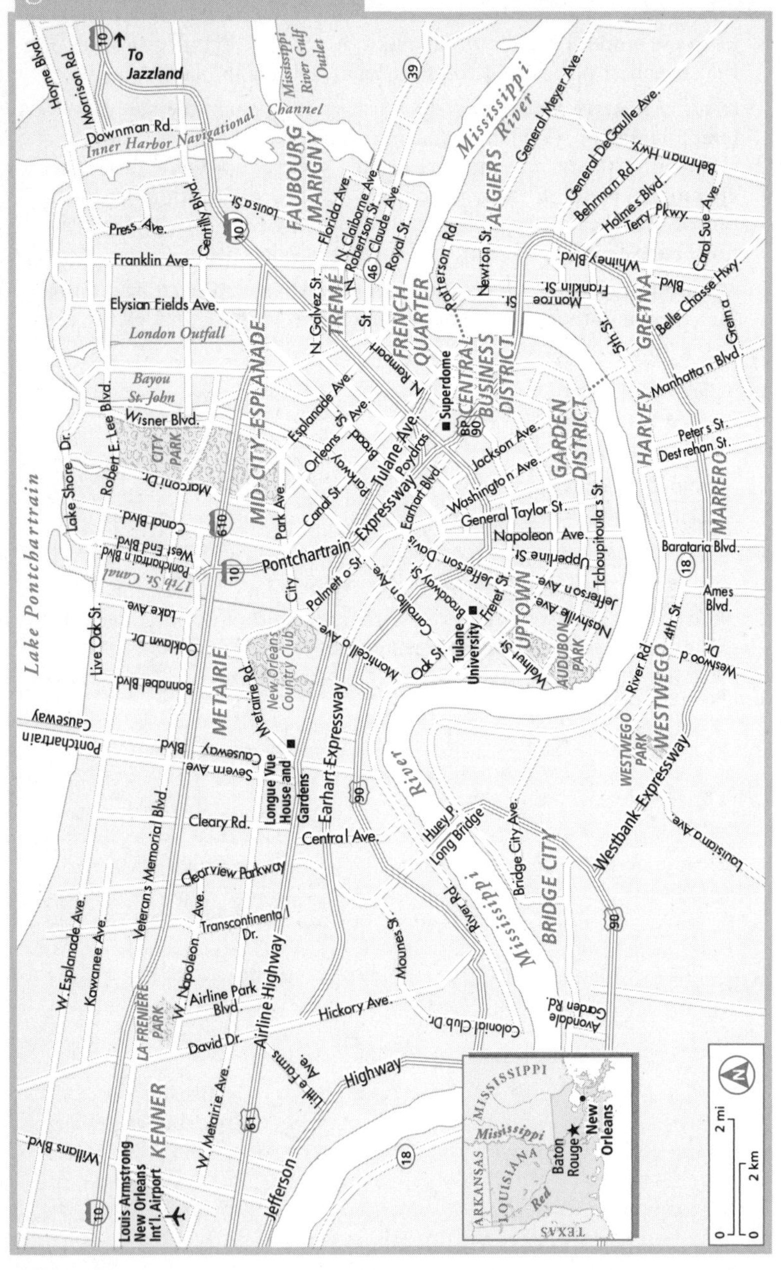
To Jazzland
Hayne Blvd.
Morrison Rd.
Downman Rd.
Inner Harbor Navigational Channel
Mississippi River Gulf Outlet
FAUBOURG MARIGNY
Mississippi River
ALGIERS
General Meyer Ave.
General DeGaulle Ave.
Behrman Hwy.
Behrman Rd.
Holmes Blvd.
Terry Pkwy.
Carol Sue Ave.
Whitney Blvd.
Franklin St.
Monroe St.
GRETNA
Belle Chasse Hwy.
Gretna Blvd.
Manhattan Blvd.
Louisa St.
Gentilly Blvd.
Press Ave.
Franklin Ave.
Elysian Fields Ave.
London Outfall
Bayou St. John
Wisner Blvd.
Robert E. Lee Blvd.
Lake Shore Dr.
CITY PARK
Marconi Dr.
Canal Blvd.
West End Blvd.
Pontchartrain Blvd.
17th St. Canal
Lake Ave.
Live Oak St.
Oakdale Dr.
Bonnabel Blvd.
Pontchartrain Causeway
Lake Pontchartrain
Florida Ave.
N. Claiborne Ave.
N. Robertson St.
Claude Ave.
Royal St.
TREMÉ
FRENCH QUARTER
N. Galvez St.
St.
N. Rampart
Patterson Rd.
Newton St.
CENTRAL BUSINESS DISTRICT
Superdome
MID-CITY
ESPLANADE
Esplanade Ave.
Orleans St.
Broad Ave.
Parkway
Canal St.
Park Ave.
Tulane Ave.
Poydras
Pontchartrain Expressway
City Park Ave.
Earhart Blvd.
Jackson Ave.
Washington Ave.
GARDEN DISTRICT
General Taylor St.
Napoleon Ave.
Upperline St.
Tchoupitoulas St.
Jefferson Davis
Jefferson Ave.
Nashville Ave.
Palmetto St.
Carrollton Ave.
Broadway St.
Freret St.
Tulane University
UPTOWN
Walnut St.
AUDUBON PARK
Oak St.
Monticello Ave.
5th St.
HARVEY
Peters St.
Destrehan St.
MARRERO
Barataria Blvd.
Ames Blvd.
4th St.
Westwood Dr.
River Rd.
WESTWEGO
WESTWEGO PARK
Westbank Expressway
Louisiana Ave.
METAIRIE
Metairie Rd.
New Orleans Country Club
Causeway Blvd.
Severn Ave.
Longue Vue House and Gardens
Earhart Expressway
Cleary Rd.
Central Ave.
River
Huey P. Long Bridge
Bridge City Ave.
BRIDGE CITY
Mississippi
River Rd.
Veterans Memorial Blvd.
Clearview Parkway
Transcontinental Dr.
W. Napoleon Ave.
W. Esplanade Ave.
Kawanee Ave.
Airline Park Blvd.
Airline Highway
Mounes St.
Hickory Ave.
Colonial Club Dr.
Avondale Garden Rd.
LA FRENIERE PARK
David Dr.
Little Farms Ave.
Jefferson Highway
KENNER
W. Metairie Ave.
Williams Blvd.
Louis Armstrong New Orleans Int'l. Airport
MISSISSIPPI
Mississippi
ARKANSAS
LOUISIANA
Red
TEXAS
Baton Rouge
New Orleans
N
0
2 mi
0
2 km

PART ONE

UNDERSTANDING *the* CITY

A TOO-SHORT HISTORY *of* *a* FASCINATING PLACE

NEW ORLEANS EXERCISES A STRANGE FASCINATION over the rest of the country, and for good reasons. It's foreign territory at heart. It has flown three national flags—four if you count the Confederate States of America—and changed hands a couple more times than that. Like several other southern cities, it was "occupied" by then-hostile Union forces, had to repulse periodic Native American raids, and might briefly have flown a British flag as well, if the Battle of New Orleans had turned out differently. (And, legend aside, it might easily have done so.) Andy Jackson notwithstanding, New Orleans's legal system is still based upon the Napoleonic code.

New Orleans has always lived an unnatural, enchanted life, an island dug out of the swamp some yards lower than the river that embraces it, tethered to the world by bridges, ferries, and causeways. Its proximity to the swamps exposed it to almost yearly epidemics; in the course of just over 100 years, between 1795 and 1905, an estimated 100,000 lives were lost to yellow fever, malaria, or cholera. The city has been flattened by hurricanes—and nearly erased by floods. And despite all that water around it, it has been destroyed twice by fire—catastrophes that wiped out almost the entire first century of construction.

New Orleans has been identified with both the most sophisticated Creole culture and good-ol'-boy corruption; it has produced a rich ethnic melting pot and the most virulent racism. Oil drillers rescued it in the first half of the 20th century, and international petroleum prices nearly strangled it in the second half. Mardi Gras is the world's most famous frat party, yet when New Orleans threw a World's Fair to celebrate itself, it nearly went bankrupt.

Somehow, as low as New Orleans gets—as much as ten feet below sea level in some places—it never quite goes under. Like that Ol' Man River that surrounds it, like those famous good times, it just keeps rollin' along.

THE FRENCH FLAG

LOUISIANA STOOD AT THE CENTER of imperial rivalries right from the beginning. Columbus had claimed the New World for Spain, but the other seagoing nations also pursued colonial territory and (as they believed) Asian trade. In 1519, the Spanish explorer Alonzo de Pindea sailed at least past, if not up, the mouth of the Mississippi River. In 1534, Cartier sailed down the St. Lawrence waterways from Canada into the Northeast. Only a few years later, Hernando de Soto established settlements along the southeastern coast and actually reached the Mississippi, but Spanish attention was distracted by the conquest of Mexico and expansion into the American Southwest and northern South America.

In the 1670s, while the British were planting Union Jacks up and down the Atlantic Coast from Maine to the Carolinas, René Cavelier, Sieur de La Salle, set out from Canada with the intention of following the Illinois River all the way to the mouth of the Mississippi River in the Gulf of Mexico and, in 1682, claimed for France all the land drained by the Mississippi. He named the land Louisiana in honor of his sovereign lord King Louis XIV, the Sun King. Spain launched a huge manhunt in an attempt to intercept La Salle (when they finally reached his settlement, mutineers had already murdered him), but by the turn of the 17th century, other Frenchmen had established settlements all over Louisiana and what is now the state of Mississippi.

In 1699, the Sieur de Bienville planted a huge cross at the bend of the Mississippi River, and 20 years later his brother, the Sieur d'Iberville, stood looking out over the Mississippi where it connected to Lake Pontchartrain through Bayou St. John and ordered the construction of his "city." He named it La Nouvelle Orleans in honor of Philippe, Duc d'Orleans, who was then the Regent of France.

It was probably fortunate that the name of the river eventually settled into Mississippi, a corruption of the name of the Mamese-Sipou tribe that lived along its banks. At various times, it was referred to as the Sassagoula, the St. Louis, the Escondido, and, most curiously for such a muddy stream, the Immaculate Conception.

Marshy, mosquito infested, and oppressively hot, New Orleans became the subject of a real-estate scam that might have inspired the Florida land boom of the 1920s. Posters and supposed eyewitness tales of the gold-rich territories flourished—most promulgated by an unscrupulous Scottish crony of the regent's with the ironic name of John Law, though even he thought Baton Rouge a likelier site. These stories lured thousands of French optimists and opportunists to the crude settlement, where they had little choice but to build the city they had been told already existed. Life in the settlement was so meager that in 1727, 88 women convicts were released from prison on the condition that they accompany the Ursuline nuns to New Orleans as mail-order brides.

These were not the only unaristocratic imports: in fact, there were probably far more exiles, common soldiers, petty thieves, intractable slaves, and indentured servants than blue-bloods, and fewer "casket girls"—the respectable but impoverished girls who also came out as wards of the Ursuline Sisters with their few belongings packed in small trunks—than street women. (It should be remembered, however, that life in Paris was very hard and that many young girls fell or were sold into prostitution as a last resort, so their records should perhaps not be held against them. They worked pitifully hard for their "freedom" in New Orleans, in any case.)

The city was laid out with the streets in a grid around a central plaza that faced the river—the Place d'Armes, now Jackson Square. *Vieux Carré* means "Old Square," and the district almost was square: it extended from the Mississippi River to Rampart Street, which was once literally a rampart or wall, and from Esplanade Avenue to Iberville. (The Vieux Carré is generally said to extend to Canal Street, but Canal Street was originally intended to be just that: a canal dividing the French Quarter from the American sector in what is now the Central Business District.) Gradually the settlement grew, and merchants, traders, and practical farmers, as well as more restless aristocrats, came to Louisiana to stay. With them came the beginning of a caste system—aristocrats, merchants, farmers, and servants—that became a hallmark of Creole society.

THE SPANISH FLAG

IN THE 1760S, TWO OTHER GROUPS ARRIVED, one in extremity and one in force. The first were the Acadians—or Cajuns—whom the British forced to leave their homes in Nova Scotia, and who settled in the bayou country west of New Orleans. Though most New Orleanians looked down on the Acadians—whom they considered countrified (to say the least) with their "uncultured" dialect—the Cajuns were French nationals driven into exile by France's enemy, Britain, and so they were accepted.

The other new arrivals were anything but welcome: the Spanish. To their dismay, the ethnically proud New Orleanians discovered that King Louis XV had secretly surrendered the Louisiana Territory to his Spanish cousin Charles III (some writers say it was used to pay off huge gambling debts). The residents violently resisted the Spanish takeover and succeeded in routing the first commissioner sent from Madrid. But in 1769, a more determined mercenary with the intriguing name of Don Alexander O'Reilly, or "Bloody Reilly," arrived with an armada of 24 warships and 2,000 soldiers. He executed several of the most prominent rebels and made swift work of the insurrection.

The Arsenal and Cabildo were erected on the square (*cabildo* means "governing body"), and French and Spanish aristocrats began inviting each other to dinner.

By the time the American colonies declared independence from Britain, New Orleans was an important Spanish outpost, which made the entrance of the Spanish on either side potentially decisive. Finally, Oliver Pollack, a New Orleans native who had become a member of the Continental Congress, persuaded Bernardo de Galvez, then-governor of New Orleans, to send a convoy of 20 supply ships to New York to aid the American revolutionaries. Great Britain then declared war on Spain, and de Galvez proceeded to roll over the British colonies along the Gulf of Mexico. Consequently, although Lafayette and the French are usually remembered as the key European allies of the American forces, the Spanish also played an essential role.

THREE FLAGS IN FORTY YEARS

UNSETTLED AS NEW ORLEANS'S FIRST 60 YEARS had been, the next 40 or so were just as dramatic.

The city was devastated by two great fires, the first in 1788 and the second, which came before the community had rebuilt, in 1794. Only a couple of buildings remain from before that time: the Old Ursuline Convent, whose age is undisputed; and Madame John's Legacy, which is the subject of some debate. Determined to prevent a third disaster, the Spanish promulgated new building codes: all roofs had to be tiled, houses were to be made of brick or plaster rather than wood, high walls had to separate gardens so one fire wouldn't spread from house to house, and alleys were eliminated to prevent a bellows effect that might feed a blaze. So what is considered classical French Quarter architecture—arches, rear courtyards, and the famous ornamental wrought iron of the balconies and fences—is actually Spanish.

Meanwhile, the city's merchants and shippers continued to prosper. The city was not only a major exchange point between the eastern and midwestern markets, but it also controlled much of the European-American import and export trade. New Orleans's strategic position, both for trade and defense, made the city highly attractive to the new government of the United States, and a source of great regret to the French government. The city remained solidly French at heart, with a royalist cast of mind—another wave of French aristocrats had fled the Revolution in 1789—and so when Napoleon set out to establish his own French empire, New Orleans became a spoil of war. In 1800, by yet another secret treaty, Spain ceded the Louisiana Territory back to France.

Napoleon became a romantic idol to the colonists, who proudly named a battalion of streets after his battle victories—Marengo, Milan, Perrier, Constantinople, Austerlitz, Cadiz, Valence, Jena, and even Forcher (after his great general)—not to mention Napoleon and Josephine themselves.

But when things began to turn sour for him, Napoleon decided to cash in the American colonies to finance his European campaigns and the effort to reclaim Santo Domingo (Haiti) after the great slave rebellion of Toussaint L'Ouverture. When President Thomas Jefferson offered to buy the port of New Orleans, Napoleon surprised him by offering to sell the entire Louisiana Territory—more than 500 million acres—for the sum of $15 million ($11 million in cash and $4 million in forgiven debt). The sale was officially transacted in the Cabildo on December 20, 1803. Louisiana became a U.S. territory, and in 1812 it was granted statehood, a fact commemorated in the arrival of the first steamboat, the *New Orleans*. It is one of those curiosities of political history that this exchange, facilitated by British and Dutch banks, provided Napoleon with funds to continue his war against those same nations.

Despite Napoleon's apparent betrayal, in 1820 loyal New Orleans Creoles plotted to rescue the deposed emperor from his prison on St. Helena, but he died before it could be attempted. His death mask, however, was delivered to his followers and is still on display at the Cabildo.

The purchase of Louisiana by the United States inspired thousands of Americans—and not-yet-Americans, recent immigrants still looking to make their home there—to ride, raft, barge, stage, and even walk to the thriving port.

In the first seven years after Louisiana became a state, the population of New Orleans more than tripled, from 8,000 to 25,000.

A huge non-Creole community sprang up just upriver of the Vieux Carré, near the older sugar plantations and sometimes on top of them, and out into what is now the Garden District. The new arrivals were not welcomed by the more-civilized-than-thou New Orleanians. The Scotch-Irish, who had already settled along the Carolina and Virginia mountains, were a new and particularly rough presence among the old Creole families; they took the word *riffing,* Gaelic for "rowing," and contemptuously referred to all the laboring men and hardscrabble farmers who poled their way down the Mississippi as "riffraff."

A huge drainage canal emptying into the river was marked out along the upriver edge of the French Quarter, ostensibly as part of the construction of the booming city but also to serve as an emotional (if not actual) barrier between the French Quarter, now also known as the First Municipality, and the American quadrant, officially the Second Municipality. In response to this subtle but elegant slight, the Americans laid out their sector, called Faubourg Ste. Marie, as a sort of mirror image of the Vieux Carré, with Lafayette Square (a seemingly polite tribute, but subtly claiming the marquis for the Americans) as a Place d'Armes; St. Patrick's as a rival to St. Louis Cathedral; and Gallier Hall, which was the official City Hall until the 1950s, in place of the old Cabildo. Each had its own mayor and council, each its own regulations. The city was not officially united until 1852.

As it happened, the canal was never built; and for a time, although it was referred to as the "neutral ground," the swath was the scene of repeated brawls between Creole residents and brash, aggrandizing newcomers. Eventually a grand boulevard, divided by a great median, was paved through the strip instead and was dubbed Canal Street. Even so, it remained the acknowledged border between the two communities, and ever since, the New Orleans term for a median strip has been "neutral ground."

"THE WHITES OF THEIR EYES"

THE WINNING OF THE BATTLE OF NEW ORLEANS has become such a touchstone of American pride that it has inspired hit songs (Johnny Horton's "Battle of New Orleans") and Hollywood epics (such as *The Buccaneer,* with Charlton Heston as Andrew Jackson and Yul Brynner as Jean Lafitte). The legend is glorious and shining—overnight excavations, secret meetings, Redcoats coming ghostlike through the fog to the banshee wailing of bagpipes, and Jackson shouting, "Don't shoot until you see the whites of their eyes!"

As is frequently the case with warfare, the truth is a little muddier. It is true, however, that the ruthless and lucky Jackson lost only 13 men while killing 2,000 British Army soldiers. It's probably true that without the combined efforts of 5,000 American, Creole, black, and Native American volunteers—not to mention the heavy arms and ammunition donated by Lafitte from his store of plunder—Jackson's Tennessee soldiers would have had a much harder time. And considering how intensely most Native Americans hated Jackson, who had commanded many brutal campaigns against the Creek and Choctaw tribes, their participation was even more remarkable.

The great irony is that the war was already over. The Treaty of Ghent had been signed a fortnight earlier. However, the campaign and victory served to unite the previously rancorous Creole and American communities, along with the smaller Scots-Irish, German, mestizo, and native-Creole outposts, and to establish New Orleans, distinctive as it might be, as an all-American city.

FREE BLACKS, SLAVES, AND MULATTOS

THE PRESENCE OF AFRICAN AND CARIBBEAN BLACKS, both free and slave, in New Orleans can be documented as far back as the early clearing of the French Quarter neighborhood. In 1721, only a couple of years after the city's founding, there were 300 slaves for only 470 Europeans, and a code noir ("black code") was enacted in 1724 as a way of regulating the slave trade.

Free blacks, people "of color" (of mixed racial heritage in almost any proportion), and slaves made up a substantial portion of the population; the free blacks of New Orleans outnumbered those of any other southern city. In fact, by 1803 there were exactly as many blacks and mixed-race residents as whites: 4,000 of each, with 1,300 (40%) of the blacks being free. By the beginning of the Civil War, there were an estimated 30,000 free blacks in New Orleans.

An elaborate caste system emerged in which those of mixed race assumed social rank according to the amount of white (Creole) ancestry they could claim. *Mulattos* were half black, half white; *quadroons* were one-quarter black (that is, they had one black grandparent); and *octoroons* were one-eighth black. Women of mixed heritage were considered exceedingly handsome, and though the Creole aristocrats would never have dreamed of marrying a black woman, it was considered a mark of wealth and good taste—another bit of conspicuous consumption—to have a well-spoken, elegantly dressed black or biracial mistress. Many of these women became heads of the Creoles' city homes, running second establishments, in effect, and if they were really lucky, might be freed at their masters' death. If not, at least their children might be recognized as illegitimate offspring and left some money.

This was such a widely recognized custom that the Creoles might even formally court these women, making semiofficial offers to their mothers or owners that included property settlements, allowances, and the like. The annual quadroon balls became notorious tableaux of young "available" beauties, something between an auction and a debutante ball. Many of these balls were held in the Orleans Ballroom, a grandiose hall built in 1817 and now a special-events site within the Bourbon Orleans Hotel.

As time went on, the *gens de couleur libre*—literally, "free people of color"—developed their own quite-sophisticated culture. The sons of Creole aristocrats were often given first-class educations befitting their (fathers') status, and some were even sent to Europe, where people of multiracial heritage were somewhat better accepted. Alexandre Dumas, the author and playwright (*The Three Musketeers* and *The Count of Monte Cristo*) was biracial, and by some accounts Napoleon's Josephine, from the island of Martinique, had some mixed ancestry as well.

Both free and slave blacks were allowed to congregate in Congo Square, near North Rampart and Orleans streets in what is now Louis Armstrong Park; as many as 2,000 gathered in this Choctaw meeting place on Sundays to sing, dance, trade, eat, fight, and perhaps practice a little voodoo until the "curfew," a cannon in the Place d'Armes, sounded. (In tribute, the first New Orleans Jazz and Heritage Festival in 1969 was held in Congo Square.)

In the years just before the Civil War, New Orleans was the largest slave market in the nation. Blacks, even well-to-do persons of color and freedmen, remained mere residents rather than citizens; blacks were not granted the right to vote until 1868, during Reconstruction and despite a campaign of terror by the Ku Klux Klan. They were effectively disenfranchised again in 1898 through a legislative maneuver requiring stringent proof of literacy. The vote was returned only in 1965, and although African Americans make up more than half of the city's population, the first black mayor, Ernest Morial, was not elected until 1978. (All mayors since have also been black.) Carnival krewes were not integrated until 1991, and some krewes boycotted or even withdrew from Mardi Gras when that happened.

THE WAR BETWEEN THE STATES AND RECONSTRUCTION

THE PORT OF NEW ORLEANS PRACTICALLY FLOATED on money in the decades after the Treaty of Ghent. Steamboats were in their prime; at the peak, there were some 11,000 plying the Mississippi; some of the luxury paddle wheelers, the "showboats," had capacities of 600 and served 500 for dinner. It was the beginning of New Orleans's tourism industry. Cotton, tobacco, and the slave trade fueled the economy. By 1840 New Orleans was the second-busiest port in the nation, after New York, and had a population of more than 100,000. The Irish Famine of 1841 sparked another flood of immigrants, who settled northwest of the American sector in what gradually became known as the Irish Channel; a large number of Germans also moved in. Unfortunately, their arrivals were offset by the yellow-fever epidemic of 1853, which killed 11,000 people and incapacitated another 40,000, becoming the most deadly epidemic in the nation's history.

But in 1861, with the secession of the Confederate States, Louisiana changed flags for the fourth time—and with the taking of New Orleans by Union forces under Admiral David Farragut in 1862, flew its sixth.

The Union occupation (as New Orleanians saw it, although officially it ceased to be an "occupation" after 1865) lasted 15 years. New Orleans fell so early that its three-year occupation by "enemy troops" is the longest unfriendly occupation of any city in the United States, and amnesty was not granted Confederate officers until 1872. Reconstruction was a period of tremendous unrest in the entire region.

It was the rapid evolution of steamboat travel that helped resurrect interest in the city. As trips became faster and shorter, a craze for unofficial river races took hold, and steamboats vied to set speed records between St. Louis and New Orleans, often with great sums wagered on the outcomes. In the summer of 1870, the then-recordholder, the *Natchez,* belonging to Thomas P. Leathers, took up the challenge of Captain John W. Cannon, owner of the *Robert E. Lee.* The two steamed out of New Orleans on June 30 with a reported $1 million, much of it from European gamblers, riding on the race. By stripping his boat to a near shell, and arranging for mid-river refueling—a very modern concept—Cannon managed to beat Captain Leathers by six and a half hours, arriving in St. Louis on Independence Day after a trip of 3 days, 18 hours, and 14 minutes. After that contest, the steam-boat race craze subsided.

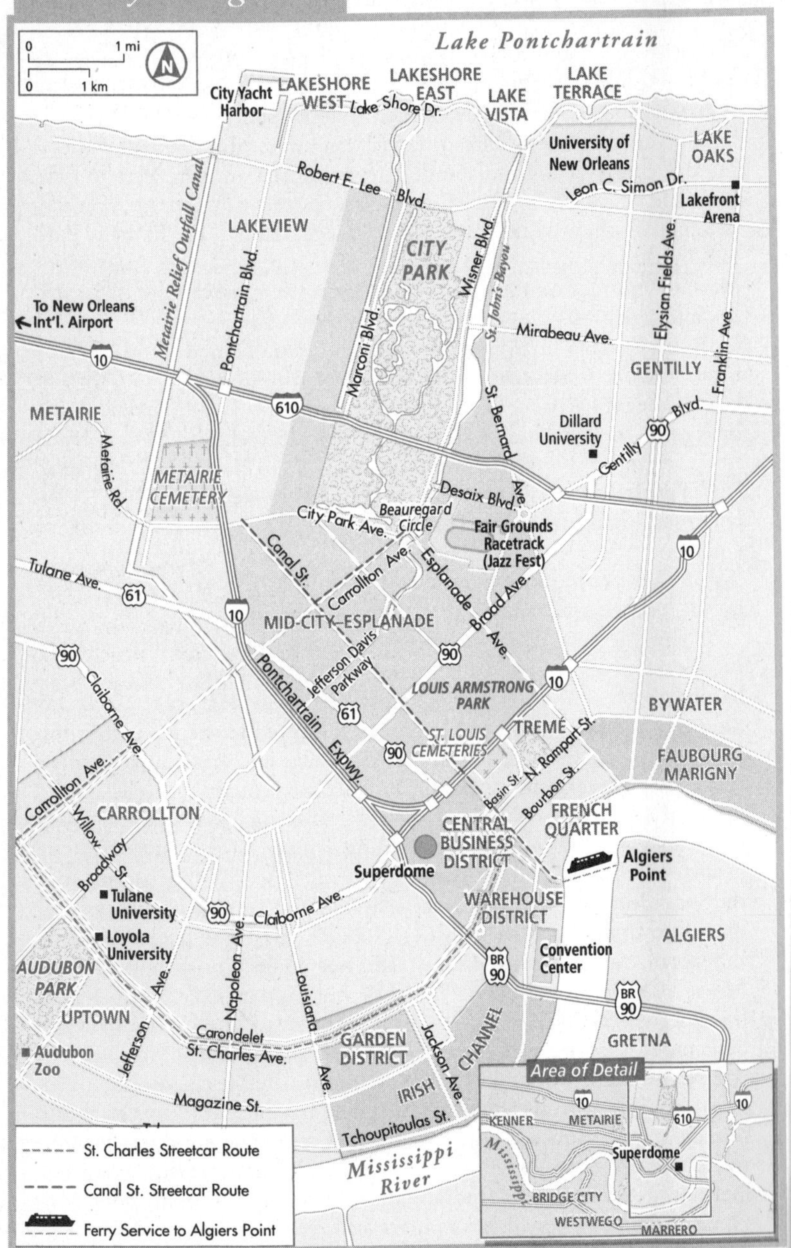

In the final two decades of the 19th century, as the reviving port began to bring new industry and pleasure seekers into the city, what might be called the Bourbon Street culture made its first bow. By 1880 there were almost 800 saloons operating in New Orleans, along with about 80 gambling parlors and even more bordellos, which, though officially banned, had never been prosecuted or even regulated. New Orleans was starting to develop a reputation as a party town, a reputation that many people resisted and resented.

In 1897, an alderman named Sidney Story proposed that all these activities be restricted to a red-light district along Basin Street adjoining the French Quarter. The business of vice prospered almost virtuously in what was dubbed "Storyville." The fanciest bordellos boasted not only elegant décor, sophisticated refreshments, and fine entertainment (these "sporting palaces" were where many of the great jazz improvisors got their start), but also well-dressed and willing ladies whose names, addresses, and racial heritage were listed in "blue books" that parodied the Social Register. One of the few surviving blue books is in the Old U.S. Mint Museum, along with several beautiful stained-glass windows from a bordello.

THE 20TH CENTURY AND THE NEW MILLENNIUM

THE CENTURY BEGAN PROMISINGLY: oil was discovered in Louisiana, and the new dredging and refining industry pumped new money into the regional economy (and pollutants into the water). In the early decades of the century, so many Italian workers moved to New Orleans to work the docks and oil fields that portions of the Quarter and Warehouse District were nicknamed "Little Palermo," and Metairie remains a hub of Italian surnames. But a second potential moneymaker, jazz, which had struck its first ragtime notes just before the turn of the 19th century, was turned out: the Storyville neighborhood, the bordello area and center of the burgeoning "jass" movement, was closed and virtually bulldozed off the face of the earth. "King" Oliver, Jelly Roll Morton, and other prominent musicians moved north to New York and Chicago, launching successful careers and a nationwide craze.

Some New Orleanians might have felt that the Great War was being fought at home. A massive hurricane struck the city in 1915, devastating the economy and widening the division between the well-to-do and the subsistence farmers; and though a cure for the dreaded yellow fever had been discovered in the early years of the century, the great influenza epidemic of 1918 killed at least 35,000 residents. In 1927 one of the worst floods in history flattened the city, ushering the Depression into the state even before it struck the rest of the nation. (Such natural disasters are a repeated chorus in Louisiana history: Hurricanes Betsy, in 1965, and Camille, in 1969, caused billions of dollars' worth of damage, and periodic floods have caused even more damage.)

Louisiana would have remained a virtual feudal society had it not been for the antiestablishment revolution of Huey Long, the "Kingfish"—populist, demagogue, and drunk—who became governor in 1928 and bullied, bludgeoned, and blackmailed the state legislature into expanding public education, roads, and hospitals. Within a year he was indicted on bribery charges, but he was cleared and subsequently elected to the U.S. Senate. He began as a vocal New Deal supporter but soon embraced a populism that bordered on socialism and alarmed even the most liberal of Washingtonians. In 1935, while on a trip home, he was assassinated, but the Long arm of family law stretched on: his brother Earl was a two-time governor, and his son Russell served in the U.S. Senate from 1948 until 1986.

The growth of industry, particularly oil and natural gas, has been a boon to the state economy, if not the ecology. By 1980 more than 40 countries maintained consular offices in New Orleans, an indication of the power of a trade port that accommodated more than 5,000 international vessels every year. But in 1984 the massive World's Fair Exposition, set up along three wharves with an eye toward the rejuvenation of the Warehouse District, ran heavily into debt and, combined with the collapse in world oil prices, came perilously close to bankrupting the city. What resulted was symbolic: the harder industries turned to the softer tourism industry for partnership. The wharf areas that were renovated for the World's Fair are now the site of the Riverwalk Marketplace and the vast and expanding Convention Center, which brings in more than a million people a year by itself. The luxury hotels along Canal Street and in the burgeoning Warehouse District owe their existence primarily to the face-lift connected to the fair. And the legalization of gambling has brought in some money to the state (although the on-again, off-again construction of the massive Harrah's casino near the foot of Canal Street bankrupted many smaller subcontractors along the way). The Morial Convention Center was the biggest and busiest in the United States. New Orleans was booming into the 21st century.

And then came Katrina.

WHEN *the* FLOODGATES OPENED

THERE IS NO UNDERESTIMATING the impact that Hurricane Katrina had, and continues to have, on New Orleans and the surrounding area. (Although much additional damage was caused by Hurricane Rita less than a month later, including the reflooding of the Lower Ninth Ward and Gentilly neighborhoods, "Katrina" is generally used as a shorthand for both calamities.) Even in a city that has withstood three centuries of plagues, fires, floods, wars, and horrific storms, August 29, 2005, looms as terrifying as September 11, 2001, in New York.

With the closure of the train stations and airports on August 28 and the fumbled fueling of school and commercial buses expected to transport locals, tens of thousands were trapped in the city. On the highways, already gridlocked traffic was immobilized as gas stations ran dry. Staffs at hospitals and health-care centers that were to have been served by those same buses were forced to evacuate as many patients as they could, and many stayed behind in shameful and rapidly degenerating circumstances. Mayor Ray Nagin's mandatory evacuation order on the 28th, many hours after the danger of a cataclysmic strike was clear, only added to the chaos.

When Katrina finally struck—and she actually made landfall three times, once as a relatively mild Category 1 in South Florida, then at near–Category 4 force, and again at Category 3 in Louisiana—she brought 8 to 10 inches of rain to the city, 15 inches to Slidell. Four-fifths of the city and surrounding areas were flooded, St. Bernard Parish entirely so. As the water rose, the Interstate 10 bridge to Slidell collapsed, and the Lake Pontchartrain Causeway was limited to emergency vehicles. Nearly a million people were without power or manner of escape, and as the water rose, hundreds struggled to hold on for rescue from attics and rooftops and boats.

If the Vietnam War was the "television war," Katrina was the broadcast catastrophe, with scenes of devastation, hunger, panic, heroics, faith, and governmental fumbling at all levels played out day after day in the public eye. The once highly efficient Federal Emergency Management Agency (FEMA), which had been incorporated into the Department of Homeland Security after 9/11, became a national laughingstock. Only days after being reassured by President Bush that "Brownie, you're doing a heckuva job," FEMA head Michael Brown was out of work. The 26,000 people shoehorned into the Superdome, designated as the city's official "refuge of last resort," quickly overwhelmed its facilities (and the roof was peeled back by the storm, causing more panic). Another 20,000 took shelter in the Morial Convention Center. Families were separated, children lost, the elderly and disabled in dire straits, the dead unmoved. Not until September 3 were buses sent to the Superdome, and it was another day before the Convention Center was completely evacuated.

So terrible was the film footage that nations around the world immediately promised money, relief workers, and supplies. Among the countries that came to America's aid were Mexico, Canada, Germany, Russia, China, India, Pakistan, the none-too-affluent Bangladesh, Sri Lanka (which was itself still reeling from the tsunami of December 2004), and even Cuba and Venezuela, along with several wealthy Arab nations. Qatar's Sheik Hamad bin Khalifa al-Thani not

only gave $100 million, including $17.5 million to historic Xavier University (the country's only black Catholic college), but he also visited New Orleans in April 2008, touring the still-devastated Ninth Ward, and offering even more assistance.

All in all, an estimated two-thirds of the city's pre-Katrina population, a disproportionate percentage of it black, was displaced by the storms. Of the more than 1,900 persons reported dead or missing afterward, nearly all were from Louisiana. One of the New Orleans area's incorporated parishes, St. Bernard, downriver to the east, lost 95% of its pre-Katrina residents, and a year later, fewer than 40% had returned.

Just as seriously, Katrina and Rita made clear the widening gaps between the well-to-do and working-class constituencies of New Orleans. (It is widely believed among many black New Orleanians that the levees were not breached but intentionally blown up, because the noise of the floodgates breaking was so explosive.) New Orleans residents in exile found it nearly impossible to claim what aid was forthcoming, many without fixed addresses or Internet access, or to acquire elaborate permits for razing or rebuilding. As many as half the transplanted former residents told surveyors they were better off in their new homes and had no plans to return.

A year after Katrina, the issues of what and how to rebuild were as raw as ever. Little of the promised federal aid had actually been delivered, and revelations that at least $2 billion of it had been siphoned off by fraud or lost to incompetence added to the debate. Nearly half the mobile homes that were to house hurricane victims stood empty on an airfield in Arkansas while FEMA paid $250,000 a month in rent; the trailers were finally given away to other aid organizations. (Those that were distributed may have cost even more: as time went on, high levels of formaldehyde and other contaminants caused widespread health problems among the people living in them.) Practically the entire Lower Ninth Ward and the Mid-City, Lakeview, and Gentilly neighborhoods remained gutted scenes of devastation; the "belts" (high-water marks) and spray-painted notes from rescue workers were still vivid, some on roofs and second floors. Whole blocks still lacked electricity. Some areas were even "highlights" of Katrina-themed bus tours—and as macabre as that may sound, it was a necessary shock for those who otherwise might have seen only the usual, and seemingly recovered, French Quarter and Garden District.

Even in better-off neighborhoods, the continuing economic problems could be glimpsed behind the gloss of new paint. Tourism and convention business was so diminished that airlines were only offering half as many seats to New Orleans as they had before the storms. Perhaps only a third of the city's restaurants had reopened, and many of those restricted their hours, partly because of slow business but also because of a critical shortage of workers (and of the employees who remained, many warned that skyrocketing rents might drive them away as well). A similar percentage of businesses were believed to be operating, with more trickling away. By the beginning of 2007, close to two-thirds of hotels had reopened, but the ripple effect of closures that was clear in New York after 9/11 was clear here as well. Produce suppliers, dishwashers, day laborers, laundry services, janitors, delivery drivers, shrimpers, and bartenders had fewer places to ply their wares and skills—and tips, which often account for a fair percentage of their earnings, were harder to come by. At the same time, landlords were raising rents, cutting even further into their incomes.

Landscape companies and construction firms were doing good business, but even they complained of widespread theft of materials; the black market for stolen copper pipes, electrical cords, and power tools was particularly strong, making it even more difficult for victims of flooding to rebuild. (An unfortunate undercurrent of racism surfaced as well, this time against the many Mexican and Hispanic laborers who came up to work for construction companies.) Street crime and the police department's continuing manpower shortage forced the state to ask for help from National Guard troops and reservists.

Medical facilities were not only overwhelmed during the crisis but also fatally contaminated by the breakdown of facilities even before the flooding. Even now, of the seven hospitals in the area, five are still closed and two are offering only emergency services. (The loss of hospital beds has more impact on residents than tourists, of course, but it emphasizes that visitors should be sure to carry prescription medicines and copies of doctor's instructions when traveling.) Hundreds of medical professionals lost positions and had to relocate, with more ripple effects on pharmacies, uniform stores, and even home health aides and 911 dispatchers. Doctors continue to warn of long-term effects from exposure to sewage-heavy floodwaters along with mold and allergens remaining in the environment. Many schools, churches, community and social-services centers, and strip malls remain unoccupied and unrepaired.

The oil and grain industries took a serious hit for several months, as did the casinos, which not only employ hundreds of workers but also provide a substantial portion of the state's tax revenues. The buskers, street artists, and fortune-tellers who once lined Jackson Square and Royal Street became few and far between, and the queue of mule-driver carriages was much reduced.

There were some better omens: by October of 2006, the 90,000-square-foot Erato Street Cruise Terminal had opened, the Julia Street Cruise Terminal was nearly completely renovated, repair of the massive Morial Convention Center was well under way, and port officials were optimistic that the cruise-tourism industry would be at 75% of prehurricane business by year's end.

But progress is slower than some would like to admit. The school system, which was already well behind the national average in both graduation rates and reading ability, was forced nearly to start from scratch. Although the city has hired a hard-charging public school superintendent from Chicago who has pledged to radically reform the system, and though it has increased the number of charter schools, 85% of students are a year or two behind their grade level, and a third are as much as four years behind.

While the overall number of restaurants is (by some estimates) larger than before the hurricanes, many are open only part-time; the chicken-and-egg effect on waiters and bartenders means that sometimes there are openings and no workers, and at other times, the opposite.

More frighteningly, a two-year, billion-dollar program to rebuild the levees, involving 3,300 workers from the Army Corps of Engineers, has improved the flood protection only by about six inches—several feet below the water another hurricane might push in. Some walls along the Industrial Canal remain at the same level as before Katrina; the Mississippi River Gulf Outlet, which many critics say worked like a funnel to increase the flooding, remains open, and controversial. (Uncertainty on the subject led officials to declare a mandatory evacuation in advance of Hurricane Gustav in August 2008, and nearly two million residents fled. Fortunately, the city endured only an indirect hit.)

But even the size of the region is radically reduced. Prehurricane erosion of the Louisiana wetlands—thanks as much to the ill-conceived redirecting of the Mississippi River by the Army Corps of Engineers as anything else—already amounted to the loss of an entire football field every 38 minutes, or 25 square miles per year. (Wetlands are essential to braking the force of wind and storm surges.) In three-quarters of a century, Louisiana had lost 1.2 million acres, or the equivalent of the state of Delaware; Katrina and Rita together stripped another 75,000 acres. Within New Orleans itself, estimates of tree loss begin at 40,000, many of them the magnolias and live oaks of legend, while the rows of palms that had long languished along Canal Street revived, making it look more like Beverly Hills than the Big Easy. In the bayous, the death of cypress trees has been epidemic.

It will take many years for New Orleans to completely recover, and it is unlikely that it will ever be quite the same. As of September 2008, the population was estimated at 272,000—less than 60 percent of the pre-Katrina figure. The French Quarter, which many already believed had become a simulacrum of itself, has lost even more of its longtime tenants. (Indeed, prior to Katrina and Rita, some locals had disputed the addition of a statue of Bourbon Street nightlife fixture Chris Owens to a park honoring Louis Armstrong, Pete Fountain, and Al Hirt; afterward, when Owens declared she would not consider moving out of the Quarter, the grumbling ceased.) The *Times-Picayune*, whose determination to continue publishing "come hell and high water" aroused the admiration of the entire media community as well as its readers, still prints long lists of phone numbers and contacts for health, reconstruction, and administrative offices.

Because of the dispersal, some of the older mixed-race neighborhoods that were gentrifying in an almost traditionally "creole" fashion, such as Faubourg Marigny and Tremé, are increasingly white; the debate over razing or redeveloping the Ninth Ward rages on. Many scientists even suggest that massive rebuilding may be a waste, since the city continues to sink, and that global warming means the Mississippi River and Gulf of Mexico will continue to rise. If New Orleans's soul was at stake before, it faces public judgment today.

PARISHES, NEIGHBORHOODS, *and* DISTRICTS

IT MIGHT SURPRISE THOSE WHO THINK that "old" New Orleans is limited to the Vieux Carré and the Garden District, but metropolitan New Orleans has 16 National Historic Districts, including Tremé and Faubourg Marigny as well as the Warehouse District and the now critically and perhaps permanently altered Ninth Ward.

These are all within Orleans Parish (the central portion of greater New Orleans), which is roughly defined by the U-shaped bowl of the Mississippi River—the eponymous "crescent"—and lines running more or less north to Lake Pontchartrain. Many of these neighborhoods were originally laid out along fairly regular street grids, easily negotiated by newcomers, but because of the snaking of the Mississippi, the overall pattern of the center city now resembles a spider's web: sets of parallel streets occasionally are "pieced out" or head off at wider angles, and a few great, long, curving thoroughfares, such as St. Charles and Claiborne avenues and Magazine Street, follow the curve of the river. It takes a little getting used to.

Greater New Orleans also incorporates Jefferson Parish to the west beyond Audubon Park and St. Bernard Parish downriver to the east. (*Parishes* are to Louisiana what counties are to the rest of America.)

Only a few of New Orleans's neighborhoods are of real interest to tourists, but a quick overview of them may help you plan your trip. These are the same areas we have used to cluster special attractions, restaurants, nightlife, entertainment, and hotels.

THE FRENCH QUARTER

ALTHOUGH *VIEUX CARRÉ* LITERALLY MEANS "OLD SQUARE," the French Quarter is not perfectly square, as it rides a hump of Mississippi sidesaddle. And because it's tilted, it's actually closer to the shape of a diamond. (Ironically, considering the Creoles' long rivalry with their American governors, the Quarter is a fair mirror image of Washington, D.C., only in miniature.) Nevertheless, it's the easiest neighborhood to grasp logistically, because the streets do proceed in a perpendicular grid, most of them one way in alternating directions.

The boundaries are Canal Street to the southwest, North Rampart Street to the northwest, Esplanade Avenue on the northeast, and the concave line of the Mississippi to the southeast. (The legal border on the southwest is Iberville Street, but we have used Canal Street as the border throughout this book.) If you look at the neighborhood square-on, with Rampart running across the top of the grid, Jackson Square and Artillery Park are in the center at the bottom, like a stem.

This is tourist central, the neighborhood of **Bourbon Street** and all-night beignets, **St. Louis Cathedral, Preservation Hall,** and **Pat O'Brien's** Hurricanes. (Along its border with Tremé are **Ernie K. Doe's Mother-in-Law Lounge** and **St. Louis Cemetery,** a perfect metaphor for the Saturday night–Sunday morning paradox.) It includes the oldest architectural examples in the city, the most inexhaustible souvenir vendors, and the finest antiques shops, plus a handful of franchised star-power hangouts à la the Hard Rock Cafe and House of Blues. The French Quarter is something of a year-round party, justly famous for strip joints and street drinking. It has also developed a second kind of "street life" in recent years, with some of the longtime street musicians giving way to groups of punk-styled teenagers and young adults, panhandlers, and vagrants, so you may want to be less freestyle with your partying. From experience, we can tell you that the no-smoking rules, though they do not affect bars as they do restaurants, nevertheless send more smokers out on to the sidewalk, and not all are too careful with their butts. There are still full-time residents here, but in general they have withdrawn to the quieter edges of the neighborhood.

For a full description, see the walking tour of the French Quarter in Part Seven, Sightseeing, Tours, and Attractions.

CENTRAL BUSINESS DISTRICT

THE CENTRAL BUSINESS DISTRICT, generally shortened to the CBD, is a cleaver-shaped area adjoining the French Quarter on the southwest side of Canal Street and also bordering it on the northwest side of North Rampart. The CBD also includes two historic neighborhoods: the Warehouse District and the Tremé neighborhood, which itself is incorporated in the Warehouse District. On our map, the area is defined by South Claiborne Avenue/Interstate 10 on the northwest side, Business 90/Pontchartrain Expressway on the southwest, and the Mississippi on the east, with a jag from Canal Street across Rampart to Esplanade. This is also the beginning of "Uptown" New Orleans, that is, upriver from Canal Street, as opposed to "Downtown."

The CBD includes the **Ernest N. Morial Convention Center,** the **Louisiana Superdome** and the **Arena, Riverwalk Marketplace, Harrah's Casino, World Trade Center,** and the **Amtrak station.**

In the beginning, the neighborhood was known as Faubourg Ste. Marie and was the site of some early sugar plantations. However, when the Americans flooded in after the Louisiana Purchase, they chopped up the old plantations and began settling on the "other" side of Canal Street. The heart of the CBD is **Lafayette Square,** the Americans' answer to Jackson Square.

The **Warehouse District** comprises much of what had once been Faubourg Ste. Marie, including some quite impressive mansions, cultural centers, churches, and theaters. (There are also even smaller historic districts within that.) But Faubourg Ste. Marie fell out of favor as a residential neighborhood after the Civil War, leaving mostly the commercial and shipping concerns. The Warehouse/Arts District, as it's now known, is a fairly recent concept. The huge old storehouses, light-industrial hangars, and factories on the streets south of Lafayette Square and west of the Convention Center originally had easy access to the docks. Many had been abandoned or allowed to fall into disrepair in the 1960s and 1970s, and the neighborhood was ripe for redevelopment. But when plans were made to transform the dock area for the World's Fair, artists and performers began moving in, turning the old structures into lofts, studios, and display galleries. Now it's a trendy area, with several hot restaurants, hotels, many of the city's best galleries, most of its museums, and more coming in around Lee Circle. A strong campaign was mounted in the early 21st century to preserve and restore the buildings rather than raze them.

Hurricane Katrina set the neighborhood back substantially—the cult favorite Confederate Motorcycle Company, which had just moved into the District, had its home so mangled that it has relocated permanently to Birmingham; and the just-opened Hotel Monaco lay barren until the Hilton corporation finally bought it—but it is quickly recovering. Proponents see the Warehouse District as the SoHo or TriBeCa of New Orleans. The trendiness of the neighborhood is one of the factors that encouraged the revitalization of Canal Street not merely as a shopping strip but as a haven for high-profile hotels. These include the Orient-Express–owned **Windsor Court;** the **Ritz-Carlton,** constructed behind the facade of the old Maison Blanche department store; and one of two **W hotels** in the neighborhood. Even the old streetcar rails have been restored down the middle of Canal Street.

Tremé is one of the old Creole neighborhoods, part of the plantation of Claude Tremé that was bought by the city for residential development in the early 19th century. It was also one of the first black neighborhoods: Tremé is where the famous Storyville red-light district was established, now the site of a disgracefully decrepit housing project. Tremé is also the area where you'll find **Louis Armstrong Park,** the **Mahalia Jackson Theatre for the Performing Arts,** and the famous **Congo Square,** home of jazz (all currently closed at press time); **St. Louis Cemetery** (Nos. 1 and 2); several small museums of African American culture; and **Our Lady of Guadalupe Chapel.** For more information, see the walking tours of both the CBD and Warehouse District in Part Seven, Sightseeing, Tours, and Attractions.

UPTOWN AND THE GARDEN DISTRICT

UPTOWN IS BORDERED ON THE NORTHWEST by Monticello Avenue, which strikes off from the rim of the river's "cup" and marks the line between Orleans and Jefferson parishes. So in one sense the area is at the far end of the Crescent City. (Some residents of suburban Metairie and Kenner would say that New Orleans's older families seem to think so, too.)

This area is also called University, sort of shorthand for the "university neighborhood," because of the adjoining campuses of **Loyola** and **Tulane universities.** It is split virtually down the middle by the St. Charles Avenue streetcar, which makes it, like the Garden District, easily accessible from the French Quarter or hotel district. Its most famous landmark is **Audubon Park,** which stretches from the universities right to the spot where the Mississippi River turns back north, with a fine view of both banks.

At the northwest edge of the area is the **Riverbend** neighborhood, which is sort of Uptown's own counter–French Quarter, with boutiques, art galleries, bookstores, and a booming restaurant scene.

The **Garden District** is New Orleans's second-most famous neighborhood, the upper-class residential portion of the old American sector, and visually as well as historically a world away from the French Quarter. Originally there were some Creole plantation homes here—this is where the streets celebrate not only Napoleon's victories but the Muses as well—but after the turn of the 19th century, as Americans moved in above Canal Street, it became incorporated as the City of Lafayette (hence **Lafayette Cemetery** at its heart). It was annexed into New Orleans in 1852. Real-estate promoters and area residents constantly stretch the description, but the true Garden District is generally considered to fall between St. Charles Avenue and Magazine Street, Jackson Avenue on the northeast, and Louisiana Avenue on the west.

Although the area's streets occasionally shift a little as the Mississippi curves back up, the Garden District is fairly gridlike within its borders and a fine residential neighborhood for exploring (see the walking tour of this area as well). **Magazine Street** had become somewhat run down, but its ongoing revitalization has made it a popular shopping area (see Part Nine, Shopping).

FAUBOURG MARIGNY

THIS AREA, WHICH ADJOINS THE FRENCH QUARTER'S east side, has suffered a great deal more than the French Quarter from the vicissitudes of time and industrial development, but it contains many fine old houses (which are rapidly being rediscovered and restored).

Blanche DuBois's famous directions—"They told me to take a streetcar named Desire, transfer to one called Cemeteries, ride six blocks and get off at Elysian Fields"—owe most of their charm to streets in or near Faubourg Marigny, although in truth the routes wouldn't intersect. The area is named for one of the greatest charmers and greatest wastrels in New Orleans lore: Bernard Xavier Philippe de Marigny de Mandeville, who gambled away an immense fortune and gradually had to sell off his vast holdings to land developers. In 1807 Marigny subdivided his own plantation (*faubourg* means something akin to "suburb" or "cluster development"), which would become the second-oldest neighborhood in the city, and it was he who named Elysian Fields Avenue. He also gave the name Rue d'Amour, or "Street of Love," to what is today the far-less-poetic Rampart Street.

These days, the western part of Faubourg Marigny, from the edge of the French Quarter past Washington Square to Elysian Fields, is a mixed but lively neighborhood of artists, gays, hip straights, musicians, and young couples working to renovate the rambling old homes, something like the downtown Riverbend, but funkier and dicier. In fact, thanks to the number of jazz clubs that have taken root, especially along Frenchmen Street, it is in many ways the closest thing to the Bourbon Street of the true good old days.

MID-CITY–ESPLANADE

WITHIN THIS AREA ARE THE **Fair Grounds** racetrack, where the Jazz and Heritage Fest is held; the **University of New Orleans;** lovely **City Park** (which includes the **New Orleans Museum of Art** and the **Botanical Gardens**); and the **Pitot House** on **Bayou St. John,** the original passage the French took moving in from Lake Pontchartrain toward the Mississippi (and a Native American route long before that). The stretch of Esplanade Avenue near the Fair Grounds and bayou, known as **Esplanade Ridge,** makes for a nice mini–walking tour.

The FICTIONAL CITY

THE STUNNING SEQUENCE OF EVENTS in 2005 obviously inspired scores of books, many by respected local historians. Of the less voluminous tomes is our favorite, a collection of *Times-Picayune* columns written by our friend and sometime collaborator Chris Rose, titled *1 Dead in Attic*. Still, fiction always seems to convey more of the atmosphere and is more fun to take along on a vacation. Some of our personal favorites (not all currently in print, but widely available in secondhand stores and libraries) include the following.

Anne Rice's books about the Vampire Lestat, the Mayfair Witches, Lasher, and other characters have New Orleans settings, but far more gripping is her historical novel, *The Feast of All Saints,* about the free people of color and their culture in the years leading up to the Civil War. (For a list of New Orleans sites that figure in Rice's novels, see "Queen of the Damned," page 132.) And if you enjoy the old-fashioned style of murder mysteries, John Dickson Carr's *Papa La-Bas,* set amid the era of Marie Laveau and the quadroon balls, is as good as a voodoo tour of the French Quarter.

The posthumously published black-humor masterpiece *A Confederacy of Dunces,* by John Kennedy Toole, contains some of the best dialect and Bourbon Street camp of all time. Ellen Gilchrist's interrelated short stories of Garden District life in "Victory over Japan" and "In the Land of Dreamy Dreams" and the contemporary crime novels of James Lee Burke are quite different, but all first rate. Burke's tales of ex-cop–turned–private-eye Dave Robicheaux showcase the still-pungent tang of Cajun bayou and middle-class Louisiana life (along with a little murder, of course).

If you can find the books of George Washington Cable, you will love his late-19th-century stories of Creole romance and adventure. One of his stories inspired the name of **Madame John's Legacy,** a historic house in the French Quarter. The same is true of the novels of Frances Parkinson Keyes, notably *Dinner at Antoine's, Steamboat Gothic* (set at San Francisco Plantation), and *Madame Castel's Lodger,* about the house she and General P. G. T. Beauregard both lived in. (See a description of this house and Madame John's Legacy, now museums, in Part Seven, Sightseeing, Tours, and Attractions.)

Walker Percy might be the city's foremost "serious" novelist, edging out William Faulkner by dint of long residence (Faulkner only stayed a few years). Percy had an almost unequaled sense of the minute degrees of social distinction, coming as he did from one of the area's most prominent clans. Most of his novels, among them *The Moviegoer* and *Love among the Ruins,* are set in the New Orleans area. Faulkner's novel *Pylon* and several of his short stories have New Orleans backgrounds, as do Tennessee Williams's *A Streetcar Named Desire, The Rose Tattoo,* and *Suddenly Last Summer,* among others. The residences of Williams, Faulkner, and several others are pointed out in the walking tour of the French Quarter described in Part Seven.

In recent years, Kate Chopin's works, particularly *The Awakening,* one of the first great feminist novels of the late 19th century (set in New Orleans), have been rediscovered, and deservedly so. William Sidney Porter, better known as O. Henry, lived in New Orleans for a little while before the turn of the 19th century, and some of his stories, including "Cherchez la Femme," are set in the city. In fact, local legend has it that he borrowed his famous pseudonym from a popular bartender, whose services were routinely summoned by a call of "Oh, Henry!" The city also makes several cameo appearances in Mark Twain's *Life on the Mississippi,* the sketches he wrote about piloting a steamboat.

Finally, if you'd like to raise a toast to your favorite writer, O. Henry fans should head to **Tujague's** (823 Decatur Street). For almost everyone else—Hearn, Twain, Walt Whitman, William Makepeace Thackeray, and even Oscar Wilde—go to the **Old Absinthe House** at 240 Bourbon Street. Ask for a Sazerac.

PART TWO

PLANNING *your* VISIT

WHEN *to* GO

PICK YOUR PARTY

METEOROLOGICALLY SPEAKING, most residents consider that New Orleans really has only two seasons: summer—a sticky, sweltering southern classic prone to afternoon showers and dramatic sunsets that lasts roughly from May 1 to October 1; and a long, cool, and almost identically damp fall-into-spring that rarely dips to the freezing point.

But in terms of tourism, New Orleans has gradually developed four major holiday "seasons": Carnival (or, as most people think of it, Mardi Gras), which leads up to that Fat Tuesday blowout somewhere between February 3 and March 9; the New Orleans Jazz and Heritage Festival, from the last weekend of April through the first weekend of May; Halloween, which boomed in the Anne Rice era; and Creole Christmas, a lower-key but increasingly popular group of events spread throughout December and lasting through New Year's Eve and the Sugar Bowl. And that doesn't even count the occasional Super Bowl or NCAA Final Four, or the dozens of other less famous festivals and celebrations around the city.

unofficial **TIP**
If you plan to visit New Orleans during Mardi Gras, you might seriously consider staying in the suburbs to avoid the almost 24-hour noise, or at least try to get something in the Garden or Warehouse Districts, where you can enjoy the traditional decorations without the full French Quarter hedonism.

If you plan to come during the four big holidays, there are a few things you ought to consider. First, the fun is only nominally free. Don't be surprised if you have to pay premium rates for hotel rooms and airline seats, especially around Mardi Gras and Jazz Fest, *if* you can get them. That's another thing to know: you'd better get a hotel reservation immediately, because most of the events are sold out well in advance, and some people make reservations for Mardi Gras more than a year ahead. Mardi Gras can fall on any Tuesday between February 3 and March 9. It falls on February 24 in 2009, February 16 in 2010, March 8 in 2011, and February 21 in 2012. (The festival moves because it is fixed 46 days before Easter, which is itself fixed by the lunar schedule, falling on the first Sunday after the first full moon after the equinox.)

A third factor is that the sheer size of the crowd may begin to sour on you after a while. Many restaurants and bars simply pack up the tables during Mardi Gras and settle for making money on the itinerant drinkers; restaurants that maintain their poise may refuse to make reservations or require you to leave a deposit or credit card number in case you fail to show up. (And realize again that with such a crowd, getting around town is really tricky.) Restrooms quickly overload, and overloaded drinkers may settle for the street. An increasing number of nicer restaurants, especially along parade routes, are opting to close entirely during the last week of Carnival.

If you're coming in a Super Bowl or Final Four year, you'll have the same problem with overcrowding: even football fans without game tickets flock to the city, either in hopes of scalping seats or just to enjoy the televised hoopla. But if you can't resist these famous events, read the special information on each in Part Three, New Orleans's Major Festivals.

If you have more general interests or want to take the family, pick a less frenetic time to go: between Easter and the Jazz Fest, usually held around late April and early May, is very quiet, and you can enjoy the French Quarter Festival, a smaller and more local jazz and heritage festival not yet quite so crowded; September and early October are warm and usually fine; in March you can enjoy another underestimated attraction: the astonishing, high-spirited, and eccentric Tennessee Williams/New Orleans Literary Festival. Even winter can be nice if you like a brisk walk, and there are certainly no crowds in the museums. If you're traveling on business, of course, you may not have much of a choice.

The good news is that except during the big festivals, you will rarely have to stand in line, except for a table. There are so many distractions in New Orleans that only a couple of attractions (the ticket booth at the Aquarium of the Americas and IMAX theater, perhaps) collect much of a queue. And you can usually avoid that by going early or buying tickets a day in advance.

WEATHER OR NOT . . .

IF YOU AREN'T USED TO SOUTHERN SUMMERS, you may find your visit to New Orleans a sticky experience. (You'll see T-shirts all over the French Quarter that read, "It's not the heat, it's the stupidity," which gives you some idea how tired the natives are of hearing tourists complain.) Thunderstorms are almost a daily occurrence in June, July, and August, but they provide only temporary relief. The epidemics

NEW ORLEANS'S AVERAGE TEMPERATURES AND PRECIPITATION

	AVERAGE HIGH	AVERAGE LOW	AVERAGE RAINFALL
January	69°	43°	4.97"
February	65°	45°	5.23"
March	71°	52°	4.73"
April	79°	59°	4.50"
May	85°	65°	5.07"
June	90°	71°	4.63"
July	91°	74°	6.73"
August	90°	73°	6.02"
September	87°	70°	5.87"
October	79°	59°	2.66"
November	70°	50°	4.06"
December	64°	45°	5.27"

of yellow fever, malaria, and cholera that used to strike from the swamp are a thing of the past, but the social and performance calendars still tend to duck the extremes of summer, and so should you, when the sun is highest. If you skim the calendar of special events, you'll see they drop off in summertime, because even in early May, during the Jazz and Heritage Festival, temperatures can hit 100°F.

On the other hand, compared to most places the climate is pretty mild. Snow is a rare and festive occurrence, and the average low temperature, even in January, is 43°F. (The average high is 69°F, which should also give you an idea of how much the mercury can swing from midnight to midafternoon.) So you can easily consider an off-peak vacation.

Late summer and early fall are, as everyone knows, hurricane season. These days, there is plenty of warning from local authorities. However, just in case you have to deal with some temporary disaccommodation because of bad weather, it's a good idea to have any essential medication on hand and perhaps to pack a small flashlight. If you're going to sign up for one of those haunting expeditions, you'll want it anyway.

GATHERING INFORMATION

BROCHURES, HISTORICAL BACKGROUND, AND UP-TO-DATE SCHEDULES are available from the **New Orleans Convention and Visitors Bureau** (2020 St. Charles Avenue, New Orleans, LA 70130; ☎ 800-672-6124 or 504-566-5011; **www.neworleanscvb.com**). For information targeted to African American visitors, contact the **New**

Orleans Multicultural Tourism Network at ☎ 504-523-5652 or check out their Web site at **www.soulofneworleans.com.** Gay and lesbian visitors may want to contact the **Lesbian and Gay Community Center of New Orleans** at ☎ 504-945-1103; **www.lgccno.net.** Jewish visitors can call the **New Orleans Jewish Community Center** at ☎ 504-897-0143; **www.nojcc.com.**

NEW ORLEANS AND THE INTERNET

THE FOLLOWING ARE THE BEST PLACES to go on the Web to launch yourself into New Orleans cyberspace:

- **www.neworleans.com** is maintained by NewOrleans.Com Media and contains advertisements, travel coupons, a hotel booking service, and articles on various subjects. Businesspeople researching New Orleans will find useful articles on banking, industry, and trade.
- **www.neworleansonline.com** is a fun Web page that is maintained by a group called the New Orleans Tourism Marketing Corporation. Subjects found on this page include music, history, people, and dining. On the practical side, you can search by amenity for a hotel room or check out the calendar of events.
- **www.nawlins.com** is an extensive Web page maintained by the New Orleans Convention and Visitors Bureau. Although this page contains helpful information for leisure travelers, meeting and convention planners will find it particularly useful.
- **www.nola.com** is maintained by the New Orleans *Times-Picayune* and offers information on news, events, entertainment, and festivals. It also offers a five-day weather forecast and a chat forum.

MAJOR TRAVEL AND RESERVATION SITES

TRAVEL AND BOOKING SITES are some of the most useful sites on the Internet today. They allow you to designate your destinations and preferences and then immediately check on a variety of available flights, cruises, tours, hotels, and rental cars.

If you make a reservation online, remember that it's just like making reservations on the phone or through your travel agent. Make sure that you are aware of any restrictions or refund policies that the sites or the related companies have in place. If you make a reservation with an airline through a Web site, you can generally assume that this airline's policies apply. If you are purchasing a vacation package or something else from one of the vacation sites, be sure to visit the policies or disclaimer sections of the site so you understand what will happen if you need to change or cancel your plans. Always check this before you submit your order.

Although there are great deals to be found on the Internet, remember that each travel provider's site is nothing more than an electronic media billboard. Be prepared for all of the hype, purple prose, and exaggeration you would find in any other kind of advertisement. Also be aware that filling out a profile will potentially make you a target for all of the provider's promotional messages. If you like to receive a lot of e-mail, fine. Otherwise, be selective.

Note: There are certain airlines, generally those that offer extra-discounted fares most of the time, that are not part of the major reservation systems. So if you want to fly on these airlines, you either have to call them directly, use your travel agent, or go to their Web sites. At the time of this writing, Southwest Airlines is one of the airlines not participating in the main reservations systems.

Listed below are some sites we find particularly useful. We are not listing all the reservation sites with booking capabilities—just the main ones as of this writing. New sites are launched every month.

www.expedia.com
www.frommers.com
www.hotels.com
www.kayak.com
www.travelaxe.com
www.travelocity.com
www.trip.com

SPECIAL CONSIDERATIONS

WHAT TO PACK

PERHAPS A LITTLE SADLY, this once most elegant of societies has become extremely informal. You probably won't see a black tie or tuxedo outside of a wedding party unless you are fortunate enough to be invited to a serious social event. Even an old, established restaurant such as Galatoire's requires only a jacket (after 5 p.m. and all day Sunday) but not a tie, and most others only recommend a jacket.

Shorts and polo shirts are everywhere, night or day, and a sundress or neat pair of khakis will make you look downright respectable. A rainproof top of some sort, a lightweight jacket, and a sweater, even a sweatshirt, may be all you'll need in the summer. Remember that you will probably be going in and out of air-conditioning as well as rain. Something along the lines of a trenchcoat with a zip-in lining or a wool walking coat with a sweater will usually do in winter. (Fur coats are not a moral issue in New Orleans, but are rarely necessary, and the constant bustle of people carrying glasses and food around on the streets might make it a risk unless you plan to spend most of the time partying in the highest fashion.)

Frankly, the two most important things to consider when packing are comfortable shoes (this is a culture of asphalt, concrete, and flagstone streets) and skirts or pants with expandable waistlines. Even if you don't think you're going to eat much, the scent of food constantly fills the air, and the Café du Monde by Jackson Square is still making those beignets—fried doughnuts dusted with powdered sugar, three for a buck—24 hours a day. Second, there is no other city in which the food is so rich and full of fat, cholesterol, salt, and calories as this, and even if you don't eat more than usual, you may temporarily feel the effects.

(Add a third item to your packing list—Alka-Seltzer.) If you don't want to pack "fat" clothes, you'd better pack your running shoes, too.

And finally, some parts of this city have a crime problem (see "Crime in New Orleans and How to Avoid It" in Part Six, Arriving and Getting Oriented), so there is no good reason to walk around flashing expensive jewelry. Leave it at home and stick to the Mardi Gras beads.

If you insist on bringing Fido or Fifi, there are a few hotels that will accept small pets, including the Loews on Poydras and the Sheraton on Canal, but it's a hot and crowded city for four-legged tourists. Consider boarding your buddy at **Zeus' Place** uptown at 4601 Freret (☎ 504-304-4718); it has Webcams so you can keep tabs on Tabby.

PLAYING HOST

IF YOU ARE COMING IN WITH A FAMILY or business group and are in charge of arranging some sort of party or reception, there are plenty of restaurants, music clubs (check out the **Voodoo Garden at House of Blues**), steamboats, and hotels with private rooms. But there are also a few less ordinary places to throw a party, if you really want to make an impression. Within City Park, for example, the New Orleans Botanical Garden has the 6,000-square-foot **Pavilion of the Two Sisters** (☎ 504-488-2896), the **Conservatory,** and various terraces where events can be catered; even **Storyland and Carousel Gardens** (☎ 504-488-2896) can be reserved for earlier events.

The **Contemporary Arts Center** (☎ 504-528-3805; **www.cacno.org**) and the **Louisiana Children's Museum** (☎ 504-586-0725; **www.lcm.org**), both within easy walking distance of the Convention Center, have spaces for rent. Blaine Kern's **Mardi Gras World** in Algiers lets party guests try on the parade masks (☎ 504-361-7821; **www.mardigrasworld.com**). The restored second-floor "Appartement de l'Empereur" at the **Napoleon House** (☎ 504-524-9752) can be reserved as well, and even though Bonaparte himself never came here, the atmosphere is quite imperial. (Since Katrina, the hours have shortened—cafe and bar: Monday to Saturday, closed Sunday; open at 11:30 a.m., cafe closes at 5:30 p.m., bar open until midnight on Friday and Saturday—but for special events it will stay open.)

PLAYING TOP CHEF

HERE'S ANOTHER IDEA THAT MIGHT either enliven a social event or provide an unusual "spouses' function" during a business convention: playing chef for a day. The only thing more famous than Mardi Gras is probably New Orleans's food, and devotees of Cajun and Creole cuisine can not only indulge in it, but also apprentice to it, at least temporarily. There are several cooking schools in New Orleans, most associated with local celebrity chefs, that offer classes during which visitors can either actively participate or simply watch and taste, depending on their ambitions.

The **New Orleans School of Cooking** at 524 St. Louis Street (☎ 504-525-2665; **www.nosoc.com**) operates Monday through Sunday and offers a two-and-a-half-hour Cajun-Creole class at 10 a.m. for $27 a person. This covers the class-cooked lunch (menu changes daily but may include jambalaya, shrimp and artichoke soup, gumbo, bread pudding, and pecan pie) and an Abita beer. Group classes and even private hands-on demonstrations are available.

The **New Orleans Cooking Experience** is guest-staffed by professional chefs. Half-day classes include two and a half hours of instruction, a four-course "dinner party," wine, and recipes ($150), and are led by such popular local chefs as Frank Brigtsen and slow-food maven Poppy Tooker. Two-day "vacations" with classes on Friday night and Saturday lunch are $290, and three-day extended classes, including dinner at Brigtsen's Restaurant, are $385. The school is located in the **House on Bayou Road,** a 1790s West Indies–style inn a short way from the French Quarter at 2275 Bayou Road (☎ 504-945-9104; **www.neworleanscookingexperience.com**).

You can even dine amid the Carnival floats at Blaine Kern's **Mardi Gras World** complex across the river in Algiers; lunch is $30 (☎ 504-361-7821; **www.mardigrasworld.com**), where a demonstration-lunch plus studio tour is $30 per person for groups of ten.

EXCHANGING VOWS

CARRIED AWAY BY THE ROMANCE OF IT ALL? There is a three-day waiting period between getting a license and being married, but the judge has the option of waiving it, so your weekend could turn out to be pretty spectacular. And he may even waive the requirement for your birth certificate if you seem sober enough. Contact the Marriage Clerk at ☎ 504-219-4611, 8:15 a.m. to 2:45 p.m. weekdays.

If you have more time to plan, the **Pharmacy Museum** has a lovely rear garden big enough for a (moderate) wedding (☎ 504-565-8027; **www.pharmacymuseum.org**), and at least part of the fee is tax deductible. The **House of Broel** in the Garden District, which houses a fantastic doll collection, is a popular wedding site and has a bridal salon onsite as well (☎ 504-522-2220; **www.houseofbroel.com**). And the courtyard at **Court of Two Sisters** restaurant (Royal Street; ☎ 504-522-7261) is extremely photogenic.

For designer gowns for the bride, her mother, and any available friends, try **Harold Clarke** (☎ 504-568-0440; **www.haroldclarke.com**) at the corner of Iberville and Dauphine in the French Quarter. For even more upscale wedding attire, head uptown to **Mimi** (5500 Magazine Street; ☎ 504-269-6464), which has the exclusive bridal wear contract with Vera Wang along with other tony designers, formal and somewhat less so (after all, there are plenty of garden spots and courtyards around). **Fleur de Paris** (523 Royal Street; ☎ 504-525-1899) can provide suitably celebratory millinery.

NEW ORLEANS FOR FAMILIES

OF COURSE, NEW ORLEANS IS MOST FAMOUS as a sort of adult playground, but if you're considering a family vacation here, don't worry. Despite all the round-the-clock bars and burlesque houses, New Orleans is full of family-style attractions, both in and out of the French Quarter. And since these are year-round, you can avoid the special-event crowds altogether.

Within the Vieux Carré is the entire **French Market.** And **Jackson Square,** with its balloon twisters, clowns, and mule-drawn carriages, is undeniably entertaining (if a bit undependable as far as historic detail is concerned). The free **Canal Street ferry** ride across the Mississippi is a perennial favorite, as is the **Musée Conti Wax Museum** (although at press time it was open to the public only on Mondays and Fridays; ☎ 504-525-2605; **www.historyofneworleans.com**). There are several doll and toy museums–stores that may attract some children, as well as the **Pharmacy Museum** (☎ 504-565-8027; **www.pharmacymuseum.org**). Kids who play dress-up will love the carnival exhibit at the Presbytere (☎ 504-568-6968), with its Aladdin's cave of crowns and pins.

unofficial **TIP**
Remember that warnings about dehydration in the city's heat go double for children.

The state-of-the-art **Louisiana Children's Museum** is in the Warehouse District (☎ 504-523-1357; **www.lcm.org**), and the new **Audubon Insectarium** in the U.S. Custom House on Canal Street has proven extremely popular—especially the insect-cooking cafe (☎ 504-581-4629). At the edge of the Riverwalk area is the Aquarium of the Americas, from which you can take a boat directly to **Audubon Zoo** in the Garden District (☎ 866-ITS-AZOO; **www.auduboninstitute.org**). The zoo is also accessible from the St. Charles streetcar, which is another family possibility.

City Park in Mid-City has an antique carousel, miniature ride-able trains, a smaller-guage train that circles a replica of the New Orleans area, the Storyland playground designed around Mother Goose characters, plus botanical gardens and a riding stable (☎ 504-482-4888; **www.neworleanscitypark.com**). Beyond the park, in eastern New Orleans, is the **Audubon Louisiana Nature Center** (**www.auduboninstitute.org**). The center once offered a planetarium, hands-on exhibits, and 86 acres of forest trails; however, it suffered much damage from Katrina and was indefinitely closed at press time.

Near the airport is a treasure trove for families, a complex of attractions called **Rivertown** (☎ 504-468-7231; **www.rivertownkenner.com**) that includes an observatory and planetarium; Mardi Gras and toy-train museums; a Native American–living museum; and the Children's Castle, where puppet and magic shows are staged. A repertory theater is also here.

(At press time, the **Six Flags** amusement park east of town was still closed and being evaluated; although no formal announcement about its future has been made, it is unlikely to reopen.)

And if you're interested in swamp and bayou life, you can either sign up for one of the several swamp tours or cruises or take a short drive to the **Barataria Preserve**—Jean Lafitte's old stronghold and now a 20,000-acre park with a Park Service visitor center, trails, and boardwalks that wind among the cypress swamps and freshwater branches (☎ 504-589-2330). Or visit the **Global Wildlife Center** near Folsom (☎ 985-796-3585; **www.globalwildlife.com**) and go nose to nose with a giraffe (see Part Seven, Sightseeing, Tours, and Attractions).

kids If you bring the kids along for the convention but have to get a little work in, contact **Accents on Children's Arrangements** (☎ 504-524-1227) to get them in on some special children's tours.

TIPS FOR INTERNATIONAL TRAVELERS

VISITORS FROM WESTERN EUROPE, the United Kingdom, Japan, or New Zealand who stay in the United States fewer than 90 days need only a valid passport, not a visa, and a round-trip or return ticket. Citizens of other countries must have a passport (good for at least six months beyond the projected end of the visit) and a tourist visa as well, available from any U.S. consulate. Contact consular officials for application forms; some airlines and travel agents may also have forms available.

If you are taking prescription drugs that contain narcotics or require injection by syringe, be sure to get a doctor's signed prescription and instructions (good advice for all travelers). Pacemakers, metal implants, and surgical pins may set off security machines, so a letter from your doctor describing your condition is a wise precaution (again, this applies to domestic travelers as well). Also check with the local consulate to see whether travelers from your country are currently required to have any inoculations; there are no set requirements to enter the United States, but if there has been any sort of epidemic in your homeland, there may be temporary restrictions.

If you arrive by air, be prepared to spend as much as two hours entering the country and getting through U.S. Customs. Canadians and Mexicans crossing the borders either by car or by train will find a much quicker and easier system. Every adult traveler may bring in, duty free, up to 1 liter of wine or hard liquor; 200 cigarettes, 100 non-Cuban cigars, or 3 pounds of loose tobacco; and $100 worth of gifts, as well as up to $10,000 in U.S. currency or its equivalent in foreign currency. No food or plants may be brought in, and the contents of personal laptops and other electronic devices may be examined. For information on sales tax refunds, see Part Nine, Shopping.

Credit cards are by far the most common form of payment in New Orleans, especially American Express, VISA (also known as BarclayCard in Britain), and MasterCard (Access in Britain, Eurocard in Western Europe, or Chargex in Canada). Other popular cards include Diners Club, Discover, and Carte Blanche. Travelers checks will be accepted at most hotels and restaurants if they are in American dollars; other currencies should be taken to a bank or foreign exchange and turned into dollar figures (the Mutual of Omaha office offers this service and wires funds in or out).

The dollar is the basic unit of monetary exchange, and the entire system is decimal. The smaller sums are represented by coins. One hundred cents (or pennies, as the 1-cent coin is known) equal one dollar; 5 cents is a nickel (20 nickels to a dollar); 10 cents is called a dime (10 dimes to a dollar); and the 25-cent coin is called a quarter (4 quarters to a dollar). There are two types of dollar coins, both nearly the same size as the quarter, but one is octagonal, with angled-off edges, and the other is a rosy gold color, not silver, so they are easily identified. Beginning with one dollar, money is in currency bills (there are both one-dollar coins and bills). Bills come in $1, $2 (uncommon), $5, $10, $20, $50, $100, $500, and so on, although you are unlikely to want to carry $1,000 or more. Stick to $20s for taxicabs and such; drivers rarely can make change for anything larger.

International visitors who shop at stores participating in the Louisiana Tax-Free Shopping (LTFS) program can get a refund on the taxes on retail purchases; see Part Nine, Shopping, for details.

If you need any additional assistance, there is an Immigration Service desk at the airport (☎ 504-467-1713). For language assistance, try the AT&T language line at ☎ 800-874-9426. You must have a six-digit client ID, provided through a business, to use this service.

And throughout the United States, if you have a medical, police, or fire emergency, dial ☎ 911, even on a pay telephone, and an ambulance or police cruiser will be dispatched to help you.

TIPS FOR TRAVELERS WITH DISABILITIES

VISITORS WHO USE WALKING AIDS SHOULD BE WARNED: only the larger museums and the newer shopping areas can be counted on to be wheelchair accessible. Many individual stores and smaller collections are housed in what were once private homes with stairs, and even those at sidewalk level are unlikely to have wider aisles or specially equipped bathrooms. Sidewalks themselves, especially the more historic flagstone or brick ones, can be uneven. The restaurants that we profile later in the book all have a disabled-access rating, but you need to call any other eatery or store in advance. Similarly, you need to call any stores you're interested in. Antiques stores in particular tend to be tightly packed and with shelving at all levels.

FOR THE NOSE THAT KNOWS

IF YOU ARE ALLERGY SENSITIVE, watch out for spring; contact-lens wearers might find backup spectacles helpful. As for smoking, it is prohibited in any public building, restaurants, on the streetcars, and in taxis. Bars that are not part of restaurants may still allow smoking at the owners' discretion. The same goes for casinos and tobacco shops, so be prepared one way or the other.

A CALENDAR *of* FESTIVALS *and* EVENTS

THESE ARE NEW ORLEANS'S MAJOR CELEBRATIONS and their approximate dates (specific ones where possible). Clearly, the long, slow recovery from the hurricanes of 2005 make many of these events problematic, so be sure to contact the various organizations before making travel plans, or ask the hotel concierge for more information. Remember, if the event requires tickets, it's best to try to arrange them before leaving home; otherwise you may find yourself paying extra or being locked out entirely. Please note that many festivals, especially in the summer, move around from year to year, and that some close down or are replaced by others; so if you are interested, contact organizers as soon as possible.

In addition to the contacts listed below, **Ticketmaster** (☎ 504-522-5555) may be able to supply tickets to particular events, although there will be an additional handling charge.

January

THE ANNIVERSARY OF THE BATTLE OF NEW ORLEANS *Early January.* The actual date is January 8, and a special mass is held on that day (see the profile for the Old Ursuline Convent in Part Seven, Sightseeing, Tours, and Attractions). However, the reenactment of the battle, with Redcoats, cannons, and encampment demonstrations, varies slightly around that. Call Chalmette Battlefield and National Cemetery at ☎ 504-589-2133, or log on to **www.nps.gov/jela.** *Note:* The battlefield and cemetery have some closed and restricted areas, though parts of the battlefield reopened in late spring of 2006. Call or visit the Web site for updates.

February

MARDI GRAS *February 24 in 2009, February 16 in 2010, March 8 in 2011, and February 21 in 2012.* (Because it is a church holiday, and is based on the lunar calendar, Mardi Gras can run into March, but it most often falls in February.) Mardi Gras—literally "Fat Tuesday," meaning the last day for observant Catholics to indulge in eating meat until Easter, is the culmination of six weeks of Carnival; see Part Three, New Orleans's Major Festivals. Contact the Convention and Visitors Bureau at ☎ 504-566-5005 and ask for the latest schedules. The day before, now called Lundi Gras or "Fat Monday," is also an organized and highly recommended event; contact Riverwalk Marketplace (**www.riverwalkmarketplace.com**), 1 Poydras Street, New Orleans, LA 70130, or ☎ 504-522-1555.

March

ST. JOSEPH'S DAY *Mid-March.* The Italian equivalent of St. Patrick's Day salutes Jesus's adoptive father and officially falls on March 19. But like St. Paddy's, the celebrations spread out a little. The symbolic gift of the feast is fava beans, which the saint is believed to have showered upon the starving people of Sicily; however, a large feast is more typical, especially for the needy. Most are private, but if you're interested in the Italian-American heritage, contact the American Italian Renaissance Foundation at ☎ 504-522-7294.

ST. PATRICK'S DAY *Mid-March.* The actual date is March 17, but the parade dates vary (and you may catch the Mardi Gras Indians in a special encore). For information on the French Quarter celebration, contact Molly's at the Market, 1107 Decatur Street, New Orleans, LA 70116, or ☎ 504-525-5169.

CRESCENT CITY CLASSIC *Late March to April (Easter weekend).* An international field runs this scenic 10K race from Jackson Square to City Park. Write the CCC at P.O. Box 13587, New Orleans, LA 70185, or call ☎ 504-861-8686. Visit the Web site at **www.ccc10k.com.**

SPRING FIESTA *Late March or early April.* A two-weekend celebration, dating back to the 1930s, featuring tours of private historic homes not usually open to the public, and culminating in a grand parade of horse-drawn carriages through the French Quarter. A featured event is the presentation of the queen and her court in Jackson Square before the big parade. Tickets for home tours are $22 in advance and $25 the day of the tour. Contact organizers at 826 St. Ann Street, New Orleans, LA 70116, or ☎ 800-550-8450, or visit **www.springfiesta.com.**

TENNESSEE WILLIAMS/NEW ORLEANS LITERARY FESTIVAL *Third week of March to early April.* This five-day event features seminars, dramatic readings (often featuring Hollywood and Broadway celebrities), theatrical productions, walking tours of the French Quarter, and the popular Stella and Stanley shouting competition in Jackson Square. Contact the Tennessee Williams/New Orleans Literary Festival, 938 Lafayette Street, Suite 514, New Orleans, LA 70113; ☎ 504-581-1144, or visit **www.tennesseewilliams.net.**

April

FRENCH QUARTER FESTIVAL *Second week of April.* This began as something of an apology to area residents (and performers) for the fact that the Jazz and Heritage Festival had gotten so large and so national. However, it's now more popular with locals than the more crowded events. Throughout the Quarter, free concerts are performed on more than 15 separate stages, and there are patio tours, fireworks, and second-line brass parades. The whole of Jackson Square and the riverfront down to the aquarium, along with the Old U.S. Mint, become a huge jazz buffet, thanks to the efforts of several dozen Cajun and Creole restaurants. Contact the French Quarter Festival office at 400 North Peters Street, Suite 205, New Orleans, LA 70130 or ☎ 504-522-5730; **www.fqfi.org.**

ZURICH CLASSIC OF NEW ORLEANS *April.* This PGA tournament sports a $6 million-dollar purse and is held at the Tournament Players Club of Louisiana on the East Bank. Call ☎ 504-342-3000 or 866-NOLA-TPC; **www.zurichgolfclassic.com.**

NEW ORLEANS JAZZ AND HERITAGE FESTIVAL *Last weekend in April and the first weekend in May.* One of the country's most popular musical events fills the Fair Grounds with food, crafts, and thousands of performers. See details in Part Three, New Orleans's Major Festivals, or contact Jazz Fest, 336 Camp Street, Suite 250, New Orleans, LA 70130, or ☎ 504-522-4786; **www.nojazzfest.com.**

May

ZOO-TO-DO *May 1, 2009 (April 24, 2009 Zoo-To-Do for Kids).* The fund-raiser for Audubon Zoo is one of the most profitable events in the country and includes food, decorations, and special performances. Call ☎ 504-861-6160 or 504-861-2537, or visit **www.auduboninstitute.org.**

GREEK FESTIVAL *Late May.* All those streets around Lee Circle didn't get to be named for the Muses for no reason. Enjoy folk dancing, Greek food, music, and crafts. Contact festival organizers at Holy Trinity Cathedral, 1200 Robert E. Lee Boulevard, New Orleans, LA 70122, or ☎ 504-282-0259, or visit **www.greekfestnola.com.**

NEW ORLEANS WINE AND FOOD EXPERIENCE *Late May.* The premier taste-of-the-town event distributes goodies from more than 75 restaurants and 200 wineries. Contact organizers at ☎ 504-529-WINE; **www.nowfe.com.**

June

THE GREAT FRENCH MARKET CREOLE TOMATO FESTIVAL *First weekend of June.* Cooking demonstrations, tastings, and music along the French Market promenade. Festival is held at French Market, 1008 North Peters Street, New Orleans, LA 70116, or ☎ 504-522-2621.

SOUL FEST *Usually held on Father's Day weekend in June.* A two-day celebration of African-American food, culture, and music at the Audubon Zoo. For information go to **www.goneworleans.about.com.**

July

ESSENCE MUSIC FESTIVAL *Early July (usually Fourth of July weekend).* A half-million people hear several days of soul, jazzy R&B, and blues in the Superdome, along with seminars, crafts, and a book fair. Visit **www.essencemusicfestival.com** for more information.

GO FOURTH ON THE RIVER *July 4.* Independence Day celebrations at various locations, including Riverwalk, Mardi Gras World in Algiers, and the French Market, include street performances, shopping specials, discounts to riverfront attractions, concerts, parades, and "dueling barges" shooting off fireworks. Visit **www.go4thontheriver.com.**

TALES OF THE COCKTAIL *Mid-July.* This rapidly expanding convention (part bartending-history seminar, part all-day cocktail party) takes place at various locations in the French Quarter; it runs through more than two tons of ice and 3,500 lime wedges a year, not to mention the booze. For information go to **www.talesofthecocktail.com.**

August

WHITE LINEN NIGHT *First Saturday in August.* Warehouse District galleries mount simultaneous openings with visual and performing arts along Julia Street. Contact the Contemporary Arts Center, 900 Camp Street, New Orleans, LA 70130, or ☎ 504-528-3805; **www.cacno.org.**

SATCHMO SUMMERFEST *First weekend in August.* Seminars, second-line parades, and a Jazz Mass are among this festival's tributes to homegrown superstar Louis Armstrong. Visit **www.fqfi.org.**

SOUTHERN DECADENCE *Last week of August through Labor Day.* This gay and lesbian Mardi Gras has grown from a mostly local fling to a national event that draws 100,000 or more to the French Quarter. It lived up to its name so successfully that conservative groups launched a campaign to ban it, but organizers managed to tone it down just enough to keep it alive. Traditional epicenter of the extravaganza is the Golden Lantern on Royal Street at Barracks. Call ☎ 504-522-8047 or go to **www.southerndecadence.com.**

DECAFEST *Last week of August through Labor Day.* This festival of gay and lesbian theater, film, music, comedy, and literary events parallels Southern Decadence and benefits HIV/AIDS organizations. Call ☎ 504-945-6789 or go to **www.decafest.org.**

September

INTERNATIONAL ARTS FESTIVAL *Second weekend in September at Scouts Island in City Park.* Music, children's activities, celebration of diverse cultures. Third-oldest festival in the New Orleans area; ☎ 504-367-1313; **www.internationalartsfestival.org.**

October

JAZZ AWARENESS MONTH *Throughout October.* Concerts, many of them free, lectures, and family events. Contact the Louisiana Jazz Federation at ☎ 504-558-6100.

NEW ORLEANS FILM FESTIVAL *Early to mid-October.* Regional and world premieres of films and screenings of award winners; the main screenings are at Canal Place Cinema. For more information, call ☎ 504-309-6633 or visit **www.neworleansfilmfest.com.**

OKTOBERFEST *Weekends throughout the month.* Venues and restaurants around town set out German food and drink; watch for polka lessons. Home base is the Deutsches Haus; call ☎ 504-522-8014.

VOODOO MUSIC EXPERIENCE *Late October.* This three-day music festival features several stages playing hip-hop, popular, alternative, and rock music. For more information, visit **www.voodoomusicfest.com.**

FRENCH QUARTER HALLOWEEN *Last weekend in October.* One of the largest gay parties of the year, and in the country, with elaborate costumes and street parading, this celebration now attracts straight participants as well.

BOO AT THE ZOO *End of October.* Annual Halloween extravaganza at the Audubon Zoo with special children's entertainment, a "ghost train," midnight "witches' races," and a haunted house. Contact the Audubon Institute, 6500 Magazine Street, New Orleans, LA 70118, or ☎ 504-861-2537. Visit **www.auduboninstitute.org.**

November

SWAMP FESTIVAL *First weekend in November.* Sponsored by the Audubon Institute and held at the zoo over two weekends, this offers close encounters with indigenous animals, a taste of Cajun food, and music and crafts. Contact the Audubon Nature Institute, 6500 Magazine Street, New Orleans, LA 70118, or ☎ 504-861-2537.

CELEBRATION IN THE OAKS *Late November to early January.* City Park kicks off the holiday season with a display of millions of lights, music, seasonal foods, and special events. Contact City Park, 1 Palm Drive, New Orleans, LA 70124, or ☎ 504-482-4888. Visit **www.neworleanscitypark.com.**

RACING SEASON AT THE FAIR GROUNDS *Mid-November to early January.* The country's oldest operating racetrack still hosts thoroughbred races Thursday through Monday during the holiday season, with 250 new slot machines and simulcasts at other times. For reservations call ☎ 800-262-7893 within Louisiana, or ☎ 504-944-5515; **www.fairgroundsracecourse.com.**

STATE FARM BAYOU CLASSIC *Late November.* One of collegiate football's long-standing rivalries, between Grambling State and Southern universities, winds up the season at the Superdome; **www.statefarmbayouclassic.com.**

December

CHRISTMAS NEW ORLEANS STYLE *Throughout the month.* See Part Three, New Orleans's Major Festivals, for details.

NEW YEAR'S EVE *December 31.* Jackson Square may not be as big as Times Square, but it holds a heck of a street party, complete with a countdown and, yes, a lighted ball—or a "Baby Bacchus" or sometimes a gumbo pot—that drops from the top of Jax Brewery. Contact the Convention and Visitors Bureau, 2020 St. Charles Avenue, New Orleans, LA 701302, or ☎ 800-672-6124.

PART THREE

NEW ORLEANS'S MAJOR FESTIVALS

MARDI GRAS MANIA

YOU COULD WRITE A BOOK ABOUT MARDI GRAS, and many people have. The big picture, you already know: it's a loud, public, and highly indulgent series of parades, formal masques and balls, and "second line" dancing. (The term refers to the parasol-wielding high-steppers who traditionally formed a second line behind the brass band, and who gradually acquire a civilian train like a comet attracting cosmic detritus.) There's partying in the streets, in the bars, in the restaurants, in the courtyards, in the parks, in the alleys—no wonder most French Quarter residents rent their homes out for the week and flee uptown, or even out of town. There's little sleep to be had, with more than a million visitors—a record two million in 2003—in town packed elbow to armpit and mug to go-cup. Tourism officials estimate that Mardi Gras spending has reached a billion dollars a year, and even the truncated celebration of early 2006 supplied an obvious boost to the city's economy as well as its spirits.

But in recent years, the ever-increasing incidents of public inebriation, fighting, nudity, petty (and occasionally greater) crime, and general vagrancy have for many people irretrievably tarnished the event; some of the oldest and most respected societies have pulled out entirely.

Some, it must be pointed out, have pulled out with less plausible excuses: after the City Council ruled in 1991 that the all-white krewes had to integrate their parades, two of the three oldest parading krewes, the venerable Comus and Momus, chose to stop parading rather than integrate. They were followed the next year by Proteus, the fourth-oldest parading krewe, though it returned to active duty in 2000. They now maintain their balls strictly as private parties. A recent Rex float, florid with flames and demons, was titled "Momus in Hades," a tribute to one of the most famous parades in Mardi Gras history: the 1877 "Hades, a Dream of Momus," which managed to insult nearly every politician at the state or national level; however, some city residents took it as a poke from Rex to its less amenable rival. (It would have been more appropriate than they knew: although it's not often mentioned, white supremacists and antifederalist groups often used Mardi Gras parades, and costume masks, as a cover for rallies and sometimes riots during Reconstruction. Some, including the Mystick Krewe of Comus, were at times virtual fronts for such groups.)

The pleading for beads and other *lagniappe* (pronounced **LAN-yap**) and the traditional cries of "Throw me somethin', mister" have degenerated to the point where members of even the highest-profile krewes knowingly twirl their fanciest prizes and demand that women bare their breasts to earn the treasure. (Worse, many female tourists don't seem to limit themselves to Mardi Gras, but flash for trash any night of the year.) Grown-ups (we use the phrase ironically) now far outperform the most spoiled and insatiable small children by stealing beads tossed to others, concealing the size of their trove, and even snatching stuffed animals and toys. Wearing the biggest and showiest beads is now a sort of measure of either testosterone or nubility, depending on the wearer. It's no wonder that the locals tend to avoid Bourbon Street and opt for smaller parties in the suburbs, or pick and choose their events. However, if you want to immerse yourself in the spirit, we can try at least to make it a little easier on you.

No city, except perhaps for Rio de Janeiro, is so closely associated with Carnival as New Orleans. In fact, it almost seems as if the city's destiny was to be the biggest Mardi Gras party town in the world: on March 3, 1699, when the Sieur d'Iberville (brother of the Sieur de Bienville) camped on the Mississippi River, the day was Mardi Gras, and that was what he named the site—Mardi Gras Point. Hedging a bit, perhaps, the city declared the 1999 Carnival season the 300th anniversary celebration. Nevertheless, it is clear that there were some rudimentary carryings-on in the area—Mobile had a Boeuf Gras, a "fatted calf" club, even before the city of New Orleans formally existed—almost from the very beginning, so observing Mardi Gras in the Crescent City is one of those things a lot of people feel they ought to do at least once.

Mardi Gras, for those who think it means "bottoms up," actually translates as "Fat Tuesday"; it's so called because it's the last day before Lent, when observant Catholics were supposed to give up meat eating (and, ideally, various other fleshly pleasures). The weeks between Twelfth Night and Lent are called Carnival, from the Latin for "farewell to meat," although the festival season certainly involves plenty of feasting—stocking up, so to speak. Although many people refer to the entire Carnival season as Mardi Gras, that title rightfully applies to only the one day, and using the term wrongly is one way to brand yourself a really green outsider. The day after Fat Tuesday is Ash Wednesday, the beginning of the sober Lenten season, which continues until Easter. In other words, Tuesday is supposed to be the last day to enjoy oneself for nearly seven weeks. Hence it became an occasion for overindulgence, followed by extreme penitence, beginning smack on the mark with midnight mass. Nowadays most people settle for the indulgences and watch the taped replay of Ash Wednesday services on television later. In fact, St. Louis Cathedral doesn't even hold midnight mass at the end of Mardi Gras any more because of the unruly crowds.

Mardi Gras is also a legal holiday in Louisiana, so get your banking done on Monday. (But be sure to check the calendar there, too; in 1999, for example, the Monday before Mardi Gras coincided with the federal holiday Presidents' Day, so there was no banking from Friday to Wednesday, and no postal service from Saturday to Wednesday. It was also Valentine's Day on Sunday, and the end of spring break for a lot of college students; so now you know how they wound up with two million people in the streets.)

Mardi Gras has a long and suitably flamboyant history in New Orleans. The French colonists celebrated Mardi Gras, or more commonly, Twelfth Night (January 6, Epiphany, when the Wise Men delivered their presents to the infant Jesus), in some form for nearly 50 years. It was Twelth Night, rather than Christmas, that was the big day, the climax to a nearly two-week reign by the Lord of Misrule. The tricolor brioche pastry now called king cake—or "couronne" meaning "crown" in French—was originally a Twelfth Night treat, as was the gateau des Rois, the Three Kings' cake, an almond cream–stuffed puff pastry still seen on some more traditional menus.

But when the city was turned over to the Spanish empire, which adhered to a much more rigorous and ascetic form of Catholicism, the governor banned the festivities—and the anti-Catholic Americans who took over after the Louisiana Purchase weren't favorably inclined toward such Papist displays, either. In fact, there was nearly a serious dustup over whether the music played at Carnival season was to be in English or in French. However, there was always at least some private partying to keep the spirit alive. By 1823 the balls were legal again, and within a few years the street parties took hold; the first walking parades were organized in 1837. As in modern times, the crowds kept swelling; a parade of mounted "Bedouins" was a huge public success in 1852, but by 1855, newspaper reports, focusing on the violence of the rabble and the drunkenness of some participants (ahem), called for an end to the celebrations.

Instead, a group of aristocratic Creoles formed the first secret krewe, the Mystick Krewe of Comus, to give the mayhem some form. It was Comus that designed the first great classical tableaux- and theme-parade floats and debuted them in early 1857. The Twelfth Night club first selected a queen and threw trinkets soon after the Civil War (during which, due to the occupation, all celebrations were cancelled). The Krewe of Rex designed the first "doubloon" in 1884. That same year, incidentally, Comus picked its first queen, Mildred Lee, daughter of the "sainted" Robert E. Lee—payback for those four years, perhaps. The theme song, the rather sappy "If Ever I Cease to Love," was a signature song of New York vaudeville star Lydia Thompson, who was performing in New Orleans in 1872. The lovesick Grand Duke Alexis of Russia followed her south, and in his honor every krewe played the number in its parade (except Momus, which fortunately had thrown its inaugural parade on New Year's Eve). Now it's not so common, but Rex and his court still begin their ball with it.

The first "electric parade" was in 1889, when the appropriately named Krewe of Electra wired the headdresses of more than 125 paraders. The first black organization, the Original Illinois Club, was founded in 1895; the first all-woman krewe, Les Mysterieuses, followed suit the next year and held a formal ball, though the first all-woman parade, by the Krewe of Venus, wasn't launched until 1941. (It has since disbanded.) The gay Krewe of Petronius threw its first ball in 1962; there are now four gay krewes. Mardi Gras has survived wars (though the only times it has been cancelled were during the Civil War and World Wars I and II), Prohibition (only Rex paraded in 1920), fires, blizzards, monsoons, epidemics (most of it was lost to yellow fever in 1879), racial tensions (with losses, as mentioned), and hurricanes (1965's Betsy chewed up a chunk of several krewes). The first post-Katrina Mardi Gras, held in 2006 (despite much controversy), was much curtailed—11 krewes did not parade, routes had to be rearranged, and many of the most popular school marching bands were so sparse they had to combine forces—but it proved a major emotional boost to the town.

The major parades include dozens of floats, punctuated by marching bands and mounted police, and may require the talents of 2,000 or 3,000 people. Mardi Gras expert Arthur Hardy, who has been publishing the semiofficial guide to Mardi Gras for more than 20 years, has calculated that the parades of Endymion, Bacchus, and Orpheus, which are held the three nights leading up to Mardi Gras, among themselves account for 3,750 members, 110 floats, 90 marching bands, and 375 units.

Most of the krewes (the only correct spelling for Mardi Gras "crews") have names and themes taken from classical mythology: Aphrodite, Pegasus, Mercury, Ulysses, Saturn (which has not rolled since the hurricanes), Rhea, Argus, Atlas, Atreus, Helios, Orion, Poseidon, Pan, Hermes, Zeus, Juno, Diana, Hercules, Venus, Midas, Mithras, Isis, Iris, Thor, and Thoth ("tote," as it's pronounced locally) have all had their own krewes, although not all survive or parade. Most members are masked, and many never even reveal their membership, especially those who belong to charitable clubs.

Although the strict secrecy has eased a little, some krewes still keep parade themes and rulers quiet until the last minute. The captain of the krewe, who is actually the executive officer, is a permanent position, but the king, queen, and court change from year to year. Rex, considered the real King of Carnival, is never publicly identified until the night before. The "dictator" of the Krewe d'État, which was formed only in 1996 and is trying to return the parades to their original political and satirical tone, is never publicly identified. Depending on the krewe, the royals may either be mature members of the business and social communities, or up-and-comers, with queens and ladies drawn from the debutante circle. In the older social families, there may be more than one generation of kings and queens, and several lesser lights.

Bacchus, on the other hand, is the most celebrity-conscious position and regularly crowns actors of, let us say, obvious appetites, such as John Goodman and James Belushi, and the verbally voracious Larry King. The Krewe of Orpheus, named after the musician so eloquent he persuaded Hades to release his dead wife (although she slipped away again), was founded in 1994 by Harry Connick Jr. as the first "super krewe" with male and female members, and its parade on Saturday night is considered one of the modern highlights. Over the years, celebrities as wide ranging as the Beach Boys, Dolly Parton, Stevie Wonder, Whoopi Goldberg, Bob Hope, Britney Spears, Toby Keith, Marisa Tomei, Sean Astin, and Jackie Gleason have been lured to the throne of parade floats.

In its heyday, and even up until fairly recently, Creole Carnival season was a much more elegant affair, with fancy-dress and masquerade balls, elaborate trinkets, and *lagniappe,* a word meaning something like "a little extra" and applied to any small gift or token, even a nibble or free drink. Nowadays, yelling "Throw me somethin', mister" may get you beads, candy, bikini pants, or almost anything—if you can wrest it away from the next guy, or the girl on his shoulders. (The familiar purple, green, and gold colors represent justice, faith, and power, and you may need all three to survive.) Even now, being a krewe member is fairly expensive; it costs more than $3,000 to ride with Krewe of America.

Obviously, you need not be a New Orleans resident to participate—the Southern Trial Lawyers Association annually schedules its convention in New Orleans to coincide with Mardi Gras so that members may parade with the Bards of Bohemia—but the most traditional dances are still sponsored by old-line krewes, and their parties are still by closely guarded invitation only, many of them doubling as the debutante balls of their members' daughters. They often get to sit in special boxes along the parade routes and be saluted by their loyal following on the floats, and some actually ride and toss themselves.

Even if somehow you do get invited to a traditional krewe ball, remember that you are not a member and can only sit in the spectator seats and enjoy the show. (The only exception is a woman guest issued a "call-out card"; she will sit with the other eligible women until the dancing begins and her escort calls her out.) And it is quite a show: the last year's court will be presented, and the costumes displayed in tableaux. The ball of the Krewe of Rex, for example, which is probably the most intently traditional, follows so rigid a line that its party directives are reprinted almost word for word as stories in the *Times-Picayune* every year—sort of an inside joke:

> *It begins about 6 p.m. the day before* Mardi Gras (Lundi Gras *or "Fat Monday") with Rex's being ferried downriver (in the 19th century it was a paddleboat; these days, he's transported by Coast Guard cutter) to land at Spanish Plaza at the foot of Canal Street. There he is greeted by the King of Zulu. Rex reads a proclamation declaring the advent of festivities—a little late, but then he is the official King of Carnival—fireworks ensue, and he and his retainers head for their ball, usually held at a downtown hotel or the convention center. The captain announces the arrival of the court, in order of precedence; the court dances the first dance and then everybody gets to join in. Around 9 p.m., however, a messenger from the Krewe of Comus is announced; he invites Rex and his Queen to visit the Comus court (usually in the neighboring ballroom), and Rex and company head over for another presentation to the King of Comus, who, unlike Rex, is never unmasked.*

Some outsiders may find all this pompous circumstance a little strange, especially in contrast to the other parties in the street. (Among the better-natured spoof parades is the annual Mystic Krewe of Barkus parade, a fund-raiser for the Louisiana Society for the Prevention of Cruelty to Animals (LSPCA) that has chosen such themes as "Lifestyles of the Bitch and Famous" and "Jurassic Bark.") However, many newer and more-liberal krewes throw more-public and less-tradition-bound "supper dances," and you may be able to get tickets to some of those. Orpheus and Tucks, for example, sell party tickets through Ticketmaster. You can even join a krewe and ride for a few hundred bucks.

> *unofficial* **TIP**
> Arthur Hardy's essential *Mardi Gras Guide* will probably be all over town when you get there, but you would be smart to have one in advance, because it includes maps, schedules, tips, gossip, features, and even the occasional coupon. Write to 602 Metairie Road, Metairie, LA 70005, call ☎ 504-838-6111, or go to **www.mardigrasguide.com**.

Carnival season in New Orleans traditionally begins with the Krewe of Twelfth Night ball held on Twelfth Night or Epiphany (January 6), but the pace gradually picks up: the last 10 or 12 days of Carnival is high parade season, when at almost any moment police sirens announce the imminent arrival of a marching band, motorcycle drill team, or horseback troupe, stilt-walking clowns, acrobats, balloon twisters, and professional and amateur dancing girls. Although these are rarely as elaborate or as lengthy as those in the final few days, they are often just as entertaining and not nearly so crowded. The French Quarter in particular erupts into walking parades of ordinary celebrants that form behind the bands and second-liners. One of the sweetest is a parade of elementary-school children, with a tiny king who sometimes loses his crown as his mule-drawn carriage turns a corner. (For renting or buying costumes, see "Mardi Gras and Music" in Part Seven, Sightseeing, Tours, and Attractions; or look in Part Nine, Shopping.)

And since any real business pretty much comes to a halt after lunch on Friday, the city has instituted a more recent celebration on Lundi Gras. It's actually one of the best things about Carnival these days, involving a whole day of music (two stages' worth) on the riverfront and in front of the Aquarium of the Americas. That's followed by the landing of Rex and the fireworks on the Spanish Plaza, a free public masquerade ball, and the lavish one-two parades of the Bards of Bohemia (all professional entertainers, including the fire swallower who was married to his assistant on the float as they passed City Hall), and the celebrity-laden Orpheus.

Though the most famous parades use St. Charles Avenue and Canal Street, not all the parades do: various routes go uptown, downtown, or into the suburbs, and some guidebooks have maps and information. (The French Quarter is no longer used for the big parades except in a few cases, and only for a couple of blocks.) The *Times-Picayune* publishes a daily list of routes and times of parades—along with anecdotes, full-color photographs, ball-queen presentations, and literally pages of trivia—throughout the Carnival season.

Mardi Gras day more or less officially kicks off with one of the real highlights, the Zulu Social Aid and Pleasure Club parade. The role of Zulu is a key one, because it brings up some racial issues still not very smoothly settled in New Orleans, as we've mentioned elsewhere. The Zulu parade dates from early in the 20th century, when a black resident named William Storey parodied the elaborately crowned Rex by strutting behind his float wearing an old lard can on his head and calling himself "King Zulu."

Gradually, however, the Zulus' plucky sense of humor, their no-holds-barred self- *and* social parody, and their very serious accomplishments (like the best of the old-line krewes, Zulu is made up of respected professionals and community activists) have given it a rare prestige. Nowadays the Zulus' gilded coconut shells are among the most coveted throws, and it is an even greater honor, especially for a white resident, to be invited to participate. Of course, they have to wear blackface and a grass skirt; but then even the black members and the king himself do the minstrel-show makeup thing.

And finally, in 1999, at "the last Mardi Gras of the millennium" as they said inaccurately but grandly, Rex not only accepted King Zulu's greeting at the river but also exchanged greetings, king to king. It was a subtle shift, but one obvious to everyone in the crowd, and it may have been the most important event of the entire festival. It was also the 50th anniversary of the year that Louis Armstrong rode as King Zulu, and that was frequently alluded to as one of Fat Tuesday's greatest moments. (Armstrong's wife returned as queen in 1973.)

unofficial **TIP**
The InterContinental hotel at 444 St. Charles is among those setting up grandstand seats for the parade of Rex and selling them in a package with buffet meals; call ☎ 504-525-5566.

So the parade of Zulu, which leads straight into Rex, is a touchstone event of the day—the inaugural event, in fact. It begins at 8:30 a.m. (theoretically) and then heads off toward downtown as the various "walking clubs" are promenading about town to set the tone. These range from the Half-Fast Walking Club, founded by legendary jazz clarinetist Pete Fountain, which walks the traditional Canal and St. Charles route; to the more daringly clad entertainers of Bourbon Street's bars and strip joints; to the fantastically beaded and befeathered black "Indians" of Kenner and Metairie, such as the revered Wild Tchoupitoulas tribe, whose chiefs are required to sew their costumes themselves and indulge in great competitions of face, style, and song. (These suits, veritable walking floats of feathers, beads, and sequins, may weigh 300 pounds.) The highly competitive Bourbon Street Awards, the gay costume competition around the intersection of St. Ann and Burgundy streets outside the Rawhide bar, warms up around midday, as less formal processions are forming all over town.

The most elaborately "classical" float, the crown-shaped vessel of Rex, King of Carnival, takes off at 10 a.m. and arrives at Gallier Hall around midday, preceded by a cohort of gold-helmeted lieutenants and white horses. Atop one of Rex's floats is a papier-mâché fatted ox, or *boeuf gras*, reminding you of the meatless days to come. The parade route goes across St. Charles Avenue starting as far back as Napoleon Street, so if you can find a place along St. Charles, you can see everything without being swamped by the Bourbon Street brawlers. There are limited bleachers put up, but the public tickets generally go on sale right after Christmas; contact the Metropolitan Convention and Visitors Bureau.

Don't worry about running dry; to accommodate early parade-goers, many bars open at 8 a.m., and the convenience stores along the parade routes do a continual carryout business. But remember, Fat Tuesday ends on Ash Wednesday, and like Cinderella's coach, it turns into a pumpkin exactly at midnight. This is the one and only time that "time" is definitely called in New Orleans, so be prepared. The police, led by the many mounted officers who warm up for duty by parading during the day, "sweep" the French Quarter in a maneuver that is as invariably part of the next day's newspaper photo spread as Miss America jumping in the Atlantic City surf the morning after the pageant.

In the meantime, try to pace yourself. Consider the paucity of restrooms; most hotels issue colored wristbands to make sure only paying guests get in, and no bar or restaurant is going to welcome you if you don't plan to purchase anything. The city does place some portable toilets around the parade routes, near the music stages along the riverfront, but they quickly become overloaded, and many people, especially the younger guys, are reluctant to go so far from their parade-side stations to use them. Unfortunately, since a lot of people will lose either patience or control, you'll have to be careful where you walk, much less sit, especially in the Quarter.

However, if you do some careful scouting early in the day, you may see a fairly new Mardi Gras phenomenon: pay-per-visit portable-restroom parks. A few clever entrepreneurs have taken to renting toilets, setting them up in strategic locations, and charging for their use. A couple of years ago, a guy put up 28 of them near Bourbon Street and Iberville, and clients paid $1 per visit during the day and $2 after 6 p.m., or bought an all-day pass for $10. In return, a host stayed on duty to maintain order, keep the johns as clean as possible, and spray them with air freshener. The next year, several more porta-parks appeared, including one right on Canal Street. Some restaurants and shops also put signs up advertising toilet privileges for $2 or $3 a trip, but the quality control leaves a lot more to be desired.

To be quite frank, the best way to enjoy Mardi Gras is to pick a couple of days, immerse yourself in the party spirit, and be gone by the time Fat Tuesday gets into high gear. You could come for Friday and Saturday, see the Endymion and Bacchus parades, among others, and get your fill of beads and friendly strangers while the bloom is still on the rose. (Traditionally, many local residents pull out on Sunday morning.) Or even come in as the first wave of hotel guests goes, spend Sunday and Monday, getting the most out of Lundi Gras, and take the early-Tuesday flights out. The detritus starts to build up pretty heavily by Monday—in 1999 street cleaners, sweeping up right behind the police, gathered an estimated 932 tons of garbage, and that's just in New Orleans alone, not counting the neighboring parishes.

But if you want to see the real thing, here are some tips on how to have fun and look like a native. If you're going to be within tossing distance at a night parade—that is, either in a stand with fairly good access or staked out right behind the barricades—you should also have a handful of quarters in your pocket to throw to the torchbearers. They are reminders of the men who once carried real flaming-pitch torches (today's torches are fueled with naphtha) for the Krewe of Comus, which was the first to figure out how to turn parading into a nighttime spectacle. The really experienced carriers not only twirl these heavy torches, called *flambeaux,* but they can also spot the glint of coin from yards away. They have to—although this traditional tribute goes back a long way, few nonnatives know about it, and so, despite the huge popularity of Mardi Gras, the cut of flambeaux carriers has been getting pretty short in recent years. If you feel like looking for dollar coins to toss, they'd be grateful.

Aside from a couple of vendor trucks offering steam-table Thai or Chinese, you'll probably have to settle for a hot dog or pizza. (This is along the parade route; there will be more of those turkey-leg and jambalaya concessionaires along the river.) Plastic containers are a lot safer than glass or metal, but since so many people will be buying alcohol as the day goes on, you'll be surrounded by both eventually, so real shoes are a good idea, too. And you should bring a lot of water or soda, because you will be dehydrated, and the markups at quick-stops are steep.

unofficial **TIP**
When it comes to food supplies during parades, it's smart to bring your own.

Veteran parade-goers take duffel bags or shopping totes to put their goodies in. You can only put so many beads over your shoulders—you will find that the cumulative weight is pretty surprising—and come the next parade, or the next morning, it starts all over again. According to "Mardi Gras Man" Arthur Hardy, just those same three parades, Endymion, Bacchus, and Orpheus, toss more than 1.5 million plastic cups, 2.5 million doubloons, and around 25 million beads. And they aren't even the only krewes parading at one time. So you might as well be picky; hold on to the good ones and let the cheapies go to the kids.

unofficial **TIP**
Think about donating left-over Mardi Gras trinkets to a shelter, a hospital children's ward, or the like.

One of the perennial mysteries of Ash Wednesday is not a spiritual but a material one: What do you do with all those trinkets? Do you ship them home? Throw them out? Try to sell them to a bead merchant for the next year? Good luck. You could decorate your Christmas tree with them, but you'll still have to store them for eight months. Trust us, a few strands will do you.

Another thing that comes in handy if you're serious about being really close to the action is goggles of the sort used in racquetball, especially for children whose reflexes may not be as quick. A slung rope of beads is like an Argentine bolo, and pretty dangerous. There are likely to be incoming missiles from several angles at once; and as the parades get more elaborate and the crowds get rowdier, you are almost certain to get a few bruises. It may come as a rude surprise, but the 50-year-old tourist trying to revive his career as a Lothario can be just as much of a toss hog as any teenager. Worse, in fact. And now that beads are bigger and heavier and the float riders start showing off by slinging out huge handfuls of them at a time, you can occasionally take quite a shot. Even large cheap sunglasses might help, if you can keep them on.

Leave your car out of the neighborhood if possible; many streets are closed off, and parking regulations are vigorously enforced. If you inadvertently drive into a parade route, it can cost you a cool $100.

First-time Mardi Gras celebrants, many of whom have never been to New Orleans at all, frequently come anticipating dinner at the famous restaurants of the French Quarter. Be sure to make your reservations

unofficial **TIP**
Don't carry a lot of cash, and put it someplace other than your pocket.

well in advance, because a fair number of the trendiest ones will be closed Tuesday or even for several days beforehand because the closing-off of parade routes makes it so hard for their patrons to get in and out that it's not worth staying open. Some give up the sit-down dishes in favor of sandwiches and salads. Others that are located in hotels, such as the Windsor Grill in the Windsor Court, are open only to hotel guests who can show their identification bands. So do some advance work. And if you get the little doll in your slice of the tricolor King Cake, you have to throw the next party.

Here's another piece of logic that often fails to dawn on outsiders: since so many of the parade routes include St. Charles Avenue and Canal Street, the streetcar doesn't run on Fat Tuesday, and not for huge parts of the days and nights beforehand. (The parade routes are not only marked off by portable fences, they are actively patrolled by police officers, who are instructed to prevent civilians crossing the road and are sometimes downright truculent about the available options.) Similarly, since many of the parades wind up down at the convention center or at major hotels where the krewe balls are held, the Riverfront Line is blocked off. So quaint as they are, and handy as it may seem, this is one time you're not going to be able to use public transportation. Cabs are going to have a hard time negotiating the area as well, so the best thing is to have a coherent plan and be ready to walk it.

And you should also realize that these parades are long, long affairs, several hours' worth—sometimes all day. For one thing, you have to beat the band. Unless you have a grandstand ticket (and to some extent, even if you do, because they are only for sections, not specific seats), you need to stake out a position along the parade route a couple of hours early. Many people who want prime territory spend all night or show up at the literal crack of dawn toting sofas, stepladders, and lawn chairs. So if, for example, you decide to view Zulu and Rex from farther uptown, and Zulu is scheduled to start off at 8:30 a.m., you need to be down on the street by 6:30 or 7 a.m., if not sooner.

Then, even if Zulu does get off on time, it will be 10:30 or 11 a.m. before it turns the corner of St. Charles onto Canal (so you need to be in position by 8:30 or 9 a.m., and then expect to have to hold your ground against invaders). Each parade takes a couple of hours to pass, followed immediately by Rex, followed by the dozen Elks Club trucks, followed by the Crescent City trucks, which are huge semis honking and wheezing, all still bearing dozens of bead-tossers, followed by the Krewe of America . . . and sometimes the police barricades never open in between. So if you stake out your position at 8 a.m., it may be 6 p.m. before you can cross the parade without going a very, very long way out of your way. Especially if you're downtown, you need to be sure which side of Canal—in the Quarter or out—you want to spend most the day. If you want to see the costume parades and balcony parties on Bourbon Street, plan to cross Canal before 9:30 a.m., catch a bit of Zulu, and cut away.

The same goes at night; if you enjoy the Lundi Gras festival at Spanish Plaza, which generally lasts until around 7:30 p.m., then get into position for Bards of Bohemia, you may be there until after midnight waiting for Orpheus to finish up. So make sure you consider the map in advance. (It's midnight: do you know where your hotel is?)

kids If you want to come to Mardi Gras and bring your kids, but don't necessarily want to take them to the parades with you (or don't think they need to get their first lessons in anatomy along Bourbon Street), there are a fair number of activities for them in addition to those mentioned earlier in "New Orleans for Families"; check the *Times-Picayune*. Several of the hotels provide kids' carnivals or parties, and the Louisiana Children's Museum offers special in-house parades, mask-making classes, and so on. You could opt for seeing the parades in Metairie or Kenner: these are much more family-style events, and the "Indian" walking parades are famously rousing, with good music and flamboyant costumes of a huge and feathered sort particularly attractive to kids. You could go out to the Fair Grounds racetrack and see an afternoon of races; in 1999, jockey Julie Kron won her 350th race on Mardi Gras and turned back flips for the crowd. Or you could skirt the entire issue: there is a rather different but fascinating Cajun Mardi Gras celebration in Lafayette, Louisiana, about three hours from the city; see "Cajun Country Festivals" at the end of this chapter.

JAZZ *and* HERITAGE FEST

THE NEW ORLEANS JAZZ AND HERITAGE FESTIVAL spans a ten-day period in late April and early May. It's usually called Jazz Fest for short, and in fact the first festival, organized over a quarter century ago by the same folks who brought you the Newport Jazz Festival, featured such superstars as Duke Ellington, Mahalia Jackson, and Al Hirt. Now, however, the folk, rock, pop, blues, gumbo, zydeco, Latin, R&B, swamp rock, brass, bounce (brass crossed with rap), ragtime-revival, bluegrass, gospel, and even klezmer performers far outnumber the jazz traditionalists; it's estimated that close to 5,000 musicians show up.

Long a favorite of lower-key visitors, in recent years it has come to rival Carnival in its crowds, although not yet in its sheer overindulgence. The main stages, a dozen of them, are erected at the Fair Grounds near City Park, with the two biggest performance stages at either end of the racetrack infield and tents all around the 25-acre site. The music is big time but wide

unofficial **TIP**

A good cooling-off tip: the gospel performers, who are often older and in any case have a hard time competing with all those amplified bands, are always in a tent of their own, with some form of air-conditioning and real chairs.

ranging: veterans include the Neville Brothers, the Marsalis brothers (and sometimes patriarch Ellis as well), Irma Thomas, Gladys Knight, Wilson Pickett, the Indigo Girls, the Dave Matthews Band, Walter "Wolfman" Washington, Raful Neal, Kenny Neal, the Radiators, the Iguanas, Beausoleil, Buckwheat Zydeco, Joan Baez, and Van Morrison. In recent years, it's even included the alternative-grunge-country Wilco, bluesy-rock Black Crowes, former Beach Boy Brian Wilson, and Susan Cowsill of Cowsills fame. And such superstars as Bruce Springsteen, Paul Simon, and Bob Dylan turned out in 2006 to ensure that the festival would not be washed away in Katrina's wake. You just wander around until something grabs your fancy. There are related concerts at clubs and venues all around the city, some even on the water, and the streets are full.

Meanwhile, parts of the Fair Grounds are spread out with scores of food concessions—not the usual fast-food junk, but gumbo, fried alligator, red beans and rice, jambalaya, crabs, oysters, poor boys, sushi, spring rolls, and even roast pig. Jewelry, handcrafted furniture, finer handcrafted instruments, decoys, beadwork, and baskets make for some of the most worthwhile souvenirs the city has to offer.

The Fair Grounds are in a constant state of ferment from 11 a.m. to 7 p.m.; tickets are $40 in advance or $50 at the gate. (Thursday tickets are $30 in advance or $40 at the gate.) Bus-shuttle tickets are available for about $16 round-trip. Nighttime concerts are held at various locations, although if you cock an ear toward the nicer hotel lounges and jazz clubs, you may pick up a free jam or two.

unofficial **TIP**
Forget driving to Jazz Fest; either take public transportation or a cab. Or hoof it.

The fest takes place actually over two long weekends (Thursday through Sunday). If you have to choose, go for the second part of the festival—on Sunday morning when New Orleans's most famous falsetto, Aaron Neville, usually steps up with the famous Zion Harmonizers at the gospel show. And since this event generally dovetails with the Cinco de Mayo festivities—an appropriate party for New Orleans, as it commemorates one of the many Spanish-French battles fought over the southern North American continent—it's even more high spirited. Also, if you don't want to spend every day—or every dollar—out at the Fair Grounds, you can see several dozen of the bands who are in town for Jazz Fest for free at two of the preeminent record stores in the French Quarter, the **Louisiana Music Factory** (210 Decatur Street; ☎ 504-586-1094) and **Peaches Records** (408 North Peters at Decatur; ☎ 504-529-4411).

For more information, contact the **Jazz and Heritage Festival** office at 336 Camp Street, Suite 250, New Orleans, LA 70130; call ☎ 504-522-4786; or check out **www.nojazzfest.com.** *Off Beat* magazine puts out a comprehensive guide to the festival every year, although after it starts, but check their Web site for hints:

www.offbeat.com. You can also buy advance tickets through **Ticketmaster:** ☎ 800-488-5252 or 504-522-5555.

Incidentally, if you're more interested in Cajun, African, and island music, consider the **Festival International de Louisiane** in Lafayette at the end of April, which takes over a five-block piece of downtown and draws about 300,000 fans. For more information, call ☎ 337-232-8086 or go to **www.festivalinternational.com.**

unofficial **TIP**
Jazz Fest frequently falls during one of the first real heat waves, so be sure to pack sunglasses, sunblock, water, and a hat or at least a bandanna.

HALLOWEEN

IF YOU WANT TO DRESS FOR THE OCCASION, there are plenty of stores that will frill you and thrill you to the utmost. The city is filled with costume, mask, and makeup shops; **Fifi Mahony's** (934 Royal Street; ☎ 504-525-4343), drag closet to the Bourbon Street stars, gives wiggy a new meaning. But if you like the more decadent retro-cavalier look (think Lestat), duck into **Trashy Diva** (829 Chartres; ☎ 504-581-4555) for the underlayers and then step across to **Violets** (808 Chartres; ☎ 504-569-0088) for the frills.

But you don't have to be invited to the coven ball to enjoy Halloween in New Orleans. If you have any love for dressing up and acting out, this is one of the most wonderful times to be in the city. It's as flamboyant as Mardi Gras but with far more wit, sheer theatricality (as opposed to theatrical classicism), and fun—and not nearly so much puking and public urination. The weather is apt to be warmer, and the restaurants stay open. And because the event has become a great draw for gay costumers and drag queens, any display of breasts is at least scientifically interesting. Drag bars have a long, illustrious history in New Orleans, going back at least a century and probably longer. And in addition to the fine professional queens in the Quarter and over in Faubourg Marigny, you are apt to be serenaded, fondled, and generally scooped up by a raft of "talented amateurs," as they used to say of *The Avengers'* Emma Peel, herself a style icon of the gay crowd here. Informal parades and smartly turned-out paraders are showered with beads and coins from the galleries just as they are during Mardi Gras. Altogether, it's a great affair, unless you're uptight about who's tight in those tights.

There are lots of costume parties, especially around the French Quarter (and any number of impromptu parades), as well as a more organized four-day celebration over Halloween weekend with concerts and cocktail parties that benefit the Lazarus Project, a home for New Orleans residents with AIDS. Concert venues include the House of Blues; for more information go to **www.halloweenneworleans.com.**

kids For kids, check out **Boo at the Zoo** (see "A Calendar of Festivals and Events" in Part Two, Planning Your Visit).

Of course, between Lestat and Marie Laveau, you can make a Halloween holiday of your own any time; see the sections on "Walking on the Dark Side" and "The Great Hereafter" in Part Seven, Sightseeing, Tours, and Attractions.

CREOLE CHRISTMAS

THIS IS THE SORT OF TOURISM-INDUSTRY CREATION that still seems a little packaged—in fact, some brochures refer to it as "New Orleans Christmas" or "Christmas New Orleans–style" because, although old Creole society supplied the inspiration for many of the events, visitors tend to lump Cajun and Creole culture together. (If you're confused yourself, see "A Too-short History of a Fascinating Place" in Part One, Understanding the City.)

unofficial **TIP**
Look for Creole Christmas specials offered by hotels and restaurants.

Gradually, however, New Orleans Christmas has developed some fine moments—and in fact, the week before Christmas is described by locals as one of the best times to be in the city. Starting at Thanksgiving, City Park's old live oaks are hung with thousands of lights in the shapes of fleur-de-lis, harps, and stars, and you can ride the miniature trains or even hire a carriage. Many fine older homes are decorated in the old style and lit up at night. Plenty of holiday events are free and perfect for a family vacation: special walking tours and concerts, parades (with Papa Noel himself heading up the second line), brass bands, museum exhibits, house tours, tree lightings, cooking and ornament-making workshops for kids, cooking exhibitions, and candlelight caroling in Jackson Square. The whole French Quarter is lit up, and street performers, jugglers, and dancers fill the parks. Costumed impersonators from New Orleans history (Baroness Pontalba, Lola Montez, Andrew Jackson, Edgar Degas, Buffalo Bill Cody, and so on) walk the street to talk with passersby. Midnight mass in St. Louis Cathedral is lovely, even if you aren't Catholic, with carols, candles, wonderful stained glass, and the like. There are almost nightly gospel concerts as well, either in St. Louis Cathedral or historic St. Mary's on Chartres. (There are also menorah lights and Kwanzaa activities and other cultural celebrations.)

On the other side of Canal Street, Harrah's Hotel stages the "Miracle on Fulton Street" festival from about Thanksgiving through Twelfth Night, with lights and "snow," a Santa shop and photo ops with the Big Guy, and lots of musical guests, including many of the local and regional favorites such as Charmaine Neville, Marva Wright, Nathan and the Zydeco Cha-Chas, and brass bands.

Many hotels, both chain and independent, offer special low "Papa Noel" or "Creole Christmas" rates, while restaurants of the quality of Arnaud's, Brennan's, Galatoire's, Broussard's, Upperline, and

Commander's Palace set out "reveillon" menus adapted from old Creole celebrations, usually including Champagne or eggnog and perhaps a little *lagniappe*. (*Reveillon* means "awakening," because the great Creole houses used to celebrate the holiday with a huge dinner after attending midnight mass on Christmas Eve.)

Probably the most famous Christmas display in town outside City Park; one that's nearly as elaborate, though not half as restrained, has been at the Metairie home of entrepreneur Al Copeland, founder of the Popeye's and Copeland's restaurant chains. Despite Copeland's death in 2008, his family will mount the display again in 2009. (Just follow the line of cars taking Veterans Highway to Transcontinental Avenue, turn right, then left onto Folse, and go two blocks. You can't miss it.) Beginning in 2010, however, the lights will move to Metairie's Lafreniere Park.

unofficial **TIP**
Homes in the country are all decked out, which makes this a really good time to plan your plantation tour.

At 7 p.m. on Christmas Eve, scores of huge bonfires are set up and down the Mississippi around the plantations (by some estimates 100 of them in 50 miles) and across the river from the French Quarter in the Algiers neighborhood, the only noncontiguous section of the city. For more about New Orleans Christmas, plus a second booklet of caroling schedules, lightings, fireworks, and so on, as well as discount coupons on shopping, dining, and attractions, call ☎ 800-474-7621 (**www.neworleansonline.com**) for the *New Orleans Official Visitors Guide*.

Of course, major party town that it is, New Orleans doesn't really surrender the Christmas season until New Year's Eve, which is another wild, woolly, loud, and lively night on the town, culminating with a giant crowd singing "Auld Lange Syne" in Jackson Square. New Year's Eve also coincides with the collegiate football championship Sugar Bowl, held in the Superdome. Just as for Mardi Gras, you need to make your hotel reservations early; however, you may be able to sneak in a good airfare by waiting to come until, say, December 27 or 28 and staying over until after New Year's Day. Or you could stay through until Twelfth Night on January 6, when the first Carnival krewe kicks off the pre–Mardi Gras season . . . or even January 8, for the annual celebration of Jackson's victory at the Battle of New Orleans. . . .

CAJUN COUNTRY FESTIVALS

THERE IS MORE AND MORE INTEREST IN CAJUN CULTURE—just notice what sort of music all those souvenir shops are blaring out onto Bourbon Street these days. What's called "Cajun Mardi Gras" in Lafayette, Louisiana, about three hours west of New Orleans, is a much more family-style festival than the Bourbon Street blowout. There the festival's sovereigns are King Gabriel and Queen Evangeline, from Longfellow's epic story of the Cajun diaspora, and several of the events are geared specifically to children. And unlike the Rex ball, the final party is open to the public (though you should still tie that black tie). You can also participate in some even older country-style events, such as house-to-house partying. For information, contact the **Lafayette Convention and Visitors Commission,** P.O. Box 52066, Lafayette, LA 70505; call ☎ 800-346-1958 or visit **www.lafayettetravel.com.**

In Eunice, Louisiana, about two hours west of Baton Rouge, the tradition of *courir de Mardi Gras* ("running of Mardi Gras") means that hundreds of costumed revelers parade in trucks and trailers from house to house, singing, dancing, busking, or begging for the ingredients of a huge, city-sized gumbo made at day's end. Family-style celebrations begin on Saturday. For more information, visit **www.eunice-la.com.**

Around mid-October, Lafayette is the site of a multitheme celebration, the **Festivals Acadiens,** spotlighting Cajun traditions and history (**www.festivalsacadiens.com** or **www.lafayettetravel.com**). The best-known part is the **Festival de Musique Acadienne,** now more than 30 years old and drawing many fans of two-step, zydeco, and traditional Cajun-French music. Set up alongside the music stages is the **Bayou Food Festival,** a mouthwatering abundance of smothered quail, oysters en brochette, boudin sausages, and other Cajun specialties, prepared by area restaurants. The **Louisiana Craft Fair** spotlights traditional methods and native materials: duck-decoy carving, caning, basket weaving, quilting, pottery making, jewelry, and even alligator skinning. Artists over 60 have their own seniors circuit, so to speak, the **RSVP** (Retired Senior Volunteer Program) **Fair,** where you get the tall tales along with the traditional crafts.

There are also Mardi Gras celebrations along the Mississippi Gulf Coast, notably in Biloxi and Gulfport. Contact the **Mississippi Gulf Coast Convention and Visitors Bureau** at P.O. Box 6128, Gulfport, MS 39506; call ☎ 888-467-4853; or go to **www.gulfcoast.org.**

And although it's not truly Cajun, the various cultural celebrations of Isleños—Louisianans descended from Canary Island fishermen—held just outside New Orleans are of unusual interest. Contact the **Canary Islands Descendants Association** (☎ 504-682-1010; **www.canaryislanders.com**) or the **Los Isleños Heritage and Culture Society** (☎ 504-523-2245; **www.losislenos.org**) about festivals and events.

PART FOUR

ACCOMMODATIONS

DECIDING WHERE *to* STAY

NEW ORLEANS, YOU MUST UNDERSTAND, has an almost palpable feel. History here is cumulative, and from the French to the Spanish to the Confederacy to the present, every sailor, gambler, barmaid, and merchant has left something for you to savor. When you are in New Orleans, you know without being told that you are someplace very different. In fact, it's not so much a place to be as a place to know. Even as a first-time tourist, your heart aches to know New Orleans intimately, to be part of its exotic rhythms and steaminess. The city never, never leaves your consciousness. You wear it and breathe it at the same time, all of it, and hundreds of years of blues in the night, chicory coffee, and sweat on the docks become part of your reality.

This reality is sustained by the river, the humidity, the narrow streets, and even by the city's grittiness and poverty. And it is reflected by its small, quirky hotels and inns. Some of the most delightful, interesting, and intimate hotels in America can be found in New Orleans. Ditto for guesthouses and bed-and-breakfasts. Zoning and historic preservation ordinances, particularly in the French Quarter, have limited the construction of modern high-rise hotels and stimulated the evolution of an eclectic mix of medium- and small-sized properties, many of which are proprietorships. In an age of standardization and cookie-cutter chain lodging, these smaller hotels, distinguished by cozy courtyards, shuttered windows, balconies, and wrought-iron trim, offer guests a truly unique lodging experience.

Hotels in New Orleans are concentrated in the French Quarter and along Canal Street between Claiborne Avenue and the river. Most of the larger, modern chain hotels are situated near the convention center at the river end of Canal Street. Smaller hotels, inns, and guesthouses are sprinkled liberally around the French Quarter and along St. Charles Avenue west of Lee Circle. Historically, there have been relatively few hotels located in other parts of town. Although today there are some hotels near the airport and along Interstate 10 east of the city, hotels outside of the Central Business District–French Quarter area are relatively scarce.

If you would like to visit during any holiday other than Mardi Gras or Jazz Fest, make your reservations six months or more in advance. For Mardi Gras (late February to early March) you need to plan nine months to one year ahead, and for the New Orleans Jazz and Heritage Festival (late April to early May), give yourself at least ten months.

While we would not dissuade you from experiencing Mardi Gras, be advised that the city is pretty much turned upside down at that time. Hotels are jammed, prices are jacked up, parking is impossible, and the streets are full of staggering drunks. In the French Quarter, many bars and restaurants dispatch their furniture and fixtures to warehouses to make room for the throng of wall-to-wall people. While Mardi Gras is a hell of a good party, it essentially deprives visitors of experiencing the real New Orleans.

If you happen to be attending one of the big conventions, book early and use some of the tips listed below to get a discounted room rate.

SOME CONSIDERATIONS

1. When choosing your New Orleans lodging, make sure your hotel is situated in a location convenient to your recreation or business needs, and that it is in a safe and comfortable area.
2. New Orleans hotels generally offer lower-quality rooms than those in most cities profiled by the *Unofficial Guides.* As a consequence of the generally lower-quality standard, newer chain hotels have not had to invest in superior rooms in order to be competitive.
3. If you plan to take a car, inquire about the parking situation. Some hotels offer no parking at all, some charge dearly for parking, and some offer free parking. Check the Hotel Information Chart at the end of this chapter for availability and prices.
4. If you are not a city dweller, or perhaps are a light sleeper, try to book a hotel on a quieter side street. In the French Quarter, avoid hotels on Bourbon Street. If you book a Central Business District or Canal Street hotel, ask for a room off the street and high up.
5. When you plan your budget, remember that New Orleans's hotel tax is 13%.
6. The ratings and rankings in this chapter are based solely on room quality and value. To determine if a particular hotel has room service, a pool, or other services and amenities, see the alphabetical Hotel Information Chart at the end of this chapter.

unofficial **TIP**
Because New Orleans thrives on tourism, weekday hotel rates are often lower than weekend rates (the opposite of most cities where business travel rules).

french quarter accommodations

1. Andrew Jackson Hotel
2. The Astor Crowne Plaza
3. Best Western French Quarter Landmark Hotel
4. Bienville House Hotel
5. Bourbon Orleans Hotel
6. Chateau Bourbon Hotel
7. Chateau Dupré Hotel
8. Chateau LeMoyne French Quarter Holiday Inn
9. The Cornstalk Hotel
10. A Creole House Hotel
11. Dauphine Orleans
12. French Quarter Courtyard Hotel
13. French Quarter Suites
14. Historic French Market Inn
15. Holiday Inn French Quarter
16. Hotel de la Monnaie
17. Hotel Monteleone
18. Hotel Provincial
19. Hotel Royal
20. Hotel St. Marie
21. Hotel St. Pierre
22. Hotel Villa Convento
23. Inn on Bourbon Ramada Plaza
24. Lafitte Guest House
25. Lamothe House
26. Le Richelieu in the French Quarter
27. Maison De Ville
28. Maison Dupuy Hotel
29. Marriott New Orleans
30. New Orleans Guest House
31. Olivier House Hotel
32. Omni Royal Orleans Hotel
33. Place D'Armes Hotel
34. Prince Conti Hotel
35. Ritz-Carlton New Orleans
36. Royal Sonesta Hotel
37. Saint Ann–Marie Antoinette
38. The Saint Louis
39. Soniat House
40. St. Peter House
41. W French Quarter
42. Westin New Orleans Canal Place

new orleans accommodations

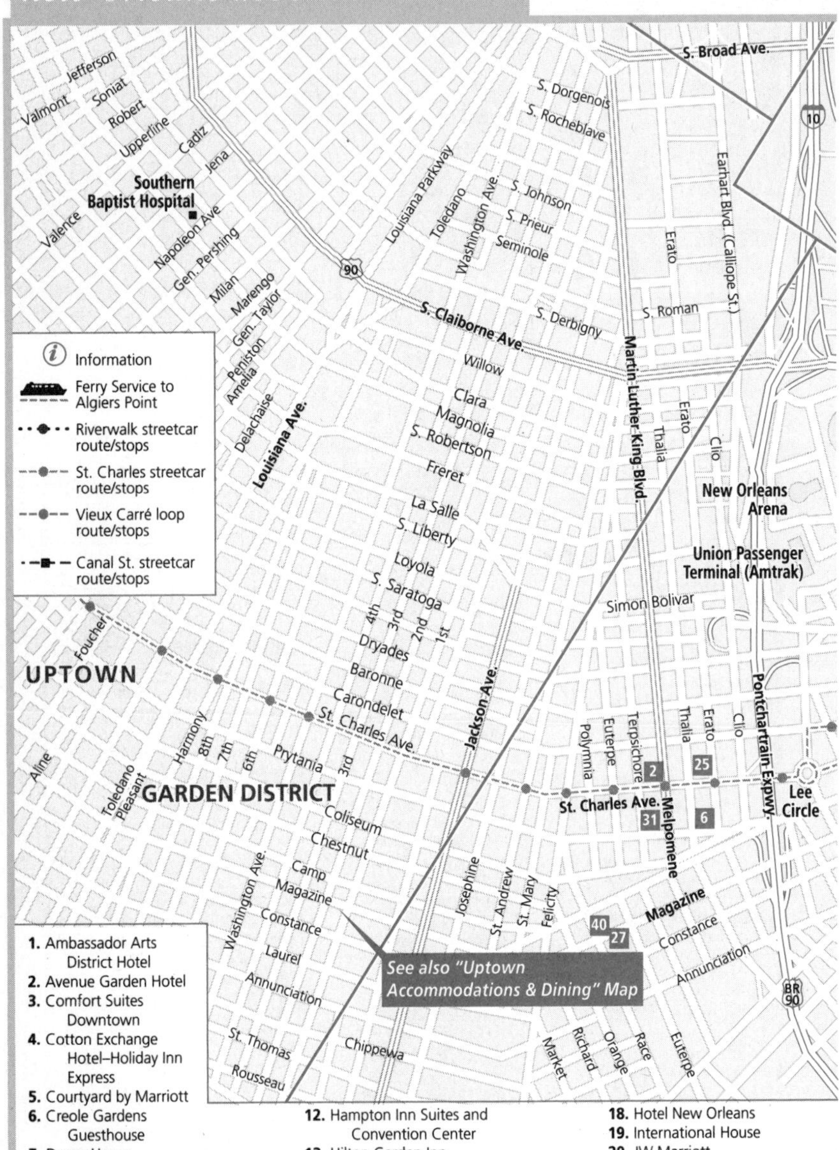

1. Ambassador Arts District Hotel
2. Avenue Garden Hotel
3. Comfort Suites Downtown
4. Cotton Exchange Hotel–Holiday Inn Express
5. Courtyard by Marriott
6. Creole Gardens Guesthouse
7. Degas House
8. DoubleTree Hotel New Orleans
9. Embassy Suites New Orleans
10. The Frenchmen Hotel
11. Hampton Inn Downtown
12. Hampton Inn Suites and Convention Center
13. Hilton Garden Inn
14. Hilton New Orleans Riverside
15. Homewood Suites by Hilton
16. Hotel Inter-Continental New Orleans
17. Hotel Le Cirque
18. Hotel New Orleans
19. International House
20. JW Marriott
21. Lafayette Hotel
22. Le Pavillon Hotel
23. Loews
24. Loft 523
25. Maison St. Charles Hotel & Suites
26. Marigny Manor House

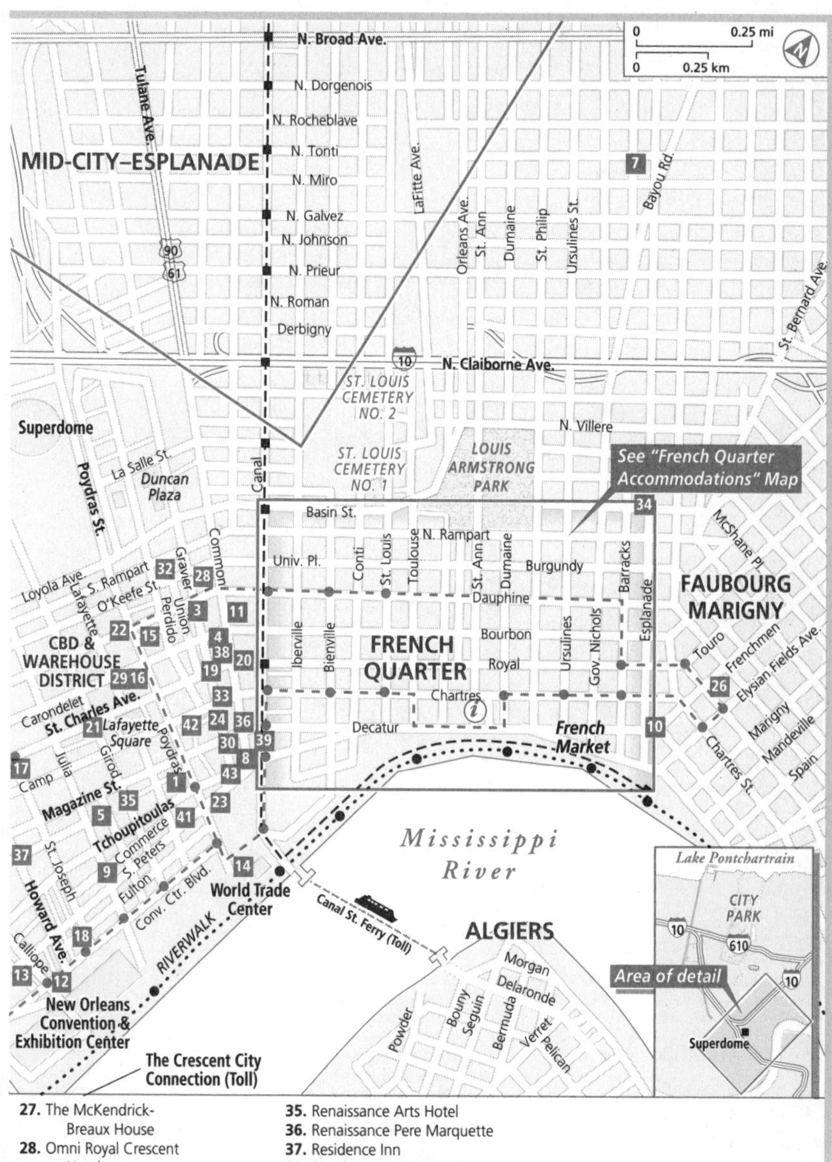

27. The McKendrick-Breaux House
28. Omni Royal Crescent Hotel
29. The Parc St. Charles
30. Pelham Hotel
31. Prytania Park Hotel
32. Quality Inn & Suites
33. Queen and Crescent Hotel
34. Rathbone Inn
35. Renaissance Arts Hotel
36. Renaissance Pere Marquette
37. Residence Inn
38. Royal St. Charles Hotel
39. Sheraton New Orleans Hotel
40. St. Vincent Guest House
41. W New Orleans
42. The Whitney
43. Windsor Court Hotel

uptown accommodations & dining

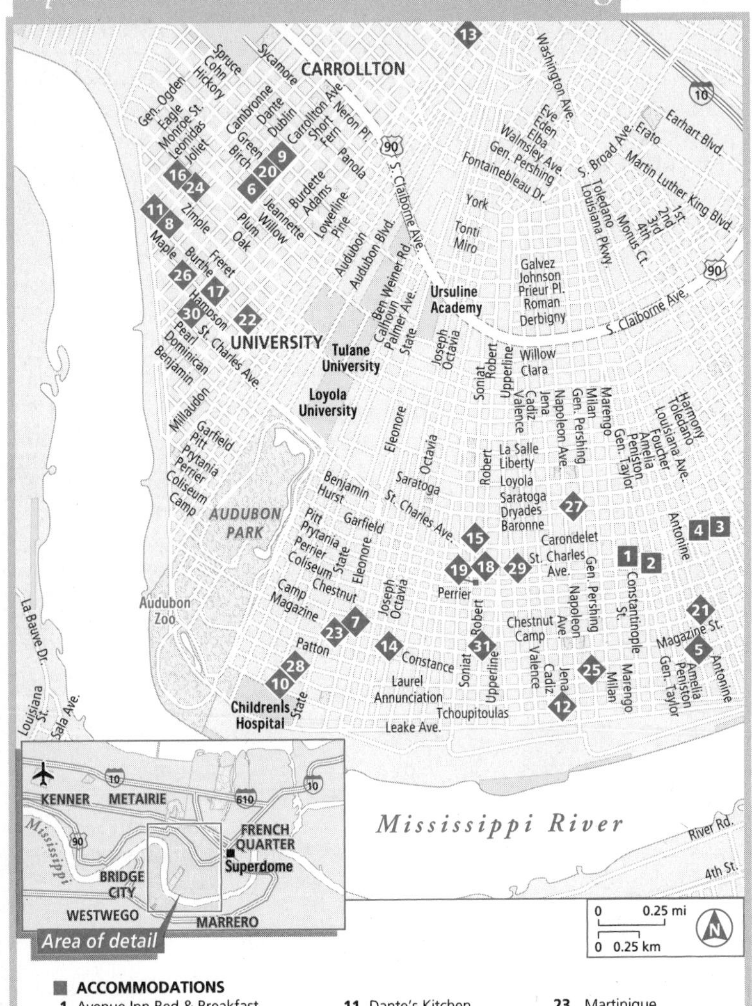

■ **ACCOMMODATIONS**

1. Avenue Inn Bed & Breakfast
2. The Columns
3. Hampton Inn
4. St. Charles Inn Best Western

◆ **RESTAURANTS**

5. Baru Bistro
6. Basil Leaf
7. Bistro Daisy
8. Brigtsen's
9. Café Grenada
10. Clancy's
11. Dante's Kitchen
12. Dick and Jenny's
13. Five Happiness
14. Flaming Torch
15. Gautreau's
16. Jacques-Imo's
17. Jamila's
18. La Crepe Nanou
19. La Thai Cuisine
20. Lebanon's Cafe
21. Lilette
22. Maple Street Cafe
23. Martinique
24. Ninja
25. Nirvana
26. One
27. Pascal's Manale
28. Patois
29. Upperline
30. Vincent's
31. Vizard's

Many of the nicest hotels in New Orleans are older properties that have found ways to cram insane amounts of luxurious amenities into shoebox-sized rooms. These hotels rely as much on their dignified reputations as on their guestroom quality to attract guests. Although extremely nice, their rooms lack the square footage to be called "luxurious" by any standard. One hotel that satisfies all requirements of space and opulence has finally made its way into the French Quarter. The **Ritz-Carlton,** on the Vieux Carré side of Canal Street, opened its doors in 2000, setting a new standard for New Orleans lodging expectations.

New Orleans is full of old hotels, some well maintained, some not. Many are situated in ancient buildings, with guestrooms in varying states of renovation and dilapidation. Lobbies of the nicer hotels are characteristically decorated in gaudy antique gilt, with old-world sculptures and crystal chandeliers. Along similar lines, you are likely to find more antique and antique-replica furniture in New Orleans hotel rooms than in most any other U.S. tourist destination. Four-poster rice beds are a particular favorite.

And it's gonna cost you. In general, New Orleans hotels are pricey. But good deals can be found, and upon inspection, a pattern emerges. With a handful of exceptions, the hotels that offer the best values are found outside the French Quarter. And within the French Quarter, those hotels found on or within one block of Bourbon Street are often outrageously expensive. So, as is often the case with urban hotels, the address of the hotel is the deciding factor in the room price.

For example, one of the most expensive hotels in New Orleans, the **Inn on Bourbon Ramada Plaza,** is located right in the middle of the Bourbon Street action. Although the Inn on Bourbon offers only a three-star room, it is continually booked due to location.

Before making any reservations, find out when the guestrooms in your prospective hotel were last renovated. Request that the hotel send you its promotional brochure. Ask if brochure photos of guestrooms are accurate and current.

GETTING *a* GOOD DEAL *on a* ROOM

SPECIAL WEEKDAY RATES

ALTHOUGH WELL-LOCATED NEW ORLEANS HOTELS are tough for the budget conscious, it's not impossible to get a good deal, at least relatively speaking. For starters, many French Quarter hotels that cater to tourists offer special weekday discount rates that range from 5 to 25% below weekend rates. You can find out about weekday specials by calling individual hotels or by consulting your travel agent.

IF YOU MAKE YOUR OWN RESERVATION

AS YOU POKE AROUND TRYING TO FIND A GOOD DEAL, there are several things you should know. First, always call the specific hotel rather than the hotel chain's national 800 number. Quite often, the reservationists at the national number are unaware of local specials. Always ask about specials before you inquire about corporate rates. Do not be reluctant to bargain. If you are buying a hotel's weekday package, for example, and want to extend your stay into the following weekend, you can often obtain at least the corporate rate for the extra days. Do your bargaining, however, before you check in, preferably when you make your reservations.

unofficial **TIP**
New Orleans's value season generally starts the first weekend in July (it seems New Orleans is not a popular Independence Day destination) and ends on the first weekend in September.

GETTING CORPORATE RATES

MANY HOTELS OFFER DISCOUNTED CORPORATE RATES (5 to 12% off rack). Usually you do not need to work for a large company or have a special relationship with the hotel to obtain these rates. Simply call the hotel of your choice and ask for their corporate rates. Many hotels will guarantee you the discounted rate on the phone when you make your reservation. Others may make the rate conditional on your providing some sort of bona fides—for instance, a fax on your company's letterhead requesting the rate, or a company credit card or business card on check-in. Generally, though, the screening is not rigorous.

THE INTERNET REVOLUTION

PURCHASING TRAVEL ON THE INTERNET has revolutionized the way both consumers and hotels do business. For you, it makes shopping for a hotel and finding good deals much easier. For the hotel, it makes possible a system of room inventory management often referred to as "nudging." Here's how it works. Many months in advance, hotels establish rates for each day of the coming year. In developing their rate calendar, they take into consideration all of the variables that affect occupancy in their hotel as well as in New Orleans in general. They consider weekend versus weekday demand; additional demand stimulated by holidays, major conventions, trade shows, and sporting events; and the effect of the four seasons of the year on occupancy.

After rates for each date are determined, the rates are entered into the hotel's reservation system. Then hotel management sits back to see what happens. If the bookings for a particular date are in accord with management's expectations, no rate change is necessary. If demand is greater than management's forecast for a given date, they might raise the rate to take advantage of higher than expected bookings. If demand eases off, the hotel can revert back to the original rate.

If demand is less than expected, the hotel will begin nudging, that is, incrementally decreasing the rate for the day or days in question until booking volume increases to the desired level. Though this sort of rate manipulation has been an integral part of room inventory management for decades, the Internet has made it possible to rethink and alter room rates almost at will. A hotel can theoretically adjust rates hourly on its own Web site. Major Internet travel sellers such as Travelocity, Hotels.com, and Expedia, among others, are fast and agile and quite capable of getting a special deal (that is, a lower rate) in front of travel purchasers almost instantaneously. For the hotel, this means they can manage their inventory on almost a weekly or daily basis, nudging toward full occupancy by adjusting their rates according to demand.

Of course, hotels don't depend entirely on the Internet. Lower rates and various special deals are also communicated by e-mail to preferred travel agents, and sometimes directly to consumers via e-mail, print advertisements, or direct-mail promotions.

Finding Deals on the Internet

By far the easiest way to scout room deals is on Internet search engines **www.kayak.com** and **www.travelaxe.com.** Kayak is a straightforward, easy-to-navigate site that scans not only Internet sellers but also national hotel-chain Web sites and sometimes individual hotel Web sites. You can organize your search by price, location, star rating, brand, and amenities. Detailed descriptions of each property along with photos, customer reviews, and a map are also available. Around 200 properties are listed for New Orleans. Kayak provides a direct link to the lowest-price sellers.

At Travelaxe, you can download free software (only runs on PCs) that scans the better Internet sites selling discounted rooms. You enter your proposed check-in and checkout dates (required) as well as preferences concerning location and price (optional), and click "Search." The program scans a dozen or more Internet seller sites and presents the discounted rates for all hotels in a chart for comparison. The prices listed in the chart represent the total you'll pay for your entire stay. To determine the rate per night, divide the total by the number of nights you'll be staying. If you decide to book, you deal directly with the site offering the best price. The software doesn't scan the individual hotel Web sites, so if you have a specific hotel in mind, you should check the hotel's site and call the hotel's reservation desk to ask about specials.

Finally, for Internet shopping, consider **www.priceline.com.** There you can tender a bid for a room. You can't bid on a specific hotel, but you can specify location (French Quarter, Garden District, etc.) and the quality rating expressed in stars. If your bid is accepted, you will be assigned to a hotel consistent with your location and quality requirements, and your credit card will be charged in a nonrefundable transaction for your entire stay. Notification of acceptance usually takes less than an hour. We recommend bidding $45 to $60 per night for a three-star hotel and $65 to $90 per night for a four-star. To gauge your chances of success, check to see if any major conventions or trade shows are scheduled during your preferred dates. Reduce your bid for off-season periods.

RESERVATION SERVICES

WHEN WHOLESALERS AND CONSOLIDATORS deal directly with the public, they frequently represent themselves as "reservation services." When you call, ask for a rate quote for a particular hotel, or for the best available deal, in your preferred area. If there is a maximum amount you are willing to pay, say so. Chances are the service will find something that will work for you, even if they have to shave a dollar or two off their own profit.

By calling the hotels ourselves, we were often able to beat the reservation services' rates when rooms were generally available. When the city was booked, however, and we could not find a room by calling the hotels ourselves, the reservation services could almost always get us a room at a fair price.

Services that frequently offer substantial discounts include:

hotels.com ☎ 800-346-8357 **www.hotels.com**

Hotel Reservations Network ☎ 800-282-7613 **www.hotelreservationsnetwork.com**

HOW TO EVALUATE A TRAVEL PACKAGE

HUNDREDS OF NEW ORLEANS PACKAGE VACATIONS are offered to the public each year. Packages should be a win-win proposition for both the buyer and the seller. The buyer has to make only one phone call and deal with a single salesperson to set up the whole vacation: transportation, rental car, lodging, meals, attraction admissions, and even golf and tennis. The seller, likewise, has to deal with the buyer only once, eliminating the need for separate sales, confirmations, and billing. In addition to streamlining sales, processing, and administration, some packagers also buy airfares in bulk on contract like a broker playing the commodities market. Buying a large number of airfares in advance allows the packager to buy them at a significant savings from posted fares. The same practice is also applied to hotel rooms. Because selling vacation packages is an efficient way of doing business, and because the packager can often buy individual package components (airfare, lodging, etc.) in bulk at a discount, savings in operating expenses realized by the seller are sometimes passed on to the buyer so that, in addition to convenience, the package is also an exceptional value. In any event, that is the way it is supposed to work.

All too often, in practice, the seller cashes in on discounts and passes none on to the buyer. In some instances, packages are loaded with extras that cost the packager next to nothing but inflate the retail price sky high. Predictably, the savings to be passed along to customers do not materialize.

unofficial **TIP**
Hotel reservationists do not usually inform you of existing hotel-package specials or offer them to you. In other words, you have to ask.

When considering a package, choose one that includes features you are sure to use; whether you use all the features or not, you will most certainly pay for them. Second, if cost is of greater concern than convenience, make a few phone calls and see what the package would cost if you booked its individual components (airfare, rental car, lodging, etc.) on your own. If the package price is less than the à la carte cost, the package is a good deal. If the costs are about the same, the package is probably worth buying just for the convenience.

If your package includes a choice of rental car or airport transfers (transportation to and from the airport), take the transfers if you plan to spend most of your time in the French Quarter or the Central Business District. If you want to run around town or go on excursions outside the city, take the car. If you take the car, be sure to ask if the package includes free parking at your hotel.

The following tour operators specialize in vacation packages to New Orleans. Book directly or through your travel agent.

Atlas Tour and Travel ☎ 504-483-0607 **www.atlastourandtravel.com**

Destination Management ☎ 800-366-8882 **www.bigeasy.com**

Travel New Orleans ☎ 800-535-8747 **www.travelneworleans.com**

Tour operators, of course, prefer to sell you a whole vacation package. When business is slow, however, they will often agree to sell you just the lodging component of the package, usually at a nicely discounted rate.

Hotel-sponsored Packages

In addition to tour operators, packages are frequently offered by hotels. Usually "land only" (that is, no airfare included), the hotel packages are sometimes exceptional deals. New Orleans hotels (especially those that are larger and closest to the convention center) seem to have good package deals that include room upgrades, special services (for example, concierge, dry cleaning, etc.) and some meals for those in town for multiple nights over large convention weekends. Many packages are specialized, offering plantation tours, jazz tours, or the like, while others are offered only at certain times of the year, such as "Papa Noel" deals during the December holiday season. Newspaper promotion of hotel specials tends to be limited to the hotel's primary markets, which for most properties are Louisiana, Texas, Alabama, Florida, Mississippi, Georgia, Arkansas, and Tennessee. If you live in other parts of the country, check individual hotel Web sites for packages.

HELPING YOUR TRAVEL AGENT HELP YOU

WHEN YOU CALL YOUR TRAVEL AGENT, ask if he or she has been to New Orleans. If the answer is no, be prepared to give your travel agent some direction. Do not accept any recommendations at face value. Check out the location and rates of any suggested hotel and make certain that the hotel is suited to your itinerary.

Because some travel agents are unfamiliar with New Orleans, they may try to plug you into a tour operator's preset package. This essentially allows the travel agent to set up your whole trip with a single phone call and still collect an 8 to 10% commission. The problem with this scenario is that most agents will place 90% of their New Orleans business with only one or two wholesalers or tour operators. In other words, it's the line of least resistance for them, and not much choice for you.

Travel agents will often use wholesalers who run packages in conjunction with airlines, like Delta's Dream Vacations or American's Fly-Away Vacations. Because of the wholesaler's exclusive relationship with the carrier, these trips are very easy for travel agents to book. However, they will probably be more expensive than a package offered by a high-volume wholesaler who works with a number of airlines in a primary New Orleans market.

To help your travel agent get you the best possible deal, do the following:

1. Determine where you want to stay in New Orleans, and if possible, choose a specific hotel that meets your needs. This can be accomplished by reviewing the hotel information provided in this guide and by checking Web sites of hotels that interest you.
2. Check out the hotel deals and package vacations advertised in the Sunday travel sections of the *Atlanta Journal-Constitution, New Orleans Times-Picayune,* or *Dallas Morning News* newspapers. Often you will be able to find deals that beat the socks off anything offered in your local paper. See if you can find specials that fit your plans and include a hotel you like.
3. Call the hotels or tour operators whose ads you have collected. Ask any questions you have concerning their packages, but do not book your trip with them directly.
4. Tell your travel agent about the deals you find and ask if he or she can get you something better. The deals in the paper will serve as a benchmark against which to compare alternatives proposed by your travel agent.
5. Choose from the options that you and your travel agent uncover. No matter which option you select, have your travel agent book it. Even if you go with one of the packages in the newspaper, it will probably be commissionable (at no additional cost to you) and will provide the

agent some return on the time invested on your behalf. Also, as a travel professional, your agent should be able to verify the quality and integrity of the deal.

HOTELS *and* MOTELS: *Rated and Ranked*

WHAT'S IN A ROOM?

EXCEPT FOR CLEANLINESS, STATE OF REPAIR, and decor, most travelers do not pay much attention to hotel rooms. There is, of course, a discernible standard of quality and luxury that differentiates Motel 6 from Holiday Inn, Holiday Inn from Marriott, and so on. In general, however, hotel guests fail to appreciate the fact that some rooms are better engineered than others.

Contrary to what you might suppose, designing a hotel room is (or should be) much more complex than picking a bedspread to match the carpet and drapes. Making the room usable to its occupants is an art, a planning discipline that combines both form and function.

Decor and taste are important, certainly. No one wants to spend several days in a room whose decor is dated, garish, or even ugly. But beyond the decor, several variables determine how livable a hotel room is. In New Orleans, for example, we have seen some beautifully appointed rooms that are simply not well designed for human habitation. The next time you stay in a hotel, pay attention to the details and design elements of your room. Even more than decor, these will make you feel comfortable and at home.

It takes the *Unofficial Guide* researchers quite a while to inspect a hotel room. Here are a few of the things we check that you may want to start paying attention to:

ROOM SIZE While some smaller rooms are cozy and well designed, a large and uncluttered room is generally preferable, especially for a stay of more than three days.

TEMPERATURE CONTROL, VENTILATION, AND ODOR The guest should be able to control the temperature of the room. The best system, because it's so quiet, is central heating and air-conditioning, controlled by the room's own thermostat. The next best system is a room module heater and air conditioner, preferably controlled by an automatic thermostat, but usually by manually operated button controls. The worst system is central heating and air without any sort of room thermostat or guest control.

The vast majority of hotel rooms have windows or balcony doors that have been permanently sealed. Though there are some legitimate safety and liability issues involved, we prefer windows and balcony doors that can be opened to admit fresh air. Hotel rooms should be odor and smoke free, and not feel stuffy or damp.

ROOM SECURITY Better rooms have locks that require a plastic card instead of the traditional lock and key. Card-and-slot systems allow the hotel, essentially, to change the combination or entry code of the lock with each new guest. A burglar who has somehow acquired a conventional room key can afford to wait until the situation is right before using the key to gain access. Not so with a card-and-slot system. Though larger hotels and hotel chains with lock-and-key systems usually rotate their locks once each year, they remain vulnerable to hotel thieves much of the time. Many smaller or independent properties rarely rotate their locks.

In addition to the entry-lock system, the door should have a deadbolt, and preferably a chain that can be locked from the inside. A chain by itself is not sufficient. Doors should also have a peephole. Windows and balcony doors, if any, should have secure locks.

SAFETY Every room should have a fire or smoke alarm, clear fire instructions, and preferably a sprinkler system. Bathtubs should have a nonskid surface, and shower stalls should have doors that either open outward or slide side to side. Bathroom electrical outlets should be placed high on the wall and not too close to the sink. Balconies should have sturdy, high rails.

NOISE Most travelers have been kept awake by the television, partying, or traffic on the street outside. Better hotels are designed with noise control in mind. Wall and ceiling construction are substantial, effectively screening out routine noise. Carpets and drapes, in addition to being decorative, also absorb and muffle sounds. Mattresses mounted on stable platforms or sturdy bed frames do not squeak. Televisions, enclosed in cabinets and outfitted with volume governors, rarely disturb guests in adjacent rooms.

unofficial **TIP**
If you are easily disturbed by noise, ask for a room on a higher floor, off main thoroughfares, and away from elevators and ice and vending machines.

In better hotels, the air-conditioning and heating system is well maintained and operates without noise or vibration. Likewise, plumbing is quiet and positioned away from the sleeping area. Doors to the hall, and to adjoining rooms, are thick and well fitted to better block out noise.

DARKNESS CONTROL Ever been in a hotel room where the curtains would not quite meet in the middle? Thick, lined curtains that close completely in the center and extend beyond the edges of the window or door frame are required. In a well-planned room, the curtains, shades, or blinds should almost totally block light at any time of day.

LIGHTING Poor lighting is an extremely common problem in American hotel rooms. The lighting is usually adequate for dressing, relaxing, or watching television, but not for reading or working. Lighting needs to be bright over tables and desks, and beside couches or easy chairs. Since so many people read in bed, there should be a separate light for each person. A room with two queen beds should have individual lights for four people. Better bedside reading lights illuminate a small area, so if one person wants to sleep and another to read, the sleeper will not be bothered by the light. The worst situation by far is a single lamp on a table between beds. In each bed, only the person next to the lamp will have sufficient light to read. This deficiency is often compounded by weak lightbulbs.

In addition, closet areas should be well lit, and there should be a switch near the door that turns on room lights when you enter. A seldom seen but desirable feature is a bedside console that allows a guest to control all or most lights in the room from bed.

FURNISHINGS At bare minimum, the bed(s) must be firm. Pillows should be made with nonallergenic fillers and, in addition to the sheets and spread, a blanket should be provided. Bedclothes should be laundered with fabric softener and changed daily. Better hotels usually provide extra blankets and pillows in the room or on request, and sometimes use a second top sheet between the blanket and spread.

There should be a dresser large enough to hold clothes for two people during a five-day stay. A small table with two chairs, or a desk with a chair, should be provided. The room should be equipped with a luggage rack and a three-quarter- to full-length mirror.

The television should be color and cable connected; ideally, it should have a volume governor and remote control. It should be mounted on a swivel base, and preferably enclosed in a cabinet. Local channels should be posted on the set and a local TV program guide should be supplied. The telephone should be touch-tone, be conveniently situated for bedside use, and have on or near it easy-to-understand dialing instructions and a rate card. Local telephone directories should be provided. Better hotels install phones in the bathroom and equip room phones with long cords.

Well-designed hotel rooms usually have a plush armchair or a sleeper sofa for lounging and reading. Better headboards are padded for comfortable reading in bed, and there should be a nightstand or table on each side of the bed(s). Nice extras in any hotel room include a small refrigerator, a digital alarm clock, and a coffeemaker.

BATHROOM Two sinks are better than one, and you cannot have too much counter space. A sink outside the bath is a great convenience when one person bathes as another dresses.

Better bathrooms have both a tub and shower with a nonslip bottom. Tub and shower controls should be easy to operate. Adjustable showerheads are preferred. The bath needs to be well lit and should have an exhaust fan and a guest-controlled bathroom heater. Towels and washcloths should be large, soft and fluffy, and plentiful. There should be an electrical outlet for each sink, conveniently and safely placed.

Complimentary shampoo, conditioner, and lotion are pluses, as are robes and bathmats. Better hotels supply bathrooms with tissues and extra toilet paper. Luxurious baths feature a phone, a hair dryer, sometimes a small television, or even a Jacuzzi.

VENDING Complimentary ice and a drink machine should be located on each floor. Welcome additions include a snack machine and a sundries (combs, toothpaste) machine. The latter are seldom found in large hotels that have restaurants and shops.

HOTEL RATINGS

OVERALL QUALITY To distinguish properties according to relative quality, tastefulness, state of repair, cleanliness, and size of standard rooms, we have grouped the hotels and motels into classifications denoted by stars. Star ratings in this guide apply to New Orleans–area properties only and do not necessarily correspond to stars awarded by Mobil, AAA, or other travel critics. Because stars carry little weight in the absence of common standards of comparison, we have linked our ratings to expected levels of quality established by specific American hotel corporations.

WHAT THE RATINGS MEAN

★★★★★	Superior Rooms	Tasteful and luxurious by any standard
★★★★	Extremely nice rooms	What you would expect at a Hyatt Regency or Marriott
★★★	Nice rooms	Holiday Inn or comparable quality
★★	Adequate rooms	Clean, comfortable, and functional without frills—like a Motel 6
★	Super-budget rooms	

Star ratings describe the property's standard accommodations. For most hotels, a "standard accommodation" is a room with either one king bed or two queen beds. In an all-suite property, the standard accommodation is either a one- or two-room suite. In addition to standard accommodations, many hotels offer luxury rooms and special suites not rated here. Star ratings are assigned without regard to whether a property has restaurant(s), recreational facilities, entertainment, or other extras.

ROOM QUALITY In addition to stars (which delineate broad categories), we also employ a numerical rating system. Our rating scale is 0 to 100, with 100 as the best possible rating, and zero (0) as the worst. Numerical ratings are presented to show the difference we perceive between one property and another. Rooms at the Hotel Royal, the Bienville House, and the Dauphine Orleans are all rated as three and a half stars (★★★½. In the supplemental numerical ratings, the Hotel Royal is rated an 82, the Bienville House an 80, and the Dauphine Orleans a 76. This means that within the three-and-a-half-star category, the Bienville House is a bit nicer than the Dauphine Orleans, and the Hotel Royal has an edge over both.

COST Cost estimates are based on the hotel's published rack rates for standard rooms. Each "$" represents $50. Thus, a cost symbol of "$$$" means a room (or suite) at that hotel will cost about $150 a night.

HOW THE HOTELS COMPARE

FOLLOWING IS A HIT PARADE of the nicest rooms in town. We've focused strictly on room quality, and excluded any consideration of location, services, recreation, or amenities. In some instances, a one- or two-room suite can be had for the same price or less than that of a hotel room.

If you use subsequent editions of this guide, you will notice that many of the ratings and rankings change. In addition to the inclusion of new properties, these changes also consider guestroom renovations or improved maintenance and housekeeping. A failure to maintain guestrooms properly or a lapse in housekeeping standards can negatively affect the ratings.

Finally, before you begin to shop for a hotel, take a look at this letter we received from a couple in Hot Springs, Arkansas:

> *We cancelled our room reservations to follow the advice in your book [and reserved a hotel room highly ranked by the* Unofficial Guide]. *We wanted inexpensive, but clean and cheerful. We got inexpensive, but [also] dirty, grim, and depressing. I really felt disappointed in your advice and the room. It was the pits. That was the one real piece of information I needed from your book! The room spoiled the holiday for me aside from our touring.*

Needless to say, this letter was as unsettling to us as the bad room was to our reader. Our integrity as travel journalists, after all, is based on the quality of the information we provide our readers. Even with the best of intentions and the most conscientious research, however, we cannot inspect every room in every hotel. What we do, in statistical terms, is take a sample: we check out several rooms selected at random in each hotel and base our ratings and rankings on those rooms. The inspections are conducted anonymously and without the knowledge of the management. Although unusual, it is certainly possible that the rooms we randomly inspect are not representative

How the Hotels Compare in New Orleans

HOTEL	STAR	QUALITY	COST
Loft 523	★★★★★	99	$$$
Loews	★★★★★	98	$$$$$$–
International House	★★★★★	97	$$$$+
W French Quarter	★★★★★	97	$$$$$+
Windsor Court Hotel	★★★★★	96	$$$$$$
Degas House: Historic Home, Courtyard, and Inn	★★★★½	95	$$$$+
InterContinental Hotel New Orleans	★★★★½	95	$$$$$
Ritz-Carlton New Orleans	★★★★½	95	$$$$$+
Royal Sonesta Hotel	★★★★½	95	$$$$$
Soniat House	★★★★½	95	$$$$$+
W New Orleans	★★★★½	95	$$$$$+
The McKendrick-Breaux House	★★★★½	93	$$$
Renaissance Arts Hotel	★★★★½	92	$$$$+
DoubleTree Hotel New Orleans	★★★★½	90	$$$+
Hotel Le Cirque	★★★★½	90	$$$–
JW Marriott	★★★★½	90	$$$$$–
Lafitte Guest House	★★★★½	90	$$$$$
Hilton New Orleans Riverside	★★★★	89	$$$$+
Hotel Monteleone	★★★★	89	$$$$$$–
Lafayette Hotel	★★★★	89	$$$$–
Marriott New Orleans	★★★★	89	$$$$$–
Omni Royal Orleans Hotel	★★★★	89	$$$$$$–
Renaissance Pere Marquette	★★★★	89	$$$$$–
Sheraton New Orleans Hotel	★★★★	89	$$$$+
Westin New Orleans	★★★★	89	$$$$$$+
Omni Royal Crescent Hotel	★★★★	88	$$$+
Astor Crowne Plaza	★★★★	86	$$$$$
Marigny Manor House	★★★★	86	$$$–
Hilton Garden Inn	★★★★	85	$$$$–
Hotel Provincial	★★★★	85	$$$$+
Chateau Bourbon	★★★★	84	$$$$$+

HOTEL	STAR	QUALITY	COST
Avenue Inn Bed & Breakfast	★★★½	83	$$$$
Courtyard by Marriott	★★★½	83	$$$
Homewood Suites by Hilton	★★★½	83	$$$$–
Le Pavillon Hotel	★★★½	83	$$$$$$$–
Residence Inn	★★★½	83	$$$$–
The Whitney	★★★½	83	$$$+
Ambassador Arts District Hotel	★★★½	82	$$+
Embassy Suites New Orleans	★★★½	82	$$$–
Hotel Royal	★★★½	82	$$+
The Parc St. Charles	★★★½	82	$$$+
Queen and Crescent Hotel	★★★½	82	$$$–
Hampton Inn Suites & Convention Center	★★★½	81	$$$$$–
Maison Dupuy Hotel	★★★½	81	$$$+
Bienville House Hotel	★★★½	80	$$$+
Hampton Inn Downtown	★★★½	80	$$$–
Hotel New Orleans	★★★½	80	$$$$+
Hotel St. Marie	★★★½	77	$$$
Bourbon Orleans Hotel	★★★½	76	$$$+
Dauphine Orleans	★★★½	76	$$$+
Holiday Inn French Quarter	★★★½	76	$$$+
Maison De Ville	★★★½	76	$$$$$+
The Columns	★★★½	75	$$$$$–
The Cornstalk Hotel	★★★½	75	$$$$+
Hotel de la Monnaie	★★★½	75	$$$–
Inn on Bourbon, Ramada Plaza	★★★½	75	$$$+
Le Richelieu in the French Quarter	★★★½	75	$$$+
Prince Conti Hotel	★★★½	75	$$$+
The Saint Louis	★★★½	75	$$$
The Frenchmen Hotel	★★★	74	$$–
Place D'Armes Hotel	★★★	74	$$$
Royal St. Charles Hotel	★★★	74	$$+

How the Hotels Compare (continued)

HOTEL	STAR	QUALITY	COST
Cotton Exchange Hotel/ Holiday Inn Express	★★★	73	$$$$–
Hampton Inn	★★★	73	$$$+
Chateau LeMoyne French Quarter Holiday Inn	★★★	72	$$$–
Creole Gardens Guesthouse	★★★	72	$$$
Rathbone Inn	★★★	72	$$$
St. Charles Inn Best Western	★★★	72	$$$–
New Orleans Guest House	★★★	71	$$–
Maison St. Charles Hotel & Suites	★★★	70	$$$–
Saint Ann/Marie Antoinette	★★★	68	$$$
French Quarter Courtyard Hotel	★★★	67	$$–
Pelham Hotel	★★★	66	$$$–
Historic French Market Inn	★★★	65	$$$$
Olivier House Hotel	★★★	65	$$$–

of the majority of rooms at a particular hotel. Another possibility is that the rooms we inspect in a given hotel are representative, but that by bad luck a reader is assigned a room that is inferior. When we rechecked the hotel our reader disliked, we discovered our rating was correctly representative, but that he and his wife had unfortunately been assigned to one of a small number of threadbare rooms scheduled for renovation.

To avoid disappointment, snoop around in advance. Check out guestrooms on the hotel's Web site or get a copy of the hotel's promotional brochure before you book. Be forewarned, however, that some hotel chains use the same guestroom photo on their Web sites and in their promotional literature for all hotels in the chain; a specific guestroom may not resemble the brochure photo. When you or your travel agent call, ask how old the property is and when your guestroom was last renovated. If you arrive and are assigned a room inferior to that which you had been led to expect, demand to be moved to another room.

THE TOP 30 BEST DEALS IN NEW ORLEANS

HAVING LISTED THE NICEST ROOMS IN TOWN, let's reorder the list to rank the best combinations of quality and value in a room.

HOTEL	STAR	QUALITY	COST
Prytania Park Hotel	★★★	65	$$$+
Avenue Garden Hotel	★★½	63	$$+
French Quarter Suites	★★½	62	$$
Andrew Jackson Hotel	★★½	56	$$+
Chateau Dupré Hotel	★★½	56	$$+
Comfort Suites Downtown	★★	55	$$–
Quality Inn & Suites	★★	55	$$$+
St. Peter House	★★	55	$$+
St. Vincent Guest House	★★	53	$$–
Best Western French Quarter Landmark Hotel	★½	47	$$+
Hotel St. Pierre	★½	46	$$$–
Lamothe House	★½	46	$$$+
A Creole House Hotel	★½	44	$$+
Hotel Villa Convento	★	37	$$$+

As before, the rankings are made without consideration of location, recreational facilities, entertainment, or amenities.

A reader recently complained to us that he had booked one of our top-ranked rooms in terms of value and had been very disappointed in the room. We noticed that the room the reader occupied had a quality rating of ★★½. We would remind you that the value ratings are intended to give you some sense of value received for dollars spent. A ★★½ room at $30 may have the same value rating as a ★★★★★ room at $85, but that does not mean the rooms will be of comparable quality. Regardless of whether it's a good deal or not, a ★★½ room is still a ★★½ room.

Listed on the next page are the best room buys for the money, regardless of location or star classification, based on averaged rack rates. Note that sometimes a suite can cost less than a single room.

The Top 30 Best Deals in New Orleans

HOTEL	STAR RATING	QUALITY RATING	COST ($=$50)
1. Loft 523	★★★★★	99	$$$
2. Hotel Le Cirque	★★★★½	90	$$$–
3. The McKendrick-Breaux House	★★★★½	93	$$$
4. Marigny Manor House	★★★★	86	$$$–
5. Ambassador Arts District Hotel	★★★½	82	$$+
6. Hotel Royal	★★★½	82	$$+
7. The Frenchmen Hotel	★★★	74	$$–
8. Doubletree Hotel New Orleans	★★★★½	90	$$$+
9. New Orleans Guest House	★★★	71	$$–
10. French Quarter Courtyard Hotel	★★★	67	$$–
11. Queen and Crescent Hotel	★★★½	82	$$$–
12. International House	★★★★★	97	$$$$+
13. Omni Royal Crescent Hotel	★★★★	88	$$$+
14. Embassy Suites New Orleans	★★★½	82	$$$–
15. Royal St. Charles Hotel	★★★	74	$$+
16. Hampton Inn Downtown	★★★½	80	$$$–
17. Renaissance Arts Hotel	★★★★½	92	$$$$+
18. Courtyard by Marriott	★★★½	83	$$$
19. Degas House: Historic Home, Courtyard, and Inn	★★★★½	95	$$$$+
20. Hilton Garden Inn	★★★★	85	$$$$–
21. Hotel de la Monnaie	★★★½	75	$$$–
22. Lafayette Hotel	★★★★	89	$$$$–
23. W French Quarter	★★★★★	97	$$$$$+
24. Hotel St. Marie	★★★½	77	$$$
25. Maison Dupuy Hotel	★★★½	81	$$$+
26. Loews	★★★★★	98	$$$$$$–
27. The Whitney	★★★½	83	$$$+
28. InterContinental Hotel New Orleans	★★★★½	95	$$$$$
29. Royal Sonesta Hotel	★★★★½	95	$$$$$
30. Sheraton New Orleans Hotel	★★★★	89	$$$$+

New Orleans Hotels by Location

French Quarter

Andrew Jackson Hotel
Astor Crowne Plaza
Best Western French Quarter Landmark Hotel
Bienville House Hotel
Bourbon Orleans Hotel
Chateau Bourbon
Chateau Dupré Hotel
Chateau LeMoyne French Quarter Holiday Inn
The Cornstalk Hotel
A Creole House Hotel
Dauphine Orleans
Degas House: Historic Home, Courtyard, Inn
French Quarter Courtyard Hotel
French Quarter Suites
Historic French Market Inn
Holiday Inn French Quarter
Hotel de la Monnaie
Hotel Monteleone
Hotel Provincial
Hotel Royal
Hotel St. Marie
Hotel St. Pierre
Hotel Villa Convento
Inn on Bourbon Ramada Plaza
Lafitte Guest House
Lamothe House
Le Richelieu
Maison De Ville
Maison Dupuy Hotel
Marriott New Orleans
New Orleans Guest House
Olivier House Hotel
Omni Royal Orleans Hotel
Place D'Armes Hotel
Prince Conti Hotel
Rathbone Inn
Ritz-Carlton New Orleans
Royal Sonesta Hotel
Saint Ann/ Marie Antoinette
The Saint Louis
Soniat House
St. Peter House
W French Quarter
Westin New Orleans

Central Business District

Ambassador Arts District Hotel
Comfort Suites Downtown
Cotton Exchange Hotel–Holiday Inn Express
Courtyard by Marriott
DoubleTree Hotel New Orleans
Embassy Suites New Orleans
Hampton Inn Downtown
Hampton Inn Suites & Convention Center
Hilton Garden Inn
Hilton New Orleans Riverside
Homewood Suites by Hilton
InterContinental Hotel New Orleans
Hotel Le Cirque
Hotel New Orleans
International House
JW Marriott
Lafayette Hotel
Le Pavillon Hotel
Loews
Loft 523
Omni Royal Crescent
The Parc St. Charles
Pelham Hotel
Quality Inn & Suites
Queen and Crescent Hotel
Renaissance Arts Hotel
Renaissance Pere Marquette
Residence Inn
Royal St. Charles Hotel
Sheraton New Orleans
W New Orleans
The Whitney
Windsor Court Hotel

Uptown and the Garden District

Avenue Garden Hotel
Avenue Inn Bed & Breakfast
The Columns
Creole Gardens Guesthouse
Hampton Inn
Maison St. Charles Hotel & Suites
The McKendrick-Breaux House
Prytania Park Hotel
St. Charles Inn Best Western
St. Vincent Guest House

Faubourg Marigny

The Frenchmen Hotel
Marigny Manor House

Hotel Information Chart

Ambassador Arts District Hotel ★★★½
535 Tchoupitoulas Street
New Orleans, LA 70130
☎ 504-527-5271
FAX 504-527-5270
TOLL-FREE ☎ 800-455-3417
www.ambassadorneworleans.com

ROOM QUALITY	82
COST ($=$50)	$$+
LOCATION	CENTRAL BUSINESS DISTRICT
NO. OF ROOMS	165
POOL	–
SAUNA	–
ROOM SERVICE	•
PARKING	VALET, $26
BREAKFAST	–
EXERCISE FACILITIES	•

Andrew Jackson Hotel ★★½
919 Royal Street
New Orleans, LA 70116
☎ 504-561-5881
FAX 504-596-6769
TOLL-FREE ☎ 800-654-0224
www.andrewjacksonhotel.com

ROOM QUALITY	56
COST ($=$50)	$$+
LOCATION	FRENCH QUARTER
NO. OF ROOMS	22
POOL	–
SAUNA	–
ROOM SERVICE	–
PARKING	LOT, FREE
BREAKFAST	CONTINENTAL
EXERCISE FACILITIES	–

Astor Crowne Plaza ★★★★
739 Canal Street
New Orleans, LA 70130
☎ 504-962-0500
FAX 504-962-0501
TOLL-FREE ☎ 800-684-1127
www.astorneworleans.com

ROOM QUALITY	86
COST ($=$50)	$$$$$
LOCATION	FRENCH QUARTER
NO. OF ROOMS	515
POOL	•
SAUNA	–
ROOM SERVICE	•
PARKING	VALET, $31
BREAKFAST	CONTINENTAL
EXERCISE FACILITIES	•

Bienville House Hotel ★★★½
320 Decatur Street
New Orleans, LA 70130
☎ 504-529-2345
FAX 504-525-6079
TOLL-FREE ☎ 800-535-9603
www.bienvillehouse.com

ROOM QUALITY	80
COST ($=$50)	$$$+
LOCATION	FRENCH QUARTER
NO. OF ROOMS	83
POOL	•
SAUNA	–
ROOM SERVICE	–
PARKING	LOT, $20
BREAKFAST	CONTINENTAL
EXERCISE FACILITIES	OFF SITE

Bourbon Orleans Hotel ★★★½
717 Orleans Street
New Orleans, LA 70116
☎ 504-523-2222
FAX 504-571-4666
www.bourbonorleans.com

ROOM QUALITY	76
COST ($=$50)	$$$+
LOCATION	FRENCH QUARTER
NO. OF ROOMS	218
POOL	•
SAUNA	–
ROOM SERVICE	•
PARKING	VALET, $30
BREAKFAST	–
EXERCISE FACILITIES	•

Chateau Bourbon Hotel ★★★★
800 Iberville Street
New Orleans, LA 70112
☎ 504-586-0800
FAX 504-586-1987
TOLL-FREE ☎ 877-999-3223
www.wyndham.com

ROOM QUALITY	84
COST ($=$50)	$$$$$+
LOCATION	FRENCH QUARTER
NO. OF ROOMS	251
POOL	•
SAUNA	–
ROOM SERVICE	•
PARKING	LOT, $26; VALET, $31
BREAKFAST	–
EXERCISE FACILITIES	•

Comfort Suites Downtown ★★
346 Baronne Street
New Orleans, LA 70112
☎ 504-524-1140
FAX 504-218-4991
TOLL-FREE ☎ 800-524-1140
www.choicehotels.com

ROOM QUALITY	55
COST ($=$50)	$$–
LOCATION	CENTRAL BUSINESS DISTRICT
NO. OF ROOMS	102
POOL	–
SAUNA	•
ROOM SERVICE	–
PARKING	LOT, $12
BREAKFAST	CONTINENTAL
EXERCISE FACILITIES	•

The Cornstalk Hotel ★★★½
915 Royal Street
New Orleans, LA 70113
☎ 504-523-1515
FAX 504-522-5558
TOLL-FREE ☎ 800-759-6112
www.cornstalkhotel.com

ROOM QUALITY	75
COST ($=$50)	$$$$+
LOCATION	FRENCH QUARTER
NO. OF ROOMS	14
POOL	–
SAUNA	–
ROOM SERVICE	–
PARKING	LOT, $15
BREAKFAST	–
EXERCISE FACILITIES	–

Cotton Exchange Hotel/ Holiday Inn Express ★★★
231 Carondelet Street
New Orleans, LA 70130
☎ 504-962-0700
FAX 504-962-0701
TOLL-FREE ☎ 888-538-5667
www.cottonhotelneworleans.com

ROOM QUALITY	73
COST ($=$50)	$$$$–
LOCATION	CENTRAL BUSINESS DISTRICT
NO. OF ROOMS	102
POOL	•
SAUNA	–
ROOM SERVICE	–
PARKING	VALET, $18
BREAKFAST	–
EXERCISE FACILITIES	•

Avenue Garden Hotel ★★½
1509 St. Charles Avenue
New Orleans, LA 70130
☎ 504-521-8000
FAX 504-528-3180
TOLL-FREE ☎ 800-379-5322
www.avenuegardenhotel.com

ROOM QUALITY	63
COST ($=$50)	$$+
LOCATION	UPTOWN AND THE GARDEN DISTRICT
NO. OF ROOMS	25
POOL	–
SAUNA	–
ROOM SERVICE	–
PARKING	GARAGE, $15
BREAKFAST	CONTINENTAL
EXERCISE FACILITIES	ADJACENT

Avenue Inn Bed & Breakfast ★★★½
4125 St. Charles Avenue
New Orleans, LA 70130
☎ 504-269-2640
FAX 504-269-2641
TOLL-FREE ☎ 800-490-8542
www.avenueinnbb.com

ROOM QUALITY	83
COST ($=$50)	$$$$
LOCATION	UPTOWN AND THE GARDEN DISTRICT
NO. OF ROOMS	17
POOL	–
SAUNA	–
ROOM SERVICE	–
PARKING	FREE LOT
BREAKFAST	CONTINENTAL
EXERCISE FACILITIES	–

Best Western French Quarter Landmark Hotel ★★½
920 N. Rampart Street
New Orleans, LA 70116
☎ 504-524-3333
FAX 504-522-8044
TOLL-FREE ☎ 888-876-8791
www.frenchquarterlandmark.com

ROOM QUALITY	47
COST ($=$50)	$$+
LOCATION	FRENCH QUARTER
NO. OF ROOMS	100
POOL	•
SAUNA	–
ROOM SERVICE	–
PARKING	LOT, $19
BREAKFAST	CONTINENTAL
EXERCISE FACILITIES	–

Chateau Dupré Hotel ★★½
131 Rue Decatur
New Orleans, LA 70130
☎ 504-569-0600
FAX 504-569-0606
TOLL-FREE ☎ 888-538-5666
www.chateauduprehotel.com

ROOM QUALITY	56
COST ($=$50)	$$+
LOCATION	FRENCH QUARTER
NO. OF ROOMS	62
POOL	–
SAUNA	–
ROOM SERVICE	–
PARKING	VALET, $25
BREAKFAST	CONTINENTAL
EXERCISE FACILITIES	–

Chateau LeMoyne French Quarter Holiday Inn ★★★
301 Rue Dauphine
New Orleans, LA 70112
☎ 504-581-1303
FAX 504-523-5709
TOLL-FREE ☎ 800-282-0244
www.ichotelsgroup.com

ROOM QUALITY	72
COST ($=$50)	$$$–
LOCATION	FRENCH QUARTER
NO. OF ROOMS	171
POOL	•
SAUNA	–
ROOM SERVICE	–
PARKING	VALET, $30
BREAKFAST	–
EXERCISE FACILITIES	–

The Columns ★★★½
3811 St. Charles Avenue
New Orleans, LA 70115
☎ 504-899-9308
FAX 504-899-8170
TOLL-FREE ☎ 800-445-9308
www.thecolumns.com

ROOM QUALITY	75
COST ($=$50)	$$$$$–
LOCATION	UPTOWN AND THE GARDEN DISTRICT
NO. OF ROOMS	19
POOL	–
SAUNA	–
ROOM SERVICE	–
PARKING	STREET
BREAKFAST	FULL
EXERCISE FACILITIES	–

Courtyard by Marriott ★★★½
124 St. Charles Avenue
New Orleans, LA 70130
☎ 504-581-9005
FAX 504-581-6264
TOLL-FREE ☎ 800-321-2211
www.marriott.com

ROOM QUALITY	83
COST ($=$50)	$$$
LOCATION	CENTRAL BUSINESS DISTRICT
NO. OF ROOMS	140
POOL	–
SAUNA	–
ROOM SERVICE	–
PARKING	VALET, $24
BREAKFAST	–
EXERCISE FACILITIES	•

Creole Gardens Guesthouse ★★★
1415 Prytania Street
New Orleans, LA 70130
☎ 504-569-8700
FAX 504-525-6555
TOLL-FREE ☎ 866-569-8700
www.creolegardens.com

ROOM QUALITY	72
COST ($=$50)	$$$
LOCATION	UPTOWN AND THE GARDEN DISTRICT
NO. OF ROOMS	24
POOL	–
SAUNA	–
ROOM SERVICE	–
PARKING	FREE LOT
BREAKFAST	FULL
EXERCISE FACILITIES	–

A Creole House Hotel ★½
1013 St. Ann Street
New Orleans, LA 70116
☎ 504-524-9232
FAX 504-523-5198
TOLL-FREE ☎ 800-535-7815
www.acreolehouse.com

ROOM QUALITY	44
COST ($=$50)	$$+
LOCATION	FRENCH QUARTER
NO. OF ROOMS	31
POOL	–
SAUNA	–
ROOM SERVICE	–
PARKING	LOT, $15
BREAKFAST	CONTINENTAL
EXERCISE FACILITIES	–

Hotel Information Chart (continued)

Dauphine Orleans ★★★½
415 Dauphine Street
New Orleans, LA 70112
☎ 504-586-1800
FAX 504-586-1409
TOLL-FREE ☎ 800-521-7111
www.dauphineorleans.com

ROOM QUALITY	76
COST ($=$50)	$$$+
LOCATION	FRENCH QUARTER
NO. OF ROOMS	111
POOL	•
SAUNA	–
ROOM SERVICE	–
PARKING	VALET, $28
BREAKFAST	CONTINENTAL
EXERCISE FACILITIES	•

Degas House: Historic Home, Courtyard, and Inn ★★★★½
2306 Esplanade Avenue
New Orleans, LA 70119
☎ 504-821-5009
FAX 504-821-0870
TOLL-FREE ☎ 800-755-6730
www.degashouse.com

ROOM QUALITY	95
COST ($=$50)	$$$$+
LOCATION	FRENCH QUARTER
NO. OF ROOMS	10
POOL	–
SAUNA	–
ROOM SERVICE	–
PARKING	FREE LOT
BREAKFAST	CONTINENTAL
EXERCISE FACILITIES	–

Doubletree Hotel New Orleans ★★★★½
300 Canal Street
New Orleans, LA 70130
☎ 504-581-1300
FAX 504-212-3141
TOLL-FREE ☎ 800-222-TREE
www.doubletree.com

ROOM QUALITY	90
COST ($=$50)	$$$+
LOCATION	CENTRAL BUSINESS DISTRICT
NO. OF ROOMS	363
POOL	•
SAUNA	–
ROOM SERVICE	•
PARKING	VALET, $35
BREAKFAST	–
EXERCISE FACILITIES	•

The Frenchmen Hotel ★★★
417 Frenchmen Street
New Orleans, LA 70116
☎ 504-948-2166
FAX 504-948-2258
TOLL-FREE ☎ 800-831-1731
www.frenchmenhotel.com

ROOM QUALITY	74
COST ($=$50)	$$–
LOCATION	FAUBOURG MARIGNY
NO. OF ROOMS	25
POOL	•
SAUNA	•
ROOM SERVICE	–
PARKING	STREET, $15–20
BREAKFAST	CONTINENTAL
EXERCISE FACILITIES	–

Hampton Inn ★★★
3626 St.Charles Avenue
New Orleans, LA 70115
☎ 504-899-9990
FAX 504-899-9908
TOLL-FREE ☎ 800-292-0653
www.neworleanshamptoninns.com

ROOM QUALITY	73
COST ($=$50)	$$$+
LOCATION	UPTOWN AND THE GARDEN DISTRICT
NO. OF ROOMS	100
POOL	•
SAUNA	–
ROOM SERVICE	–
PARKING	FREE LOT
BREAKFAST	CONTINENTAL
EXERCISE FACILITIES	–

Hampton Inn Downtown ★★★½
226 Carondelet Street
New Orleans, LA 70130
☎ 504-529-9990
FAX 504-529-9996
TOLL-FREE ☎ 800-HAMPTON
www.hamptoninn.com

ROOM QUALITY	80
COST ($=$50)	$$$–
LOCATION	CENTRAL BUSINESS DISTRICT
NO. OF ROOMS	187
POOL	–
SAUNA	–
ROOM SERVICE	–
PARKING	VALET, $28
BREAKFAST	FULL
EXERCISE FACILITIES	•

Historic French Market Inn ★★★
501 Rue Decatur
New Orleans, LA 70130
☎ 504-561-5621
TOLL-FREE ☎ 888-538-5651
www.neworleansfinehotels.com

ROOM QUALITY	65
COST ($=$50)	$$$$
LOCATION	FRENCH QUARTER
NO. OF ROOMS	126
POOL	•
SAUNA	–
ROOM SERVICE	–
PARKING	LOT, $25
BREAKFAST	–
EXERCISE FACILITIES	•

Holiday Inn French Quarter ★★★½
124 Royal Street
New Orleans, LA 70130
☎ 504-529-7211
FAX 504-522-7930
TOLL-FREE ☎ 800-447-2830
hineworleans-frenchquarter.felcor.com

ROOM QUALITY	76
COST ($=$50)	$$$+
LOCATION	FRENCH QUARTER
NO. OF ROOMS	374
POOL	•
SAUNA	–
ROOM SERVICE	•
PARKING	LOT, $26
BREAKFAST	–
EXERCISE FACILITIES	•

Homewood Suites by Hilton ★★★½
901 Poydras Street
New Orleans, LA 70122
☎ 504-581-5599
FAX 504-581-9133
TOLL-FREE ☎ 800-CALL-HOME
www.homewoodsuitesneworleans.com

ROOM QUALITY	83
COST ($=$50)	$$$$–
LOCATION	CENTRAL BUSINESS DISTRICT
NO. OF ROOMS	166
POOL	•
SAUNA	•
ROOM SERVICE	–
PARKING	LOT, $17
BREAKFAST	FULL
EXERCISE FACILITIES	•

Embassy Suites New Orleans ★★★½
315 Julia Street
New Orleans, LA 70130
☎ 504-525-1993
FAX 504-522-3044
TOLL-FREE ☎ 800-EMBASSY
www.embassyneworleans.com

ROOM QUALITY	82
COST ($=$50)	$$$–
LOCATION	CENTRAL BUSINESS DISTRICT
NO. OF ROOMS	372
POOL	•
SAUNA	–
ROOM SERVICE	•
PARKING	VALET, $30
BREAKFAST	FULL
EXERCISE FACILITIES	•

French Quarter Courtyard Hotel ★★★
1101 N. Rampart
New Orleans, LA 70116
☎ 504-522-7333
FAX 504-522-3908
TOLL-FREE ☎ 800-290-4233

ROOM QUALITY	67
COST ($=$50)	$$–
LOCATION	FRENCH QUARTER
NO. OF ROOMS	51
POOL	•
SAUNA	–
ROOM SERVICE	–
PARKING	LOT, $12
BREAKFAST	CONTINENTAL
EXERCISE FACILITIES	–

French Quarter Suites ★★½
1119 N. Rampart Street
New Orleans, LA 70116
☎ 504-524-7725
FAX 504-522-9716
TOLL-FREE ☎ 800-457-2253
www.frenchquartersuites.com

ROOM QUALITY	62
COST ($=$50)	$$
LOCATION	FRENCH QUARTER
NO. OF ROOMS	18
POOL	•
SAUNA	–
ROOM SERVICE	–
PARKING	LOT, $22
BREAKFAST	CONTINENTAL
EXERCISE FACILITIES	–

Hampton Inn Suites & Convention Center ★★★½
1201 Convention Center Blvd.
New Orleans, LA 70130
☎ 504-566-9990
FAX 504-566-9997
TOLL-FREE ☎ 866-311-1200
www.hamptoninn.com

ROOM QUALITY	81
COST ($=$50)	$$$$$–
LOCATION	CENTRAL BUSINESS DISTRICT
NO. OF ROOMS	288
POOL	•
SAUNA	–
ROOM SERVICE	–
PARKING	VALET, $28
BREAKFAST	FULL
EXERCISE FACILITIES	•

Hilton Garden Inn ★★★★
1001 S. Peters Street
New Orleans, LA 70130
☎ 504-525-0044
FAX 504-525-0035
TOLL-FREE ☎ 800-HILTONS
www.hiltongardeninn.com

ROOM QUALITY	85
COST ($=$50)	$$$$–
LOCATION	CENTRAL BUSINESS DISTRICT
NO. OF ROOMS	284
POOL	•
SAUNA	•
ROOM SERVICE	•
PARKING	VALET, $22
BREAKFAST	–
EXERCISE FACILITIES	•

Hilton New Orleans Riverside ★★★★
2 Poydras Street
New Orleans, LA 70140
☎ 504-561-0500
FAX 504-584-1721
TOLL-FREE ☎ 800-HILTONS
www.hilton.com

ROOM QUALITY	89
COST ($=$50)	$$$$+
LOCATION	CENTRAL BUSINESS DISTRICT
NO. OF ROOMS	1,616
POOL	•
SAUNA	•
ROOM SERVICE	•
PARKING	VALET, $36; LOT, $30
BREAKFAST	–
EXERCISE FACILITIES	•

Hotel de la Monnaie ★★★½
405 Esplanade Avenue
New Orleans, LA 70116
☎ 504-947-0009
FAX 504-945-6841
www.hoteldelamonnaie.com

ROOM QUALITY	75
COST ($=$50)	$$$–
LOCATION	FRENCH QUARTER
NO. OF ROOMS	53
POOL	•
SAUNA	–
ROOM SERVICE	–
PARKING	STREET
BREAKFAST	–
EXERCISE FACILITIES	•

Hotel Le Cirque ★★★★½
936 St. Charles Avenue
New Orleans, LA 70130
☎ 504-962-0900
FAX 504-962-0901
TOLL-FREE ☎ 800-684-9525
www.neworleansfinehotels.com

ROOM QUALITY	90
COST ($=$50)	$$$–
LOCATION	CENTRAL BUSINESS DISTRICT
NO. OF ROOMS	137
POOL	–
SAUNA	–
ROOM SERVICE	–
PARKING	LOT, $20
BREAKFAST	–
EXERCISE FACILITIES	–

Hotel Monteleone ★★★★
214 Rue Royale
New Orleans, LA 70130
☎ 504-681-4413
FAX 504-681-4413
TOLL-FREE ☎ 800-535-9595
www.hotelmonteleone.com

ROOM QUALITY	89
COST ($=$50)	$$$$$$–
LOCATION	FRENCH QUARTER
NO. OF ROOMS	600
POOL	•
SAUNA	–
ROOM SERVICE	•
PARKING	LOT, $27
BREAKFAST	–
EXERCISE FACILITIES	•

Hotel Information Chart (continued)

Hotel New Orleans ★★★½
881 Convention Center Boulevard
New Orleans, LA 70130
☎ 504-524-1881
FAX 504-528-1005
TOLL-FREE ☎ 888-524-1881
www.hotelneworleansconvention center.com

ROOM QUALITY	80
COST ($=$50)	$$$$+
LOCATION	CENTRAL BUSINESS DISTRICT
NO. OF ROOMS	168
POOL	–
SAUNA	–
ROOM SERVICE	•
PARKING	VALET, LOT, $26
BREAKFAST	–
EXERCISE FACILITIES	•

Hotel Provincial ★★★★
1024 Rue Chartres
New Orleans, LA 70116
☎ 504-581-4995
FAX 504-581-1018
TOLL-FREE ☎ 800-535-7922
www.hotelprovincial.com

ROOM QUALITY	85
COST ($=$50)	$$$$+
LOCATION	FRENCH QUARTER
NO. OF ROOMS	94
POOL	•
SAUNA	–
ROOM SERVICE	–
PARKING	VALET, $18
BREAKFAST	CONTINENTAL
EXERCISE FACILITIES	–

Hotel Royal ★★★½
1006 Rue Royal
New Orleans, LA 70116
☎ 504-524-3900
FAX 504-558-0566
TOLL-FREE ☎ 800-776-3901
www.melrosegroup.com/melroseroyal

ROOM QUALITY	82
COST ($=$50)	$$+
LOCATION	FRENCH QUARTER
NO. OF ROOMS	30
POOL	–
SAUNA	–
ROOM SERVICE	–
PARKING	LOT, $25
BREAKFAST	–
EXERCISE FACILITIES	–

Inn on Bourbon, Ramada Plaza ★★★½
541 Bourbon Street
New Orleans, LA 70130
☎ 504-524-7611
FAX 504-568-9427
TOLL-FREE ☎ 800-535-7891
www.innonbourbon.com

ROOM QUALITY	75
COST ($=$50)	$$$+
LOCATION	FRENCH QUARTER
NO. OF ROOMS	186
POOL	•
SAUNA	–
ROOM SERVICE	•
PARKING	LOT, $25
BREAKFAST	–
EXERCISE FACILITIES	•

InterContinental Hotel New Orleans ★★★★½
444 St. Charles Avenue
New Orleans, LA 70130
☎ 504-525-5566
FAX 504-523-7310
TOLL-FREE ☎ 800-327-0200
www.new-orleans.intercontinental.com

ROOM QUALITY	95
COST ($=$50)	$$$$$
LOCATION	CENTRAL BUSINESS DISTRICT
NO. OF ROOMS	479
POOL	•
SAUNA	–
ROOM SERVICE	•
PARKING	VALET, $45; LOT, $29
BREAKFAST	–
EXERCISE FACILITIES	•

International House ★★★★★
221 Camp Street
New Orleans, LA 70130
☎ 504-553-9550
FAX 504-200-9560
TOLL-FREE ☎ 800-633-5770
www.ihhotel.com

ROOM QUALITY	97
COST ($=$50)	$$$$+
LOCATION	CENTRAL BUSINESS DISTRICT
NO. OF ROOMS	119
POOL	–
SAUNA	–
ROOM SERVICE	–
PARKING	LOT, $26
BREAKFAST	–
EXERCISE FACILITIES	•

Lamothe House ★½
621 Esplanade Avenue
New Orleans, LA 70116
☎ 504-947-1161
FAX 504-943-6536
TOLL-FREE ☎ 888-696-9575
www.lamothehouse.com

ROOM QUALITY	46
COST ($=$50)	$$$+
LOCATION	FRENCH QUARTER
NO. OF ROOMS	30
POOL	•
SAUNA	–
ROOM SERVICE	–
PARKING	LOT, $15
BREAKFAST	CONTINENTAL
EXERCISE FACILITIES	–

Le Pavillon Hotel ★★★½
833 Poydras Street
New Orleans, LA 70112
☎ 504-581-3111
FAX 504-620-4130
TOLL-FREE ☎ 800-535-9095
www.lepavillon.com

ROOM QUALITY	83
COST ($=$50)	$$$$$$$–
LOCATION	CENTRAL BUSINESS DISTRICT
NO. OF ROOMS	226
POOL	•
SAUNA	–
ROOM SERVICE	•
PARKING	LOT, $32
BREAKFAST	–
EXERCISE FACILITIES	•

Le Richelieu in the French Quarter ★★★½
1234 Chartres Street
New Orleans, LA 70116
☎ 504-529-2492
FAX 504-524-8179
TOLL-FREE ☎ 800-535-9653
www.lerichelieuhotel.com

ROOM QUALITY	75
COST ($=$50)	$$$+
LOCATION	FRENCH QUARTER
NO. OF ROOMS	86
POOL	•
SAUNA	–
ROOM SERVICE	–
PARKING	FREE LOT
BREAKFAST	–
EXERCISE FACILITIES	–

Hotel St. Marie ★★★½
827 Toulouse Street
New Orleans, LA 70112
☎ 504-561-8951
FAX 504-581-3802
TOLL-FREE ☎ 800-366-2743
www.hotelstmarie.com

ROOM QUALITY	77
COST ($=$50)	$$$
LOCATION	FRENCH QUARTER
NO. OF ROOMS	103
POOL	•
SAUNA	–
ROOM SERVICE	•
PARKING	VALET, $26
BREAKFAST	–
EXERCISE FACILITIES	–

Hotel St. Pierre ★½
911 Burgundy Street
New Orleans, LA 70116
☎ 504-524-4401
FAX 504-593-9425
TOLL-FREE ☎ 800-225-4040
www.hotelsaintpierre.com

ROOM QUALITY	46
COST ($=$50)	$$$–
LOCATION	FRENCH QUARTER
NO. OF ROOMS	74
POOL	•
SAUNA	–
ROOM SERVICE	–
PARKING	FREE LOT
BREAKFAST	CONTINENTAL
EXERCISE FACILITIES	–

Hotel Villa Convento ★
616 Ursulines Street
New Orleans, LA 70116
☎ 504-522-1793
FAX 504-524-1902
TOLL-FREE ☎ 800-887-2817
www.villaconvento.com

ROOM QUALITY	37
COST ($=$50)	$$$+
LOCATION	FRENCH QUARTER
NO. OF ROOMS	25
POOL	–
SAUNA	–
ROOM SERVICE	–
PARKING	LOT, $12
BREAKFAST	–
EXERCISE FACILITIES	–

JW Marriott ★★★★½
614 Canal Street
New Orleans, LA 70130
☎ 504-525-6500
FAX 504-525-1128
TOLL-FREE ☎ 888-364-1200
www.marriott.com

ROOM QUALITY	90
COST ($=$50)	$$$$$–
LOCATION	CENTRAL BUSINESS DISTRICT
NO. OF ROOMS	494
POOL	•
SAUNA	•
ROOM SERVICE	•
PARKING	VALET, $32
BREAKFAST	–
EXERCISE FACILITIES	•

Lafayette Hotel ★★★★
600 St. Charles Avenue
New Orleans, LA 70130
☎ 504-524-4441
FAX 504-523-7327
TOLL-FREE ☎ 888-856-4706
www.thelafayettehotel.com

ROOM QUALITY	89
COST ($=$50)	$$$$–
LOCATION	CENTRAL BUSINESS DISTRICT
NO. OF ROOMS	44
POOL	–
SAUNA	–
ROOM SERVICE	•
PARKING	VALET, $19
BREAKFAST	–
EXERCISE FACILITIES	NEARBY

Lafitte Guest House ★★★★½
1003 Bourbon Street
New Orleans, LA 70116
☎ 504-581-2678
FAX 504-581-2677
TOLL-FREE ☎ 800-331-7971
www.lafitteguesthouse.com

ROOM QUALITY	90
COST ($=$50)	$$$$$
LOCATION	FRENCH QUARTER
NO. OF ROOMS	14
POOL	–
SAUNA	–
ROOM SERVICE	–
PARKING	FREE LOT
BREAKFAST	CONTINENTAL
EXERCISE FACILITIES	–

Loews ★★★★★
300 Poydras Street
New Orleans, LA 70130
☎ 504-595-3300
FAX 504-595-3310
TOLL-FREE ☎ 800-235-6397
www.loewshotels.com

ROOM QUALITY	98
COST ($=$50)	$$$$$$–
LOCATION	CENTRAL BUSINESS DISTRICT
NO. OF ROOMS	285
POOL	•
SAUNA	•
ROOM SERVICE	•
PARKING	VALET, $29
BREAKFAST	–
EXERCISE FACILITIES	•

Loft 523 ★★★★★
523 Gravier Street
New Orleans, LA 70130
☎ 504-200-6523
FAX 504-200-6522
www.loft523.com

ROOM QUALITY	99
COST ($=$50)	$$$
LOCATION	CENTRAL BUSINESS DISTRICT
NO. OF ROOMS	18
POOL	–
SAUNA	–
ROOM SERVICE	•
PARKING	LOT, $22
BREAKFAST	–
EXERCISE FACILITIES	•

Maison De Ville ★★★½
727 Rue Toulouse
New Orleans, LA 70130
☎ 504-561-5858
FAX 504-528-9939
TOLL-FREE ☎ 800-634-1600
www.maisondeville.com

ROOM QUALITY	76
COST ($=$50)	$$$$$+
LOCATION	FRENCH QUARTER
NO. OF ROOMS	23
POOL	•
SAUNA	–
ROOM SERVICE	–
PARKING	VALET, $34
BREAKFAST	CONTINENTAL
EXERCISE FACILITIES	–

Hotel Information Chart (continued)

Maison Dupuy Hotel ★★★½
1001 Rue Toulouse
New Orleans, LA 70112
☎ 504-586-8000
FAX 504-525-5334
TOLL-FREE
www.maisondupuy.com

ROOM QUALITY	81
COST ($=$50)	$$$+
LOCATION	FRENCH QUARTER
NO. OF ROOMS	200
POOL	•
SAUNA	–
ROOM SERVICE	•
PARKING	VALET, $28+
BREAKFAST	–
EXERCISE FACILITIES	•

Maison St. Charles Hotel & Suites ★★★
1319 St. Charles Avenue
New Orleans, LA 70130
☎ 504-522-0187
FAX 504-529-4379
TOLL-FREE ☎ 800-831-1783
www.maisonstcharles.com

ROOM QUALITY	70
COST ($=$50)	$$$–
LOCATION	UPTOWN AND THE GARDEN DISTRICT
NO. OF ROOMS	130
POOL	•
SAUNA	•
ROOM SERVICE	–
PARKING	STREET, $17
BREAKFAST	–
EXERCISE FACILITIES	–

Marigny Manor House ★★★★
2125 N. Rampart Street
New Orleans, LA 70116
☎ 504-943-7826
FAX 504-943-7826
TOLL-FREE ☎ 877-247-7599
www.marignymanorhouse.com

ROOM QUALITY	86
COST ($=$50)	$$$–
LOCATION	FAUBOURG MARIGNY
NO. OF ROOMS	4
POOL	–
SAUNA	–
ROOM SERVICE	–
PARKING	LOT
BREAKFAST	CONTINENTAL
EXERCISE FACILITIES	–

Olivier House Hotel ★★★
828 Toulouse Street
New Orleans, LA 70112
☎ 504-525-8456
FAX 504-529-2006
TOLL-FREE ☎ 866-525-9748
www.olivierhouse.com

ROOM QUALITY	65
COST ($=$50)	$$$–
LOCATION	FRENCH QUARTER
NO. OF ROOMS	42
POOL	•
SAUNA	–
ROOM SERVICE	–
PARKING	FREE LOT
BREAKFAST	–
EXERCISE FACILITIES	–

Omni Royal Crescent Hotel ★★★★
535 Gravier Street
New Orleans, LA 70130
☎ 504-527-0006
FAX 504-571-7575
TOLL-FREE ☎ 800-843-6664
www.omnihotels.com

ROOM QUALITY	88
COST ($=$50)	$$$+
LOCATION	CENTRAL BUSINESS DISTRICT
NO. OF ROOMS	97
POOL	•
SAUNA	–
ROOM SERVICE	•
PARKING	VALET OR LOT, $27
BREAKFAST	–
EXERCISE FACILITIES	•

Omni Royal Orleans Hotel ★★★★
621 St. Louis Street
New Orleans, LA 70140
☎ 504-529-5333
FAX 504-529-7089
TOLL-FREE ☎ 888-444-OMNI
www.omnihotels.com

ROOM QUALITY	89
COST ($=$50)	$$$$$$–
LOCATION	FRENCH QUARTER
NO. OF ROOMS	346
POOL	•
SAUNA	–
ROOM SERVICE	•
PARKING	VALET, $28
BREAKFAST	–
EXERCISE FACILITIES	•

Prince Conti Hotel ★★★½
830 Conti Street
New Orleans, LA 70112
☎ 504-529-4172
FAX 504-581-3802
TOLL-FREE ☎ 800-366-2743
www.princecontihotel.com

ROOM QUALITY	75
COST ($=$50)	$$$+
LOCATION	FRENCH QUARTER
NO. OF ROOMS	76
POOL	–
SAUNA	–
ROOM SERVICE	•
PARKING	VALET, $25
BREAKFAST	–
EXERCISE FACILITIES	–

Prytania Park Hotel ★★★
1525 Prytania Street
New Orleans, LA 70130
☎ 504-524-0427
FAX 504-522-2977
TOLL-FREE ☎ 888-498-7591
www.prytaniaparkhotel.com

ROOM QUALITY	65
COST ($=$50)	$$$+
LOCATION	UPTOWN AND THE GARDEN DISTRICT
NO. OF ROOMS	62
POOL	–
SAUNA	–
ROOM SERVICE	–
PARKING	STREET, FREE
BREAKFAST	CONTINENTAL
EXERCISE FACILITIES	OFF SITE

Quality Inn & Suites ★★
210 O'Keefe Avenue
New Orleans, LA 70112
☎ 504-525-6800
FAX 504-525-6808
TOLL-FREE ☎ 877-525-6900
www.qualityinn.com

ROOM QUALITY	55
COST ($=$50)	$$$+
LOCATION	CENTRAL BUSINESS DISTRICT
NO. OF ROOMS	100
POOL	–
SAUNA	–
ROOM SERVICE	–
PARKING	LOT, $17
BREAKFAST	CONTINENTAL
EXERCISE FACILITIES	–

Marriott New Orleans ★★★★
555 Canal Street
New Orleans, LA 70140
☎ 504-581-1000
FAX 504-523-6755
TOLL-FREE ☎ 888-364-1200
www.marriott.com

ROOM QUALITY	89
COST ($=$50)	$$$$$–
LOCATION	FRENCH QUARTER
NO. OF ROOMS	1,329
POOL	•
SAUNA	–
ROOM SERVICE	•
PARKING	VALET, $32
BREAKFAST	–
EXERCISE FACILITIES	•

The McKendrick-Breaux House ★★★★½
1474 Magazine Street
New Orleans, LA 70130
☎ 504-586-1700
FAX 504-522-7138
TOLL-FREE ☎ 888-570-1700
www.mckendrick-breaux.com

ROOM QUALITY	93
COST ($=$50)	$$$
LOCATION	UPTOWN AND THE GARDEN DISTRICT
NO. OF ROOMS	9
POOL	–
SAUNA	–
ROOM SERVICE	–
PARKING	FREE LOT
BREAKFAST	CONTINENTAL
EXERCISE FACILITIES	–

New Orleans Guest House ★★★
1118 Ursulines Street
New Orleans, LA 70116
☎ 504-566-1177
FAX 504-566-1179
TOLL-FREE ☎ 800-562-1177

ROOM QUALITY	71
COST ($=$50)	$$–
LOCATION	FRENCH QUARTER
NO. OF ROOMS	14
POOL	–
SAUNA	–
ROOM SERVICE	–
PARKING	FREE LOT
BREAKFAST	CONTINENTAL
EXERCISE FACILITIES	–

The Parc St. Charles ★★★½
500 St. Charles Avenue
New Orleans, LA 70130
☎ 504-522-9000
FAX 504-522-9060
TOLL-FREE ☎ 888-856-4489
www.neworleansfinehotels.com

ROOM QUALITY	82
COST ($=$50)	$$$+
LOCATION	CENTRAL BUSINESS DISTRICT
NO. OF ROOMS	123
POOL	•
SAUNA	–
ROOM SERVICE	–
PARKING	LOT, $25
BREAKFAST	–
EXERCISE FACILITIES	•

Pelham Hotel ★★★
444 Common Street
New Orleans, LA 70130
☎ 504-522-4444
FAX 504-539-9010
TOLL-FREE ☎ 888-856-4486
www.neworleansfinehotels.com

ROOM QUALITY	66
COST ($=$50)	$$$–
LOCATION	CENTRAL BUSINESS DISTRICT
NO. OF ROOMS	60
POOL	–
SAUNA	–
ROOM SERVICE	•
PARKING	VALET, $19
BREAKFAST	–
EXERCISE FACILITIES	–

Place D'Armes Hotel ★★★
625 St. Ann Street
New Orleans, LA 70116
☎ 504-524-4531
FAX 504-581-3802
TOLL-FREE ☎ 800-366-2743
www.placedarmes.com

ROOM QUALITY	74
COST ($=$50)	$$$
LOCATION	FRENCH QUARTER
NO. OF ROOMS	83
POOL	•
SAUNA	–
ROOM SERVICE	–
PARKING	VALET, $26
BREAKFAST	CONTINENTAL
EXERCISE FACILITIES	–

Queen and Crescent Hotel ★★★½
344 Camp Street
New Orleans, LA 70130
☎ 504-587-9700
FAX 504-587-9701
TOLL-FREE ☎ 800-975-6652
www.queenandcrescenthotel.com

ROOM QUALITY	82
COST ($=$50)	$$$–
LOCATION	CENTRAL BUSINESS DISTRICT
NO. OF ROOMS	196
POOL	–
SAUNA	–
ROOM SERVICE	–
PARKING	VALET, $26
BREAKFAST	CONTINENTAL
EXERCISE FACILITIES	•

Rathbone Inn ★★★
1244 Esplanade Avenue
New Orleans, LA 70116
☎ 504-309-4479
FAX 504-947-7454
TOLL-FREE ☎ 866-729-8140
www.rathbonemansions.com

ROOM QUALITY	72
COST ($=$50)	$$$
LOCATION	FRENCH QUARTER
NO. OF ROOMS	14
POOL	•
SAUNA	–
ROOM SERVICE	–
PARKING	FREE LOT
BREAKFAST	CONTINENTAL
EXERCISE FACILITIES	–

Renaissance Arts Hotel ★★★★½
700 Tchoupitoulas Street
New Orleans, LA 70130
☎ 504-613-2330
FAX 504-613-2331
TOLL-FREE ☎ 800-431-8634
www.marriott.com

ROOM QUALITY	92
COST ($=$50)	$$$$+
LOCATION	CENTRAL BUSINESS DISTRICT
NO. OF ROOMS	217
POOL	•
SAUNA	•
ROOM SERVICE	•
PARKING	VALET, $28
BREAKFAST	–
EXERCISE FACILITIES	•

Hotel Information Chart (continued)

Hotel	Room Quality	Cost ($=$50)	Location	No. of Rooms	Pool	Sauna	Room Service	Parking	Breakfast	Exercise Facilities
Renaissance Pere Marquette ★★★★ 817 Common Street New Orleans, LA 70112 ☎ 504-525-1111 FAX 504-525-0688 TOLL-FREE ☎ 800-372-0482 www.marriott.com	89	$$$$$–	CENTRAL BUSINESS DISTRICT	272	•	•	•	VALET, $28	–	•
Residence Inn ★★★½ 345 St. Joseph Street New Orleans, LA 70130 ☎ 504-522-1300 FAX 504-522-6060 TOLL-FREE ☎ 800-331-3131 www.marriott.com	83	$$$$–	CENTRAL BUSINESS DISTRICT	231	•	–	–	VALET, $18	BUFFET	•
Ritz-Carlton New Orleans ★★★★½ 921 Canal Street New Orleans, LA 70112 ☎ 504-524-1331 FAX 504-524-7675 TOLL-FREE ☎ 800-241-3333 www.ritzcarlton.com	95	$$$$$+	FRENCH QUARTER	452	•	–	•	VALET, $36	–	•
The Saint Louis ★★★½ 730 Bienville Street New Orleans, LA 70130 ☎ 504-581-7300 FAX 504-679-5013 TOLL-FREE ☎ 888-508-3980 www.stlouishotel.com	75	$$$	FRENCH QUARTER	97	–	–	–	LOT, $15; VALET, $30	–	–
Sheraton New Orleans Hotel ★★★★ 500 Canal Street New Orleans, LA 70130 ☎ 504-525-2500 FAX 504-595-5552 TOLL-FREE ☎ 888-625-4988 www.sheratonneworleans.com	89	$$$$+	CENTRAL BUSINESS DISTRICT	1,110	•	•	•	LOT, $25	–	•
Soniat House ★★★★½ 1133 Chartres Street New Orleans, LA 70116 ☎ 504-522-0570 FAX 504-522-7208 TOLL-FREE ☎ 800-544-8808 www.soniathouse.com	95	$$$$$+	FRENCH QUARTER	33	–	–	–	VALET, $25	–	–
W French Quarter ★★★★★ 316 Chartres Street New Orleans, LA 70130 ☎ 504-581-1200 FAX 504-523-2910 TOLL-FREE ☎ 800-448-4927 www.starwoodhotels.com	97	$$$$$+	FRENCH QUARTER	98	•	–	•	VALET, $32	–	NEARBY
W New Orleans ★★★★½ 333 Poydras Street New Orleans, LA 70130 ☎ 504-525-9444 FAX 504-581-7179 TOLL-FREE ☎ 877-946-8357 www.starwoodhotels.com	95	$$$$$+	CENTRAL BUSINESS DISTRICT	423	•	•	•	VALET, $28	–	•
The Westin New Orleans Canal Place ★★★★ 100 Rue Iberville New Orleans, LA 70130 ☎ 504-566-7006 FAX 504-553-5029 TOLL-FREE ☎ 800-937-8461 www.starwoodhotels.com	89	$$$$$$+	FRENCH QUARTER	438	•	–	•	VALET, $30	–	•

Royal Sonesta Hotel ★★★★½
300 Bourbon Street
New Orleans, LA 70130
☎ 504-586-0300
FAX 504-586-0335
TOLL-FREE ☎ 800-SONESTA
www.sonesta.com

ROOM QUALITY	95
COST ($=$50)	$$$$$
LOCATION	FRENCH QUARTER
NO. OF ROOMS	483
POOL	•
SAUNA	–
ROOM SERVICE	•
PARKING	LOT, $31
BREAKFAST	–
EXERCISE FACILITIES	•

Royal St. Charles Hotel ★★★
135 St. Charles Avenue
New Orleans, LA 70130
☎ 504-587-3700
FAX 504-587-3701
TOLL-FREE ☎ 800-268-9749
www.royalsaintcharles.com

ROOM QUALITY	74
COST ($=$50)	$$+
LOCATION	CENTRAL BUSINESS DISTRICT
NO. OF ROOMS	147
POOL	–
SAUNA	–
ROOM SERVICE	–
PARKING	VALET, $26
BREAKFAST	–
EXERCISE FACILITIES	•

Saint Ann/ Marie Antoinette ★★★
717 Rue Conti
New Orleans, LA 70130
☎ 504-581-1881
FAX 504-524-8925
TOLL-FREE ☎ 800-535-9111
www.stannmarieantoinette.com

ROOM QUALITY	68
COST ($=$50)	$$$
LOCATION	FRENCH QUARTER
NO. OF ROOMS	66
POOL	•
SAUNA	–
ROOM SERVICE	–
PARKING	LOT, $19
BREAKFAST	–
EXERCISE FACILITIES	–

St. Charles Inn Best Western ★★★
3636 St. Charles Avenue
New Orleans, LA 70115
☎ 504-899-8888
FAX 504-899-8892
TOLL-FREE ☎ 800-489-9908
www.bestwestern.com

ROOM QUALITY	72
COST ($=$50)	$$$–
LOCATION	UPTOWN AND THE GARDEN DISTRICT
NO. OF ROOMS	40
POOL	–
SAUNA	–
ROOM SERVICE	–
PARKING	STREET
BREAKFAST	CONTINENTAL
EXERCISE FACILITIES	•

St. Peter House ★★
1005 St. Peter Street
New Orleans, LA 70116
☎ 504-524-9232
FAX 504-523-5198
TOLL-FREE ☎ 800-535-7815
www.stpeterhouse.com

ROOM QUALITY	55
COST ($=$50)	$$+
LOCATION	FRENCH QUARTER
NO. OF ROOMS	29
POOL	–
SAUNA	–
ROOM SERVICE	–
PARKING	LOT, $15
BREAKFAST	CONTINENTAL
EXERCISE FACILITIES	–

St. Vincent Guest House ★★
1507 Magazine Street
New Orleans, LA 70130
☎ 504-523-3411
FAX 504-566-1518
www.stvguesthouse.com

ROOM QUALITY	53
COST ($=$50)	$$–
LOCATION	UPTOWN AND THE GARDEN DISTRICT
NO. OF ROOMS	78
POOL	•
SAUNA	–
ROOM SERVICE	–
PARKING	FREE LOT
BREAKFAST	–
EXERCISE FACILITIES	–

The Whitney ★★★½
610 Poydras Street
New Orleans, LA 70130
☎ 504-581-4222
FAX 504-207-0100
TOLL-FREE ☎ 800-WYNDHAM
www.wyndham.com

ROOM QUALITY	83
COST ($=$50)	$$$+
LOCATION	CENTRAL BUSINESS DISTRICT
NO. OF ROOMS	93
POOL	–
SAUNA	–
ROOM SERVICE	•
PARKING	VALET, $25
BREAKFAST	CONTINTENTAL
EXERCISE FACILITIES	•

Windsor Court Hotel ★★★★★
300 Gravier Street
New Orleans, LA 70130
☎ 504-523-6000
FAX 504-596-4513
TOLL-FREE ☎ 888-596-0955
www.windsorcourthotel.com

ROOM QUALITY	96
COST ($=$50)	$$$$$$
LOCATION	CENTRAL BUSINESS DISTRICT
NO. OF ROOMS	322
POOL	•
SAUNA	•
ROOM SERVICE	•
PARKING	VALET, $32
BREAKFAST	–
EXERCISE FACILITIES	•

PART FIVE

VISITING *on* BUSINESS

LODGING *for* BUSINESS TRAVELERS

THE PRIMARY HOTEL CONSIDERATIONS for business travelers are affordability and proximity to the site or area where you will transact your business. Identify the area(s) where your business will take you, and then use the hotel chart to cross-reference the hotels located in that area. Once you have developed a short list of possible hotels that are conveniently located, fit your budget, and offer the standard of accommodations you require, you can make use of the cost-saving suggestions discussed in Part Four to obtain the lowest rate.

LODGING CONVENIENT TO MORIAL CONVENTION CENTER

IF YOU ARE ATTENDING A MEETING or trade show at the **Morial Convention Center,** the most convenient lodging is in the Central Business District or in the French Quarter. Closest to the convention center are the **Hampton Inn and Suites** and the **Hilton Garden Inn** directly across the street, and the **Residence Inn** on St. Joseph. Next are the **Embassy Suites** and the **Hotel New Orleans.** The hotels on Canal Street and those on the western side of the French Quarter are also within decent proximity. Two Vieux Carré shuttle-bus routes combine with the Riverfront streetcar to make commuting from the French Quarter to the convention center easy. It takes about 10 to 12 minutes to walk from the exhibit halls to the river end of Canal Street and about 5 to 12 minutes more to reach hotels in the upper Quarter (between St. Peter and Canal streets).

unofficial **TIP**
Parking is available at the convention center, but it is expensive and not very convenient. We recommend leaving your car at home and using shuttles, streetcars, or cabs.

If at all possible, you should avoid commuting to Morial Convention Center from the suburbs or the airports during rush hour. If you want a room near the convention center, book early—very early. If you need a room at the last minute, try a reservation service or one of the strategies listed below.

CONVENTION RATES: HOW THEY WORK AND HOW TO DO BETTER

IF YOU ARE ATTENDING A MAJOR CONVENTION or trade show, the meeting's sponsoring organization has probably negotiated convention rates with a number of hotels. Under this arrangement, hotels agree to block a certain number of rooms at an agreed-upon price for conventioneers. Sometimes, as in the case of a small meeting, only one hotel is involved. In the event of a large convention at Morial Convention Center, however, a high percentage of Central Business District and larger French Quarter hotels will participate in the room block.

Because the convention sponsor brings a lot of business to the city and reserves a large number of rooms, it usually can negotiate a volume discount on the room rate, a rate that should be substantially below rack rate. The bottom line, however, is that some conventions and trade shows have more bargaining clout and negotiating skill than others. Hence, your convention sponsor may or may not be able to obtain the lowest possible rate.

Once a convention or trade-show sponsor has completed negotiations with participating hotels, it will send its attendees a housing list that includes all the hotels serving the convention, along with the special convention rate for each. When you receive the housing list, you can compare the convention rates with the rates obtainable using the strategies listed below. If the negotiated convention rate doesn't sound like a good deal, you can try to reserve a room using a half-price club, a reservations service, or a tour operator. Remember, however, that many of the deep discounts are available only when the hotel expects to be at less than 80% occupancy, a condition that rarely prevails when a big convention comes to town.

Strategies for Beating Convention Rates

There are several tactics for getting around convention rates:

1. Reserve early. Most big conventions and trade shows announce meeting sites one to three years in advance. Get your reservation booked as far in advance as possible. If you book well ahead of the time the convention sponsor sends out the housing list, chances are good that the hotel will accept your reservation.

2. Compare your convention's housing list with the list of hotels presented in this guide. You may be able to find a suitable hotel that is not on the housing list.

3. Use a local reservations service, a wholesaler, or a room consolidator. This is also a good strategy to employ if you need to make reservations at the last minute. Local reservations services, wholesalers, and consolidators almost always control some rooms, even in the midst of a huge convention or trade show.

The ERNEST N. MORIAL CONVENTION CENTER

THE ERNEST N. MORIAL CONVENTION CENTER is located at 900 Convention Center Boulevard, New Orleans, LA 70130 (☎ 504-582-3023; fax 504-582-3032; **www.mccno.com**). Though it suffered an estimated $200 million in damage in the aftermath of Katrina—it was an all-too-familiar sight on national television, with its hundreds of distraught and angry inhabitants—its importance to the city's economic recovery made its repair a priority, and it has been back in business since last summer.

The Morial Convention Center includes 1.1 million square feet of contiguous exhibit space under one roof since its third-phase expansion was completed in early 1999. All this muscle backs up to and stretches out along the bank of the Mississippi. The front of the center runs along South Front Street, also called Convention Center Boulevard, reached easily from Interstate 10 by the Tchoupitoulas/ St. Peter exit. For pedestrians attending an event at the convention center, the battle is won after you've found the front door. For many attendees coming from the Canal Street major hotels and the French Quarter lodgings, the way in is simply not clear from a distance, nor is it distinctly marked once you come to it. The primary entrance is on Convention Center Boulevard, but the doors are actually perpendicular to the street, not parallel to the facade. The entrance is not marked by a plaza, flags, sculpture, or a fountain—nothing really shouts, "Enter here!"

This only poses a problem on that first critical day of registration when many people still feel disoriented. The best advice is to head for the Riverwalk Marketplace shopping center, which is highly visible on the Mississippi at Canal, Poydras, and Julia streets. As you face it (and the river), go to your right and have faith that the door will appear. It is a low-key ramp leading to a series of glass doors. Once you're inside, the facility is very well marked. The exhibit halls are alphabetically labeled, with "A" nearest the main entrance.

If the original architect missed the downbeat, the convention center administration does its best to set the right tempo. Clear, handsome promotional literature is readily available by calling the marketing and sales department office. The publication details the floor plans of the facility, including the capacities of the various spaces. There are 55

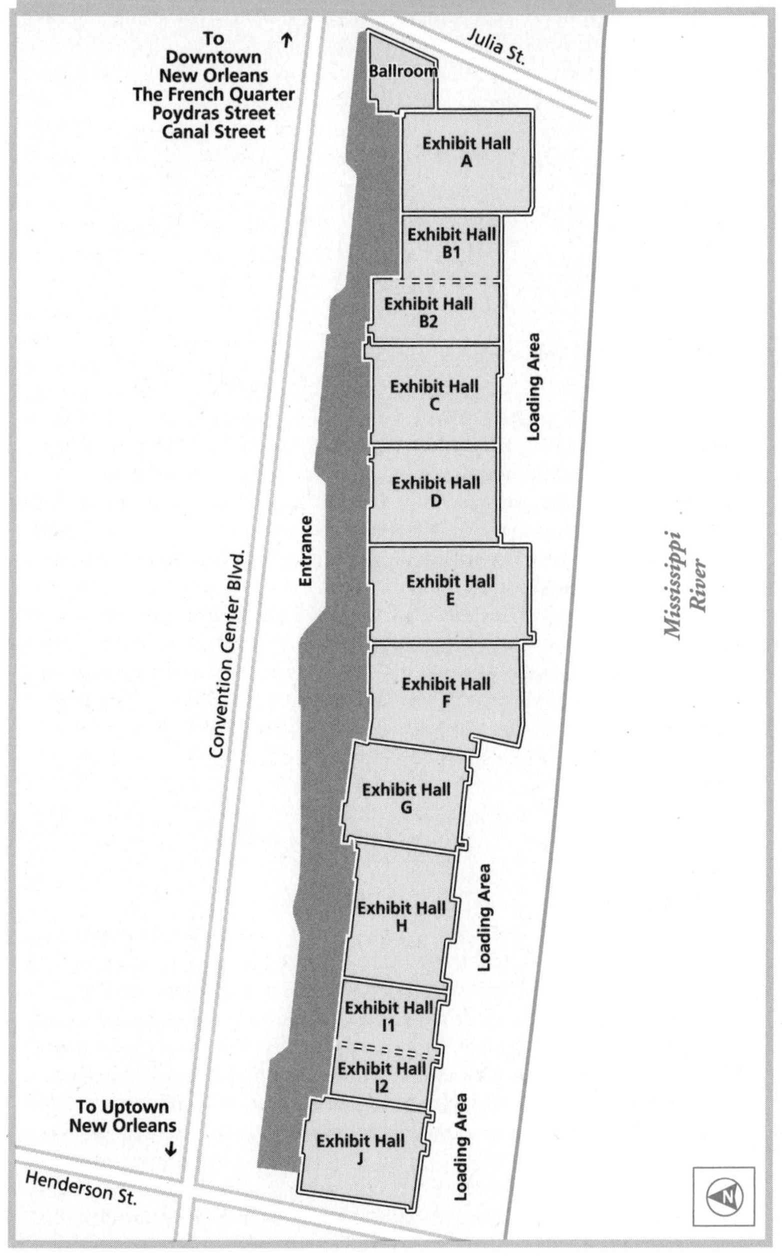
ernest n. morial convention center
To Downtown New Orleans The French Quarter Poydras Street Canal Street
Julia St.
Ballroom
Exhibit Hall A
Exhibit Hall B1
Exhibit Hall B2
Exhibit Hall C
Exhibit Hall D
Exhibit Hall E
Exhibit Hall F
Exhibit Hall G
Exhibit Hall H
Exhibit Hall I1
Exhibit Hall I2
Exhibit Hall J
Loading Area
Loading Area
Loading Area
Entrance
Convention Center Blvd.
Mississippi River
To Uptown New Orleans
Henderson St.
N

spaces for highway vans and 13 freight drive-in entrances. The same brochure specifies the dimensions of these entrances, the floor-load capacity (350 pounds per square foot), and a host of other details needed by exhibitors. The facility is nonunion.

Another handy piece to help you get around is "Walking Tours of the Warehouse District and Lafayette Square: Art, History and Architecture," produced by the Downtown Development District in cooperation with the Warehouse District Arts Association. (Ask the convention center or the Chamber of Commerce for it. You can also find it in hotel lobby racks.) The convention center borders this district, and this brochure lists museums and institutions, galleries, landmarks, hotels, cafes and restaurants, and the St. Charles streetcar route, all within walking distance of the center.

GETTING FOOD

THE FOOD IN THE CENTER is definitely above average, and the promo literature makes much of their prize-winning chef, Leon West, who supervises the production of two kitchens, each of which can produce 20,000 meals in a 24-hour period. In the 400-seat **Atrium/Restaurant Lounge** you can order Cajun and Creole favorites. There are conventional concession-refreshment areas located off each exhibit-hall floor. Prices are not as high as they could be, but no bargains can be found either.

If you can break free, there are several good restaurants within a 10- to 15-minute walk. **Ernst Cafe** (600 South Peters Street; ☎ 504-525-8544; **www.ernstcafe.net**) offers plate lunches and sandwiches. Businesspeople needing a quieter atmosphere can dine at the **Sugar House Restaurant** (inside the Embassy Suites Hotel at 315 Julia Street; ☎ 504-525-1993). The muffuletta joints across the street from the convention center are another quick option. There are also many choices, some featuring local cuisine on short order, at the **Bon Fête Food Court** inside the Riverwalk Marketplace next door to the convention center.

Among the most popular new restaurants in the neighborhood for heartier dining are **Drago's,** an offshoot of the popular Metairie creator of grilled oysters, in the lobby of the Hilton Riverside Hotel (2 Poydras Street; ☎ 504-584-3911); **Ruth's Chris Steakhouse** in the Harrah's Hotel (525 Fulton Street; ☎ 504-587-7099); and Todd English's **Riche** (528 Fulton Street; ☎ 504-533-6000). Slightly more casual is the **Gordon Biersch** brewpub (200 Poydras; ☎ 504-522-2739). And of course, no visit to New Orleans would be complete without breakfast—at any hour—at **Mother's** (401 Poydras; ☎ 504-523-9656).

PART SIX

ARRIVING *and* GETTING ORIENTED

COMING *into the* CITY

NOTHING SPOILS A VACATION QUICKER THAN A TRAFFIC JAM, a missed connection, or a too-long walk with luggage—the sorts of misadventures that are often overlooked in the excitement of planning a trip. New Orleans happily abandons its claim to mystery when it comes to making tourists comfortable: It's well supplied with public transportation; the airport is new and efficient but not impersonal or intimidating; and once you sling a little lingo, you can get directions from anyone. Just take a few minutes to get organized before you cut loose.

BY PLANE

Louis Armstrong New Orleans International Airport (☎ 504-464-0831; **www.flymsy.com**) is located about ten miles west of New Orleans, in Kenner. At four feet above sea level, it's a frequent source of jokes about "high-flying" airstrips and so on, but it is relatively high and dry, at least compared to the surrounding area—and if you fly in, watching the complex gradually take shape from the swampland around it, you'll see why that's important.

The airport is fully wheelchair accessible, and the telephone banks in each concourse have TDD phones. Ticket counters are in the center on the upper level, with the four concourses at the ends, and information counters, concessions, and gift stands scattered about. A full-service Whitney National Bank, 24-hour automated-teller machines (ATMs), and a post office drop box are in the main central hall. There is a **Visitor Information Services booth** (☎ 504-464-2752) in the west end of the lobby. The **TravelEx Business Center** (☎ 504-465-9647) office and an American Express travelers-check machine are in the ticket lobby. Transportation and baggage claim are downstairs, with additional ATMs; there are elevators at each end. The airport-shuttle desk downstairs (☎ 504-522-3500) is staffed 8 a.m. to 11 p.m.; after hours, travelers can purchase a ticket with cash from a driver outside.

New Orleans is served by more than ten airlines. **Northwest** and **USAirways** use Concourse A. **Southwest Airlines** uses Concourse B. **American Airlines, Airtran,** and **United Air Lines** all use Concourse C, and **Delta, Continental,** and **JetBlue** use Concourse D.

Incidentally, the restrooms in the airport are very nice. The toilets are automatically sanitized with each flush, and motorized seat covers slip over the seats at the push of a button. All faucets are touch free as well, operated by electric eyes.

Getting to the City from the Airport

To get from the airport to the city, you may take the **Airport Shuttle** (☎ 504-522-3500) for $15 per person; the van, which operates around the clock, will take you directly to your hotel. If you want to have the shuttle pick you up and take you back to the airport, call 24 hours in advance with your flight-departure information, and they will schedule a pickup.

unofficial **TIP**
Never accept an offer for a cab or limo made by a stranger in the terminal or baggage claim. At best, you will be significantly overcharged for the ride. At worst, you may be abducted.

Taxi fare from the airport is currently $28 for one or two passengers, and $12 per person for three or more plus a $2 gas tariff. You can either pick one up off the line or contact **United Cabs** in advance (☎ 504-522-9771) and arrange to have a driver waiting for no additional charge. A limo can be ordered from the airport shuttle service, or a luxury-class stretch limo can be hired from **Carey Signature Livery** (☎ 504-523-6511) or **Bonomolo** (☎ 504-522-7565). Rates from the airport to the Central Business District (CBD)–French Quarter range from about $125 and up (plus 15 to 20% for the driver) for a six-passenger limo. *Hint:* If you want a showy chauffeur during any of the special events in town (for example, the Super Bowl or Mardi Gras), better call in early.

A **Jefferson Transit** (☎ 504-818-1077; **www.jeffersontransit.org**) express bus to the CBD puts you within a few blocks' walking distance of many of the newer hotels along Canal Street; it costs only $1.60 to go to downtown New Orleans, which may be the best choice if you're not lugging tons of baggage. The bus leaves the airport every 20 minutes or so, but it is available only between 5:20 a.m. and 9:20 p.m. on weekdays and 6:20 a.m. and 9:20 p.m. on Saturday and Sunday. The terminus is on Tulane and Loyola avenues on weekdays, and on weekends the bus runs only to the Tulane and Carrollton stop.

Regular **Regional Transit Authority** buses may also serve your route; call RTA at ☎ 504-248-3900 for exact times; or visit the Web site at **www.norta.com** (For more on RTA passes, see "Public Transportation" on page 109.)

The rental-car counters are in the lower level of the airport: **Hertz** (☎ 800-654-3131, **www.hertz.com**), **AVIS** (☎ 800-230-4898, **www.avis.com**), **Budget** (☎ 800-527-0700, **www.budget.com**), **National** (☎ 800-227-7368, **www.nationalcar.com**), and **Enterprise Rent-a-Car** (☎ 800-261-7331, **www.enterprise.com**) are all on site and also have second offices downtown, if for some reason you don't want to return the car to the airport. **Alamo** (☎ 800-GO-ALAMO, **www.alamo.com**), **Thrifty** (☎ 800-847-4389, **www.thrifty.com**), and **Dollar Rent a Car** (☎ 800-800-3665, **www.dollar.com**) have an airport lot only. From the rental-car lots, signs will direct you onto Interstate 10 to the city (be sure to read "By Car" below).

For Private Planes

There is a small private airstrip for those who fly or charter their own aircraft. **New Orleans Lakefront Airport,** on the south side of Lake Pontchartrain, also has some rentals; call ☎ 504-243-4010 or 504-241-9400, or visit **www.lakefrontairport.com** for more information.

BY CAR

NEW ORLEANS IS CONNECTED to the interstate highway system by **Interstate 10,** which goes pretty much right through the city east and west, with a few tricky spots. One thing to remember is that I-10 makes an unusual V-dip toward the French Quarter and CBD, while **Interstate 610** sails straight across the Mid-City region and dumps you back out on I-10 at the east end of town; it won't get you where you want to go, and it is a rush-hour trap of the first order. The other thing to know is that there is no marked French Quarter exit off I-10; it's marked Vieux Carré, Exit 235A. (If your hotel is along Canal Street in the CBD, take the Poydras Street exit.) Signage is not particularly good here in any case, and turn-signal indicators seem to be a lost art, so be careful.

If you are driving in from the east along I-10, there is a **Visitors Information Center** at the Paris Road exit where you can pick up brochures, maps, discount coupons, and coffee, and make last-minute hotel reservations, if necessary.

East–west **US 61** is **Airline Highway,** the older route from Kenner into the city, and becomes **Tulane Avenue** heading to the CBD near the French Quarter. **US 90,** also called the Old Spanish Trail, makes a squiggly circle around the river, curving around uptown and the Westbank before scooting back south and west toward New Iberia and Lafayette. (US 90 is the scenic route to Cajun country, but you can take I-10 nearly to Lafayette and on to Baton Rouge.)

Interstate 12 runs east–west as well, but along the north shore of Lake Pontchartrain, as if putting a lid on the bowl of I-10. From I-12 you can take either Interstate 59 or Interstate 56 south. The 24-mile-long **Lake Pontchartrain Causeway** (toll road) is the world's longest over-water bridge, and it's a beautiful drive; sometimes you can see nothing but sky and water, and sometimes even glimpses of the skyline or sailboat fleets. The causeway comes straight south and joins I-10, US 61/Airline Highway, US 90/Claiborne Avenue, and so on. **Interstate 59** (north–south) intersects I-10 east of the city; **I-56** from Jackson, Mississippi, joins I-10 west of the city.

BY BUS OR TRAIN

Greyhound Bus Lines coaches (☎ 800-231-2222; **www.greyhound.com**) roll into **Union Terminal** at Loyola and Howard avenues at the edge of the Central Business District, not far from the Superdome. Ticket counters are open daily 5:15 a.m. to 1 p.m. and 2:30 to 7 p.m.

Union Terminal is also the **Amtrak** station (☎ 800-872-7245; **www.amtrak.com**), with connections to New York, Washington, Los Angeles, and Chicago. Ticket counters are open 5:45 a.m. to 10 p.m. daily (check for senior-citizen discounts and special fares). There is a taxi stop outside the terminal, of course.

WHERE TO FIND TOURIST INFORMATION IN NEW ORLEANS

YOU CAN GET AN AMAZING AMOUNT OF MATERIAL and background from the **New Orleans Convention and Visitors Bureau** (2020 St. Charles Avenue, New Orleans, LA 70130; ☎ 800-672-6124; **www.neworleanscvb.com**), which also operates information centers within each terminal of the Louis Armstrong New Orleans International Airport. For specialized information, contact the **New Orleans Multicultural Tourism Network** (☎ 504-523-5652; **www.soulofneworleans.com**). In the French Quarter itself, there is a **Louisiana State Welcome Center** right on Jackson Square in the Pontalba Apartments (529 St. Ann Street; ☎ 504-568-5661) that has hundreds of brochures on attractions and tours and street maps. And the visitors bureau also distributes these brochures on a motorized cart that stops during the day at such gathering spots as Union Terminal, Aquarium of the Americas, Spanish Plaza, the Louisiana Children's Museum, and the 600 block of Canal Street.

Once you are in town, the main source of information on special events, sports, arts, and tours is the *Times-Picayune,* which has an entertainment calendar every day and a special pull-out section on Fridays, called "Lagniappe," devoted to recreation and family fun. Among the free magazines you'll see around town and in hotel and restaurant lobbies are *OffBeat,* which covers the local music and nightlife scene (you can peruse it in advance at **www.offbeat.com**), *Gambit Weekly,* and *Where. Ambush* magazine (**www.ambushmag.com**) is a gay-and-lesbian publication. Or check in bookstores for *New Orleans Magazine* and the African American–oriented monthly *New Orleans Tribune.*

GETTING ORIENTED

NEW ORLEANS GEOGRAPHY IS CONFUSING (even for locals), because it conflicts with our notion of U.S. geography and our basic sense of north–south orientation. Louisiana is shaped like an L. New Orleans is at the bottom of the L on the east end and is sandwiched between Lake Pontchartrain to the north and the Mississippi River to the south. Most folks picture the Mississippi River as flowing due south and emptying into the Gulf of Mexico. While this is correct, generally speaking, the river happens to snake along in west–east fashion as it passes New Orleans, not veering south again until after Chalmette, where the Battle of New Orleans was fought in the War of 1812. To the surprise of many, the mouth of the Mississippi River is actually more than five hours south of New Orleans by boat.

If you spend time in New Orleans, the presence of the lake and the river are inescapable. As you begin to explore, you will discover that much of the city is tucked into one long bend of the river and that many of the streets and highways follow the curve of that bend. The curve in question, when viewed in the customary north–south orientation, is shaped like the smile of a happy face. Although suburbs and industrial areas parallel the river both east and west of the smile (and also across the river—south of the smile), the areas of the city most interesting to visitors are located within the curve. This curve, or smile, as we put it, is why New Orleans is called the Crescent City.

The oldest part of the city, the **French Quarter,** or Vieux Carré, is situated at the right (east) corner of the smile, while **Uptown,** aka the **University District,** with Tulane and Loyola universities, is located at the left (west) corner. Moving from the right corner toward the bottom of the smile, you will leave the French Quarter, cross Canal Street, and enter the **Warehouse** and **Central Business districts.** The Central Business District is New Orleans's *real* downtown. The warehouses line the river and serve the city's bustling port.

If you look at a map of downtown, you will notice that all the streets emanating from the French Quarter change names after they cross Canal Street. Royal Street in the French Quarter becomes St. Charles Avenue in the business district (easy to remember if you think of King Charles) and parallels the river like a mustache above the smile. On St. Charles, you can drive or take the St. Charles streetcar around the curve of the smile to visit some of New Orleans's most interesting neighborhoods. As you work down the smile to the bicuspids and incisors, you will encounter the Warehouse District, the Irish Channel, the Garden District, and finally the University District, including Audubon Park (described in Part Seven, Sightseeing, Tours, and Attractions).

If you are driving in New Orleans, picture holding a fan upside down over the happy face. Position the fan so that the handle points north toward the lake and the curved spread of the fan aligns with the bend in the river (the smile). Tchoupitoulas Street runs at the edge of the fan along the river. A few blocks inland is St. Charles, paralleling both Tchoupitoulas and the river. Farther away from the river toward the handle is Claiborne Avenue, following the same crescent-shaped route. The sides of the fan angling up to the handle are Esplanade on the right (east) and Carrollton on the left (west). The handle of the fan extends to the lake and includes City Park. Tourists, convention-goers, and most business visitors spend the vast majority of their time within the area of the fan.

Just outside the fan to the west is **Metairie,** where you can access the Lake Pontchartrain Causeway. Farther west are **Kenner** and the airport. To the northeast are **Elysian Fields** and **Gentilly,** where you will find Dillard and Southern universities, the University of New Orleans, and Pontchartrain Park. To the southeast along the river are the Chalmette National Battlefield, Jean Lafitte National Historic Park, and Pakenham Oaks.

FINDING YOUR WAY AROUND THE FRENCH QUARTER

WHILE ORIENTATION IN THE GREATER NEW ORLEANS area tends to be confusing, finding your way around the French Quarter is a cinch. The French Quarter is rectangular and arranged in a grid, like midtown Manhattan. The river forms one long side of the rectangle, and Rampart Street forms the other. The short sides of the rectangle are Canal Street, the main downtown thoroughfare, and Esplanade Avenue.

The longer streets paralleling the river are the French Quarter's primary commercial, traffic, and pedestrian arteries. Moving from the river inland, these streets are Decatur, Chartres, Royal, Bourbon, Dauphine, Burgundy, and Rampart. The more commercially developed blocks toward Canal Street are traditionally known as the Upper Quarter, while the quieter, more residential blocks toward Esplanade are called the Lower Quarter.

As recently as 30 years ago, upper **Decatur,** next to the river, was the domain of visiting sailors and home of the fabled Jax Brewery. Lower Decatur then, as now, was home to the French Market. With the closing of the brewery and the advent of the Riverwalk promenade, Decatur was effectively sanitized and turned into a souvenir-shopping mall and restaurant venue. **St. Louis Cathedral** and **Jackson Square** face Decatur, with most of the modern tourist development between Jackson Square and Canal Street. Moving down Decatur toward Esplanade is a rejuvenated **French Market,** the timeless **Café du Monde,** and the **Central Grocery,** with its signature Italian sandwich, the muffuletta.

unofficial **TIP**
Sections of the French Quarter—specifically parts of Bourbon and Royal streets, and some areas around Jackson Square—are often closed to cars, encouraging pedestrian traffic.

Heading away from the river, you'll come to **Chartres,** with its galleries, restaurants, cozy taverns, and small hotels. Chartres, perhaps more than any other French Quarter street, has maintained its historic identity. Commerce rules here, as elsewhere, but it's softer, less crass, and much more respectful of its heritage.

Royal, the next street over, has always been the most patrician of the Quarter's main thoroughfares. Lined with antiques and art galleries, as well as some of the city's most famous restaurants, hotels, and architecture, Royal Street is the prestige address of the Vieux Carré.

One block walking takes you from the grand and sophisticated to the carnal and crass: you have arrived on **Bourbon Street.** While Bourbon Street has always appealed to more primitive instincts, it did so within the worn, steamy context of its colorful past. But today, Bourbon Street is a parody of itself, a plastic corporate version of the honky-tonks, burlesque shows, and diners that molded its image. Between the T-shirt shops, trendy bars, and upscale strip clubs, you can still find a few survivors from Bourbon Street's halcyon days, but they are an endangered species.

Burgundy and **Dauphine,** the two streets between Bourbon and the boundary of the French Quarter at Rampart Street, were once primarily residential. During the past two decades, however, homes have made way for small hotels, shops, and restaurants. While less architecturally compelling than Royal or Chartres, these streets are nonetheless lovely, and they remain quieter and less commercial than the streets between Bourbon and the river, providing a glimpse of what the Quarter was like when it was still mainly a thriving neighborhood.

Rampart Street, like Canal and Esplanade, is essentially a border street: broad, heavily trafficked, and very different from the streets within the French Quarter. Twelve streets run from Rampart to Decatur, intersecting the main commercial thoroughfares discussed above and completing the grid.

St. Peter and **St. Ann** streets bisect the Vieux Carré halfway between Canal and Esplanade. St. Peter, especially the block between Bourbon and Royal, is regarded by many as the "heart of the Quarter." Most of the tourist and commercial activity in the French Quarter occurs toward Canal Street, and from Bourbon Street down to the river. Except for lower Decatur and the French Market, the Esplanade half of the Vieux Carré remains residential, albeit with an increasing number of proprietary hotels and guesthouses.

PUBLIC TRANSPORTATION

NEW ORLEANS IS A VERY HANDS-ON, HOSPITABLE CITY. And the main neighborhood attractions, especially for tourists, are accessible by public transportation, give or take a taxi or two. But you will probably be asking for directions and addresses, and those are two of the most peculiar things about this idiosyncratic city. Names can be unrecognizable, and maps can seem upside down.

As we pointed out earlier, you probably don't need or want a car in the city. Most of the time, whether you're in the French Quarter or any other neighborhood, you'll be walking. If you think you'll want a car, you should figure out exactly what excursions you want to take outside the city and only rent one for those days. Otherwise you'll have to worry about parking lots, parking tickets, and perhaps vandalism—not to mention being impounded. (If you are, call the **Public Works Auto Pound** at ☎ 504-565-7450.) If you're staying at one of the larger hotels around Canal Street or in the suburbs, it may have parking (which may or may not be free). But most visitors will find the buses, streetcars, and taxis handy to any place they want to go.

By far the nicest way to get from one neighborhood to the other, or to rest your feet after a good promenade, is the streetcar.

Locals always used to call them "trolleys," but perhaps because of the heavy promotion the lines are getting these days, the word "streetcar" is gradually winning out. Still, you will sound less like a tourist if you refer to them as trolleys.

The **Riverfront streetcar,** which originates near Esplanade Avenue, runs along the river to the border of the French Quarter. Each one-way trip costs $1.25. The Riverfront streetcar operates from 7 a.m. to 10:30 p.m. and updates are available at **www.norta.com.** A second streetcar runs down the center of Canal Street to the top of the French Quarter; a transfer between this trolley and the Riverfront streetcar is 25 cents.

The more famous **St. Charles Avenue streetcar** originates at Canal Street and runs 24 hours a day through the Garden District past Audubon Park and Riverbend. Another line takes you up Canal Street all the way to City Park, or to the Greenwood and Metairie cemeteries. These alternate on the track, so check with the operator. Each one-way trip is $1.25. Kids under age 2 ride free.

unofficial **TIP**

Although the St. Charles line has cars running about every 18 minutes most of the day, it runs only once an hour after 11 p.m., so keep that in mind if you have a late dinner planned. Also remember that the Canal Street line alternates routes, so the wait can be substantial. When you get off at City Park or the cemeteries, ask the conductor what the scheduled return times are and time your visit accordingly.

City bus trips are also $1.25 and transfers are also 25 cents. Both the streetcars and the buses are operated by the Regional Transit Authority, and you can get one- or three-day VisiTour passes good for unlimited rides on any of them. A one-day pass is $5, and a three-day pass is $12. Most hotels and information centers, and many shops, sell the RTA passes, or you can buy them at the Gray Line Tours kiosks around town. For bus routes and times, call the 24-hour RTA RideLine at ☎ 504-248-3900 or visit **www.norta.com.**

Taxicabs are pretty easy to find in the French Quarter, especially around hotels, but if you're out somewhere without a lift, call **White Fleet** (☎ 504-822-3800), **Yellow-Checker Cabs** (☎ 504-525-3311), or **United Cab** (☎ 504-524-9606). New Orleans cabs run on meters—base charge $4.50, plus $1.60 a mile—but if you come during a special event, such as Jazz and Heritage Fest, there may be a base $5 or more charge in effect. Additionally, most cab companies charge an extra $1 per person after the first passenger. Taxis can also usually be hired for a flat rate if a group of several people want to tour a few attractions; call the dispatcher's office and see what sort of deal you can get. Or if you happen to be picked up by one of the really friendly ones (and New Orleans cabbies can be hilariously well informed), find out if he freelances.

You can also rent a bicycle and combine touring and exercise: **Bicycle Michael's** has a variety of mountain bikes, three-speeders, and even bicycles built for two (622 Frenchmen Street; ☎ 504-945-9505; **www.bicyclemichaels.com**).

THINGS *the* NATIVES ALREADY KNOW

NEW ORLEANS CUSTOMS AND PROTOCOL

NEW ORLEANS IS A CITY THAT PRIDES ITSELF on Southern hospitality, and most residents and business owners have learned to be very patient with tourists. They need to be. And so may you.

To be blunt about it, for all the mutterings about crime you will hear from locals (see "Crime in New Orleans and How to Avoid It," page 116), it's almost certain that the biggest problem you'll run into in New Orleans is other tourists, particularly on Bourbon Street. Women will have to be prepared for a few juvenile remarks from the inebriated and the eternally self-deluded (amazing how attractive some people seem to consider themselves). An increasing percentage of students tend to drift toward the French Quarter bars on the weekends, many still under the impression that "flashing" for Mardi Gras beads is a local tradition. There is a vital gay community here, and gay and lesbian visitors are welcome, but as always, there may be a few ill-mannered heteros to ignore. And a few visitors may be taken aback by the number of extravagantly dressed punksters on the streets, with their Technicolor spiked hair and heavy leathers. Longtime locals seem to find them a little scary, but they don't seem particularly interested in bothering anyone so far as we can tell. There are fewer panhandlers than there used to be, at least for the time being, and most of them will spin you a tale rather than just accost you.

Otherwise, just go by what you might call the flip side of the Golden Rule: do nothing unto others that would be embarrassing if done unto you.

Many intersections have stop signs in both directions (these are one-way streets, remember). But don't let that lead you into dropping your guard on other streets. Just be aware of where you are, or you may find yourself stepping in front of a moving vehicle.

TALKING THE TALK

IRONICALLY, FOR A CITY WITH SO MANY OBVIOUS European influences, New Orleans talks with a very American accent. (So American, in fact, that a lot of "dese guys," especially the ones with roots in the Irish Channel and Metairie, sound as if they just disembarked from Brooklyn or New Jersey, because they come from the same river-roustabout stock.)

What that means for outsiders is that local names can be wildly confusing, not to mention the name of the city itself. Much has been written about how to say it—and to be fair, there isn't an easy answer—but what it is *not* is **N'awlins** in two syllables, or **Noo Or-LEENS** in three or **New OR-lee-uns** in four. It's something in between: **Noo-AW-lins,** or, in what's left of the Creole dialect, **New-YAW-yuns,** with the first two syllables blending together, sort of two and a half beats. Unfortunately, the *Orleans* in Orleans Avenue and Orleans Parish is pronounced **Or-LEENS.**

Then comes the *Vieux Carré* (**View Kah-RAY**), literally "Old Square," the original name for the French Quarter; it's one of the few things around that are still pronounced with a French accent aside from *beignets* (**ben-YAYS**), *Arnaud's* (**Ar-KNOWS**), and *Tremé* and *Faubourg Marigny* (**TRUH-may, FOH-burg MARE-in-yee**), the neighborhoods adjoining the Vieux Carré. *Metairie* is pronounced **MET-uh-ree**; *Pontchartrain* is **PAWN-cha-tren.** And *Marie Laveau* is **mar-EE lah-VOH,** *Jean Lafitte* is **ZHAWN lah-FEET,** and *Mardi Gras* is **MAR-dee GRAH,** of course.

Most confusing of all are the street names, which have in many cases been translated first from Spanish to French (memorialized on blue-and-white-tile signs on the sides of buildings at intersections throughout the French Quarter), and then from French to fractured French, or to Italianese, or occasionally to English (for example, most people say "Royal Street" now, though you will still see "Rue Royale" on some business cards and on French Quarter street signs).

Burgundy is pronounced **bur-GUN-dee,** *Conti* is **con-TIE,** *Chartres* is **CHAR-ters,** *Esplanade* is **es-pluh-NAYD,** *Carondelet* is **kuh-ron-duh-LETT** (not LAY), *Milan* is **MY-lun,** and *Iberville* is **EYE-ber-ville.**

Even worse is what happened to the classic Greek names of the Muses east of the Garden District: *Terpsichore* is **TERP-si-kore,** *Calliope* is **KAL-ee-ope,** *Clio* is **KLEYE-oh,** *Melpomene* is **MEL-poe-mean,** and so on.

The Indian-derived *Tchoupitoulas* is easier than it looks, like an old tomahawk joke on *Laugh-In:* **chop-it-TOOL-us** or even **chap-it-TOOL-us.**

As for the city's various nicknames—"The Big Easy," "The Crescent City," or the older "Paris of America" and "The City That Care Forgot"—none is particularly popular, and you probably will never hear a local use one.

Incidentally, although it works wonderfully in a literary sense to speak of Desire, as in *A Streetcar Named Desire,* the line's destination (the Desire Area, a neighborhood near Faubourg Marigny) was originally pronounced **dez-ih-RAY,** after Désirée, one of the daughters of the man who developed this section of New Orleans back in the 19th century.

WALKING THE WALK

MUCH OF NEW ORLEANS CAN BE COVERED ON FOOT, and that's a good thing, because it means you can settle for pedestrian directions such as "turn right" and "go three blocks on." What you don't want to get into is traditional directions—north, south, etc.—because in New Orleans, it just isn't very helpful. Because of the Mississippi River's snaking, the city somewhat resembles an open fan: although various neighborhoods have right angles within themselves, including the Garden District and the French Quarter, just about the only intersection that aligns with the compass is Napoleon Avenue and Tchoupitoulas Street.

So directions in New Orleans are given according to the biggest landmarks around: the Mississippi River and Lake Pontchartrain. Locals speak of going "toward the river" or of something's being "riverside"; an address "toward the lake" might also be "lakeside"—very roughly north. "Uptown" is above—that is, more or less west of—Canal Street, while "downtown" is said to be below, or on the French Quarter side of Canal. That also helps tell you which is "upriver"—toward uptown—versus "downriver." Audubon Park is upriver, as are the River Road plantations, but the French Quarter is downriver from the Garden District. Got it?

Other apparently specific directions are merely relative. South Claiborne actually goes mostly northwest, and North Claiborne swings in a curve that runs mostly east and southeast. As for the Westbank . . . it's south and east of the city, somewhere between Algiers and Gretna. The Eastbank, naturally, is to the west.

DRESS

IN A TOWN AS HOT AND HUMID AS NEW ORLEANS, only bankers, lawyers, and maître d's regularly wear suits. That's something of an exaggeration, but not much: what it really boils down to is that self-respecting New Orleanians dress, tourists don't. Decades of Southern culture still persuade many women to wear dresses and hose, and you'll notice that the docents and information guides at museums and historic houses usually do. The minimum "dress" for women is nice earrings and long pants rather than shorts, shoes rather than athletic wear or sandals for men. (Some restaurants, including Commander's Palace and Brennan's, will not serve women in shorts, even longer ones.) But again, this is a tourist town and you're on vacation, so you can decide how much you care about sticking out or fitting in. Except for social occasions, you're not likely to be penalized for wearing shorts or sports clothes anywhere around town. It's just that those who do dress neatly may get better treatment or tables than those who don't.

Even at night, only a few restaurants require men to wear a jacket, mostly the older standbys such as Antoine's and Arnaud's. But "dressy casual" is the style at most of the popular spots such as Dickie Brennan's Steakhouse and Mr. B's, and you may feel more comfortable in a jacket, even wearing it over a golf shirt or nice T-shirt—that is, unmarked and monotone, à la Don Johnson. The most famous exception is Galatoire's, which continues to demand jacket and tie at dinner and all day Sunday.

EATING IN RESTAURANTS

NEW ORLEANS FARE MAY BE FAMOUS, but it's not all that varied. Continental, Creole (which is very similar but has kept more traditional rich cream sauces than modern Continental), and Cajun styles dominate, particularly in the areas tourists are most likely to visit. And to be honest, you may find several days of such food not only filling but a trifle too rich; go slow. Most other restaurants are either new American or Italian (or franchised) in style.

Compared to many cities, the number of restaurants in New Orleans that do not accept reservations is fairly high. (During Mardi Gras, you may not find anybody willing to take a reservation.) Standing in line at Galatoire's, where the host is amazingly deft at juggling parties in his head, and at K-Paul's Louisiana Kitchen, where you may share your table with another party, is the stuff of legend. (K-Paul's now takes reservations for its upstairs dining room.)

As a rule, the restaurants that require reservations tend to be the same ones that require a jacket. In the same way, however, many of those would be willing to seat you, perhaps at the bar, if you are dressed at least neatly.

It shouldn't require saying, but having seen too many slightly overexuberant tourists trying to slip into restaurants past the queue, we will say it: please be considerate and stay in place. Besides, these hosts are pros; they'll catch you.

TIPPING (AND STRIPPING)

NEW ORLEANS IS A SERVICE-ORIENTED ECONOMY, and you should expect to recognize that. The going tip rate for bartenders or waiters and taxi drivers is 15 to 20%, although if you use them as sources of local information—which is always a good bet—add a dollar for luck. At your hotel, you should leave the maids at least

$1 per day of your stay, ideally $2 per day (and if the room is tended twice a day, it's nice to tip both shifts). If there is a bellman, give him $1 per suitcase, and while it isn't quite rude not to slip the doorman a buck for getting you a taxi, it never hurts. After all, it might be a longer wait next time.

You should also consider how many bars and restaurants have cut their hours. That means the waiters' and bartenders' wages are down, as are their cumulative tips—even as rents are climbing. So be a little generous; a dollar more makes a lot of difference at the end of the day. And the same goes for street performers; with fewer visitors, take-home goes down.

As for tipping strippers, it's usually $1 in one of the older, cheaper joints, or $5 for something special (you will probably be offered a "table dance," which offers a sort of up-close-and-personal view). In the really upscale places, such as Maiden Voyage or Rick's, the going rate may be a little higher, but it's up to you. Total nudity is prohibited, so there will be some sort of G-string, skimpy bathing suit, or garter to tuck it into.

However, there are a few strip-joint no-nos you should be aware of (all common sense, but as we've said, the behavior of some tourists will astound you): absolutely no fondling of the dancers is allowed, and you may find the dancers ready to retaliate if you try. If you visit a burlesque house (this reminder more often applies to women who are escorted by men), behave yourself; don't make faces, denigrate the dancers, or pull on your escort to get away. If you are offended by the spectacle, don't go.

NEW ORLEANS ON THE AIR

ASIDE FROM THE USUAL BABBLE OF FORMAT ROCK, talk, easy-listening, and country-music stations, New Orleans is home to a few

NEW ORLEANS'S RADIO STATIONS

STATION	FREQUENCY	FORMAT
WWNO	89.9 FM	National Public Radio
WWOZ	90.7 FM	Lots of music with local history
WQUE	93.3 FM	Hip-hop, soul, R & B
WKBU	95.7 FM	Classic rock
WEZB	97.1 FM	Conventional top-40 radio
WNOE	101.1 FM	New Orleans's country-music flagship
WLMG	101.9 FM	Adult contemporary
KKND	106.7 FM	Modern country
WWLT	870 AM/105.3 FM	News, talk, sports

stations that really stand out for high-quality broadcasting. Tune in to what hip locals are listening to.

PUBLIC ACCOMMODATIONS

THE *UNOFFICIAL GUIDES* ARE STARTING to get a reputation for worrying about restrooms, or rather, about your being able to find them. This is a tribute to the relatively short staying power of our founder, Bob Sehlinger, and someday we'll stop teasing him about it. But he has a good point: being uncomfortable doesn't help you enjoy a walking tour or a museum. And especially in summer, when New Orleans can be so hot, it's tempting to drink a lot. (When, while in New Orleans, is it not tempting to drink a lot?)

The greatest concentration of restrooms in the French Quarter is down near the water (no pun intended, surely): Riverwalk, Jax Brewery–Millhouse Complex, and Canal Place all have good, clean bathrooms, as does the French Market (two sets, in the 900 and 1200 blocks). Across from Jackson Square, there are restrooms in Woldenberg Riverfront Park. City Park and the Audubon Park tennis courts also have public restrooms. Museums and department stores are equipped as well. Some places have pay toilets, so it's a good idea to keep some emergency change around; and where there is an attendant, it's considered polite to leave a tip, though you need leave only a quarter or so—cheap by big-city standards.

The large-hotel lobbies usually have restrooms, although you should only take advantage of them in an emergency, and when you are reasonably well dressed. If you are really in a pinch, go to a bar and at least order a soda before you hit the john.

CRIME *in* NEW ORLEANS *and* HOW *to* AVOID IT

FROM THE NEWS CLIPS OF MARDI GRAS, New Orleans may seem like an X-rated Disney World, but this is real life—and it's real life in a city with big gaps in income levels and housing. That, combined with a history of police corruption, translates into a dire and long-standing crime problem from which the city was just beginning to recover.

New Orleans was in an unfortunate contest with Washington, D.C., for that infamous title Murder Capital of the Nation; its murder rate was five times that of New York City, and only about a third of New Orleans murders were being solved. In 1994, homicides hit a record high of 421. New Orleans's poverty level is the third worst in the country. It is legal in New Orleans to carry a concealed weapon. And since the 1980s, crack cocaine has been big bad business here, fueling tensions and gang machismo. Now new "territories" are up for grabs by local gangs. Even with so many people displaced by Hurricanes Katrina and Rita, street crime has once again spiked, forcing state and federal authorities to increase the presence of state troopers and National Guard troops.

While the overwhelming majority of violent crimes still occur in the poorest parts of town, around the housing projects, you cannot take for granted that you are safe even in the French Quarter. After all, that's where the rich—or at least those who appear rich by housing-project standards—are to be found.

To make matters worse, the New Orleans Police Department has a long history of notorious corruption. In the last decade, NOPD officers were convicted of having witnesses beaten and even executed, of robbery and murder, and of institutional extortion.

Such reports made things sound pretty bad, and local authorities finally began to take them—and their effect on the city's reputation—seriously. The hiring of former Washington, D.C., deputy police chief Richard Pennington in 1994 began a reform in the police department. Pennington launched a number of highly publicized police initiatives, as well as numerous anticorruption efforts, firing or disciplining hundreds of officers, hiring hundreds more, and raising salaries and standards. A private coalition of New Orleans businesses and residents hired consultants Jack Maple, former deputy commissioner of the New York Police Department, and John Linder to set up a computerized "map" of the city's highest-crime spots; the same method is credited with having cut the New York murder rate in half since 1993.

In June of 2000, New Orleans was given the City Livability Award by the United States Conference of Mayors, placing the city first among 14 other major cities. The award came as a result of police reform and crime reduction.

In 2004, Pennington moved to Atlanta to take on that city's police department, and a flamboyant career member of the New Orleans force, Edwin P. Compass III, was named to replace him. Compass, who has been credited with implementing much of the new program, has presided over continued improvement in crime statistics. Though still above national averages, most categories of violent crime went down from 2003 to 2004.

But nothing could have prepared even the jauntiest cop for Katrina. Within hours, police headquarters was inoperable. Communications and transportation completely broke down; first responders were getting contradictory information. In some areas, journalists on the scene and ham-radio operators were asked by public officials for updates.

More than 250 officers—many of whom had families in harm's way—deserted before the storm, some of them in patrol cars. Another 300 patrol cars were flooded and unusable; officers were then reported stealing cars from automobile dealerships. There were no "shifts." Officers worked until they dropped, and then some.

With all law-enforcement resources stretched to their limit, subsistence raiding of groceries and drugstores by flood victims rapidly progressed to looting of luxury boutiques, electronics stores, and gun shops. In many cases, the criminal activity took place under the nose of exhausted and outnumbered police officers unwilling to challenge the perpetrators. Desperate to escape or determined to resist evacuation, residents attacked relief helicopters (inexplicably firing at some of them), makeshift ambulances, boat patrols, bus convoys, police, and military troops. As tensions rose, reports of police brutality vied with video evidence of widespread theft, and a few were even taped apparently looting. Finally on September 1, backup National Guard troops arrived to supplement those on the ground, and the next day Governor Kathleen Blanco requested that another 30,000 be dispatched.

In the aftermath of the hurricane, the New Orleans police force was devastated. The officers who had deserted their posts were either suspended or fired, leaving the force drastically shorthanded. Veterans took early retirement; younger officers resigned and moved away. Of the officers who remained on the force, 80% had lost their own homes.

The department's budget was slashed by one-fifth, which, along with the sudden shortage of affordable housing, made recruitment even more difficult. Evidence from many pending criminal investigations was contaminated or lost. Although funds were promised to replace lost uniforms, patrol cars, and supplies, it was many weeks before a semblance of order was established. Still under enormous pressure, the department was accused of excessive force and/or negligence, but residents of the better-off neighborhoods rallied to their defense.

Compass himself worked tirelessly in the weeks after the hurricane, and announced his intention to form a tribunal to investigate and punish those officers that had abandoned their posts. (He was also beginning to suffer some health problems.) But there was resistance to his plan—Mayor Ray Nagin, for example, wanted to name a civilian commission—and Compass resigned at the end of September. He was succeeded by his deputy, Warren Riley, another longtime member of the force.

In July 2006, shortly after a widely publicized rise of violent crime, including the shooting of five teenagers, a task force of 300 National Guard members and 60 state troopers returned to New Orleans to patrol New Orleans East, the Lower Ninth Ward, Lakeview, and Gentilly. During the first months of revived convention business, the sight of groups of uniformed officers in the French Quarter and Warehouse District became commonplace, and reaction was generally positive. And despite periodic spikes in criminal behavior, the murder rate is down, street crime in tourist areas has fallen, and a campaign to target known drug dealers and gang members is showing progress.

unofficial **TIP**
Jackson Square is a good bet at all hours, thanks to the round-the-clock crowd at the Café du Monde.

You should be careful, as you would in any major city. The whole French Quarter is pretty safe during the day, but after dark you should stick to the more populated streets—Bourbon, Royal, Chartres, Decatur, Canal, Dauphine, and Burgundy between Dumaine and Canal—and even then you should be wary of the outer blocks. Avoid walking alone outside the commercial areas, and be sure not to flash your personal belongings if you do. Still, travel in a group or take a cab; if you aren't sure how safe an area is, ask one of the locals.

unofficial **TIP**
Although the St. Charles streetcar runs 24 hours a day, it's best to use it in the wee hours only if your destination is within sight of the stop, or perhaps if you just want to take a round-trip to view the great houses of the Garden District lit up.

The cemeteries may seem pretty quiet, but they have become particularly dangerous to visitors wandering about; even in daylight, you should go only with a tour or at least several friends. In fact, even though there is a police station right beside the entrance to St. Louis No. 1, and there are frequently police cars idling nearby, officers will still recommend you wait for a group to join. Audubon Park and City Park are both fine and busy during the day, but again, you shouldn't be strolling through them after sunset.

Don't leave a lot of money or traveler's checks in your hotel room; even though the employees are probably dependable, the older, smaller buildings are not exactly inaccessible. And if you buy any valuable antiques of the sort that can be easily pawned, such as silver or gems, ask the hotel to lock them in the safe.

Unless you drove into the city, you will find that you don't really want a car. Wait until you're headed into the country to rent one, or just take a cab. Parking can be tough, and several days' worth is quite expensive; traffic customs carry more weight than laws in some cases. Tickets are stiff, and unless you're familiar with all the one-way roads and eccentric highway signage, you can make things harder on yourself. Besides, a parked car is just another target for criminals and drunks.

The worst time, not surprisingly, is around Mardi Gras, when the throngs and alcohol-stoked revelry invite pickpockets. In any case, if you are accosted by a thief, don't argue; try to stay calm, and hope he or she does, too.

PART SEVEN

SIGHTSEEING, TOURS, *and* ATTRACTIONS

THE NICE THING ABOUT SIGHTSEEING is that you can choose your own pace, looking closely at what intrigues you, and pushing right on past what stirs not a flicker of interest. New Orleans is particularly well suited to walking tours, and that's what we recommend. So the latter portion of this chapter is given over to introductory walks around the most important (at least, to visitors) neighborhoods, with a little background flavor and a few landmarks for orientation. We've also suggested ways to customize your visit according to your own interests, by zeroing in on just the military sites, the otherworldly media, etc. The "inside stuff"—the museums, historic houses, and so on—is described in more detail in the next section, "New Orleans Attractions," which also includes some general walking-tour tips.

But as we said before, we know that not everybody prefers do-it-yourself tours. Some people find it distracting to read directions and anecdotes while walking, and others use packaged tours as a way of getting a mental map of the area. So first we'll run through some of the guided tours available. (These are surely not all of them: tourism is a boom industry in New Orleans, and you'll see fliers for new tours every month.) If you want to take a guided tour, check through the material at the information desks and visitors' centers or even in your hotel lobby; you're likely to find a discount coupon. (Some of the tour companies are even willing to accept competitors' coupons.) Also, Louisiana residents should check with the state-owned museums; some offer free admission on certain days.

In New Orleans, you can tour by land or by sea, by mule carriage or coach, by Segway or airboat. You can download walking tours from the Web directly to your iPod (**www.traveltoe.com** or **www.audisseyguides.com**). You can see historic spots or haunts, literary sites or cemeteries, battlefields or bayous. And you can pay nothing or, well, something.

The last thing to consider is that New Orleans is not a one-size-fits-all town. Walking is wonderful if you're young and fit, but despite the many recent repairs and repavings, many areas are uneven underfoot, so if your party includes children or seniors, make sure to pace yourself. Build in a timely stop in a park; split the touring day into shifts, so that those with less stamina can head back to the hotel for a rest while the others continue. Or lay out the schedule on the democratic scheme—that is, plan to visit the attractions everyone wants to see first, the could-be-missed ones later, and the only-for-fanatics excursions last. That way, whoever wants to drop out can.

If each member of the party has his own must-sees, then set a particular hour to split up and a clearly understood place to regroup—General Jackson's statue, for example. If you're worried about a teenager getting wound up in whatever museum or exhibit he's into and losing track of the time, schedule this separate tour session just before lunch; there are few things that can override a kid's stomach alarm. Finally, because the food-and-beverage lures are everywhere, better carry a supply of snacks in plastic bags.

Below are an assortment of general-interest, historic, special-interest and even quirky tours, both guided and self-guided. You can enjoy the whole menu, or put together a sampling to your own taste. (Of course, tour companies come and go, especially the esoteric fields, so be sure to call ahead.)

GUIDED SIGHTSEEING

WALKING TOURS

MEMBERS OF THE NONPROFIT **Friends of the Cabildo** lead two-hour walks that focus on the more important historic exteriors and some of the state's museums such as Madame John's Legacy and the 1850 House (see more details on the Louisiana State Museums in "Neighborhood Walking Tours," page 134, and in the attraction profiles at the end of this chapter). Admission is called a "donation," and the quality of the work done on the museums in recent years gives resonance to the word. Besides, it costs only $12 for adults and $10 for those over age 62 or between ages 13 and 20 (free for children 12 and under). You can buy tickets in advance at the Museum Store on St. Ann Street in Jackson Square (☎ 504-523-3939; **www.friendsofthecabildo.org**) or just arrive there with the funds in hand. Tours begin daily at 10 a.m. and 1:30 p.m., except Mondays and holidays.

Rangers from the **Jean Lafitte National Historical Park** (of which the Vieux Carré is part) also lead tours from their visitors center at 419 Decatur Street (☎ 504-589-2636). The tour leaves at 9:30 a.m., lasts about an hour, and covers about a mile of the French Quarter. This tour is limited to 25 people, so each person must pick up his or her (free) pass by about 9.

One of the most interesting tours is **Le Monde Créole,** which explores the intertwined lives of the white and black, free and slave societies within the two sides (and four generations) of the family that owned Laura Plantation (see the description in "Plantation Tours and Excursions," page 151). The family also owned seven town houses in the Quarter, some of which the tour can access; tours are also available in French and German. Walks are offered at 10:30 a.m. daily from 624 Royal Street. The tour costs $20 for adults and $16 for students; reservations are required (☎ 504-568-1801).

Segways are the hot tour trend these days, and might also be the answer for those who like to walk but tire early in the heat. **Segway New Orleans Tours** start with lessons and then roll you out through the French Quarter and across the ferry to Algiers and Blaine Kern's Mardi Gras World. The 2 ½-hour session is $70 a person and advance reservations are required; passengers must be between ages 14 and 75 and weigh between 100 and 300 pounds (☎ 504-942-1970 or **www.segwaynola.com**).

BUS TOURS AND TROLLEYS

THERE IS NO SHORTAGE OF TOUR COMPANIES—you'll find fliers at any visitors center and in most hotel lobbies—but you may wish to ask a concierge or one of the volunteers at a state- or city-information booth which tour operators are the more reliable.

Gray Line Tours (☎ 504-569-1401 or 800-535-7786; **www.grayline neworleans.**com), one of the largest tour operators nationwide, offers a variety of packages, including walking tours of the French Quarter and Garden District, a drive-through tour of some hurricane-damaged neighborhoods, plantation tours, and a combination tour with lunch aboard the steamboat *Natchez*. The bus tour covers the whole city, but you don't get out and explore; on the plus side, large groups can arrange a tour in advance, and buses make pickups from the major hotels.

Louisiana Swamp Tours (☎ 504-689-3599 or 888-30-SWAMP; **www.louisianaswamp.com**) offers tours of cemeteries, the French Quarter and Garden District neighborhoods, and of areas affected by the hurricanes. So does **Cajun Encounters Tours** (☎ 504-834-1770).

unofficial **TIP**
Tourists who really want to see the areas hit hardest by Katrina might prefer to hire a private driver (most cabbies are willing to hire out for a few hours). In any case, visitors should be polite and discreet: wave when waved to, not before, and ask permission before taking photos.

The tours of neighborhoods devastated by Hurricanes Katrina and Rita are geographically limited—no group tours are allowed into the Lower Ninth Ward (by law), and the buses don't venture to Metairie or the farther-out stretches of Bayou St. John. Nevertheless, three hours of vacant middle- and lower-class neighborhoods can be surprisingly grim, so the more susceptible might want to think twice.

CARRIAGE TOURS

THESE ARE BECOMING MORE COMMON in many cities around the country (and elsewhere—imagine Florence by open buggy), and they're the sort of thing that grabs at your nostalgic heartstrings every once in a while. The French Quarter, especially at night, lends itself to such time travel. A relatively quick two-mile route does help orient you a little, and children will definitely enjoy this.

Most of the carriages line up along Decatur Street around Jackson Square; the cost ranges from about $15 to $70, depending on the length of the ride and number of passengers. There are a few things to note about such tours: Local color definitely doesn't stop at the bridle ribbons. The quality—the factual accuracy, not necessarily the entertainment quotient—varies tremendously, which is one reason there is a movement to license carriage drivers as entertainers rather than as tour guides. And most of the horses are really mules, which doesn't really affect the ride but might affect your view of the ride's authenticity. (Some seem more aromatic than horses, but that may be our imagination.) On the other hand, drivers usually stick around until midnight, so you can fit this into your schedule at almost any time.

If you want a more elaborate (more expensive) personal tour, contact **Royal Carriages** (☎ 504-943-8820), which offers tours not only of the French Quarter but also St. Louis Cemetery No. 1 (a relatively safe way to go), the Garden District, Faubourg Marigny, and—inevitably—a Ghost and Mystery Tour.

SPECIAL-INTEREST TOURS

THE "FACULTY" OF **Magic Tours** (☎ 504-588-9693) will customize tours geared to a variety of special interests, including literary history, women's contributions, and sex scandals. Retired University of New Orleans professor Kenneth Holditch, of **Heritage Literary Tours,** will lead you through a tour of literary-interest sites and homes (by appointment, ☎ 504-949-9805); having known several of the city's literary lions personally, he can customize a tour around a favorite author (though Anne Rice fans can do it for themselves; see page 132).

Roberts Batson's **Gay Heritage** tours dish the gossip on Tennessee Williams, Truman Capote, Clay Shaw, and Ellen DeGeneres. Tours are $20, but schedules vary, so call ☎ 504-945-6789 or go to **www.decafest.com.** If you read the French Quarter self-guided walking tour we've laid out below, you'll find quite a few of the literary spots listed. The **Hermann-Grima–Gallier Historic Houses** (☎ 504-525-5661) offer a special tour on "The Urban Black Experience: 19th-Century New Orleans" throughout the month of February and year-round to groups of ten or more.

Taste of New Orleans Tours

Drinking and dining (and cooking) are such an integral part of the New Orleans experience that many people try to pack in as much of them as possible. There are any number of stores, especially along the Decatur Street strip and the French Market, that stock scores of hot sauces along with season packets by Paul Prudhomme and Emeril Lagasse. And you can't miss the **Cafe du Monde,** of course, which sells its coffee and beignet mix. But here are some sentimental stops you might want to make, and a few guided tours as well. (If you happen to pass the headquarters of **Emeril Inc.** at 829 St. Charles Street, you can pick up a saucepan or two, but the selection is pretty limited.)

The muffaletta, a combination of Italian deli meats, cheeses, and olive-pepper relish, is the signature sandwich at **Central Grocery** (923 Decatur Street; ☎ 504-523-1620), where, local legend has it, Sicilian immigrant Salavatore Lupe, owner of the market, created it to limit the "spread" of his more dramatically gesticulating lunch clients. The huge round-loaf concoction is about $14 or about $8 for a substantial half. And don't worry—if you find yourself seriously addicted, they'll ship them to your home.

Jules Alciatore, who succeeded his father, Antoine, as chef of Antoine's toward the end of the 19th century, claimed to have invented oysters Rockefeller, and no one's disproved it yet (713 St. Louis Street; ☎ 504-581-4422).

Plenty of people have laid claim to inventing the **po'boy**, on the other hand; but most historians credit brothers Clovis and Benjamin Martin, former streetcar conductors who had opened their own restaurant on St. Claude. When the drivers went on strike in 1929, the Martins started provided those "poor boys" with affordable sandwiches of bread, roast beef trimmings, and gravy. You can't find the original restaurant, but you should have one for luck during your visit.

When it comes to pepper sauces, local loyalties are somewhat divided, but **Tabasco** is certainly among the most famous names. There is an elaborate merchandise store with Tabasco and hot pepper T-shirts, cookware, candies, and sauces at St. Ann Street in Jackson Square; but real fanatics can drive to the Tabasco plantation on Highway 329 in Avery Island, Louisiana—which is also a famous bird sanctuary and wetlands preserve—and take the free factory tour (☎ 337-365-8173 or **www.tabasco.com**).

Those with a sweet tooth might want to look in at the **Pontchartrain Hotel** (2031 St. Charles Avenue); it's being renovated as a luxury retirement residence, but the Bayou Bar and its famous murals are open to the public. The house creation here was not a drink, but a dessert: the original mile-high pie.

Rum might not be the first spirit you associate with New Orleans (and it actually was something of a late arrival); but "Don the Beachcomber," who claimed to have invented the mai tai, was a native. For about 15 years, the **Celebration Distillation** distillery has been turning out Old New Orleans Rum, and currently produces a white rum and aged rum and a spiced version. Tours are Monday through Friday and include a few tastings for those eligible (2815 Frenchmen Street; ☎ 504-945-9400 or **www.neworleansrum.com**).

The **Southern Comfort Cocktail Tour** (☎ 504-569-1401; **www.graylineneworleans.com**) winds through the French Quarter to track the evolution of such famous New Orleans concoctions as the Sazerac, the Hurricane, and, of course, Southern Comfort, which was invented by Martin Wilkes Heron for the New Orleans Exposition of 1885. Tours leave from the Gray Line office on Toulouse at 4 p.m. daily ($24).

The annual **Tales of the Cocktail** convention now extends over several days and involves local and celebrity chefs as well as bartenders and spirit guides (so to speak); check it out at **www.talesofthecocktail.com.**

You can, of course, arrange your own cocktail-history tour—by visiting **Pat O'Brien's, Antoine's,** and the bar at the **Renaissance Hotel.** During Prohibition, when rum was cheap and whiskey steep, the original Pat O'Brien, then proprietor of a speakeasy called Cafe Tipperary, created a rum-based drink called the Hurricane. "Storm's brewing," warned the menu. *Café brûlot,* flaming spiced coffee, was created by a waiter at Antoine's in 1890. While you can't get a Sazerac at Doc Paychaud's anymore, cocktail historian Chris McMillian at the Renaissance Hotel lounge can rattle off its history, and that of most classic concoctions, like a professor. One with a martini shaker, that is.

Walking on the Dark Side

Haunted tours, voodoo tours, and cemetery tours are all the rage in New Orleans, and you can go at practically any hour (and with guides in full capes and pointy-toothed glory, if you want). They cover essentially the same ground, so to a great extent, you just pick your style.

On the straight side is **Save Our Cemeteries** (☎ 504-525-3377 or 888-721-7493; **www.saveourcemeteries.org**), a nonprofit group whose proceeds go toward the restoration of these "cities of the dead." SOC offers a serious and informative tour of Lafayette Cemetery in the Garden District every Monday, Wednesday, Friday, and Saturday at 10:30 a.m. Tickets are $6 adults, $5 seniors and students; meet at the Washington Street gate. There is also a tour of St. Louis Cemetery on Sunday at 10 a.m., for which prices are $12 adults, $10 seniors, $6 students, and free for kids age 11 and younger (meet at 501 Basin Street).

Historic New Orleans Tours not only takes groups through Lafayette Cemetery and other Garden District sites, but also leads a voodoo and cemetery tour that includes a temple visit and explores St. Louis No.1. Robert Florence, a former park ranger (and now playwright) who has written books on the New Orleans way of death, personally leads many of the tours. The French Quarter tour leaves from the Bourbon Café Beignet at 311 Bourbon Street every day at 10:30 a.m. The Garden District tours leave from the Garden District Book Shop at Prytania and Washington at 11 a.m. and 1:45 p.m.

daily. Nightly Haunted French Quarter tours meet inside the Bourbon Orleans Hotel at 7:30 p.m., and Cemetery-Voodoo Tours begin at 10 a.m. and 1 p.m. Monday through Saturday and at 10 a.m. only on Sunday (meet at the Café Beignet at 334-B Royal Street). Reservations for tours are not required, but come 15 minutes early. Prices for all tours are $15 for adults, $13 for seniors and students, $7 for kids ages 6 to 12, and free for those under age 6. For more information, call Historic New Orleans Tours at ☎ 504-947-2120 or visit **www.tourneworleans.com.**

Magic Tours (☎ 504-588-9693) also offers a similar barrage of mystery-history—a voodoo tour and haunted-house roundup and cemetery tours, in addition to some relatively straight neighborhood walks—but they are mostly accurate as such things go (they do not mistake one old mansion with a calm history for its sanguine neighbor, as do some self-anointed tour guides). You need to make reservations, so call ahead. Adult tickets are $18, seniors and students are $15, and kids under age 6 are free.

New Orleans Spirit Tours also runs a Cemetery and Voodoo Tour that leaves the Royal Blend Coffee and Tea House at 621 Royal Street Sunday at 10:30 a.m. and Monday through Saturday at 1:15 p.m. The Ghost and Vampire Tour meets every night at 8:15 p.m. at the Toulouse Royale gift shop at 601 Royal Street. Tours last about two hours ($20 adults, $18 seniors and students, and $10 kids 12 and under); call ☎ 504-314-0806 or visit **www.neworleanstours.net.**

The **Haunted History Tours** are by far the most theatrical of the bunch—the Lafitte-cum-Lestat hosts of the vampire tours can't be beat—but they do cover a lot of ground, and in grand Gothic style. (And why not? The owners, believers both, threw themselves a vampire wedding.) The Journey into Darkness Vampire Tour, which focuses both on real-life sites and cinematic backgrounds, leaves every night at 8:30 p.m. from St. Louis Cathedral near the Jackson Square gates (hey, even Lestat went to church there). The Cemetery Tour leaves from Rev. Zombie's Voodoo Shop at 723 St. Peter Street daily at 10 a.m. and Monday through Saturday at 1:15 p.m. The Voodoo Tour leaves at 7:30 p.m. on Saturday night only. The Haunted History Tour, which focuses on reported hauntings and paranormal readings, also leaves from Zombie's at 6 p.m. and 8 p.m. nightly. The Garden District Tour, which includes both architectural discourse and the obligatory salute to Anne Rice and Lafayette Cemetery, leaves from the Pontchartrain Hotel at the corner of St. Charles and Josephine (daily, 10 a.m. and 1:30 p.m.). Another Garden District Ghosts and Legends tour leaves the Pontchartrain at 3:30 p.m. daily. All Haunted History Tours are $20 ($17 for students and seniors, $10 for children ages 6 to 12, and free for kids age 6 and under) and last about two hours. For reservations and more information, call ☎ 504-861-2727 or 888-6-GHOSTS or visit **www.hauntedhistorytours.com.**

SWAMP TOURS

THE BAYOUS OF LOUISIANA are among the nation's great natural treasures, filled with herons and ospreys, bald eagles, wild hogs, turtles, nutria, mink, deer, bear, and, of course, alligators. Several companies offer guided boat tours.

Dr. Wagner's Honey Island Swamp Tours of Slidell (☎ 504-242-5877 or 985-641-1769; **www.honeyislandswamp.com**) offers professional naturalists as guides through this rich area. The cost is $23 for adults, $15 for children under age 12 (with hotel pickup, $45 and $32); reservations are required.

Cajun Pride Swamp Tours offers visits to the Manchac bayou, several plantations, city tours, and combo swamp-plantation tours. Call ☎ 504-467-0758 or 800-467-0758 or visit **www.cajunprideswamptours.com** for details. **Louisiana Tour Company's** swamp tours (☎ 504-689-3599 or 888-30-SWAMP; **www.louisianaswamp.com**) have combo packages for Destrehan plantation, airboat tours, and cruises, with costs ranging up to $139.

Airboat Adventures tours offer a wacky twist on petting zoos (kids may get to pat a baby alligator) and also offer a combo swamp-plantation excursion (☎ 888-GO-SWAMP, 504-865-7325, or **www.airboatadventures.com**).

Other swamp tours are offered by **Jean Lafitte Swamp Tours** (☎ 504-587-1719) and Gray Line (☎ 504-569-1401 or **www.graylineneworleans.com**). For fishing tours of the bayou, see Part Ten, Exercise and Recreation.

If you prefer the walking-tour approach to wildlife, the **Barataria Unit of the Jean Lafitte National Park** (☎ 504-589-2330) has trails and boardwalks through three different ecosystem routes: bottomland hardwoods, a cypress swamp, and a freshwater marsh. There are fine exhibits in the visitors center as well; take US 90 south and west of the city to LA 45/Barataria Boulevard and continue about seven miles.

Almost directly across Lake Pontchartrain from New Orleans, about 45 miles away on Highway 51, is the **Joyce Wildlife Management Area.** There, a 1,000-foot boardwalk strikes deep into Manchac Swamp and offers great vistas for bird-watching, nature photography, and sketching. It's open sunrise to sunset. Stop by the Tangipahoa Parish visitors center (☎ 985-542-7520; **www.tangi-cvb.org**) at the Exit 28 ramp from I-55 for a free map and birding and animal guide.

A little farther away is the **Global Wildlife Center** (☎ 985-796-3585; **www.globalwildlife.com**) on Highway 40, about 15 miles east of Interstate 55, one of only three preserves for endangered and threatened species of birds and animals in the country. It covers 900 acres and is devoted to safe breeding and free ranging of zebras, giraffes, camels (one hump and two), llamas, impalas, and even kangaroos. Staffers will drive you right up to the animals for a photo op, and since many of the animals have learned to beg for treats, you may get quite a close-up—

maybe even a frog. The one-and-a-half-hour tour costs $17 for adults, $13 for seniors over age 62, and $10 for children ages 2 to 11.

RIVER CRUISES

SEVERAL BOATS CRUISE THE NEARBY MISSISSIPPI RIVER, some with meals, some with music, but to put it bluntly, a port is not the most scenic of sites. Huge tankers, rusting wharves, and old smokestacks are not exactly what Mark Twain saw when he fell in love with "Life on the Mississippi."

The paddle-wheeler steamboat ***Creole Queen*** (☎ 800-445-4109 or 504-529-4567; **www.creolequeen.com**), for example, offers one-and-a-half-hour cruises at 3 p.m. Fridays and Saturdays at the Canal Street dock. It is an authentic reproduction of a late-19th-century passenger vessel. Enjoy the Captain's narration of famous landmarks, history, and river lore as you cruise through one of America's busiest ports. View the historic French Quarter, Jackson Square, St. Louis Cathedral, and the French Market. Take note of the current port activities, including foreign ships and tugboats plying the river, as well as the unloading of cargo at the wharfs located up and down the Mississippi. This relaxing journey gives you the opportunity to see a host of New Orleans landmarks, cruise the mighty Mississippi River, and hear interesting facts about the past and present—with plenty of time to enjoy the rest of your day. The cruise is $20 for adults and $10 for kids ages 6 to 12.

Creole Queen also offers a jazz dinner cruise daily at 7 p.m.; $64 for adults and $25 for kids ages 6 to 12. Buy your tickets at the booth by the berth in front of the IMAX Theatre. Reservations are strongly recommended for the jazz cruise.

The ***Natchez*** (☎ 800-233-BOAT or 504-586-8777), a three-deck stern-wheeler that docks behind the Jax Brewery, also offers daytime and jazz dinner cruises with a buffet.

The best cruise, especially for those with children (since a couple of hours can be a long time to have to sit still), is probably the free ***Canal Street Ferry*** across to Algiers (and perhaps Blaine Kern's Mardi Gras World). The ***Canal Street Ferry*** just putters back and forth every day except Christmas to Algiers, touching the foot of Canal Street every half hour from 6 a.m. to 11:30 p.m., with the last trip returning at midnight. (The ferry spends the night in Algiers, which you don't want to do.) If you want to visit Mardi Gras World, you can pick up a free shuttle bus at the Algiers dock.

You may be able to take various overnight trips on the paddle wheelers ***Delta Queen, Mississippi Queen,*** and their younger sibling, the ***American Queen.*** The ***Delta Queen*** is a true wooden ship, while the two larger ones are steel ribbed, but all have etched glass, bright trim, antebellum-costumed staff, and so on. The ships are owned by Majestic America Line, which was for sale at press time, so the future of these ships is uncertain. Call ☎ 800-543-1949 or visit **www.majestic americaline.com** for current information.

SELF-GUIDED TOURS

EXPLORING NEW ORLEANS'S DIVERSITY

NEW ORLEANS HAS A PLEASANT CASE of multiple-personality syndrome. Even in between the big festivals, you can indulge in self-designed tours spotlighting Mardi Gras, music or literature, Creole society, or history; or you can fill your days (and nights) dabbling in that suddenly pervasive supernatural stuff, hauntings, and voodoo and vampire lore. If you're sticking to the family-rated attractions, such as those mentioned in Part Two, Planning Your Visit, you'll be pleased to see how many of them are indoors, so you won't have to worry about the rainy-day blahs, which always hit kids the hardest.

Of course, not all attractions are encased in cemetery stone or museum glass. One easy thing to do is to check through the local papers for announcements of the week's cultural offerings (this is true for music, garden, church, and home tours, as well as special receptions and taste-of-the-town events, many of which may be held in historic sites or houses of special interest).

The *Times-Picayune* newspaper produces a special section on Friday called "Lagniappe," which lists the best events—concerts, exhibits, tastings, art openings, even flea markets—of the weekend; this is also where you'll find cultural calendars. And remember that bookstores and coffee shops are traditionally neighborhood "bulletin boards" for such events.

But for a few informal do-it-yourself tour ideas, read on. Most of the sites in boldface are described in more detail in the attraction profiles later in this chapter or in Part Nine, Shopping.

Mardi Gras and Music

Hangover-wary veterans of Carnival celebrations, or those who prefer the more sophisticated Mardi Gras parades of earlier decades, can get their fill of the frills by visiting the **Presbytere** and the free **Germaine Cazenave Wells Mardi Gras Museum** at Arnaud's Restaurant, both in the French Quarter; **Blaine Kern's Mardi Gras World** across the river, where the floats are made; **Backstreet Cultural Museum** in Tremé, and perhaps the smaller **Mardi Gras Museum** in Rivertown.

If you're interested in the history of jazz, surprisingly, there isn't as much as you might expect. The first museum stop for you is the **Old U.S. Mint** (☎ 504-568-6968), which has a rare collection of early instruments; then browse the bins at area record stores (see Part Nine, Shopping). There is no trace of the famed Storyville red-light district, where jazz is generally said to have been born, although there is a re-creation and figures of some famous musicians in the **Musée Conti Wax Museum** (☎ 504-581-1993). **Congo Square** in Armstrong Park is currently gated up and awaiting renovation, but there are plans to stage some concerts there in the future. At night, however, be sure to check out **Preservation Hall** on St. Peter Street, a sort of living-history music museum (☎ 888-946-JAZZ).

Cruise Bourbon Street and you can still find a little Dixieland struggling to be heard through the rock-and-roll din. Try the **Famous Door** at Bourbon and Conti Streets (☎ 504-598-4334). **Donna's Bar and Grill** on North Rampart presents only brass bands, but very good ones (☎ 504-596-6914). Sunday jazz brunches are popular all over town; the **Court of Two Sisters** offers a jazz buffet for lunch every day (☎ 504-522-7261). If you're more into zydeco or Cajun or gumbo music, be sure to check the schedules at the legendary **Tipitina's** on Napoleon Avenue (☎ 504-895-TIPS) or the **House of Blues** on Decatur (☎ 504-310-4999). For more on jazz and music clubs, see the nightclub profiles in Part Eleven, Entertainment and Nightlife.

Despite the city's history, literary tours are a little harder when self-directed, primarily because only a few of the former writers' haunts are identifiable from the street (but we've pointed some out in the walking tours). Your best bet is to see the "Special-interest Tours" section earlier in this chapter.

History and Culture

American-history buffs have an easy time setting their agendas: the **Cabildo** and **Presbytere** complex on Jackson Square; the **Historic New Orleans Collection;** the **World War II Museum;** the **Civil War Museum at Confederate Hall; Jackson Barracks Military Museum** (still closed for repairs); and **Chalmette National Battlefield.**

As for historic houses, there are a number that are maintained as museums and decorated with original or period furnishings. For a quick-time dance through New Orleans history, compare the 1792 **Merieult House** of the New Orleans Historic Collection; the West Indies plantation–style **Pitot House,** circa 1800 (☎ 504-482-0312); the **Hermann-Grima House,** which shows the influence of early-19th-century American society on traditionally Creole architecture (☎ 504-525-5661); the 1857 **Gallier House Museum,** home of one of the city's premier architects; the **Beauregard-Keyes House,** an 1826 raised cottage that in its time sheltered both General P. G. T. Beauregard and novelist Frances Parkinson Keyes (☎ 504-523-7257), and the similar but simpler **Madame John's Legacy.** There is also the **1850 House,** a restored middle-class residence in the Pontalba Apartments on Jackson Square (☎ 504-568-6968), and **Longue Vue Gardens** (☎ 504-488-5488), which offers a glimpse of the last great gilded age of New Orleans between the wars. All these sites are profiled in other chapters, along with a few others that are open for viewing only by appointment. And throughout the book, certain buildings of interest are cited as you may come upon them.

As famous as the Garden District is, few buildings there are actually open to the public—but then, the exteriors are what really distinguish them. We have put together a limited walking tour of the area and a bit of streetcar touring later in the chapter.

If you have time, take an excursion to the great plantations west of town, but that requires some extra planning, especially if you want to spend the night in the country, or need professional guidance—see "Plantation Tours and Excursions" below. Similarly, if you're captivated by Cajun culture, you'll want to head a few hours west to Lafayette and its environs, but that almost certainly requires two days. See "Cajun Country Festivals" in Part Three, New Orleans's Major Festivals.

Don't overlook the **New Orleans Museum of Art** in City Park (☎ 504-488-2631). On the off chance that you happen to be a fan of the Impressionist painter Degas, note that the **Edgar Degas House** at 2306 Esplanade Avenue, where he may have finished as many as 17 works, has recently been restored as a bed-and-breakfast, but visitors are welcome to look around (☎ 504-821-5009 or **www.degashouse.com**). In fact, there are several houses in town with Degas connections: The building that now houses Brennan's Restaurant was originally built for his great-grandfather, Don Vincenze Rilleaux, and the Pitot House for his great-grandmother, Maria Rilleaux. The **Musson House,** at 1331 Third Avenue (☎ 800-755-6730) in the Garden District, was built for his uncle, who later built the Degas House; and some sources claim that the Waldhorn & Adler building on Royal Street at Conti was built for Don Vincenze Rilleaux, too. The offices pictured in Degas's masterpiece *A Cotton Office in New Orleans* were at 407 Carondelet in Factor's Row. There's a tour in itself.

If your preferences run to the literary, there are plenty of traces of **Tennessee Williams** about (several are mentioned in the self-guided walking tours of the French Quarter following) and an annual festival dedicated to Williamsesque stories, drinking, and bellowing contests ("Stellaaaaa!"). For festival information, call ☎ 504-581-1144.

In Tremé you'll find the **New Orleans African American Museum,** housed in the Meilleur-Goldwaithe home (1418 Governor Nicholls; ☎ 504-566-1136). Exhibits change periodically, so call ahead to find out what will be on display at the time of your visit.

One of the world's largest collections of arts and letters on race history is at **Tulane University's Amistad Research Center** (☎ 504-862-3222), which now incorporates many of the archives of Fisk University in Nashville; but it's really for the serious scholar. More general tourists interested in black Southern culture and contemporary black art should check into **La Belle Galerie** (309 Chartres Street; ☎ 504-529-5538), **Ya Ya** (601 Baronne Street; ☎ 504-529-3306), **Barrister's Gallery** (1724 O. C. Haley Boulevard; ☎ 504-525-2767), and the **Stella Jones Gallery** in the Bank One Center (201 St. Charles Avenue; ☎ 504-568-9050). And although not all "outsider art" is by black artists, the collection at **Peligro** (305 Decatur Street; ☎ 504-581-1706) includes fabulous folk fantasies.

The Great Hereafter

If you love old churches, make sure to see **St. Louis Cathedral** in Jackson Square, **St. Patrick's** in the Warehouse District, and the remarkable but only partly restored **St. Alphonsus** at 2045 Constance Street in the Irish Channel. This was Anne Rice's family church (her parents were married there, and her confirmation name is Alphonsus) as well as the fictional Mayfair family's; and it houses some of the most astonishing stained-glass panels you'll ever see, plus a replica of the Black Madonna; the tomb of Redemptorist Father Francis X. Seeles, who is credited with several miracles; and at least one of the purported graves of Pere Antoine. Notice the shamrocks in the tile work, too. Contact the **Preservation Resource Center** (923 Tchoupitoulas Street; ☎ 504-581-7032; **www.prcno.org**) to see when its next Stained Glass in Sacred Places Tour is scheduled.

For quirkier saints, visit **Our Lady of Guadalupe and Chapel of St. Jude** in the Central Business District and the **Chapel of St. Roch's** east of the French Quarter (Our Lady of Guadalupe is profiled below).

If, on the other hand, it's cemeteries you love, you can either experience them straight or gussied up with vampire and voodoo lore. You can visit several of the "cities of the dead," the most famous being **St. Louis Cemetery No. 1** (where the tomb of the city's fabled voodoo priestess Marie Laveau still receives nightly petitions) and **Lafayette Cemetery** in the Garden District (where Anne Rice creation Lasher is "buried" in a cast-iron tomb), but you should never go after dark, and preferably go in a group even during the day. Your best bet is to drive out to **Lake Lawn Metairie Cemetery,** which has all the extravagant tombs you could want to see, or wander through the Cypress Grove and Greenwood cemeteries by City Park (take the trolley).

If voodoo queens and vampire lovers are your thing, you can, uh, drink your fill. There are now probably as many "haunted," "voodoo," or "magic" tours of New Orleans as general history ones, though not all are particularly serious; see "Walking on the Dark Side" (page 125) for more information. Or stop into the **Voodoo Spiritual Temple** (828 North Rampart Street; ☎ 504-522-9627; **www.voodoospiritualtemple.org**).

Queen of the Damned

Anne Rice's physical presence may no longer be felt in New Orleans—she has sold her various historic properties since the death of her artist husband, Stan, and moved to her equally famous (to *Witching Hour* fans) home in San Francisco—but Lestat, Lasher, those Mayfair girls, and so on, live on. Rice used her native city not only as inspiration but frequently as an exact model, so even though you won't have a chance to see the Queen of the Undead emerge onto her balcony anymore, you can still lay out quite an itinerary of Rice- and vampire-related sites. You can stay up to date at **www.annerice.com.**

Until recently, Rice made her home at **1239 First Street** in the Garden District at an 1857 mansion, also known as the Rose-Brevard House, from whose balcony she sometimes made surprise appearances to fans gathered outside the gate. That mansion is the obvious model for the Mayfair home. As a child, Rice lived at **2301 St. Charles Avenue,** and as a teenager in the Dameron-Claiborne cottage at **2524 St. Charles,** the house featured in *Violin.* She purchased St. Elizabeth's Orphanage at **1314 Napoleon Avenue,** and used it to house her extensive doll and church-relic collection (including the famous coffin she used to arrive at parties in). It also served as the office for her short-lived tour company, a home for some of her aging relatives (in a private wing), a guesthouse—one of the rooms had twin gold-lamé canopy beds and animal-print upholstery worthy of *Sunset Boulevard*—and as an exhibit space for Stan's paintings. St. Elizabeth's is currently being developed into luxury, and perhaps spirited, condominiums. (She doesn't own St. Alphonsus, of course, but it's a must-see for fans.)

Other well-known Garden District landmarks featured in Rice's novels include **Commander's Palace** restaurant and the nearby **Lafayette Cemetery No. 1,** the old Pontchartrain Hotel at **2031 St. Charles,** and the Coliseum Theater at **1233 Coliseum Street.** And still another site, what is now Copeland's restaurant at **2001 St. Charles Avenue,** was the subject of a locally famous feud between Rice and popular restaurateur Al Copeland: it was originally a Mercedes-Benz dealership whose window Lestat used as a portal out of this world. Rice had wanted to turn the building into a vampire-themed cafe; when Copeland opened his trendy restaurant (then called Straya) there, Rice took out a full-page ad in the *Times-Picayune* criticizing it as a sort of historic disfigurement. "Lestat" then took out his own ad praising it. Rice later considered other locations in the neighborhood for a cafe and for a children's theater, but neither project has yet taken shape.

Lestat and his vampire "family" have used a number of famous places in the French Quarter as haunts, obviously including **St. Louis Cemetery No. 1,** where Louis has his tomb (and, according to local gossip, Rice has purchased one for herself). The **Hotel Monteleone, Galatoire's Restaurant, Café du Monde, Court of Two Sisters, Pontchartrain Hotel,** and the **Omni Royal** (formerly the St. Louis Hotel) all appear in *The Witching Hour,* among others. The **Gallier House** is believed to have been the model for the home Lestat and Louis share in *Interview with the Vampire,* although the movie version uses **Madame John's Legacy** as the backdrop.

The **Marsoudet-Caruso House** on Esplanade at Claiborne also appears in *Interview.* **Jackson Barracks, Jackson Square,** and **Destrehan Manor** plantation house in Kenner appeared in the Hollywood version.

NEIGHBORHOOD WALKING TOURS

OKAY, THIS IS THE FUN PART, at least as far as we're concerned—putting the "tour" back in the "tourist," so to speak. We've designed three routes for you, one in the French Quarter, one giving the flavor of the Garden District, and a third to help orient you to the newer pleasures of the Warehouse District and a bit of the Central Business District (CBD) at the same time.

How long they will take you depends on your pace and whether you stick to the sidewalk; you can, of course, stop at any museum or site that interests you. But none is either exhausting or exhaustive (to be frank, we think most walking tours tell you more than you need or want to know). These are just pleasant, informative, and intriguing strolls—a little history, a bit of legend, some literary notes, architectural details, and anecdotes. The French Quarter walk is the longest, of course, but then there are the greatest number of opportunities to sit, get something to eat or drink (remember, alcohol dehydrates), or duck into a store. The Garden District tour is the shortest, but it opens onto several other options, including Audubon Park, the zoo, the Riverbend neighborhood, and other sights.

The French Quarter (*Vieux Carré*)

It's nicer to think of the Quarter as the "old block" because there are so many influences at play on the tour: Spanish, German, American, and African-Caribbean, as well as French. Our route is divided into two looping halves, with the two middle parts beginning, meeting, and ending at St. Louis Cathedral. The longer part comes first, so that you can stop midway if you like and have an easier return. (This is also designed to help you get the layout of the Quarter in your head and not worry about going too far astray, because the loops go out and come back within view of the cathedral spire.)

The tour begins in the heart of **Jackson Square** (**www.jacksonsquare.com**), with a mental salute to the statue of General Andrew Jackson. As pointed out in "A Too-short History of a Fascinating Place," in Part One, this was originally called Place d'Armes by the French, reaccented to Plaza de Armas by the Spanish, and altered permanently after the glorious victory of 1815. It was also the "inspiration," or in-spite-ation, for Lafayette Square in the American sector. The statue was erected to honor the hero of 1815, of course, but the inscription, which reads, "The Union must and shall be preserved," was added by federal forces during the Civil War occupation. (To be fair, it is an accurate expression of Jackson's political sentiments.)

Straight before you is **St. Louis Cathedral,** the oldest active cathedral in the United States—and even at that, this is the third church to occupy that space since 1718. Constructed in 1794, it was partially remodeled in the late 1840s. The flagstone piazza just outside the church doors is officially called Place Jean Paul Deux, to commemorate the 1987 visit of Pope John Paul II.

Among the cathedral's beauties are a mural of the eponymous St. Louis (King Louis IX) announcing the Second Crusade; the clock bell, named Victoire by Pere Antoine himself, which has tolled to mark every hour for 90 years; and the extensive stained glass portraits of the saints (including, of course, Joan of Arc). A sweet but often overlooked small memorial at the right end of the entryway is a tribute to Henriette Delille, a free woman of color—and one who is likely to become the first New Orleans–born saint—who founded the first black congregation and worked tirelessly on behalf of both free and enslaved blacks in the city. She was proposed for canonization in 1988, and one of the new necessary miracles has been adjudged to be authentic.

To the left of the cathedral is the **Cabildo,** so named because during the Spanish administration, the governing council, or Cabildo, met here. It transferred to the French authorities, of course, and the Louisiana Purchase was ratified here (the elaborate pen used on that occasion makes those little ballpoints American presidents hand out look absurd). To the left of that is the **Arsenal,** built in 1803 on the site of what had been a Spanish prison, and now, like the Cabildo, it is part of the Louisiana State Museum complex.

Walk around the corner of the Arsenal onto St. Peter, and then turn right into the short **Cabildo Alley** and left again into **Pirates Alley.** This is one of several places in which Jackson and Jean Lafitte are frequently said to have plotted strategy for the Battle of New Orleans, but unfortunately, the alley wasn't cut through until 1831. Its real name is Ruelle d'Orleans, Sud—Little Orleans Way, South. However, there are two spots of interest here. **Faulkner House Books,** at 624 Pirates Alley, is not only a fine Southern literature bookstore but also the house where Faulkner lived while working on his first novel.

It borders **St. Anthony's Garden,** officially named Cathedral Garden but long considered a memorial to the Capuchin Father Antonio de Sedella (the beloved "Père Antoine," as the Creoles rechristened him), who arrived in 1779 and served the colony as pastor of the cathedral for nearly a half century. (The good father's garden was also, oddly, the most popular dueling ground for young aristocrats.) The statue of Jesus Christ in the garden was slightly damaged by Hurricane Katrina, losing part of a thumb and finger; but locals say that was the result of His brushing the storm away from the basilica. The smaller monument was erected by the government of Napoleon III to honor 30 French marines who died serving as volunteer nurses during one of the great yellow-fever epidemics.

Pirates Alley ends at Royal Street; turn left onto Royal and cross St. Peter Street. On your right at 613 Royal is the **Court of Two Sisters,** which a century ago was the dry-goods shop of Emma and Bertha Camors and is now a restaurant and jazz bar with its own fine courtyard and informal aviary. (The Camors sisters are a classic Southern Gothic story: they opened the fancy notions shop near the end of the

19th century, lived together—neither married—into their 80s, and died within a month of one another; they are buried side by side in **St. Louis Cemetery** No. 3.) The 600 block of Royal Street is sometimes called Governors Row, as it has, in its time, housed five governors, two Louisiana Supreme Court justices, one future U.S. Supreme Court Justice (Edward Douglass White, who served from 1910 to 1921, after having been elected senator and governor), and one future President, the young Zachary Taylor. The first inhabitant at the Two Sisters' address, in fact, was the Spanish Colonial governor.

At the next intersection, turn right onto Toulouse Street. On the left at 710 Toulouse Street is the house known as the **Court of Two Lions,** named for the two royal beasts that mount the gate pillars. It was bought in 1819 by Vincent Nolte, whose autobiography inspired the huge, and at one point hugely popular, novel-turned-movie *Anthony Adverse.* Next door at 722, the 1788-era **Adams House,** which was a boardinghouse during the Depression, a young Tennessee Williams paid $10 a month for a room (and worked as a waiter in his landlady's restaurant to pay even that). In the 1940s, a little better off, he took an apartment at 632 St. Peter Street, where he wrote *A Streetcar Named Desire.* But in the 1950s and 1960s, with both money and fame to support his writing habit, he moved back to 727 Toulouse Street, specifically to room 9 at the **Hotel Maison de Ville.**

At the next corner, turn left onto Bourbon Street; the French Opera House, one of the first great music venues in the nation, was built here before the Civil War. Stay on Bourbon for one block; then turn right again onto St. Louis Street. Halfway up on the left at 820 St. Louis is the **Hermann-Grima House,** one of the finest examples of early American architectural shifts and well worth coming back to tour.

At the corner of Dauphine Street, look catty-corner across to 509 Dauphine and the **Audubon Cottages,** also run by the Hotel Maison de Ville; John James Audubon lived in No. 1 while writing and painting his 1821 masterpiece, *Birds of North America.*

The largish white house you can see beyond that is the Greek Revival–style **Xiques House;** built in 1852, it has had a checkered career, serving at various times as a merchant's mansion, the Spanish consulate, a boardinghouse, cigar warehouse, bottling plant, and gambling den. There—the history of New Orleans in a single address!

Turn left onto Dauphine Street. In the next block are some buildings with equally colorful histories: at 415 Dauphine is the Dauphine Orleans, whose lounge, **May Bailey's Place,** used to be a bordello (and they can prove it). And at the corner of Conti Street is the **Déjà Vu** bar, said to be haunted and more reliably said to have housed an 1880s opium den.

At the corner of Conti look right; halfway up the block is the **Musée Conti Wax Museum,** but it's not worth staring at unless you're ready to visit it. If not, keep strolling along Dauphine to Bienville Street and turn left, back toward Bourbon Street. Halfway down on the left at 801 Bienville is the **Arnaud's** complex. It includes not only the restored old mansion as a restaurant (potted palms and ceiling fans, leaded glass, and mosaic tile), dining rooms filled with krewe memorabilia, and a fine old-fashioned bar, but also the **Germaine Wells Mardi Gras Museum** upstairs, where you can view for free the fine collection of Carnival costumes.

When you get to Bourbon Street, turn left one block back to Conti and right again to Royal Street; stop at the intersection. Now, remember that Royal Street was once the financial center of town. On your right, at 343 Royal Street, is the **Waldhorn & Adler Antiques** store, a huge, balconied, and wrought iron–decorated Spanish colonial edifice built around 1800 as the Bank of the United States. Facing you at 334 Royal Street is the **French Quarter Police Station,** housed in the 1826 Bank of Louisiana building (it has also served as the state capitol, among other things, and has a visitor-information center inside). On the left, on the opposite corner of Conti Street, is a building designed in 1818 by U.S. Capitol architect Benjamin Latrobe as the Louisiana State Bank (look for the "LB" entwined in the forged ironwork on the balcony) and now called Latrobe's in his honor. And across from that, the huge white building that takes up the whole **400 block of Royal** was built just after the turn of the 19th century as the civil-courts building. Later it housed the Louisiana Department of Wildlife and Fisheries and its wildlife museum, as well as the U.S. Circuit Court of Appeals for the Fifth Judicial District; most recently (having been wrested back from the feds by the state) it was expensively renovated for the Louisiana Supreme and Superior Courts and a Federal Court of Appeals. It was also used as a set for Oliver Stone's film *JFK*. Turn left back on Royal. At 417 Royal Street is the celebrated **Brennan's Restaurant,** originally built for Edgar Degas's Spanish grandfather. A few years later it was sold and became yet another bank office, the Banque de la Louisiane, gaining its own wrought-iron monogram in the balcony, a "BL." A few years after that, it was sold again, this time becoming the private residence of the socially prominent Martin Gordon (Andrew Jackson danced here several times when he returned to the city in 1828). But when Gordon went bankrupt, it was sold yet again, at auction, to Judge Alonzo Morphy (perhaps not coincidentally, he was the son-in-law of the auctioneer). In the 1850s, Morphy's son Paul became the world chess champion at 21, and having grown up in what is now the Beauregard-Keyes House, he too became the subject of one of Frances Parkinson Keyes's biographical novels (see page 169).

At **437 Royal,** in what is now the Cohen rare-coins gallery, was the Masonic Lodge where pharmacist Antoine Peychard served his fellow Masons his special after-dinner drink, poured out into little egg cups. The word for the cups was *coquetier,* which some people believe became "cocktail," and Peychard himself became immortalized as a brand of bitters. (His tonic included absinthe and Sazerac-de-Forge Cognac, the original Sazerac cocktail.)

Stay on Royal across St. Louis Street and peer into the porthole at 519 Royal; it looks in on the wine cellar of Antoine's restaurant. Across the street at **520 Royal,** walk through to the fine four-sided courtyard; take note of the *S* worked into the fan-shaped ironwork at the left corner of the third-floor balcony. In the early 19th century, this was built for wine merchant and furniture maker François Seignouret, who always used to carve that same initial into his furniture. The building at **536 Royal** was constructed just after the second great fire in 1794; the (somewhat dilapidated) three-story **Maison LeMonnier** at **640 Royal Street,** built in 1811, was considered the city's first "skyscraper." (The fourth story was added in 1876.) Note the initials "YLM," for Dr. Yves LeMonnier, in the wrought iron of the balcony.

Across the street, at 533 Royal Street is the **Historic New Orleans Collection** and the **Merieult House.** The Collection, which faces onto Royal, often has fine historical exhibits (a small but first-class assortment of Mardi Gras costumes, early propaganda posters promising streets of gold to would-be settlers, etc.) and is open and free. It also houses the finest research archives in the city, open to scholars only. Behind it is the late-18th-century Merieult House, one of only two important structures to survive the great fire of 1794, and a 19th-century cottage, which are now open for tours with paid admission. Madame Merieult, née Catherine McNamara, had hair of Irish copper that made her the toast of New Orleans. And when she and her husband visited Paris, Napoleon offered her her own castle in return for parting with her hair, which he wanted to make into a wig to woo the Sultan of Turkey (who himself wanted to woo a reluctant harem lady) into an alliance. The high-spirited Merieult refused, however.

Go another block along Royal Street and stop at the corner of St. Peter Street. The three-story redbrick building, one of the most popular postcard and photograph subjects in town, is sometimes called the **LaBranche House,** and its oak-and-acorn-pattern wrought-iron balconies are in very fine condition. (Actually, there are 11 LaBranche row houses altogether, built in the 1830s by a sugar planter, that run from the corner of Royal around the block of St. Peter toward Pirates Alley.)

Turn right down St. Peter Street. On the right, at the corner of Chartres Street, is **Le Petit Théâtre du Vieux Carré,** home to the country's oldest continuously operating community theater (dating from a 1916 production in the Pontalba Apartments). The whole building is a sort of theatrical set: built in 1922, it's a faithful reproduction of the 18th-century residence of Joseph Xavier de Pontalba, the last Spanish governor of New Orleans. The chandeliers and the courtyard fountain are of more recent origin; the wrought-iron balcony rail inside the theater is real, though, made in 1796. Le Petit Théâtre is believed to be haunted by a *Phantom*-like, well, phantom, in the balcony, who has been "photographed"; the now-defunct Society for Paranormal Research claimed to have recorded him several times.

Glance across the corner at the back of the Arsenal, and you will see that we have looped back toward Jackson Square for the first time. Now turn your back again and head out along Chartres Street, which is full of strange and wonderful shops and old facades.

At **617 Chartres,** for instance, is one of the city's oldest remaining buildings. The Boisque House was built in 1795 for the father-in-law of William Claiborne, the first U.S. state governor; but it replaced an even older important residence, that of the Spanish Royal governor Bernardo de Galvez, whose statue stands at the foot of Canal Street. The older home was destroyed in the great Good Friday fire of 1788.

After you cross Toulouse, look left; at 514 Chartres is the **New Orleans Pharmacy Museum,** housed in the 1816 shop (believed to have been designed by architect J. N. B. DePouilly) of apothecary Louis Defilho Jr. A little beyond, at the corner of Chartres and St. Louis streets is the **Napoleon House,** which may look as though the entire plaster interior is about to collapse, has probably seen more hard living than even its French Quarter peers and remains a favorite of locals despite the tourists. It owes its name to the loyal sentiments of pirate Jean Lafitte and his "general" Dominique You (who was probably really Lafitte's brother using an alias), New Orleans mayor Nicholas Girod, who owned both the two- and three-story buildings, and various other Creole leaders who fixed up the 1797 house and offered it to the deposed emperor, who was then languishing on the island of St. Helena. A plot was under way to rescue him when he died in 1821. (The third-floor "Appartement de l'Empereur" has been restored in real style, but can only be rented for private functions.) Make sure you look beyond the aging bar to the ageless courtyard.

If you're a fan of Paul Prudhomme, you can walk one more block and sniff the spicy air outside **K-Paul's Louisiana Kitchen** at 416 Chartres Street; then turn left at Conti Street and head toward Decatur Street. In the small triangle bordered by Conti, Decatur, and North Peters is a 26-foot-tall, two-ton bronze depicting New Orleans's founder Jean Baptiste le Moyne, the Sieur de Bienville, his priest Father Athanase, and a Native American. The memorial was moved here from Union Passenger Terminal in 1997, and now stands quite near where Bienville is believed to have made his landing.

Turn left again onto Decatur. As you head back toward Jackson Square, you pass the Hard Rock Cafe, the Crescent City Brewhouse, the Millhouse–Jax Brewery, and so on. By the time you make it to the square, and see those silly mules in their hats and ribbons, you'll be delighted to look right and mount the steps up to **Washington Artillery Park** and the **Moonwalk** overlooking the river.

Now settle yourself in for a cup of reviving coffee at the **Café du Monde** (or a carryout cup from **Café Pontalba**), tour the caricaturists, or just relax in **Jackson Park.** This is the end of Loop 1, and intermission time for the tour.

When you're ready to start again, turn up St. Ann Street from Decatur Street toward Chartres, looking up at the **Pontalba Apartments.** These twin Parisian-inspired complexes were built by the formidable Baroness Micaela Almonester Pontalba, daughter of Don Andres Almonester y Rojas, one of the city's wealthiest and most influential patrons. A good Eurocentric Creole, she married a cousin and moved to Paris, but when her father-in-law attempted to force her to turn over her very substantial properties (and shot her in the hand when she refused), she defied convention by packing up and returning home, where she became a shrewd businesswoman. Note the intertwined "A" and "P" initials in the wrought iron medallions along the balconies.

Halfway up the block, at 525 St. Ann Street, is the **1850 House,** a restored three-story apartment showing how a middle-class Creole family lived at the time the Baroness Micaela Almonester Pontalba built her groundbreaking and still-sought-after apartments. This is another part of the Louisiana State Museum, and tickets can be bought in the gift shop. Right next to it, at 529 St. Ann Street, is a **Louisiana Office of Tourism center,** which has scores of brochures, maps, and coupons. Intriguingly, while the state of Louisiana owns the block of apartments along St. Ann, the city of New Orleans owns the identical block of apartments on the other side of Jackson Square along St. Peter Street, including No. 540, where in the mid-1920s playwright Sherwood Anderson wrote *Dark Laughter.*

At the corner of St. Ann and Chartres streets is the **Presbytere,** the fourth Louisiana State Museum property right on Jackson Square, and the most conventional of the buildings in that it hosts both permanent and rotating exhibits about New Orleans and Louisiana history, maritime culture, society, portraiture, and decorative arts. Its most famous possession is Napoleon's death mask.

Walk past the door of the Presbytere and turn right up the 1830s flagstone walkway called **Père Antoine Alley,** which borders St. Anthony's Garden on the other side. (Like Pirates Alley, its official name is more pedestrian: Ruelle d'Orleans, Nord—Little New Orleans Way, North.) Jog left onto Royal and then right onto Orleans Street to the **Bourbon Orleans Hotel** on your right. The **Orleans Ballroom,** which has now been restored within the hotel complex, was built by entrepreneur John Davis in 1817 to house theatrical productions and opera. Although some of the official walking tours don't mention it, it was also the site of the famous quadroon balls, where Creole aristocrats formally courted mixed-race beauties to be their concubines. It apparently served, as did many public buildings, as a hospital during the Civil War, and in 1881 was acquired by an order of black nuns to serve as an orphanage and school. The order sold the building about 30 years ago to the hotel, and there have been rumored ghost sightings around the place, including one of a Confederate soldier and another of a young woman.

Turn right at Bourbon Street and there on the corner of St. Ann is **Marie Laveau's House of Voodoo,** one of the more popular spots for tarot readings, charms, and souvenirs. Keep strolling past Dumaine Street toward St. Philip; on the left, at 941 Bourbon Street, is **Lafitte's Blacksmith Shop Bar,** yet another probably apocryphal site but much loved. The story is that the Lafitte brothers, Jean and Pierre, used the blacksmith shop as a front for their smuggling and slaving network, but though there are deeds of ownership on the property dating to the early 1770s, none indicates a smithy. Still, it's architecturally interesting—one of the last bits of post-and-brick construction, which means that the bricks were set inside a wooden frame because the local clay was so soft—and is still a great candlelight jazz bar that draws locals even more than tourists. (It's such an old reliable that a few years ago, three sheriff's deputies were moonlighting behind the bar when a fugitive came in for a drink; they arrested him on the spot.) It was also the favorite watering hole of Tennessee Williams.

Continue down Bourbon two more blocks to Governor Nicholls Street and turn right. At 721 Governor Nicholls Street is the **Thierry House,** built around 1814 to a design proffered by Benjamin Latrobe when he was only 19 years old. Its neoclassical Greek style inspired the whole Greek Revival that characterized Creole architecture.

At the end of the block, turn the corner right again onto Royal. On the left corner, at 1140 Royal Street, is what is still known as the **LaLaurie Apartments,** and to tour guides as *the* Haunted House. In the early 1830s, it was the home of Delphine LaLaurie, a sort of Creole Elizabeth Báthory who hosted many brilliant and elaborate soirées there, which despite their popularity fueled gossip about the pitiable appearance of many of her servants. Several of these slaves committed suicide, or so LaLaurie said. One neighbor reported that LaLaurie had savagely beaten a young black girl, who shortly thereafter "fell" from the roof to her death, but a court merely fined her. But on April 10, 1834, when the house caught fire, neighbors, hearing the screams of slaves, broke in to find seven of them chained in a secret garret, starving and bearing the marks of torture. Rumors spread that Madame LaLaurie herself might have set the fire. The house was stormed, and she and her family barely escaped, making their way to Europe. She never returned, although the house was rebuilt, but her body was smuggled back to New Orleans and secretly buried. Some people swear they have heard the shrieking of slaves and the snapping of whips at night, and it is a very popular late-night tourist stop for ghost hosts. Madame LaLaurie is so infamous, in fact, that she is memorialized at the Musée Conti Wax Museum.

> *unofficial* **TIP**
> It's worth remembering that Bourbon Street was named not for the alcohol but for the aristocracy, and the lower blocks of Bourbon and its surroundings have many lovely buildings from throughout the city's history.

The neighboring buildings have a much finer reputation, fortunately. Just alongside at 1132 Royal Street is the **Gallier House Museum,** built in 1857 by James Gallier Jr., son of the architect of the city hall and a prominent architect himself. He designed the building with many ingenious and then-rare fixtures. The house is administered as a museum by Tulane University.

Continue on Royal, past St. Philip, to 915 Royal Street, where the wrought-iron fence that gives the **Cornstalk Hotel** its name holds court. It was cast in the 1830s in Philadelphia for Dr. Joseph Biamenti as a present for his homesick midwestern wife, and its near-twin can be seen in the Garden District in front of the house at 1448 Fourth Street.

Across the street at **900, 906,** and **910 Royal** are the three **Miltenberger houses,** built in 1838 and now housing art galleries. The granddaughter of one Miltenberger was Alice Heine, the Barbara Hutton or Pamela Harriman of her day; she married first the Duc de Richelieu and then moved on to Prince Louis of Monaco.

Turn right onto Dumaine and duck up to the **New Orleans Historic Voodoo Museum** at 724 Dumaine Street, which is part museum (some pretty grisly), part souvenir shop–fortune-telling temple, and part tour central. Then double back down a block to 632 Dumaine Street and **Madame John's Legacy,** which is put forth by many historians as the oldest existing building in the lower Mississippi River valley. It was originally built between 1724 and 1726 for Don Manuel Lanzos, the captain of the regiment; but it was either repaired or entirely rebuilt to the same design (hence the debate) after the Good Friday fire of 1788. In either case, it is a fine example of French colonial architecture of the style called a raised cottage, with a steeply pitched room and dormers, living quarters high above flood level, half timbering on the back of the rear stairs on the second floor (called columbage), and storage below. The name comes from "Tite Poulette," a short story by the 19th-century writer George Washington Cable, about a beautiful quadroon whose white lover wills her the house on his deathbed. It is now part of the state museum complex.

At the corner of Chartres, glance right—there it is, Jackson Square—and then turn left onto Chartres Street. At Ursulines Street, turn the corner just long enough to peek at the **Hotel Villa Convento,** 616 Ursulines Street. It's a respectable guesthouse now, but legend points to it as the famous House of the Rising Sun bordello. Cross Ursulines to 1113 Chartres Street, the **Beauregard-Keyes House,** built by wealthy auctioneer Joseph Le Carpentier and his son-in-law Judge Alonzo Morphy (see Brennan's, above). In its time it was home to Confederate hero General P. G. T. Beauregard and novelist Frances Parkinson Keyes. Keyes wrote two novels about previous occupants while living here (perhaps she was haunted). The better-known novel is about General Beauregard and is titled *Madame Castel's Lodger;* the second one, titled *The Chess Player,* is about Paul Morphy.

Across the street on the corner of Ursulines and Chartres streets is the **Old Ursuline Convent,** the other candidate for the title of "oldest building in Louisiana." Designed in 1745 and completed in 1752, it is the only structure that we know for sure survived the great fires at the end of the 18th century. (The Sisters of St. Ursula themselves arrived in 1727, and lived in the meantime in a building at Bienville and Chartres.) It was not only the first nunnery in the state; it was the first orphanage, the premier school for Creole children, and the first school for black and Native American children as well. Between 1831 and 1834 it housed the state legislature—the ultimate proof of charity.

Continue down Chartres to Governor Nicholls and turn right on Decatur back toward Jackson Square. The gold-plated warrior astride her fearless steed is, of course, Joan of Arc, the patron saint of France, and a gift to this still-French city from the French government. It is an exact replica of a statue that has stood in the Place de Pyramides in Paris since 1880.

The **French Market** runs along your left, with the tracks of the Riverfront streetcar beyond. Shops and restaurants line Decatur on both sides. At St. Philip Street look left and locate the National Park Service office peeking through from North Peters Street; then keep on, back to the Café du Monde, or stop at any of the little cafes along the way. Even better, stop by the legendary **Tujague's** on Decatur at Madison; the long stand-up bar is a New Orleans tradition. The bar itself, which came from Paris back in 1827, is nearly 300 years old. And it was probably here that O. Henry, if he did borrow the pseudonym from a bartender, first got the idea, because he was a regular.

The Garden District

Although some guidebooks list scores of homes in the Garden District as historically or architecturally important, they are mainly so to real devotees, especially as virtually all are private residences and can only be glimpsed from the outside. You may well see all you want to see by staying on the St. Charles Avenue Streetcar on the way to Audubon Park. So we have designed a fairly limited walk-through that will give you the flavor of the district and several of the celebrity highlights. If you go in the later morning, you may find a lunch stop at the famous—and just extravagantly restored—**Commander's Palace** convenient. If you are enjoying the stroll, you can just keep wandering and admiring the facades. (If the present owners are working in their yards, you might stop and ask if they know much about the histories of their homes; most homeowners are quite knowledgeable.) If you are seriously interested, contact the New Orleans Visitors Bureau about the **Spring Fiesta,** which starts the Friday after Easter and includes many garden and house tours.

The Garden District is the second-largest historic district in the United States, encompassing 10,700 structures—some with as many as 30 rooms. It is usually said to be bounded by St. Charles Avenue and Magazine Street (on the north and south sides, more or less) and Jackson and Louisiana avenues on the east and west. But neighboring streets continue to claim relationship, and there is now what is sometimes called a "Lower Garden District"—lower as in downtown—to the east back toward Lee Circle. The look of the Garden District is so different from the French Quarter that it almost seems like another country, and in fact it almost was. This was the "American Quarter," the area where the rich, the *nouveau riche*, and the well connected from all over the United States built extravagant mansions to show up their new fellow citizens of the Creole aristocracy.

We suggest you start by taking the St. Charles streetcar to Jackson Avenue. At 2220 St. Charles is the **House of Broel,** a longtime dollhouse collection, as well as a bridal and haute couture salon now open only for weddings or catered events. It was originally built as a two-story pied-à-terre for a planter and his family, but in the 1890s, tobacco tycoon Simon Hernsheim had the whole building lifted and added a new Victorian first floor (☎ 504-522-2220).

Across Phillip, at **2336 St. Charles** is a Greek Revival raised cottage designed by James Gallier Sr. Almost facing it, at **2265 St. Charles,** is a house that was designed by his son, James Gallier Jr., for Lavinia Dabney in the late 1850s, about the time his own home in the Vieux Carré was completed. Gallier designed it as Greek Revival; the Ionic columns and side galleries were added later.

At the corner of First Street, turn left, walk a block to Prytania, looking left through the fences for a view; then turn the corner to get a better one. At 2343 Prytania is the Beaux Arts–style **Louise S. McGehee School,** also known as the Bradish Johnson House after the wealthy sugar planter for whom it was built in 1872, for a then-astonishing $100,000, probably by New Orleans–born, Paris-trained architect James Freret. It has been a prestigious girls' school since 1929; the carriage house is the gymnasium, and the stables have been turned into a cafeteria. According to an odd legend, none of the girls, or anyone else, has been born, died, or married within its walls.

Across the street from the school at 2340 Prytania is what is sometimes called **Toby's Corner,** built sometime before 1838 for Philadelphian Thomas Toby, and believed to be the oldest house in the Garden District. (Toby went bankrupt backing Sam Houston's Texas campaign.)

Continue down First Street, noting the ornate cast iron in front of the circa 1869 Italianate home at **1331 First Street** and the matching galleries at the remarkably similar house at **1315 First Street.** Both were designed by Irish immigrant Samuel Jamison in 1869.

Just past Chestnut Street, on the corner at **1239 First Street,** is the 1857 mansion once known as the Rose-Brevard House; it was built for merchant Albert Brevard, and its elaborate ironwork has a rose pattern. It's now far more famous as the residence of former novelist Anne Rice and the setting of the best-selling book *The Witching Hour*. The original structure cost only $13,000 (the hexagonal wing was added a few years later); restoring the gates alone would cost that now.

Across the street, at **1236 First Street,** is a gorgeous Greek Revival mansion built as a wedding gift in 1847. Walk another block to Camp

Street and look across the corner to the house at **1134 First Street,** built about 1850 for Judge Jacob Payne (who may have designed it himself and in any case had slaves from his Kentucky plantation transported to construct it). It is also the home where—although the memorial stone on the sidewalk doesn't make specific reference to the sad event—Jefferson Davis, onetime U.S. senator and former president of the Confederate States of America, died in 1889.

Turn right onto Camp Street and walk to Third Street, turning right at the corner. The mansion with the magnificent arches at **1213 Third Street** was built during the Reconstruction for Irish carpetbagger Archibald Montgomery, president of the Crescent City Railroad. Continue on to the Italianate home at **1331 Third Street,** designed in 1850 by James Gallier Sr., for New Orleans postmaster Michel Musson, whose sister was Edgar Degas's mother. (The elaborate cast-iron or "iron lace" galleries were added later.)

Another block on, past Coliseum at **1415 Third Street** is the **Robinson House,** one of the Garden District's largest and most attractive homes: its curving front seems especially spacious because both stories are the same height. It was built just before the Civil War by architect Henry Howard for Virginia tobacco trader Walter Robinson, and is thought to have been one of the first homes in New Orleans to have indoor plumbing.

Go back to Coliseum; turn left onto Coliseum and walk two blocks to Washington Street. On the corner is **Commander's Palace,** where you can stop for lunch or just cast an admiring glance at the courtyard (no shorts, remember). This stately old-liner of the Brennan's fleet, a restaurant for well over a century, owes its name not to a naval officer but to owner Emile Commander. It's terribly respectable now, but back during Prohibition, the second story was a high-stakes, high-society bordello.

Behind the high brick walls of Washington and Coliseum is **Lafayette Cemetery No. 1,** named for the American sector it served, then the City of Lafayette. Laid out in 1833, the cemetery was designed for the well-to-do Protestants; its wide aisles were intended to carry extravagant funeral processions to elaborate tombs. However, it was nearly filled within 10 years by victims of repeated epidemics. The cemetery has many fine examples of the above-ground tombs that are New Orleans trademarks, including the cast-iron tomb Anne Rice uses for the elemental spirit Lasher (the cemetery itself served as a setting for scenes from the movie version of *Interview with the Vampire*). The Jefferson Fire Company No. 22 tomb with its bas-relief fire truck is also here, as are other monuments that might look familiar to fans of the seminal film *Easy Rider*. (Eternal rest or eternal bliss? In 1980, a Neiman Marcus executive and his bride were married here, on Friday, the 13th of June, wearing full black. And Rice threw herself a "burial" here in 1995 as a publicity stunt for the publication of *Memnoch the Devil*.) Unfortunately, even this cemetery is not always safe to wander without company, and in any case the gate may be locked. However, if you are waiting at the Washington Avenue gate at 10:30 a.m. Monday, Wednesday, or Friday, you can hook onto the Save Our Cemeteries tour; or contact one of the commercial tour groups mentioned previously in "Walking on the Dark Side."

Walk along the Washington Avenue cemetery wall to Prytania, and turn back to the right. Glance down Fourth Street to No. 1448 if you want to see the wrought-iron fence that is the near-twin to the one at the Cornstalk Hotel in the French Quarter. It's not actually identical, but from the same catalogue. And be sure to stop at the "historical marker" at **2805 Prytania Street,** which reads, "On this day in 1897, nothing happened."

Continue on to **2605 Prytania** at the corner of Third Street: the guesthouse of this pointy-arched Gothic Revival house, designed by the senior Gallier for a gambler (who later reneged) in 1849, though somewhat altered now, was a perfect miniature of the main house.

Just across Third Street at 2521 Prytania is the former Redemptorist Fathers chapel, **Our Lady of Perpetual Help**—"former" because the Italianate home, built in 1857 for a coffee merchant, had fallen into disrepair before being purchased, like several other dilapidated historic buildings in the district, by Anne Rice. Across from that, at 2520 Prytania, is the **Gilmour-Parker Home,** a Palladian-fronted house built in 1853 for an English cotton trader named Gilmour and later sold to John Parker, father of a future governor. The building around the corner at **1417 Third Street** used to be its carriage house, but later was considerably expanded.

It's a private home, but the mansion at **2507 Prytania,** built in the early 1850s for *New Orleans Daily Crescent* publisher Joseph. H. Maddux, is a palace that brings all past glories to life. Among its treasures are 14-foot ceilings, a fireplace of hand-painted tiles depicting a dreamy bayou landscape, huge murals of Louisiana flora and fauna, a 440-foot-long ballroom with twin Baccarat chandeliers, and so on. The **Women's Opera Guild House,** a Queen Anne–Greek Revival hybrid on the far end of the block at 2504 Prytania Street, was designed by William Freret in 1858, except for the octagonal turret, which was added toward the end of the century and holds a music room and bedrooms. It was bequeathed to the Opera Guild by its last inhabitant, Nettie Seebold, and houses a collection of 18th- and 19th-century antiques, along with some Guild mementos. (At press time it was closed for renovation, but the plan is to open for tours again in spring 2009.)

Turn left onto Second Street, walk back to St. Charles, and turn left again. At 2524 St. Charles, on the corner of Third Street, is what is known both as the **Dameron House** and more romantically—and far more widely, thanks to the publication of Anne Rice's *Violin*—as the **Claiborne Cottage.**

Rice's story has it that the Greek Revival raised cottage was the home of the son and daughter-in-law of Bernard Xavier Philippe de Marigny de Mandeville, one of the wealthiest and more influential Creoles of old New Orleans society. Mandeville de Marigny married Louise Claiborne, daughter of the diplomat who would become the first American governor of Louisiana. Their match marked the first great union of the two societies of New Orleans, but Marigny, who had inherited much land and money, gambled so obsessively that he is said to have lost a million dollars—not in modern money, but a million dollars *then*—by the time he was 20. In fact, it may have been Marigny who brought back dicing from England: it became known to the Americans as "Johnny Crapaud's game," something like "the Frog's game," and eventually "craps." (Marigny tried to name Burgundy Street "Craps Street," but it didn't take.) Unfortunately, the more people he taught the game to, the more people he lost money to. He still managed to live well, but by the time he died at 83, he was a pauper; the neighborhood of Faubourg Marigny is almost the last reminder of his huge holdings. Meanwhile, the house became a convent, a guest house, a rectory, and a school, and was nearly razed several times under various development schemes. However, in the 1950s, when Anne Rice was a teenager, her parents rented the house for several years, and *Violin* was inspired by her memories of the place. Needless to say, she later purchased the property.

And here you are back at the streetcar.

The Warehouse and Central Business Districts

This is a somewhat-mixed tour, primarily pointing out historical buildings, but with a few art sites thrown in. The neighborhood is undergoing such a dramatic transformation with constant redevelopment and construction that some sites may not be visible or open at all times. If you are a more serious student of contemporary art, you should also plan to take a walk up and down Julia Street, from Commerce to St. Charles, where there are many fine galleries and studios.

This might be called the international history tour, and not only because it starts at the World Trade Center. In a way, it mirrors the city's history, with memorials to the Spanish, French, British, Italian, and American communities.

Start by the WTC near the Algiers ferry landing. (The WTC no longer has a rotating top floor with a view for the public, but on weekends it sometimes operates as a nightclub.) The gentleman on perpetual guard between the ferry and the Harrah's carpetbaggers is Bernard de Galvez, the first colonial governor (1777–1786). Walk along Convention Center Boulevard toward Lafayette Street. At Poydras Street flash a victory "V" sign back at the **statue of Winston Churchill** (the green is called English Place).

Turn right at Lafayette, much of which has been restored as a pedestrian walk. In the open space at Fulton Street, stop to admire the new gazebo-shaped memorial to the old-line **New Orleans musicians** on your right. If you have time, stick your head into the Ruth's Chris Steakhouse and ask to see the "courting booths" (sometimes called "adultery booths"). They're new, but old in spirit.

Continue up Lafayette to South Peters Street. Just to the right at 537 South Peters is the **Italian American Museum** (☎ 504-522-7294) that has a small but intriguing collection that explores the role of Italian immigrants in Mardi Gras, Dixieland jazz, and the feast of St. Joseph's Day, held every March 19. (Among the more interesting personalities featured is Diamond Jim Moran, whose Italian restaurant used to tuck diamonds into the meatballs.)

Continue on Lafayette one more block to Commerce Street and the **Piazza d'Italia.** The Piazza d'Italia was designed by Charles Moore, and its fountain (shaped like Italy) and partial arches were supposed to suggest a classical ruin. Nearby construction had taken a toll on the park, but it has since been beautifully restored.

Continue on Lafayette to Camp Street and the edge of **Lafayette Square,** laid out in 1788 and named for the noble marquis who had joined the American Revolution. On the right is a 1974 **sculpture** by Clement Mead entitled ***Out of There,*** and straight ahead, just inside the park, is the **Benjamin Franklin monument** created in 1871 by Hiram Powers. The **statue** in the center of the park of statesman **Henry Clay,** dedicated in 1860, originally stood at the intersection of St. Charles and Canal, and the place of honor in this park once belonged to a statue of the king of Spain. Clay was moved here in 1901, after serving as a gathering place for repeated anti-integration riots.

Turn left onto Camp Street and notice the building on the left between Lafayette and Capedeville. The more or less Italian Renaissance building is now the **U.S. Court of Appeals for the Fifth Circuit,** but was built in 1914 as the post office. (Even funnier, it has been named after the modestly named justice John Minor Wisdom.) The four corners of the pergola atop the building are marked by statues of women representing industry, agriculture, history, and art.

Continue on Camp past Girod Street to **St. Patrick's Church** and its rectory. The high and narrow Gothic Revival building, built in the 1830s and for many years the undisputed high point of the area, was modeled after England's Yorkminster Cathedral by Irish architects Charles and James Dakin, and meant as a rival and rebuke to the French communicants of St. Louis Cathedral. (The shorthand for the Creole aristocrats' attitude was, "God speaks only in French," though how He felt about canonical Latin is unclear.)

Their revenge was complete in 1851, when St. Louis Cathedral was being rebuilt, because Bishop Antoine Blanc had to be ordained as archbishop in St. Patrick's. (And apparently the grudge was forgotten, as the cathedral now has its own statue of Saint Joan.)

The design was completed by James Gallier Sr. (born James Gallagher in Dublin), who was responsible for the high, vaulted interior—the nave is 85 feet high, the tower 185 feet—and the ribbed sanctuary ceiling with floral bosses. The stained glass over the altar and three large murals, painted in 1840 by Leon Pomarede, are very fine. (The one on the left shows St. Patrick baptizing the princesses of Ireland; take that, St. Louis!) The cathedral's pastor was so partisan a Confederate that he led public prayers for victory. And according to legend, when occupying Union General Benjamin "Beast" Butler demanded to know if it were true he had refused burial to a Union soldier, the good father instantly retorted that he would "be happy to bury them all!" The Italianate rectory to the church's left was built by Garden District and plantation architect Henry Howard in 1874. The pews, incidentally, are cypress.

At the end of the block, catty-corner across Julia Street, you can see what's called **Julia Row** or the **Thirteen Sisters,** a block of 13 red-brick row houses of a type that was extremely popular among upper-class residents of the American sector from about 1825 (these were built in the early 1830s) to about 1885. Notice the fan-light transom windows, attic cornices, and iron balconies. Many of these are now art galleries, but whether or not you want to browse the studios you should look into **Louisiana Products** at 618 Julia Street; this combination carryout-convenience store-community gossip center is an institution.

At 743 Camp you'll see (you can't miss) the lighthouse-shaped building that now houses **Lighthouse Glass Art** gallery, where you can not only buy fine art glass but take a glassblowing lesson (☎ 504-529-4494).

Continue along Camp past St. Joseph Street to 900 Camp Street and the **Contemporary Arts Center.** This renovated, 40,000-square-foot, turn-of-the-19th-century warehouse is both a "living museum," with studios for practicing artists and rotating exhibits, and a theater, with two stages and sometimes concerts. Even the furniture is art—the glass-wave front desk, the lobby information board, the elevator panels, and the lighting sconces are all creations of fine local artists.

Across the street at 925 Camp Street is Goldring Hall, the modern section of the **Ogden Museum of Southern Art.** Developer Roger Ogden collected more than 1,200 works by 400 Southern artists, sculptors, and printmakers and donated them to the city for this two-part complex that also includes the **Howard Memorial Library,** which is still under renovation. This structure, which opens onto Lee Circle, is an 1888 sandstone extravaganza by Romanesque Revival champion Henry Hobson Richardson and has a fabulous wood-paneled rotunda; at press time, it was still under renovation.

Tucked under the elbow of the Ogden, and clearly also designed by Richardson, is the **Civil War Museum at Confederate Hall,** which has the second-largest collection of Confederate memorabilia (after Richmond's Museum of the Confederacy) in the nation. It is also the oldest museum in the state, designed in 1891 with a cypress hallway, 24-foot ceiling, and fireproof cases for its collection of restored battle flags. The body of Jefferson Davis, who died here in 1889 (see the Garden District tour preceding), lay in state at the museum before being taken to Richmond, and many of his family effects are here, along with uniforms, weapons, insignia, and photographs.

Look left at the corner of Andrew Higgins Drive through the parking lot to the **National World War II Museum** at 945 Magazine Street; it has become one of the city's most important tourist attractions, and you are likely to want to come back for a longer visit.

Turn the corner right onto Higgins Avenue and you will see the greatest Confederate of them all, **Robert E. Lee,** on eternal vigilant guard against invasion from the north in the center of **Lee Circle.** (Talk about revered—he's not just on a pedestal, he's on a 60-foot pedestal.) The memorial was dedicated in 1884, at which time the former Tivoli Circle was renamed in his honor, and Jefferson Davis and New Orleans hometown hero P. G. T. Beauregard were still around for the ceremony. (Curiously, while Lee faces north, the melancholy Jeff Davis, from his vantage in Mid-City at Basin Street and Jefferson Parkway, looks south, as if in regret.)

If you're a fan of modern art, walk clockwise around Lee Circle. Most of the sculptures that were on display at the **K-B Plaza** at St. Charles Avenue have been moved to City Park, but among those remaining is a huge Isamu Noguchi fountain representing the Mississippi River.

Facing the circle to the left of Howard Avenue is the future **Lee Circle Center for the Arts,** an ambitious complex of working artists studios, including print facilities, sculptures, and even a full-size forge.

Swing around Lee Circle back onto St. Charles. You'll notice a lot of new residential construction, hotels and condos, and restaurants.

At 545 St. Charles, looking out toward Lafayette Square, is **Gallier Hall,** designed in the late 1840s by the senior James Gallier as City Hall for the Second Municipality (that is, the American Sector) and later of the united city. It is considered one of the most beautiful examples of the Greek Revival style in the city—and many believe in the entire country. The figures on the pediment represent justice, liberty, and commerce (the one toting barges and lifting bales). A popular special-events venue, at press time it was undergoing renovations.

Facing Gallier at the edge of Lafayette Square is the **John McDonogh monument,** portraying the philanthropist surrounded by grateful children. McDonogh endowed several public schools in the mid-19th century; until his will was known, he was just considered a cranky old miser with radical ideas about educating slaves.

Stay on St. Charles Avenue for several blocks—past the **Hilton Hotel,** formerly a Masonic temple—to Common Street; turn left, walk two blocks, and then go right onto Baronne Street. At 132 Baronne is the outlandish Alhambra-Moscovy romantic **Church of the Immaculate Conception,** informally known as the Jesuit Church. The original church, erected in the mid–19th century, had so much wrought and cast iron, some 200 tons of it, that it had nearly collapsed after five years. It was replaced in 1930 by an almost identical structure, which still has the old church's cast-iron pews and the bronze-gilt altar, designed by James Freret, which won first prize at the Paris Exposition of 1867. And except for the rude intervention of the French Revolution of 1848, the statue of the Virgin Mary that adorns it would have been installed at the Tuileries.

Go to the corner, turn right onto Canal Street, and head back toward the river. This was for many years *the* shopping area for upper- and middle-class New Orleanians ("I wore white gloves to come here," says one native), and after a dispiriting decline, Canal Street is coming back to life with a raft of brand-name shops and luxury hotels.

Past Decatur, at 423 Canal Street, is the partly restored Egyptian–Greek Revival **U.S. Customs House,** begun in the 1840s (when the Mississippi was within eyeshot) but not usable until 1889, and not fully completed until 1913. Henry Clay, still in favor, broke the ceremonial ground; later, it housed Confederate prisoners of war during the Union occupation. The huge third-floor Marble Hall, with its 55-foot skylight and 14 marble columns, is breathtaking. The new **Audubon Insectarium** is in the old carriage house area.

And now you are in sight once again of Harrah's and the World Trade Center.

PLANTATION TOURS *and* EXCURSIONS

THERE ARE SOME GOOD TOUR PACKAGERS who can take you by bus to a few of the houses, such as **New Orleans Paddlewheels** (☎ 504-592-0560 or 800-543-6332). **Gray Line Tours** (☎ 504-569-1401 or 800-535-7786) offers a tour of **Oak Alley Plantation** and **Laura Plantation. Old River Road Plantation Adventure** manages seven plantations (☎ 866-671-8687; **www.adventuresinneworleans.com**). There are also steamboat tours, but they offer no more than a glimpse of the houses from the water, and so are not very satisfying for the time they require.

unofficial **TIP**
It is unlikely that you'll have enough time to visit the plantations as part of a business trip, and unless you've figured such an excursion into your family vacation schedule (and are planning to rent a car), you may have to settle for a half-day group tour.

You can even see several of the closer plantations in only a couple of hours, notably **Destrehan** and **Oak Alley.** However, if you have time and would like to strike out by yourself, we have laid out a few options, including a half-day drive, a full-day tour, and an overnight route that would be a romantic highlight.

There are a half-dozen houses along what is called **River Road,** and a seventh house a bit to the south (plus many smaller houses, churches,

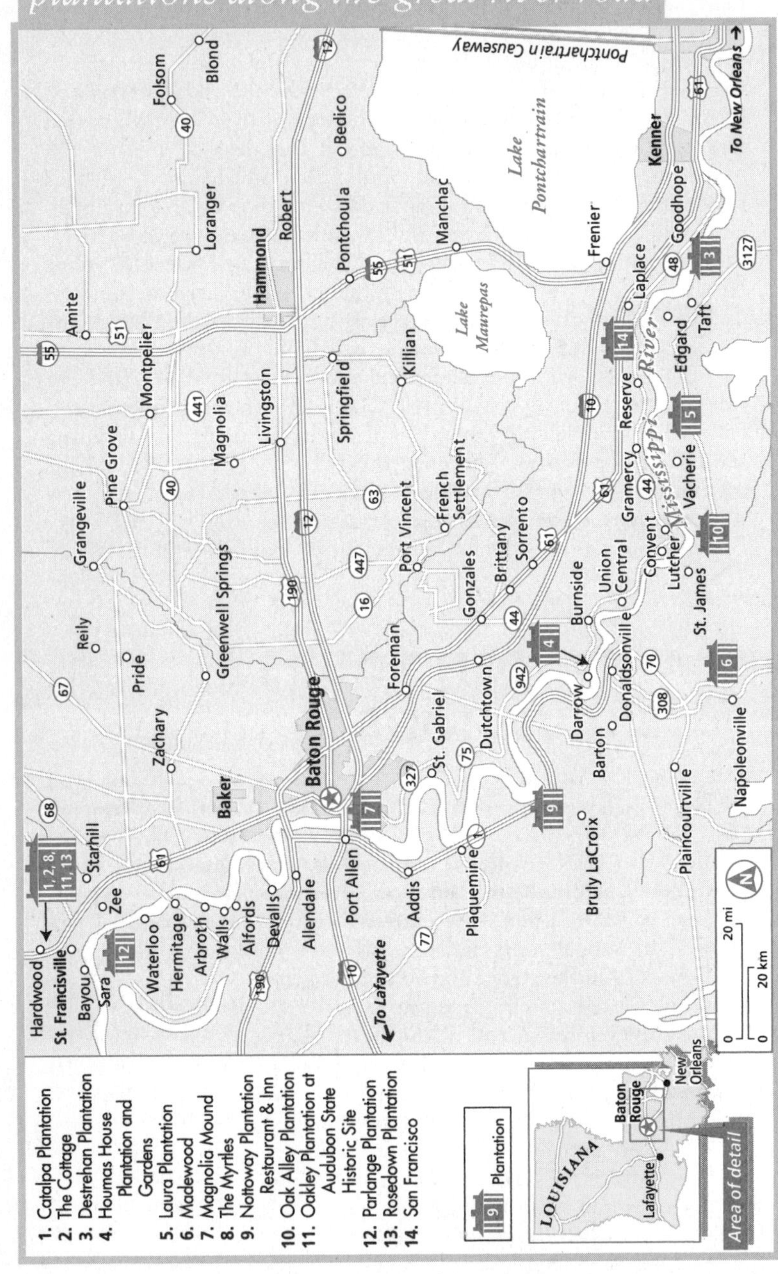
plantations along the great river road
1. Catalpa Plantation
2. The Cottage
3. Destrehan Plantation
4. Houmas House Plantation and Gardens
5. Laura Plantation
6. Madewood
7. Magnolia Mound
8. The Myrtles
9. Nottoway Plantation Restaurant & Inn
10. Oak Alley Plantation
11. Oakley Plantation at Audubon State Historic Site
12. Parlange Plantation
13. Rosedown Plantation
14. San Francisco
Plantation
LOUISIANA
Lafayette
Baton Rouge
New Orleans
Area of detail
Lake Pontchartrain
Lake Maurepas
Mississippi River
Pontchartrain Causeway
To New Orleans
To Lafayette
Baton Rouge
Hammond
Kenner
Baker
St. Francisville
Hardwood
Bayou Sara
Zee
Starhill
Waterloo
Hermitage
Arbroth
Walls
Alfords
Devalls
Allendale
Port Allen
Addis
Plaquemine
Bruly LaCroix
Plaincourtville
Napoleonville
Zachary
Pride
Reily
Grangeville
Pine Grove
Greenwell Springs
Montpelier
Amite
Magnolia
Livingston
Springfield
Robert
Pontchoula
Loranger
Folsom
Blond
Bedico
Manchac
Killian
Frenier
Laplace
Goodhope
Taft
Edgard
Reserve
Gramercy
Vacherie
Convent
Lutcher
St. James
Union
Central
Burnside
Donaldsonville
Darrow
Barton
Dutchtown
St. Gabriel
Foreman
Gonzales
Brittany
Sorrento
Port Vincent
French Settlement
0 20 mi
0 20 km

and so on). What makes this statement a little misleading is that some are on one side of the Mississippi and the rest on the other. In fact, there is no great single "River Road." There is instead a pair of two-lane River Roads, one on each side of the river—generally Route 44 or 75 on the north bank and Route 18 on the south—called various names as you continue west. Just try to keep a sense of where the river is, and watch for the house signs. It's not as difficult as it may sound—these are, after all, major tourist attractions and are well marked.

Because the tour companies are on tight schedules, they usually take Interstate 10 at least part of the way into plantation territory. However, we suggest you try a slightly more scenic route: Head west out of New Orleans on River Road (also marked as Route 44 or Jefferson Highway) and stay on the north side of the Mississippi River past **Destrehan Plantation, San Francisco Plantation,** and **Houmas House.** Then cross the Sunshine Bridge (Route 70) to the southern bank of the river, taking Route 1 a bit farther west to **Nottoway Plantation** and then heading back east, mostly on Route 18 past **Oak Alley,** the newly opened **St. Joseph's** and **Laura** plantations and then back to the city.

The ideal trip would be overnight, stopping for lunch at **Nobiles** on Main Street in Lutcher near the **St. James Historical Museum**—a "village" well worth a turn off—and taking a room at **Nottoway Plantation Restaurant & Inn,** or, even better, at **Madewood** and making dinner reservations at the hot new **Latil's Landing** at **Houmas House Plantation and Gardens** (see next page).

All the plantation homes described here have been immaculately restored and are open for tours. However, if you keep your eyes open, you will see many other fine old homes that are still private residences.

The first and closest is **Destrehan Plantation** at 13034 River Road/ LA 48, just eight miles west of the airport in Kenner (☎ 985-764-9315). Built in 1787 in the French Colonial style by a free man of color, it was given its wings just after the turn of the 19th century and renovated by the next generation into a Greek Revival style. Its Doric columns, double porch, and hipped roof will look very familiar to fans of the film *Interview with the Vampire,* and many of the haunted–New Orleans tours mention sightings and even alleged photos of phantasmic shapes here. Restored in 1970, Destrehan is the oldest plantation still intact in the entire lower Mississippi valley (and the only one to have installed an elevator to take handicapped visitors upstairs). It also boasts an official document signed by Thomas Jefferson in 1804 naming Jean Noel Destrehan to the territorial council. Admission is $10 adults, $5 ages 6 to 17; open daily 9 a.m. to 4 p.m. except major holidays; for more information, consult **www.destrehanplantation.org.**

San Francisco Plantation (☎ 985-535-2341 or 888-322-1756; **www.sanfranciscoplantation.org**), on Highway 44 a little ways outside

Reserve, is an old and elaborately Gothic Creole–style home begun in the mid-1850s by a planter named Edmond Marmillion and finished in the most fantastical manner—double galleries, widow's walk, highly decorative moldings and painting, carved woodwork—by his sons, one of whom remarked at the end of the construction that he was now *sans fruscin*, or "without a penny." So the house was first called "St. Frusquin," which was eventually corrupted to "San Francisco." Its elaborate, almost paddle-wheeling look inspired the setting of Frances Parkinson Keyes's *Steamboat Gothic*. Admission: $15 adults, $7 students ages 6 to 17, age 5 and under free; open daily except major holidays. Tours every 20 minutes, 9:40 a.m. to 4:40 p.m. April through October, 9 a.m. to 4 p.m. November through March.

A couple of miles farther along Highway 44/River Road at Highway 942 is **Houmas House Plantation and Gardens** (☎504-473-9380; **www.houmashouse.com**). It was named for the Native Americans who originally owned the land and was for decades the largest sugar plantation in Louisiana, extending over 300,000 acres: at its height, it was producing 20 million pounds every year, and so was nicknamed "The Sugar Palace." The original mid-1700s plantation house had only four rooms; what looks like the main house now, the two-and-a-half-story Greek Revival mansion with columns around three sides, was begun in 1840. Built to the fancy of a South Carolinian, it, too, was a film set, in this case for the Southern Gothic thriller *Hush . . . Hush, Sweet Charlotte*, with Bette Davis. It has also supplied romantic backdrops for soap-opera diva Susan Lucci of *All My Children*. The hexagonal houses on either side, called *garçonnières*, were used by the bachelor sons of the family (*les garçons*, or "the boys") or by houseguests. Admission: $20 mansion and garden, $10 garden only; open Monday and Tuesday, 9 a.m. to 5 p.m., Wednesday through Sunday, 9 a.m. to 8 p.m.

Houmas House has a cafe with garden views serving lunch, but the fine dining at Latil's Landing, in the original 18th-century building, is rapidly becoming a destination in its own right, so reserve ahead (☎ 225-473-9380).

Retrace Highway 44 to near Tezcuco, cross the Sunshine Bridge (so named because a former Louisiana governor, Jimmy Davis, wrote the song "You Are My Sunshine") over the Mississippi River to Donaldsonville, and look right toward Frontage Street. There you'll see a famous restaurant called **Lafitte's Landing**, which burned in late 1998 but has since reopened for catered business (available only for parties or groups of six or more guests) and as a B&B (404 Claiborne Avenue; ☎ 225-473-1232). It has interest, as you may have guessed, from the name. Formerly known as the Old Viala Plantation, it was supposed to have been one of the pirate's bases. In any case, Lafitte's son and entrepreneurial successor, Jean Pierre Lafitte, married the Viala heiress.

From Lafitte's Landing, turn onto Highway 1/Mississippi River Road and head west again for about 15 miles. Near White Castle on

Highway 405 is **Nottoway Plantation Restaurant & Inn,** a spectacular and almost unique building that was called "the white castle" and so gave its name to the town. Nottoway, built in 1859 by John Hampden Randolph, is the largest plantation home in the South, a hybrid neoclassical beauty with 64 rooms, 22 enormous columns, and a series of staggered porches and bays. Inside is a spectacular all-white ballroom with hand-carved Corinthian columns, plaster friezes, and crystal chandeliers, and a surprising list of then-rare conveniences such as hot and cold running water and gas lights. As the name suggests, you can have lunch or dinner (and swim in the walled garden that once held roses), or stay overnight with breakfast and a tour tossed into the $105 to $250 room rate. Otherwise, the admission is $10, $4 kids ages 5 to 12, kids age 4 and under free; open daily except Christmas, 9 a.m. to 5 p.m. (dinner until 9 p.m.); for information call ☎ 225-545-2730 or ☎ 877-688-4376; **www.nottoway.com.** (At press time **Nottoway Plantation** was closed for renovations. Improvements may include the addition of a museum, which would increase ticket prices for tours.)

(Incidentally, when you get as far as Nottoway Plantation, you are only about another 30 miles from Baton Rouge, around which are other plantations and attractions. If you want to go on, contact the Baton Rouge Area Convention and Visitors Bureau, P.O. Box 4149, Baton Rouge, LA 70801, ☎ 225-383-1825, or **www.visitbatonrouge.com,** and ask for their tour brochures.)

Here's another option: if you have the time, or you haven't worn out yet, you could instead go south from Donaldsonville on Highway 308 to **Madewood Plantation** on Bayou Lafourche (☎ 985-369-7151; **www.madewood.com**), a widely admired 1848 Greek Revival manor whose modern travel mag–style restoration has earned it high ratings from *Travel & Leisure,* etc. (How Creole is this region? See Napoleonville just across the river.) Again, you can stay in the main house—very romantic—or the cottages and have dinner in the original dining room, cocktails and nightcaps in the parlor, and a Continental breakfast before moving on. Overnight accommodations start at about $259 (and include breakfast and dinner). Otherwise, admission is $10 adults, $6 children under 12; open daily except major holidays, 10 a.m. to 4 p.m. Incidentally, while it may not have been visible in the movie *Interview with the Vampire,* it gets at least a half-star rating: Brad Pitt used it as his headquarters.

If you prefer to head back toward New Orleans, take Highway 18 from near the Sunshine Bridge about 15 miles to the east and look for the signs to **Oak Alley Plantation** (☎ 866-231-6664 or ☎ 225-265-2151), another Greek Revival beauty whose long drive between rows of 300-year-old live oaks, which gave it its nickname, has become famous through photographs as an example of antebellum architecture. (The real name was Bon Séjour, or "pleasant sojourn.") Built in 1839, it has as many Doric columns, 28, as the oaks themselves. It stood in for the Florida governor's family home in the movie version of *Primary Colors,* and, yes, it's done *Vampire* backdrop duty. It also has several outbuildings that have been turned into overnight rooms ($95 to $175) and a restaurant open for breakfast and lunch if you just want to drive over from New Orleans. Admission is $15 adults, $7.50 children ages 13 to 18, $4.50 ages 6 to 12; kids age 5 and under free; open 9 a.m. to 5:30 p.m. daily except major holidays.

A few miles south of Oak Alley on Highway 18 is the beautifully preserved and recently restored 1805 West Indies–style plantation **Laura,** where Louisiana's multicultural heritage is even more obvious. Built by Senegalese craftsmen, it was situated on 12,000 acres deeded to a French Catholic family by the King of Spain. The house is furnished with nearly 400 original artifacts covering two centuries. The guided tour explores Southern Creole life and includes discussions of German immigrants, slave history (there are slave cabins among the historic buildings), and the particular role of women landowners. (The Laura folks claim that it was here that Joel Chandler Harris heard and recorded the adventures of "Compare (*sic*) Lapin" and transformed them into the tales of Br'er Rabbit. However, most scholars believe that Harris's character was an amalgam of three elderly cooks, particularly one known as "Uncle" George Terrell, whom Harris knew as a teenage laborer on the Turnwold Plantation in Putnam County, Georgia, during the Civil War.) Tours are also in French; call ahead for a schedule. Admission is $15 adults, $5 ages 6 to 17; open daily 10 a.m. to 5 p.m., with the last tour at 4 p.m. (all visitors to **Laura** must take the guided tour); ☎ 225-265-7690 or 888-799-7690; **www.lauraplantation.com.**

You can take Highway 18/River Road back to the intersection of Route 90, then take the Huey Long Bridge across the Mississippi back into New Orleans. Or go the other way, southwest, on Highway 18 to Route 641, cross the bridge to I-10 and go back that way.

NEW ORLEANS ATTRACTIONS

AS YOU CAN TELL FROM THE WALKING TOURS and our suggestions in Part Two, Planning Your Visit, about designing your own special-interest tour, New Orleans is a lot more, and a lot more interesting, than Bourbon Street. Some of the finest attractions, such as City Park and the New Orleans Museum of Art, the Historic New Orleans Collection, the Jackson Barracks Museum, and Longue Vue House and Gardens, are often overlooked as tourists rush to the more obvious sites. So we've tried to evaluate most of the attractions in a way that may help you choose what you want to see depending on who's in the party, what your interests are, and how in-depth you would like to get.

We begin with general information about some of the areas not already covered elsewhere, then continue with attraction profiles listed alphabetically by name. However, keep in mind that some modes of transportation—the St. Charles Avenue streetcar and the Canal Street ferry—are attractions in themselves.

THE CENTRAL BUSINESS DISTRICT

WE'VE SAID SEVERAL TIMES that you should not venture into the **St. Louis Cemetery** without a tour group or at least several friends, even during daylight hours. Officers at the New Orleans police station on North Rampart Street catty-corner from St. Louis No. 1 suggest that if you are alone or only two, you should wait near the entrance for a tour to come through and hang on the fringe.

> *unofficial* **TIP**
> Most museums are closed on state as well as federal holidays, and in New Orleans that also means Mardi Gras and frequently All Saint's Day (November 1) as well as the more familiar dates such as Christmas. Many places have group-ticket rates, so if you are traveling with more than just your immediate family, call ahead and ask about discounts. Speaking of tickets, prices have a way of inching up without warning, so carry a little extra cash or call in advance.

One way to get a truly unusual glimpse of its setting and historic role is to visit **Our Lady of Guadalupe,** which was once used as a virtual assembly line for yellow-fever victims (see the profile below). The other important site in this area, **Louis Armstrong Park** (future site of the New Orleans Jazz National Historic Park), is currently closed for massive redevelopment.

On the other side of Canal Street, toward the Superdome and Arena, there are two overlooked but rather intriguing spots that might be of special interest to some visitors. In the neutral ground on Loyola Avenue where Lafayette Avenue would dead-end is the **Cancer Survivors Memorial,** a combination of lifelike statues, a mini labyrinth for meditation, and a series of columns representing various architectural elements through history (Doric, Arabic, African, etc.). It was funded by Richard Bloch, one of the founders of H&R Block, who himself suffered from colon and lung cancer.

The otherwise severely bland **Union Passenger Terminal** a couple of blocks farther up on Loyola at Howard Avenue holds a surprising artistic gem, rather like an architectural geode. All around the walls of the waiting room are mystical, semi-abstract, graphic, and extraordinarily impressive fresco murals created in the 1950s by Conrad Albrizio, a transplanted New Yorker. It took Albrizio two years to research the panels and two more to complete them. Albrizio later said that one of the four panels evokes the Age of Exploration and the arrival of the European powers; another the Age of Colonization, specifically the building of the city and the institution of slavery; the third the Age of Conflict, including the War of 1812 and the Civil War; and the fourth called the Modern Age and alluding to the threat of atomic power and the lure of outer space.

new orleans attractions

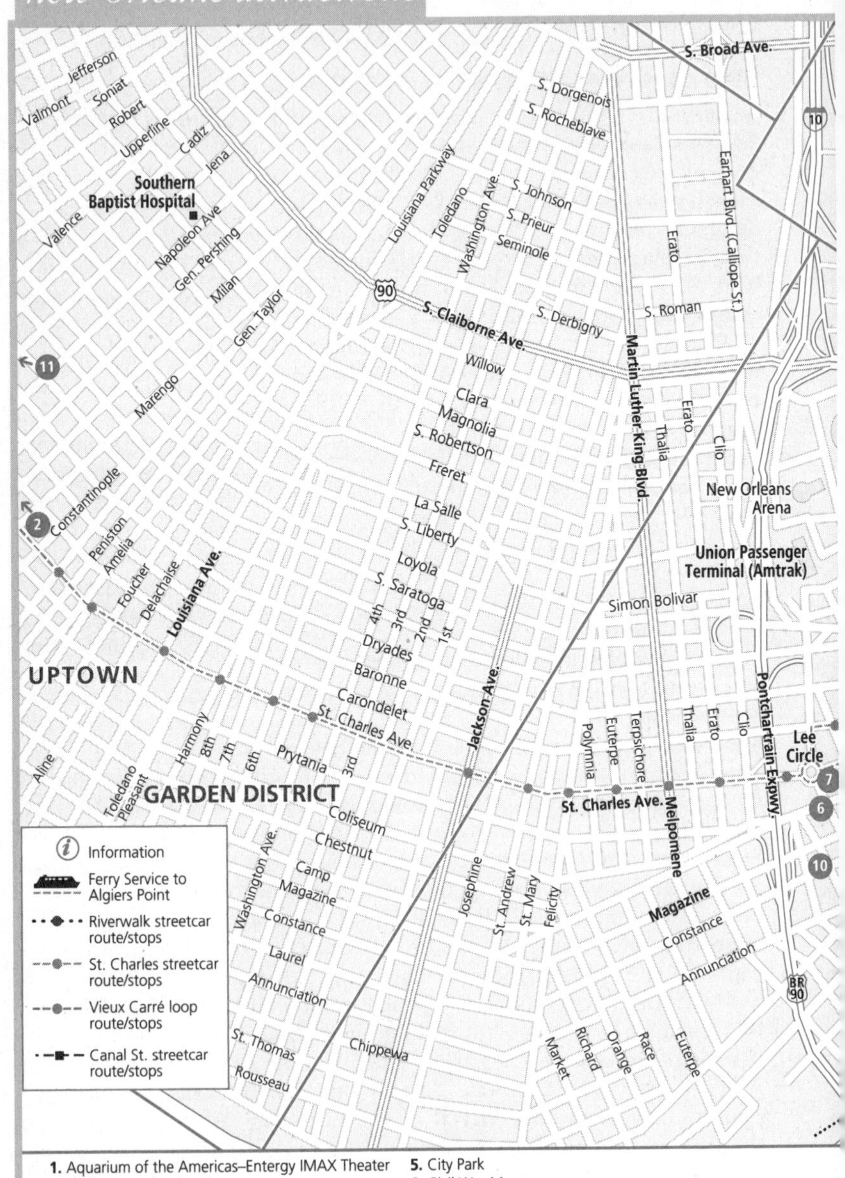

1. Aquarium of the Americas–Entergy IMAX Theater
2. Audubon Park and Zoo
3. Blaine Kern's Mardi Gras World
4. Chalmette Battlefield and National Cemetery
5. City Park
6. Civil War Museum
7. Contemporary Arts Center of New Orleans
8. Jackson Barracks Military Museum
9. Louisiana Children's Museum

N. Broad Ave.
N. Dorgenois
N. Rocheblave
N. Tonti
N. Miro
N. Galvez
N. Johnson
N. Prieur
N. Roman
Derbigny
Tulane Ave.
MID-CITY–ESPLANADE
LaFitte Ave.
Orleans Ave.
St. Ann
Dumaine
St. Phillip
Ursulines Ave.
Bayou Rd.
St. Bernard Ave.
See "Mid-City Attractions & Nightlife" Map
N. Claiborne Ave.
ST. LOUIS CEMETERY NO. 2
ST. LOUIS CEMETERY NO. 1
LOUIS ARMSTRONG PARK
N. Villere
See "French Quarter Attractions" Map
Superdome
Poydras St.
La Salle St.
Duncan Plaza
Canal
Basin St.
N. Rampart
Univ. Pl.
Conti
St. Louis
Toulouse
St. Ann
Dumaine
Burgundy
Dauphine
Barracks
Esplanade
McShane Pl.
FAUBOURG MARIGNY
Loyola Ave.
S. Rampart
O'Keefe St.
Lafayette
Gravier
Common
Union
Perdido
Iberville
Bienville
FRENCH QUARTER
Bourbon
Royal
Ursulines
Gov. Nicholls
Chartres
Decatur
French Market
Touro
Frenchmen
Elysian Fields Ave.
Marigny
Mandeville
Spain
Chartres St.
WAREHOUSE DISTRICT
CENTRAL BUSINESS DISTRICT
Carondelet
St. Charles Ave.
Lafayette Square
Julia
Girod
Poydras
Camp
Magazine St.
Tchoupitoulas
Commerce
S. Peters
Fulton
Conv. Ctr. Blvd.
St. Joseph
Howard Ave.
Calliope
RIVERWALK
World Trade Center
Mississippi River
Canal St. Ferry (Toll)
New Orleans Convention & Exhibition Center
Ernest N. Morial Convention Center
The Crescent City Connection (Toll)
ALGIERS
Morgan
Delaronde
Bermuda
Verret
Pelican
Seguin
Bouny
Powder
Lake Pontchartrain
CITY PARK
Area of detail
Superdome
0 0.25 mi
0 0.25 km

10. National World War II Museum
11. Rivertown

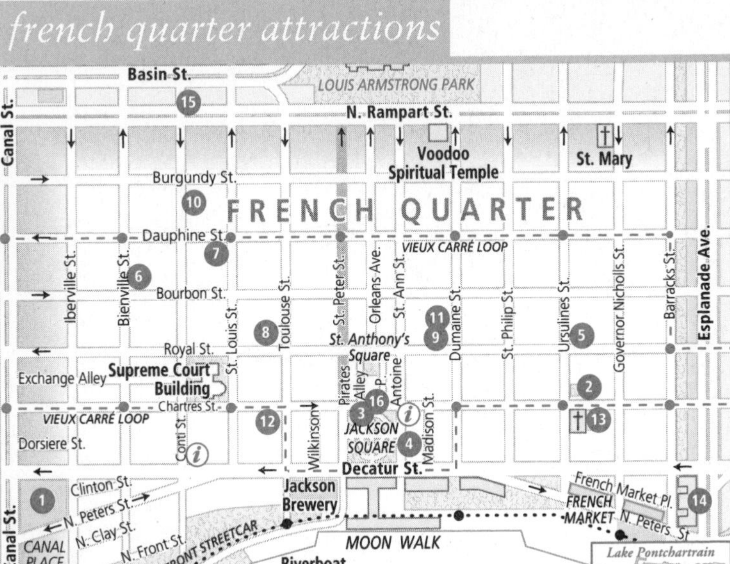

1. Audubon Insectarium
2. The Beauregard-Keyes House
3. The Cabildo and Arsenal
4. The 1850 House
5. Gallier House Museum
6. Germaine Wells Mardi Gras Museum
7. Hermann-Grima House
8. Historic New Orleans Collection
9. Madame John's Legacy
10. Musée Conti Wax Museum
11. New Orleans Historic Voodoo Museum
12. New Orleans Pharmacy Museum
13. Old Ursuline Convent–Archbishop Antoine Blanc Memorial
14. The Old U.S. Mint
15. Our Lady of Guadalupe–Shrine of St. Jude
16. The Presbytere

UPTOWN AND THE GARDEN DISTRICT

UNLESS YOU HAVE SEVERAL DAYS, are making a return trip, or have a real shopping "jones," it is unlikely you will spend much time around here. The run of Magazine Street from the Central Business District to **Audubon Park** is often touted as the new antiques center, though it is extremely drawn out; you could get off the St. Charles streetcar and walk about three blocks south (that is, turning left as you face uptown from the French Quarter). If you love stained glass, however, jump off at St. Andrew Street and walk four blocks to Constance for **St. Alphonsus,** Anne Rice's family church.

Although they do not qualify as "attractions" in the usual sense, the campuses of both **Loyola University** and **Tulane University** make for nice strolling if you happen to be in the neighborhood. They sit

mid-city attractions & nightlife

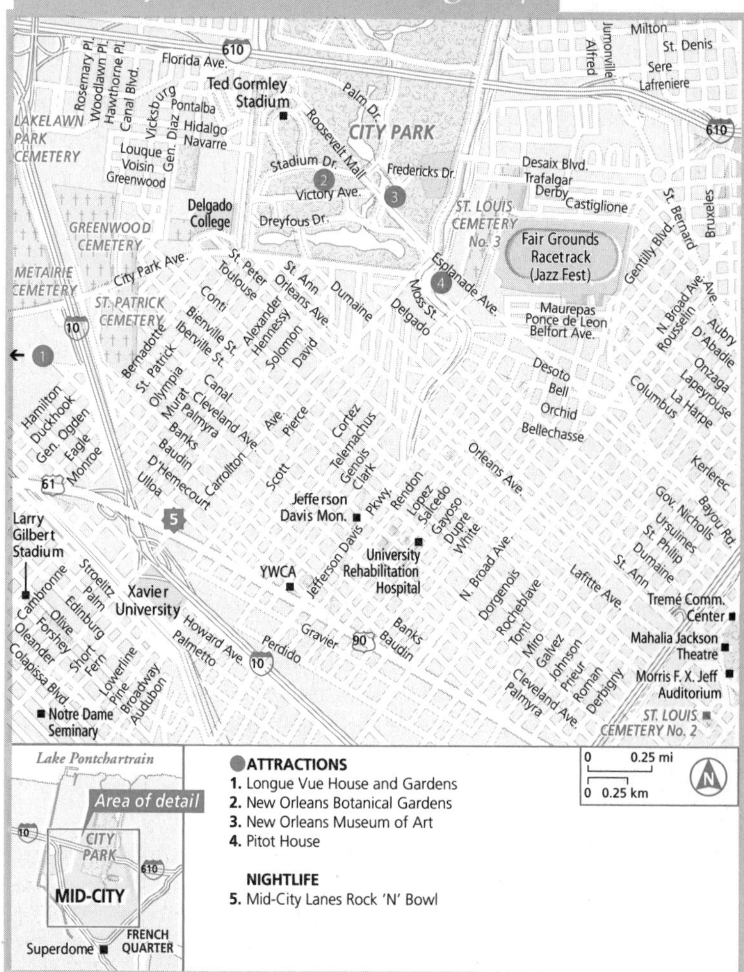

virtually side by side at streetcar stops 36 and 37 on St. Charles Avenue across from **Audubon Park**. (The statue that greets you at the entrance to Loyola, which seems to be running with its arms flung high, has been known on campus for decades as "the touchdown Jesus.") Tulane is home to the **Newcomb Art Gallery** (☎ 504-865-5328), which has a collection of Newcomb Pottery housed along with rotating exhibits and is free to the public. And there are a few Tiffany studio stained-glass windows at Tulane's **Myra Clare Rogers Memorial Chapel,** which is about four blocks off St. Charles on Audubon Place.

New Orleans Attractions by Type

TYPE & NAME	LOCATION	RATING
FUN AND CURIOSITIES		
Blaine Kern's Mardi Gras World	Algiers	★★★
Musée Conti Wax Museum	French Quarter	★★½
Rivertown	Kenner	★★★★
HISTORIC PLACES		
The Beauregard-Keyes House	French Quarter	★★★
Chalmette Battlefield and National Cemetery	Chalmette	★★★
The 1850 House	French Quarter	★½
Hermann-Grima House	French Quarter	★★★
Madame John's Legacy	French Quarter	★★★
Old Ursuline Convent/ Archbishop Antoine Blanc Memorial	French Quarter	★★½
Our Lady of Guadalupe/ Shrine of St. Jude	Central Business District	★★½
Pitot House	Mid-City/Esplanade	★★★
MUSEUMS AND CULTURE		
Aquarium of the Americas/ Entergy IMAX Theater	French Quarter	★★★★
Audubon Insectarium	French Quarter	★★★
The Cabildo and Arsenal	French Quarter	★★½
Civil War Museum	Central Business District	★★★

If you take the St. Charles Avenue streetcar out to Audubon Park, you may want to take note of a few buildings (though there are so many fine fronts that the ride itself qualifies as an attraction). At 3811 St. Charles, between Peniston and General Taylor streets, is the sweeping, double-porch-fronted **Columns Hotel** (☎ 504-899-9308) designed by architect Thomas Sully in 1883 for a wealthy tobacco merchant and used as the setting for, among other movies, *Pretty Baby*. (If you want to jump off and admire the interior, *Esquire* magazine once rated its Victorian Lounge the best bar in the city; look for the "private" room.) Across the street is **Touro Synagogue,** built in 1828 and named for Newport, Rhode Island, real-estate developer Judah Touro, who provided the funds. (Author Truman Capote was born at the nearby Touro Infirmary, also founded by the philanthropist.) At **4010 St. Charles,** between General Taylor and Constantinople streets, is the Queen Anne home Sully designed for himself. He also designed

TYPE & NAME	LOCATION	RATING
MUSEUMS AND CULTURE (CONTINUED)		
Contemporary Arts Center of New Orleans	Central Business District	★★★★
Gallier House Museum	French Quarter	★★★½
Germaine Wells Mardi Gras Museum	French Quarter	★★★
Historic New Orleans Collection	French Quarter	★★★
Jackson Barracks Museum	Chalmette	★★★★
Longue Vue House and Gardens	Near City Park	★★★★★
Louisiana Children's Museum	Central Business District	★★★★
National World War II Museum	Central Business District	★★★★★
New Orleans Historic Voodoo Museum	French Quarter	★★★
New Orleans Museum of Art	In City Park	★★★★★
New Orleans Pharmacy Museum	French Quarter	★★★
The Old U.S. Mint	French Quarter	★★★
The Presbytere	French Quarter	★★★
PARKS AND GARDENS		
Audubon Park	Uptown and the Garden District	★★★★½
Audubon Zoo	Uptown and the Garden District	★★★★★
City Park	City Park	★★★★★
Longue Vue House and Gardens	Near City Park	★★★★★
New Orleans Botanical Gardens	In City Park	★★★★

some three dozen houses along St. Charles, but unfortunately only a few remain. What is now the **New Orleans Public Library** (Latter Branch) at 5120 St. Charles (☎ 504-596-2625), between Soniat and Dufossat streets, is a fine turn-of-the-19th-century house that was home to, among others, aviator Harry Williams and his film-star wife Marguerite Clark; the reading rooms still have their ceiling murals and chandeliers. And just past the edge of the park at Walnut Street is the **Park View Guest House** (☎ 504-861-7564), an ornate Victorian that was originally built to accommodate visitors to the 1884 World Cotton Exposition in Audubon Park.

Finally, you may want to spend a few hours wandering the **Riverbend neighborhood** for a window-shopping variety as nice as the Quarter's but much less touristy. Take the St. Charles streetcar just past the big right turn onto South Carrollton Avenue (or ask for stop 44), and start strolling up and down Maple Street and then a little

New Orleans Attractions by Location

ATTRACTION	TYPE	RATING
CENTRAL BUSINESS DISTRICT		
Civil War Museum	Civil War museum	★★★
Contemporary Arts Center of New Orleans	Arts and performing arts centerl	★★★★
Louisiana Children's Museum	Children's activity center	★★★★
National World War II Museum	Military museum and veterans' memorial	★★★★★
CHALMETTE		
Chalmette Battlefield and National Cemetery	Scene of Battle of New Orleans	★★★
Jackson Barracks Museum	Military museum	★★★★
FRENCH QUARTER		
Aquarium of the Americas	Marine museum/ EntergyIMAX Theater	★★★★
Audubon Insectarium	Hands-on insect home	★★★
The Beauregard-Keyes House	Restored home of general and novelist	★★★
The Cabildo and Arsenal	Flagship of Louisiana State Museum complex	★★½
The 1850 House	Mid-19th-century apartment	★½
Gallier House Museum	Period-correct restored home	★★★½
Germaine Wells Mardi Gras Museum	Costume and jewelry collection	★★★
Hermann-Grima House	Restored Federal-style home	★★★
Historic New Orleans Collection	Complex of free exhibits	★★★
Madame John's Legacy	Part of Louisiana State Museum Complex	★★★
Musée Conti Wax Museum	History, horror, and Mardi Gras in wax	★★½

farther along Carrollton. There are fine artisan shops here, including boutiques from both Mignon Faget and Yvonne LaFleur, cafes and coffee shops, bookstores, and bars. **Brigtsen's Restaurant** (723 Dante Street; ☎ 504-861-7610) is a local favorite; it's two blocks from stop 44 (chef Frank Brigtsen is a protégé of Paul Prudhomme).

NEAR FAUBOURG MARIGNY

WE REMIND YOU AGAIN THAT CEMETERIES, as distinct a New Orleans feature as they are, can be dangerous places for solitary visitors or even small groups. However, if you are seriously intrigued by

ATTRACTION	TYPE	RATING
FRENCH QUARTER (CONTINUED)		
New Orleans Historic Voodoo Museum	Part museum/part souvenir shop	★★★
New Orleans Pharmacy Museum	Restored apothecary	★★★
The Old U.S. Mint	Part of Louisiana State Museum complex	★★★
Old Ursuline Convent/Archbishop Antoine Blanc Memorial	250-year-old religious sites, gardens, archives	★★½
Our Lady of Guadalupe–Shrine of St. Jude	Chapel of "St. Expedite"	★★½
The Presbytere	Part of Louisiana State Museum complex	★★★
KENNER		
Rivertown	Family amusement and education complex	★★★★
MID-CITY/ESPLANADE		
Pitot House	19th-century home	★★★
NEAR CITY PARK		
City Park	Municipal park	★★★★★
Longue Vue House and Gardens	Historic home, museum, gardens	★★★★★
New Orleans Botanical Gardens	Gardens and conservatory	★★★★
New Orleans Museum of Art	Fine and decorative arts	★★★★★
UPTOWN AND THE GARDEN DISTRICT		
Audubon Park	Public green, pool, playgrounds	★★★★½
Audubon Zoo	Zoo	★★★★
WEST BANK (ALGIERS)		
Blaine Kern's Mardi Gras World	Mardi Gras floats and costumes	★★★

the offbeat, stop by **St. Roch Cemetery** (☎ 504-945-5961) at Derbigny Street and St. Roch Avenue, modeled on Campo Santo dei Tedeschi near the Vatican in Rome. The story begins with the French-born St. Roch (or Rocco) who, at the beginning of the 14th century, gave away all his possessions and turned to nursing victims of the plague, often curing them by making the sign of the cross. When he himself fell ill, he was kept alive by a dog who brought him food (he's the patron saint of dog lovers); nevertheless, he was so altered that when he went home he was thrown into prison (he's also the patron of prisoners). Visited in his cell by an angel for five years, he finally died there. In Europe,

"VSR" ("*Vive St. Roch*") was often carved over doorways to ward off disease.

When yellow fever broke out in 1861 (and again in 1868), Father Thevis of nearby **Holy Trinity Church** prayed to St. Roch, promising to build a monument with his own hands if the saint would intercede. The epidemic ended, and Father Thevis built this little chapel, which is now absolutely crammed with prostheses, crutches, glass eyes, plastic body parts, and bandages from those who have come here praying for recovery from their injuries. What you see is just what's arrived recently; there are hundreds of such offerings in storage.

ATTRACTION PROFILES

Aquarium of the Americas–Entergy IMAX Theater ★★★★★

APPEAL BY AGE PRESCHOOL ★★★ GRADE SCHOOL ★★★★ TEENS ★★★★ YOUNG ADULTS ★★★★ OVER 30 ★★★ SENIORS ★★★

Along the Mississippi riverfront at the foot of Canal Street; ☎ 504-581-IMAX or 800-774-7394; www.auduboninstitute.org French Quarter

Type of attraction A state-of-the-art interactive marine museum with a good mix of science and fun. **Admission** Aquarium alone: $17.50 adults, $13 seniors, $10.50 kids ages 2–12. IMAX alone: $8.50 adults, $7.50 seniors, $5.50 kids age 12 and under. Combination tickets: $22.50 adults, $17.50 seniors, $12.50 children. Additional discount tickets available for aquarium-zoo packages, aquarium-insectarium packages, zoo-aquarium-IMAX packages, and more. **Hours** Aquarium: Tuesday–Sunday, 10 a.m.–4 p.m.; IMAX (shows every hour): Tuesday–Sunday, 10 a.m.–5 p.m. **When to go** Early, if not to see it before it gets crowded, at least to get timed tickets for later in the day, when the air-conditioning may be welcome. **Special comments** Of the 1990s generation of marine installations, very pleasant and user friendly, and a best bet for mixed-age groups. **How much time to allow** At least 1 hour for the aquarium, even if you have restless children; 2 hours for IMAX, counting standing in line.

DESCRIPTION AND COMMENTS It's hard to go wrong here unless you are so blasé that you can't get a thrill out of stroking the tough suede skin of a small sand shark (one of the most popular queues) or of marveling at the beautiful, transparent, and snowflake-complex bodies of lacy jellyfish, one of the more astounding exhibits. The museum houses several large permanent exhibits, including a multilevel, multispecies Amazon rain forest, a penguin house, Caribbean reef and Mississippi River environments, and a 400,000-gallon saltwater mini–Gulf of Mexico with 14-foot-tall glass walls and all the sharks and stingrays any kid could desire. The IMAX rotates at least two movies a day, many on historical or environmental themes (even if they are sometimes the Disney version); a few viewers may find the super-realistic wide-angle photography (and sometimes 3-D effects) dizzying. Though it has no

3-D effects, the *Hurricane on the Bayou* film, begun before Katrina but with some real and re-created footage added after, is very moving.

TOURING TIPS Wear comfortable shoes with no-slip soles; although the ramps in and out of various environments are not slick, you may be distracted by all that's going on around you. This is a nice spot to meet in the afternoon if the party wants to split up during the day, because you can buy timed IMAX tickets in advance. Another fact worth noting in a city as old and often inconvenient as New Orleans, everything is wheelchair accessible.

Audubon Insectarium ★★★

APPEAL BY AGE PRESCHOOL ★★★ GRADE SCHOOL ★★★ TEENS ★★★
YOUNG ADULTS ★★★ OVER 30 ★★★ SENIORS ★★

423 Canal Street in the old U.S. Customs House; ☎ 504-246-5672 or 800-774-7394; www.auduboninstitute.org French Quarter

Type of attraction Hands-on insect home and "cafe." **Admission** $15 adults, $12 seniors, $10 children 2–12. **Hours** Tuesday–Sunday, 10 a.m.–6 p.m. **When to go** Anytime. **Special comments** This may have a "yuck" factor for some, but most people seem to find at least part of it fascinating. **How much time to allow** 1–2 hours.

DESCRIPTION AND COMMENTS Insects may be the name, but not the only game, as spiders, worms, and centipedes get plenty of face time here. There are some see-through exhibits (ant farms, for example), colorful displays (butterflies and oversize flies), boxes of critters well camouflaged in their surroundings, quizzes, a little 3-D film fun, and some rather silly name-association jokes, such as one of Disney's Love Bugs. Not surprisingly, given the long local battle with termites, they are the subject of a full room of exhibits. (Ditto the mosquito, which carried so many of the city's fatal plagues.) And that indomitable dinosaur, the roach, gets quite a bit of coverage as well. But although it's clearly expected that kids will be the main audience, adults with any attention span will be amazed at some of the "detail" of this natural artwork.

TOURING TIPS The more squeamish members of the party should avoid the Bug Appetit Café, where local chefs dish up grasshopper herb dip, chocolate "chirp" cookies (with crickets), deep-fried worms, and the like. The Tiny Termite Café in the gift shop has more ordinary snacks, plus beeswax and honey-based cosmetics, butterfly-embroider bags, jewelry, etc.

Audubon Park ★★★★½

APPEAL BY AGE PRESCHOOL ★★★ GRADE SCHOOL ★★★ TEENS ★★★
YOUNG ADULTS ★★★★★ OVER 30 ★★★★ SENIORS ★★★

Entrances at 6800–7000 St. Charles Avenue and 6500 Magazine Street; ☎ 504-581-4629 Uptown and the Garden District

Type of attraction Public green and pedestrian retreat with riding stables, conservatory, playgrounds, golf course, bandstands, soccer fields, and jogging path. **Admission** Free. **Hours** 6 a.m.–10 p.m. **When to go** Anytime except after dark, no matter what the signs say. **Special comments** One of the reasons to choose to stay in the Garden District instead of the French Quarter; not quite as fine a facility as City Park but very close. If you're staying in town long enough to seek out exercise and recreation, this is prime; even a jog or an hour's reading in one of the shady gazebos can be an essential break for a visiting executive. **How much time to allow** Varies by activity.

DESCRIPTION AND COMMENTS This is the classic ideal of a public green, built on what was originally a sugar plantation (in the very beginning, it belonged to the Sieur de Bienville himself) and which still boasts live oaks from before the city's founding, along with magnolias, lagoons, formal plantings, hothouse flowers (the Heymann Memorial Conservatory), benches, and trails. The 365-acre park was laid out in the 1890s by John Olmstead, son of the architect of New York's Central Park, after the Cotton Exposition of 1884 (which introduced the streetcar) was held there. Cars are prohibited around the St. Charles end, so you can wander without fear. Across the railroad tracks toward the Mississippi is the less-publicized area called River View, popular for picnics or jogging. For more on the sport and exercise facilities, see Part Ten, Exercise and Recreation.

TOURING TIPS Most of the more organized activities and the zoo are at the Magazine Street end of the park. It's a fairly long walk from St. Charles Avenue if you're only trying to get from here to there, but the zoo operates a shuttle van from St. Charles around to the parking lot.

kids Audubon Zoo ★★★★★

APPEAL BY AGE PRESCHOOL ★★★ GRADE SCHOOL ★★★★ TEENS ★★★
YOUNG ADULTS ★★★★ OVER 30 ★★★ SENIORS ★★★

6500 Magazine Street in Audubon Park; ☎ 866-ITS-A-ZOO or 866-581-4629; www.audubon institute.org **Uptown and the Garden District**

Type of attraction Popular and professionally acclaimed zoological park with naturalistic environments, hands-on exhibits, a tropical-bird house, live-animal feedings, and more. **Admission** $12.50 adults, $9.50 seniors, $7.50 kids ages 2–12. **Hours** Tuesday–Sunday 10 a.m.–4 p.m. daily (ticket booths close at 4 p.m.). **When to go** Anytime. **Special comments** Extremely well designed and stocked, with huge family appeal. **How much time to allow** 2–3 hours.

DESCRIPTION AND COMMENTS There are nearly 2,000 animals here, many of them rare or endangered species, in carefully re-created environments such as the 6.5-acre Louisiana Swamp, crisscrossed with boardwalks so you can spy on the white alligators. It's only a short stroll to other continents, however: the Asian Domain, with its Indian temple, rhinos, elephants, and a white tiger; the African Savannah; the South American pampas; the primate house . . . well, you get the idea. For kids of the *Jurassic Park* generation, there's good info on dinosaurs, a group of "living dinosaurs," namely Komodo dragons, and so on. And all around, the keepers offer chances to stroke or feed the tamer animals.

TOURING TIPS The Cypress Knee Café has great food. The number of steps and escalators in the park may make you wish you hadn't brought the stroller; piggybacking may save some trouble.

The Beauregard-Keyes House ★★★

APPEAL BY AGE PRESCHOOL – GRADE SCHOOL ★★ TEENS ★★★
YOUNG ADULTS ★★★ OVER 30 ★★★ SENIORS ★★★★

1113 Chartres Street; between Ursulines and Governor Nicholls streets; ☎ 504-523-7257 French Quarter

Type of attraction Restored 19th-century raised cottage and former residence of General P. G. T. Beauregard and novelist Frances Parkinson Keyes, with personal effects and open gardens. **Admission** $5 adults, $4 seniors and students, $2 kids ages 6–12, kids age 5 and under free. **Hours** Monday–Saturday, 10 a.m.–3 p.m.; tours are given on the hour. **When to go** Anytime. **How much time to allow** No more than an hour, including guided tour and stroll around the gardens.

DESCRIPTION AND COMMENTS This is a lovely old home, even without its many historical connections. It was built in 1826 in raised-cottage style with a lovely twin staircase, Doric columns, and elegant side gallery. The formal gardens probably date back to the 1830s, when it belonged to the Swiss consul. It was a boardinghouse during the Civil War, and when Confederate general and native son Pierre Gustave Toutant Beauregard returned to the area, his own plantation in ruins, he and several members of his family lodged there for about 18 months. It was almost demolished in the 1920s, but a group of ladies lobbied for its restoration, and in 1944 the novelist Frances Parkinson Keyes (rhymes with "eyes") moved in and began meticulous reconstruction, eventually turning the big house over to a charitable foundation and living in the rear cottage, also part of the tour. Many of the furnishings and personal effects belonged to Beauregard. The gift shop has copies of most of Keyes's books, many of them historical novels dealing with Creole society and the house itself.

TOURING TIPS Like many New Orleans homes, this is strictly a guided tour, with costumed docents. But now that PBS has made *The Civil War* so lively again, even students may find Beauregard's old study intriguing. The gardens make for a nice respite as well.

kids Blaine Kern's Mardi Gras World ★★★

APPEAL BY AGE PRESCHOOL ★★★ GRADE SCHOOL ★★★ TEENS ★★★★
YOUNG ADULTS ★★★★ OVER 30 ★★★ SENIORS ★★★

233 Newton Street (across the river from the World Trade Center); ☎ 504-361-7821 or 800-362-8213; www.mardigrasworld.com Algiers

Type of attraction Year-round factory of flamboyant Mardi Gras floats and costumes. **Admission** $17.50 adults, $13.50 seniors and students with school

ID, $10.50 children ages 4–11. **Hours** Daily, 9:30 a.m.–4:30 p.m.; last tour 4:30 p.m. **When to go** Anytime. **Special comments** One of the four major year-round ways to experience Mardi Gras, and a surefire kids' favorite, especially combined with the free ferry ride. **How much time to allow** 1.5–2 hours.

DESCRIPTION AND COMMENTS Blaine Kern is known as "Mr. Mardi Gras," and for good reason. He made his first float in 1947 at the age of 19 and since then has become probably the busiest float maker in the world. He is responsible for not only more than half of the floats and multistory-sized figures for Mardi Gras, which brings in a reported $20 million a year alone, but also for Macy's Thanksgiving Day parade, the Bastille Day celebrations in Cannes, France, and more than 40 other parades around the world. This factory even makes sculptures and props for Disney. The sculpture company was founded right before the 1984 World's Fair in New Orleans to build the giant characters for that event, and now works for amusement parks all over the world. These huge warehouses, more than 500,000 square feet of them, called "dens," are filled with props, celebrity statues, royal regalia, and the artists creating them; you can even dress in costume and have your picture taken alongside one of the characters.

TOURING TIPS Take the Canal Street Ferry across and look for the shuttle bus. For older visitors, the architecture of the Algiers neighborhood may hold some interest, and the area near the ferry has several churches and buildings of historic interest, but it is still not a great area to walk around late in the day. *Note:* At press time, Kern was planning to build a new and larger Mardi Gras World along the river at the end of Convention Center Boulevard.

The Cabildo and Arsenal ★★½

APPEAL BY AGE	PRESCHOOL –	GRADE SCHOOL ★★	TEENS ★★
YOUNG ADULTS ★★★	OVER 30 ★★★	SENIORS ★★★	

On Chartres Street facing Jackson Square; ☎ 504-568-6968 or 800-568-6968; lsm.crt.state.la.us French Quarter

Type of attraction Flagship building of the Louisiana State Museum complex in the city. Entrance to the Arsenal, which only occasionally has exhibits, is through the Cabildo. **Admission** $6 adults; $5 seniors, students, and active military; kids age 12 and under free. **Hours** Tuesday–Sunday, 9 a.m.–5 p.m., closed all legal holidays. **When to go** Anytime. **Special comments** Check at the front desk for information on changing exhibits or exhibits in the Arsenal. Not terribly engaging and sometimes stiffly explained, but if you skim through, picking up the more intriguing exhibits, particularly some of the more subtle folk-art pieces, it's mildly entertaining. **How much time to allow** 30–60 minutes.

DESCRIPTION AND COMMENTS This is not a very hands-on museum, and compared with the new-generation facilities, it can be rather dry; you will probably find yourself skimming through unless you stop to watch videos. But there are a few particular exhibits that may hold even a child's attention, such as the Native American pirogue; weapons and uniforms from the Civil War and the Battle of New Orleans; that apocryphal symbol of slavery, the cotton gin; a lock of Andy Jackson's hair; antique medical tools, including a leech jar; a young child's casket; and Napoleon's death mask, sporting a dark and surprisingly philosophical visage unfamiliar from the typical portraits. African Americans and Native Americans may find the exhibits devoted to their contributions a little stiff but well intentioned. The building itself has historical significance: the official transfer of the Louisiana Territory from France to the United States was signed here, and since it also housed the State Supreme Court from 1868 to 1910, it saw the arguing of several famous legal cases, including *Plessy v. Ferguson.*

TOURING TIPS The Cabildo is wheelchair accessible and even offers wheelchairs for use; visitors with other disabilities should check in at the front counter for assistance.

Chalmette Battlefield and National Cemetery ★★★

APPEAL BY AGE PRESCHOOL – GRADE SCHOOL ★★ TEENS ★★ YOUNG ADULTS ★★★ OVER 30 ★★★ SENIORS ★★★

8606 St. Bernard Highway; ☎ 504-589-2133; www.nps.gov/jela
Chalmette

Type of attraction Scene of the Battle of New Orleans, Jackson's famous victory over the British in 1815. **Admission** Free. **Hours** Daily 9 a.m.–4:30 p.m., closed Christmas Day. **When to go** January 7–8 to see battle reenactment; otherwise anytime. **Special comments** Although the car gate closes at 4:30 p.m., there is a pedestrian entry near the cemetery. Admittedly, battlefields (and military cemeteries) don't appeal to everyone, but if you do find wandering such grounds moving, this is an unusually reassuring and well-marked route. It's an unalloyed, Hollywood-cheerful victory, not a haunting experience like revisiting Antietam, for example. And you can't beat the scenery. **How much time to allow** 1–2 hours. *Note:* At press time, the visitor center was still being reconstructed, but the Beauregard House had weathered the hurricanes like the aristocrat it is.

DESCRIPTION AND COMMENTS The bare bones of this battle, so to speak, are familiar to most Americans, by film and pop-music history, if nothing else. Here, on January 8, 1815, British forces under Lieutenant General Edward Pakenham, brother-in-law of the great Duke of Wellington, were crushed (and Pakenham killed) by the ragtag coalition of Tennessee volunteers, other Southern regiments hustled down for support, free men of color, and Barataria pirates under the able and often-ruthless Andrew Jackson. More than 2,000 British were killed on that last day (there had been skirmishes since before Christmas), but only 13 Americans were lost, all but 2 of them black. The other ironies are almost as well known: The Treaty of Ghent, ending the war, had been signed on Christmas Eve, making the battle moot; Jackson made several errors in judgment that might easily have thrown the victory the other way; and Jackson, who had unsuccessfully tried to persuade President Jefferson to name him governor of Louisiana, wound up far more famous as a result of the battle—the city threw him a triumphal parade modeled on those of the conquering Caesars—which was in effect the first great stroke of his own presidential campaign. It also marked a great turning point in the city's history, uniting Creoles and Americans (and pirates) against a common threat. The annual reenactment is highly theatrical, beginning the night before with staged spying on Pakenham and Jackson. Oddly, the adjoining Chalmette National Cemetery dates from the Civil War and holds only two veterans of the Battle of New Orleans; most of the other bodies, some 14,000 of them, are Union soldiers.

TOURING TIPS You can just drive past the landmarks, but the Beauregard House, once the plantation home of René Beauregard, son of the general, holds good exhibits that help you understand the battle's waves, your choice of a 15-minute or half-hour film, and well-informed rangers. Be sure to walk over to the levee and look onto the Mississippi River.

kids City Park ★★★★★

APPEAL BY AGE PRESCHOOL ★★★ GRADE SCHOOL ★★★★★ TEENS ★★★ YOUNG ADULTS ★★★★★ OVER 30 ★★★★★ SENIORS ★★★

1 Palm Drive off I-10 (City Park/Metairie exit); ☎ 504-482-4888; www.neworleanscitypark.com Mid-City–Esplanade

Type of attraction Municipal park with a variety of recreational and cultural attractions. **Admission** Park free; museum, botanical gardens, and some recreational centers have fees. **Hours** Sunrise to sunset. **When to go** Anytime. **How much time to allow** 1–4 hours.

DESCRIPTION AND COMMENTS This is an unrivaled family venue, with attractions for kids, jocks, picnickers, nature lovers, and general romantics. It's also an extraordinary municipal gift—1,500 acres from the old Allard Plantation. It was presented to the city by John McDonogh, whose statue stands in Lafayette Square, and is home to the largest stand of mature live oaks in the world (though many were damaged by Katrina). City Park has an almost unequaled variety of recreational facilities, golf courses, tennis courts, batting cages, riding stables, lagoons, etc., plus a bandstand (the Beatles played here in 1964), the New Orleans Museum of Art, the Botanical Gardens, the new Sculpture Garden (moved from the old K&B Plaza on Lee Circle) with its $25 million worth of Henry Moore, George Segal, et al., and the famous Dueling Oak beneath which hundreds of formal duels were fought during the 19th century. The park also has many simpler attractions, including Storyland, an old-fashioned but swell children's fairyland where kids can climb over, around, and into the larger-than-life storybook exhibits (created by Mardi Gras float king Blaine Kern) and hear the out-loud stories straight from the "books' " mouths. *Child* magazine calls this one of the top ten playgrounds in the United States. Next door is Carousel Gardens, known to locals as The Flying Horses, one of the few surviving carved wooden merry-go-rounds in the country. And beyond that are a kid-scaled Ferris wheel, miniature trains, bumper cars, a roller coaster, and so on. The train, a G-scale track with perhaps 100 engines, cars, and streetcars, runs along a replica of the city complete with miniatures of St. Louis Cathedral and Jackson's Statue, typical Garden District and Carrollton houses, Metairie Cemetery monuments, even a paddle-wheeler steamboat. *Note:* At press time, the larger miniature train, the one youngsters can sit on, was open again, but on weekends only.

TOURING TIPS From the end of November through end of December, millions of tiny lights are strung among the trees, and the Carousel and train stay lighted and alive into the evening. Long lines of locals make this an annual holiday event. That's the beloved P. G. T. Beauregard at the front gate. Also be sure to notice the Works Progress Administration (WPA) symbols, chisels, hammers, and so on, worked into the iron of the bridges around the grounds.

Civil War Museum at Confederate Memorial Hall ★★★

APPEAL BY AGE PRESCHOOL – GRADE SCHOOL ★ TEENS ★★
YOUNG ADULTS ★★★★ OVER 30 ★★★★ SENIORS ★★★★★

929 Camp Street, at Howard Avenue; ☎ 504-523-4522; www.confederatemuseum.com **Central Business District**

Type of attraction Traditional but unusually large and somber Civil War museum. **Admission** $5, $4 students and seniors, $2 kids age 12 and under. **Hours** Wednesday–Saturday, 10 a.m.–4 p.m. **When to go** Anytime. **Special comments** At press time the museum was closed for renovations; check the above Web site for updates. **How much time to allow** 1.5 hours.

DESCRIPTION AND COMMENTS "Everybody thinks it's a church, but it's not," says the staffer about this medievally somber shrine to the Glorious Cause, the oldest Civil War museum in the country. Homegrown architect Thomas Sully designed it as a complement to the Romanesque Howard Memorial Library next door (itself being renovated for the Ogden Museum of Southern Art, as noted in the walking tour of the Warehouse District), and it looks every bit the sepulcher—as it surely must have in 1893 when 50,000 mourners came to pay respects to the body of Jefferson Davis. There's no substitute for artifacts in a museum: that ineffable dignity that lingers in objects handled by long-dead humans suffuses the most sophisticated installation, and in such items the museum, also known as Confederate Memorial Hall, is rich indeed. Its collection, the second largest in the country, turns arms and armaments into an eloquent commentary on the social impact of the war on men and women alike. Among the most moving items are the frock coats worn by generals Beauregard and Braxton Bragg, whose physical slightness provides a poignant counterpoint to the magnitude of the conflict; the modest headgear of one Landon Creek, who survived seven battles and three wounds to make it to his 15th birthday; a pair of boots, long interred with its owner and now on eerie, empty display; a child's Zouave-style jacket from Marshall Field's, a high-fashion flirtation with rebellion; and part of Lee's battlefield silver. Among the women honored here are those who resisted the occupation of "Beast" Butler's troops by spitting or recoiling in their presence.

TOURING TIPS Street parking available.

Contemporary Arts Center of New Orleans ★★★★

APPEAL BY AGE PRESCHOOL ½ GRADE SCHOOL ★★ TEENS ★★★ YOUNG ADULTS ★★★★ OVER 30 ★★★★ SENIORS ★★★★

900 Camp Street, at St. Joseph Street; ☎ 504-528-3805; www.cacno.org Central Business District

Type of attraction Multidisciplinary performing-arts complex. **Admission** to gallery $5 adults, $3 seniors and students, free for children 15 and under. Performance ticket prices vary. Gallery hours Thursday–Sunday, 11 a.m.–4 p.m. **When to go** After lunchtime on weekdays to avoid school groups. **How much time to allow** 1–1.5 hours.

DESCRIPTION AND COMMENTS The CAC's gallery spaces total 10,000 square feet and rotate about every two to three months. with international as well as national and local artists' exhibits. It also includes spaces for theatrical, musical, and dance performances, as well as some cutting-edge performance art. Call for a schedule of events. That's the upside. The slight downside is that this somewhat-raw, accessible renovated warehouse can be very loud when groups of school kids come in.

TOURING TIPS Street parking available.

The 1850 House ★½

APPEAL BY AGE PRESCHOOL – GRADE SCHOOL ★ TEENS ★ YOUNG ADULTS ★★ OVER 30 ★★ SENIORS ★★

In the Pontalba Apartments at 523 St. Ann Street facing Jackson Square; ☎ 504-568-6968 or 800-568-6968; lsm.crt.state.la.us French Quarter

Type of attraction Mid-19th-century middle-class apartment with period furnishings. **Admission** $3 adults; $2 seniors, students, and active military; kids age 12 and under free. **Hours** Tuesday–Sunday, 9 a.m.–5 p.m. **When to go** Anytime, though this might qualify as rainy-day stuff. **Special comments** One of the most intriguing things about these apartments is that they are still occupied, and there's still a waiting list. Also note the Spring Fiesta Association house at 826 St. Ann Street; open during the annual Spring Fiesta, but at other times by appointment only for group tours of 10 or more people (☎ 504-581-1367). **How much time to allow** 15–20 minutes.

DESCRIPTION AND COMMENTS This is a sort of single museum exhibit expanded over several stories, a real-sized dollhouse in a way. If you are not curious about the evolution of American social customs, you may not get much out of it; what's more, it's oddly chilly—less palpably lived-in than the Hermann-Grima and Gallier houses (see profiles following). Some of its antiques, particularly the rococo revival bedroom furniture and the rare complete 75-piece set of Vieux Paris tableware will be very significant to some and merely pretty to others. What is intriguing is the apartments' history: Baroness Micaela Almonester de Pontalba, daughter of the Spanish grandee who rebuilt the Presbytere, Cabildo, and Cathedral after the great fires of the late 18th century, had survived not merely the financial shenanigans of her husband (and cousin), who fleeced her, but an attempted assassination by his father. Restored to her independence, she wanted both to transform the square from a military-parade ground into a European-style public plaza and to improve the value of her land in the declining old city. She went through several of New Orleans's best architects, including James Gallier Sr. and Henry Howard, and micromanaged the contractors who survived (if you see the portraits of the baroness in the Presbytere, you won't be surprised); but the row houses were ultimately a great success, 16 on each side and all with storefronts on the sidewalk level, just as they are today. Note the cartouche with the entwined *A* and *P*—for Almonester de Pontalba—in the balcony railing.

The apartments did eventually become fairly run-down, but were restored by massive WPA projects. The State of Louisiana owns the Lower Pontalbas (the side including the 1850 House), and the city owns the Upper Pontalbas.

TOURING TIPS This museum is not wheelchair accessible, and the rather steep and narrow stairs may be difficult for older or physically limited visitors. The booklet given to visitors for the self-guided tour offers a great deal of information about the original facilities and decoration.

Gallier House Museum ★★★½

APPEAL BY AGE	PRESCHOOL –	GRADE SCHOOL ★	TEENS ★
YOUNG ADULTS ★★	OVER 30 ★★★	SENIORS ★★★	

1132 Royal Street, between Ursulines and Governor Nicholls streets; ☎ 504-525-5661; www.hgghh.org French Quarter

Type of attraction Period-correct restoration of the house designed by prominent architect James Gallier Jr. for his own family. **Admission** $10 adults, $8 seniors and students, kids under age 8 free; $18 adults and $15 seniors and students includes **admission** to both Gallier and Hermann-Grima houses. **Hours** Monday, Tuesday, Thursday, Friday, 10 a.m.–3 p.m. (tours begin at 10, 11, noon, 2, and 3); Saturday noon–4 p.m. (last tour begins at 3 p.m.). **When to go** Anytime, although unlike most historic houses, it's difficult in the rain because you have to go along the upstairs gallery. **Special comments** Particularly interesting because Gallier designed so many more elaborate homes in the Garden District for American patrons. His aesthetic is both gracious and clever, crammed full of fine architectural and decorative detailing. **How much time to allow** 30–45 minutes.

DESCRIPTION AND COMMENTS This is one of the most meticulously correct restorations in town, partly because Gallier's own designs and notes have been preserved. Though perhaps not as wealthy as many of his patrons, Gallier would certainly qualify as comfortably well-off. His house was very up-to-date in many ways—the chandeliers were gas-burning, the bathroom had hot running water, and the whole house had a sort of primitive air-conditioning system with vents and ice-cooled air—but it is also revealing about customs of the times, with its servants' quarters, dish pantry, summer matting versus winter carpets, children's sickroom, high brick garden walls, etc. The faux painting of the cypress to resemble pine is also very characteristic. The decorative molding and plasterwork, gilded capitals, 12-foot ceilings, marble, and paneling are very fine, and the docents here are extremely knowledgeable about the entire inventory. The work on outbuildings continues. Be sure to admire the carriage in the alley between the two buildings.

TOURING TIPS Not truly wheelchair accessible, but not impossible.

Germaine Wells Mardi Gras Museum ★★★

APPEAL BY AGE PRESCHOOL ★ GRADE SCHOOL ★★ TEENS ★★
YOUNG ADULTS ★★★ OVER 30 ★★★ SENIORS ★★

Upstairs at Arnaud's Restaurant, 813 Bienville Street, between Bourbon and Dauphine streets; ☎ 504-523-0611 or 866-230-8895; www.arnauds.com/museum.html French Quarter

Type of attraction Costume and jewelry collection. **Admission** Free. **Hours** When restaurant is open. Restaurant hours 6 p.m.–10 p.m., daily; Sunday brunch, 10 a.m.–2:30 p.m. **When to go** Anytime. **Special comments** These elaborate his-and-her gowns speak volumes about the lost sophistication of old New Orleans. As a fast, free diversion, it's hard to beat. **How much time to allow** 20 minutes.

DESCRIPTION AND COMMENTS The family of restaurateur Arnaud Cazenave, and particularly his daughter, Germaine Cazenave Wells, were mainstays of the old-society Carnival for decades; Germaine alone reigned as queen of nearly two dozen balls, more than anyone else in history. Her collection of royal outfits and jewelry, many of them astonishingly luxurious and accompanied by pictures of the corresponding ball, has been rescued and placed in glass cases in a pretty but simple wing. When you find the spangled gown she wore as the 1954 Queen of Naiades, tip your hat: she loved the gown so much she was buried in a replica of it. A small case outside displays some of her almost equally exuberant Easter bonnets.

TOURING TIPS The costumes are fragile, so the air-conditioning is often turned up pretty high.

Hermann-Grima House ★★★

APPEAL BY AGE PRESCHOOL – GRADE SCHOOL ★ TEENS ★★
YOUNG ADULTS ★★★ OVER 30 ★★★ SENIORS ★★★

820 St. Louis Street between Bourbon and Dauphine streets; ☎ 504-525-5661; www.hgghh.org French Quarter

Type of attraction Beautifully restored home from the early Federal period, with unusually extensive outbuildings. **Admission** $10 adults, $8 seniors and students, kids under age 8 free; $18 adults, $15 seniors and students for combined ticket to Gallier House. **Hours** Monday, Tuesday, Thursday, Friday, 10 a.m.–3 p.m., Saturday, noon–4 p.m. (last tour leaves at 3 p.m. on all days). **When to go** Anytime. **Special comments** Every Thursday from October through May, there are special cooking demonstrations in the rear kitchen; ask at the ticket counter in the carriage house. **How much time to allow** 45 minutes–1 hour.

DESCRIPTION AND COMMENTS This is an unusual home in that it represents the style of the so-called Golden Age of New Orleans, meaning the first great commercial boom under U.S. administration. Though it's usually hard to get younger people interested in old homes, the peculiarities of this one—the shared bathroom, the outdoor kitchens, the young woman's furnishings—make it more accessible than most. The house was built in 1831 for a wealthy merchant named Samuel Hermann. It was constructed in the Federal style, with a central doorway and divided rooms rather than the 18th-century side-hall style; the exterior plaster is scored to look like brick, which was very expensive and showy. (Much of the decorative work was produced by free men of color whose craft was then flourishing in New Orleans.) The house was sold in 1844 to Judge Felix Grima, whose family remained there for five generations. The period furniture is very fine. The master bedroom actually faces the street and has a pocket-door opening to the middle hall and second bedroom for ventilation. The long garden, outbuildings for cooking and household work, and even the original carriage house (the one used for tickets and souvenirs was attached to the house next door) are finely restored. There are special black-history tours available throughout February or year-round for groups of ten or more.

TOURING TIPS Although there is no elevator, the courtyard and lower-floor rooms are sufficiently intriguing that even those with wheelchairs or walking limitations will enjoy it.

Historic New Orleans Collection ★★★

APPEAL BY AGE PRESCHOOL – GRADE SCHOOL ★ TEENS ★★
YOUNG ADULTS ★★★★ OVER 30 ★★★★ SENIORS ★★★

533 Royal Street between Toulouse and St. Louis streets;
☎ 504-523-4662; www.hnoc.org French Quarter

Type of attraction A complex of free exhibits, a late-18th-century residence, and a 19th-century residence remodeled for 1940s society. **Admission** Williams galleries, free; Williams residence and Louisiana History Galleries in the Merieult House, $5. **Hours** Tuesday–Sunday, 10 a.m.–4:30 p.m.; excluding holidays. **When to go** Anytime, but calling ahead is recommended. **Special comments** If you want to get a flavor of the social, cultural, and historical evolution of New Orleans, this is *the* tour to take. **How much time to allow** Up to 2 hours including tours.

DESCRIPTION AND COMMENTS This is partly a research center, partly a group of restored architectural gems, and a bit of an art gallery as well. The entrance-level Williams galleries have first-class rotating exhibits on Mardi Gras, renovation, arts and crafts, etc., that are free for the browsing. Behind that is the glorious 1792 Merieult House of romantic legend, whose airy rooms now house rare materials from the landmark collection of the late Kemper and Leila Williams, including maps, documents concerning the Louisiana Purchase, wildly inflated propaganda posters, rare photographs, and so on. (The extraordinary bulk of their collection is now housed in its own lovely library, the Williams Research Center, at 410 Chartres Street; this collection is free and open to the public Tuesday–Saturday, 9:30 a.m. to 4:30 p.m.) The 19th-century brick cottage at the end of the beautiful courtyard was the Williamses' residence, which they had renovated to suit their own high standards of comfort and hospitality.

TOURING TIPS This is a one-stop whirlwind tour of New Orleans history, and a particularly evocative one, since you literally step off Royal Street into a gracious residence of two centuries' standing. Wheelchair access available; ask at the counter.

kids Jackson Barracks Military Museum ★★★★

APPEAL BY AGE PRESCHOOL ★ GRADE SCHOOL ★★★★ TEENS ★★★
YOUNG ADULTS ★★★★ OVER 30 ★★★★ SENIORS ★★★★

6400 St. Claude Avenue (Rampart Street extended); ☎ 504-278-8242; www.122nd.com Chalmette

Type of attraction Military museum with antique and modern armaments and aircraft from the Revolutionary War through the Middle East operations. **Admission** Free. **Hours** Monday–Friday, 8 a.m.–4 p.m.; Saturdays and group tours are by appointment only; closed on holidays. **When to go** Anytime. **Special comments** Fantastic variety of exhibits in a small space, and virtually guaranteed to make kids happy. And because even a Phantom jet and a Russian-made tank abandoned in the Gulf War are here, veterans or students of any war in U.S. history will find something to marvel at. **How much time to allow** 1.5 hours. *Note:* At press time, the museum was closed for renovations.

DESCRIPTION AND COMMENTS Tanks, artillery, jets, battle flags, decorations, uniforms, maps . . . this military museum seems to have acquired relics from every skirmish and siege in the nation's history, but without the sometimes-morbid touch of the Confederate Museum. The museum's main building is a powder magazine dating to 1837, but not surprisingly, it had to expand into an annex. The presence of Guardsmen may make this even more realistic for youngsters.

TOURING TIPS This is now headquarters for the National Guard, and subject to "internal business," so it wouldn't hurt to call ahead. As you pass the Jackson Barracks next door, you may feel the ghosts even more strongly: the base was built by order of President Andrew Jackson, and Civil War generals Robert E. Lee, P. G. T. Beauregard, Ulysses S. Grant, and George McClellan were all stationed here as young West Point graduates.

Longue Vue House and Gardens ★★★★★

APPEAL BY AGE PRESCHOOL ½ GRADE SCHOOL ★ TEENS ★★
YOUNG ADULTS ★★★ OVER 30 ★★★★★ SENIORS ★★★★★

7 Bamboo Road off I-10 (Metairie Road exit); ☎ 504-488-5488; www.longuevue.com Mid-City–Esplanade

Type of attraction Historic home, decorative-arts museum, and formal gardens. **Admission** $10 adults, $9 seniors, $5 students and children. **Hours** Monday–Saturday, 10 a.m.–4:30 p.m. (last tour at 4 p.m.); Sunday, 1–5 p.m. (last tour at 4 p.m.). **When to go** Anytime, but flowering gardens peak in spring. **How much time to allow** 2 hours (1 each for house and gardens).

DESCRIPTION AND COMMENTS The sumptuous Greek Revival home of philanthropist Edgar Bloom Stern and Edith Rosenwald Stern, daughter of Sears tycoon Julius Rosenwald, was constructed with the express idea that it would be left as a museum. It was designed by William and Geoffrey Platt, and the gardens were laid out by Ellen Biddle Shipman, who also oversaw much of the interior decoration, which features important antiques, rice-paper wall coverings, needlework, Oriental carpets, and Wedgwood creamware. The house also offers rotating exhibits in its galleries. Among the gardens, which may be even more interesting, are the Spanish Court (modeled after the gardens of the Alhambra), the Portuguese Canal, the Wild Garden, and the Walled Garden.

TOURING TIPS The home is wheelchair accessible and a good choice for older visitors. Tour-guide brochures are available in French, German, Italian, Spanish, and Japanese, as well as large print. Educational programs are offered for both children and adults; inquire at the desk.

kids Louisiana Children's Museum ★★★★

APPEAL BY AGE PRESCHOOL ★★★★★ GRADE SCHOOL ★★★★★ TEENS ½ YOUNG ADULTS ½ OVER 30 ½ SENIORS ½

420 Julia Street; ☎ 504-523-1357; www.lcm.org
Central Business District

Type of attraction State-of-the-art children's activity center. **Admission** $7. **Hours** Tuesday–Saturday, 9:30 a.m.–4:30 p.m.; Sunday, noon–4:30 p.m. (These are school-year hours; in summer, open additional days and extended hours; check the Web site). **When to go** After lunchtime, when the day-trippers and school groups have left. **Special comments** The way early learning is supposed to be—exciting and fun. Truly accessible for kids. **How much time to allow** 1.5–2 hours.

DESCRIPTION AND COMMENTS In a colorful, noisy converted warehouse, this science- and math-oriented facility teaches kids the inner workings of things by letting them simply have a good time. Pulleys, gears, wind machines, bubble rings, and sound-wave amplifiers are offered, along with an innovative and kindly minded exhibit introducing kids to the difficulties of handicapped—but not limited—life: they shoot baskets from a wheelchair, stack blocks wearing thick, clumsy gloves, etc. There are Sesame Street–style areas, such as the cafe where they can pretend to cook, a grocery store, a Cajun cottage, and an art gallery. There's a special room for toddlers, so siblings don't feel tied down.

TOURING TIPS Being subjected to constant battering means some of the hands-on exhibits need maintenance; just move on to the next thing. Food is limited to vending machines. Street parking available.

Madame John's Legacy ★★★

APPEAL BY AGE	PRESCHOOL ★★	GRADE SCHOOL ★★	TEENS ★★
YOUNG ADULTS ★★★	OVER 30 ★★★	SENIORS ★	

632 Dumaine Street, at Royal Street; ☎ 504-568-6968
French Quarter

Type of attraction Believed to be the oldest residence in the Mississippi Valley, recently reopened after extensive renovation as an architectural model; not a historic home in the usual sense. **Admission** Free. **Hours** Tuesday–Saturday, 9 a.m.–5 p.m. **Special comments** A wonderful example of how early Louisiana residents coped with both summer swelter and winter chill. **How much time to allow** 30–45 minutes.

DESCRIPTION AND COMMENTS This landmark West Indian–style raised cottage not only survived the fire of 1794, it was likely a close copy of the previous structure, which dated to 1730 (and may have itself been copied from an older home) and was lost in the Good Friday fire of 1788. The house owes its name, however, to an 1873 short story by George Washington Cable called "Tite Poulette," about a beautiful quadroon called Zalli, or "Madame John," who inherits the house from her wealthy lover. (Unfortunately, she sells it and puts her money into a bank that fails.)

The house, the main portion of which is raised on nine-foot piers to avoid flooding, has dirt floors in the basement rooms; exposed-brick walls that serve as a gallery for exhibits and photos; painted wood paneling and inset cabinets in the second-floor bedrooms; a breezeway in front and a gallery with stairs in back; and a garden and courtyard. Children may be fascinated by the four separate chimneys (and seven fireplaces). The lot was first recorded as belonging to a Provençal sea captain named Jean Pascal, who was killed in an Indian uprising near Natchez in 1729 before he could build on the property; his widow married the next-door neighbor and built the cottage as an inn. Later it belonged to the family of buccaneer René Beluche, who was born in the house (and who later fought for both Jean Lafitte and Venezuelan revolutionary hero Simón Bolivar); a Spanish Creole officer; and a Belgian-born lawyer. It also belonged to a wealthy cattle rancher's widow, one of whose sons owned Oak Alley Plantation and another of whom became governor, and whose daughter married another plantation owner: the son of Governor William Claiborne, after which the property began to go down.

TOURING TIPS Note that only part of the house is wheelchair accessible.

Musée Conti Wax Museum ★★½

APPEAL BY AGE	PRESCHOOL ★★	GRADE SCHOOL ★★★	TEENS ★★★
YOUNG ADULTS ★★★	OVER 30 ★★★	SENIORS ★★	

917 Conti Street, between Dauphine and Burgundy streets; ☎ 504-525-2605 or 800-233-5405; www.historyofneworleans.com **French Quarter**

Type of attraction Pretty much what it sounds like: a Madame Tussaud's of New Orleans history with a little requisite scary stuff mixed in and some surprising Mardi Gras outfits as a lagniappe. **Admission** $7 adults, $6.50 seniors, $6 kids ages 4–17, kids age 3 and under free. **Hours** Monday, Friday, and Saturday, 10 a.m.–4 p.m. **When to go** Anytime, though this makes a very diverting rainy-day stop and a cool one on the hottest afternoons. **Special comments** This is not the sort of attraction to visit twice (unless you're a kid), but the first time around it has its fun moments. **How much time to allow** 45 minutes.

DESCRIPTION AND COMMENTS Wax museums may be corny, but they have a certain appeal to even the youngest of kids, who are fascinated by their immovability, and to seniors, for whom they represent the attractions of an earlier, more innocent age. These are pretty good as such things go, with German glass eyes, human hair imported from Italy, and figures straight from Paris. Many of the exhibits are purely historical—Andy Jackson and Jean Lafitte (and the Battle of New Orleans in panorama), and the hilarious vision of the Emperor Napoleon, ensconced in his bathtub, impulsively offering to sell the entire Louisiana Territory—while others are more theatrically gory (Marie Laveau leading a voodoo ritual and lovely Delphine LaLaurie gloating over her chained slaves). A few are downright cheerful—there are wax models of Louis Armstrong, Pete Fountain, Huey Long, and Mardi Gras Indian Chief Montana. Even the long-lost Storyville has its moment in the artificial sun. Dracula, the Wolf Man, Frankenstein, and two dozen or so of their friends are kept off to one side, so young or easily frightened kids don't have to see them.

TOURING TIPS Consider before taking small children; a few will find the peculiar, almost-real quality of these mannequins spooky even before they get to the chamber of horrors. International travelers may be surprised at the variety of translated tours available for rent.

National World War II Museum ★★★★★

APPEAL BY AGE PRESCHOOL ★ GRADE SCHOOL ★★★ TEENS ★★★
YOUNG ADULTS ★★★ OVER 30 ★★★★ SENIORS ★★★★

945 Magazine Street (entrance on Andrew Higgins Drive);
☎ 504-527-6012; www.ddaymuseum.org Central Business District

Type of attraction Military museum and veterans' memorial. **Admission** $14 adults, $8 seniors and students, $6 children ages 12 and under; military in uniform, free. **Hours** October–June, open daily 9 a.m.–5 p.m.; July–September, Tuesday–Sunday 9 a.m.–5 p.m.; closed on major holidays. **When to go** Anytime. **Special comments** Even-handed presentations; film more effective than exhibits. **How much time to allow** 2–3 hours.

DESCRIPTION AND COMMENTS Housed in an old warehouse that has been effectively opened up into exhibit space that almost suggests barracks and aerodromes, this still-unfinished museum—an ambitious, $300 million plan will ultimately give it 230,000 square feet, almost quadrupling its current space—combines the now-familiar "voices" (taped recollections of veterans played as background) with uniforms, weapons, rebuilt barracks bunks, radio and newspaper clips and recruitment and bonds posters into a simple but, especially for those who lived through World War II, moving tribute. So far, the museum is comprised of two "theaters" of war, the Atlantic and Pacific. The Atlantic's introductory half-hour film, narrated by David McCullough (the new Walter Cronkite of documentaries) is laudably free of bias and respectful; children may find a few scenes of battlefield casualties upsetting, but they'll probably be fascinated by the helmet with the bullet hole, etc. Some of the exhibits are a little hard to follow. The Pacific's corresponding film is narrated by the late Stephen Ambrose, one of the museum's premier supporters. The museum gift shop has some rather intriguing items, ranging from the inexpensive soldier paper dolls and reproduction pin-up posters to action figures and vintage recordings to personalized leather jackets for $550. The nicest gift for a veteran, however, would probably be a memorial brick for the Road to Victory; the $200 fee is tax deductible.

TOURING TIPS Good wheelchair access, though the exhibits twist and turn a little. There's a cafe–coffee shop on site.

New Orleans Botanical Garden ★★★★

APPEAL BY AGE PRESCHOOL ★ GRADE SCHOOL ★★ TEENS ★★ YOUNG ADULTS ★★★★ OVER 30 ★★★★ SENIORS ★★★★★

Victory Avenue, City Park, across from the tennis center; ☎ 504-483-9386; www.neworleanscitypark.com **Mid-City–Esplanade**

Type of attraction Formal gardens and conservatory. **Admission** $6 adults, $3 kids ages 5–12, kids age 5 and under free. **Hours** Tuesday–Sunday, 10 a.m.–4:30 p.m. **When to go** Anytime; seasonal exhibits. **Special comments** A quiet respite, not as elaborate as Longue Vue Gardens, but only a few minutes' stroll from the New Orleans Museum of Art and emotionally well paired with it. **How much time to allow** 15 minutes–1 hour.

DESCRIPTION AND COMMENTS This was the city's first public classical gardens, an Art Deco–style WPA creation marrying art and nature. Today its 10 acres house about 2,000 varieties of plants grouped into themed areas and settings, among them a tropical conservatory, an aquatic gardens, an azalea and camellia garden, a rose garden, cold frames, and horticultural trails.

TOURING TIPS The Garden Study Center offers 60-minute educational and how-to programs for about $10 n fall and spring; check the above City Park Web site for class listings.

New Orleans Historic Voodoo Museum ★★★

APPEAL BY AGE PRESCHOOL ★ GRADE SCHOOL ★★ TEENS ★★★ YOUNG ADULTS ★★★ OVER 30 ★★ SENIORS ★★

724 Dumaine Street, at Royal Street; ☎ 504-680-0128; www.voodoomuseum.com **French Quarter**

Type of attraction Part museum, part weird-camp souvenir shop—or to put it simply, part shock, part schlock. **Admission** $7 adults, $5.50 seniors, students, and military (all tours of museum are self-guided); check the Web site for guided walking tours. **Hours** 10 a.m.–6 p.m. **When to go** Anytime. **Special comments** One of the hot spots for psychic readings and gris-gris charms as well as "voodoo tours," this absolutely requires that you get into the spirit of things; think of it as an adventure rather than as a museum per se. **How much time to allow** 30 minutes.

DESCRIPTION AND COMMENTS If something like the Historic New Orleans Collection is the quintessential aboveboard museum, this is the height of neo–New Orleans exotica—rather grim and sometimes-grisly artifacts, strange bones and potions, a voodoo altar, plenty of Marie Laveau lore, stuffed cats and live snakes, low light, and sometimes local low life as well. If you like atmosphere, you'll love this; in fact, if it weren't so dim and dilapidated, they'd have to curse it.

TOURING TIPS Children are generally fascinated by the grotesque, but take your own kids' sensitivities into account. Teens and novice occultists will probably think it very cool, but seniors may find it all a little too grim. The museum staff not only arranges readings and tours, but also occasional "rituals."

New Orleans Museum of Art ★★★★★

APPEAL BY AGE PRESCHOOL ★ GRADE SCHOOL ★★★ TEENS ★★★
YOUNG ADULTS ★★★★★ OVER 30 ★★★★★ SENIORS ★★★★★

1 Collins Diboll Circle; ☎ 504-488-2631; www.noma.org
Mid-City–Esplanade

Type of attraction Wide-ranging fine- and decorative-arts collection. **Admission** $8 adults, $7 seniors and students, $4 children ages 3–17; free admission for Louisiana residents only. **Hours** Wednesday noon–8 p.m.; Thursday–Sunday 10 a.m.–5 p.m. **When to go** Anytime. **Special comments** Art lovers should not miss this. **How much time to allow** 1–3 hours.

DESCRIPTION AND COMMENTS This neoclassical building, commissioned in 1910 by Jamaican-born New Orleans philanthropist Isaac Delgado to benefit "rich and poor alike," lives up to its mission, housing more than 35,000 works by not only the premier American and European artists—including Picasso, Miró, and Degas, whose studio was nearby—but African, Japanese, Chinese, and Native American art as well. Its "Art of the Americas" collection, ranging from pre-Columbian through Spanish Colonial times, is one of the largest, as is its decorative glass works. There are miniatures, furnishings, and regional arts and crafts from the 19th century to today. Sketching of these masterworks is welcome, but in dry media only (pencil, charcoal, and the like) and on a single tablet no larger than legal size. One wing is devoted to rotating exhibits. General tours and special exhibition lectures are offered on an irregular schedule; check the Web site.

TOURING TIPS Free parking. The streetcar is fun, but make sure you know the schedule or you could have quite a wait.

New Orleans Pharmacy Museum ★★★

APPEAL BY AGE PRESCHOOL ★ GRADE SCHOOL ★★ TEENS ★★
YOUNG ADULTS ★★ OVER 30 ★★ SENIORS ★★★

514 Chartres Street, between Toulouse and St. Louis streets; ☎ 504-565-8027; www.pharmacymuseum.org French Quarter

Type of attraction Restored apothecary with period exhibits, old potions, and pharmaceutical supplies. **Admission** $5 adults, $4 seniors and students, kids age 5 and under free. **Hours** Tuesday and Thursday, 10 a.m.–2 p.m.; Wednesday, Friday, and Saturday, 10 a.m.–5 p.m. **When to go** Anytime; good rain alternative. **Special comments** This is another of those atmospheric venues that has to draw you. The subject may seem somewhat limited, but it's quite intriguing if you're not squeamish. **How much time to allow** 30 minutes.

DESCRIPTION AND COMMENTS This was the pharmacy of the very first apothecary to be licensed in the United States, Louis Dufilho, who was certified in 1816 and opened this store in 1823. It's an impressive piece of restoration, with German mahogany cases, antique handblown canisters and apothecary jars, a leech pot, and such famous patent medicines of the past as Pinkham's pills, the vitamin concoctions of Miss Lydia Pinkham that were supposed to resolve both ladies' vapors and, though not said openly, sexual indifference; and Spanish fly, the male equivalent still hotly sought after today. The black-and-rose-marble soda fountain, made in Italy in 1855, is a nostalgic highlight.

TOURING TIPS Bring your sense of humor. This will be of some interest to most ages, since the idea of applying leeches and trepanning skulls to relieve pressure (or possession) has a perverse appeal. The courtyard is a nice place to sit for a few minutes, and with the revival of interest in botanicals and alternative medicine, almost trendy. In a funny way, however, this has more appeal to older visitors who recognize more of the names and may even remember tales of defunct medical techniques.

The Old U.S. Mint ★★★

APPEAL BY AGE PRESCHOOL ★★ GRADE SCHOOL ★★ TEENS ★★
YOUNG ADULTS ★★★★★ OVER 30 ★★★ SENIORS ★★★★

400 Esplanade Avenue, at Decatur Street; ☎ 504-568-6968; lsm.crt.state.la.us/mintex.htm French Quarter

Type of attraction Another part of the Louisiana State Museum complex, an imaginatively reconditioned installation housing two of the city's best-kept secret exhibits. **Admission** $6 adults; $5 seniors, students, and active military; kids age 12 and under free. **Hours** Tuesday–Sunday, 9 a.m.–5 p.m. **When to go** Anytime. **Special comments** Because of its music exhibits, the museum sometimes hosts concerts of jazz, big band, spiritual, and early ballroom music; inquire at the desk. This is virtually the only exhibit on New Orleans music and requires perhaps a little personal knowledge for the fullest effect. Fans of Newcomb Pottery will think this collection a must-see. **How much time to allow** 1–2 hours.

DESCRIPTION AND COMMENTS The building itself, a huge but not clumsy Greek Revival facade with Ionic details, was designed during Andrew Jackson's administration by William Strickland, the most prominent public architect of the day. (Its copper roof took something of a beating from Katrina, and some of the jazz memorabilia was damaged, but the building has been repaired and most of the exhibits restored.) Its polished flagstone floors, double staircase, and rear galleries are still pretty impressive, although it has to be admitted that engineer P. G. T. Beauregard—not then the local hero he would be after the Civil War—had to be called in to perform a little face lift in the 1850s. One side of the second floor holds the jazz collection, which arranges old photographs of Jelly Roll Morton, King Oliver, Sidney Bechet, and Fate Marable's Orchestra alongside early instruments (including Louis Armstrong's first cornet), sheet music, and other memorabilia. Snatches of vintage recordings play overhead, and the often-overlooked women of early music are also saluted. (Be sure to notice the copy of the notorious "Blue Book," the Social Register of Storyville ladies, and the delicate stained-glass panels rescued from a demolished bordello.) The other side of the building houses the Newcomb Pottery exhibit, a collection of the Art Nouveau and Art Deco pottery created by students at Sophie Newcomb College (the women's division of Tulane University, dissolved in an academic reorganization following Katrina). Down in the basement, where the remnants of the mint equipment can be seen, are a few intriguing exhibits as well, including the carved hearse, built at the turn of the 19th century.

TOURING TIPS This is good wheelchair-access territory, with wide aisles and new bathrooms. And if you like old homes, take the time to wander up and down Esplanade Avenue. Although the neighborhood is in midrevival, it is likely to be the next Garden District. Take particular note of the house at 704 Esplanade, at Royal Street: the Gauche House (so called for owner John Gauche) was built in 1856 supposedly from a drawing by Albrecht Dürer, including cast-iron balconies, cupids, and all. Also note that you are very near the end of the Riverfront streetcar line, if you're getting tired or want to get across the Quarter easily.

Old Ursuline Convent–Archbishop Antoine Blanc Memorial ★★½

APPEAL BY AGE PRESCHOOL – GRADE SCHOOL – TEENS ★ YOUNG ADULTS ★ OVER 30 ★★ SENIORS ★★

1100 Chartres Street, at Ursulines Street; ☎ 504-529-3040
French Quarter

Type of attraction A 250-year-old complex incorporating several religious sites, formal gardens, and archives. **Admission** $5 adults, $4 seniors, $3 students, kids age 6 and under free. **Hours** Monday–Saturday, 10 a.m.–4 p.m. **When to go** Anytime. **Special comments** Not a lively, elaborate, or particularly varied site, but oddly atmospheric; obviously appeals more to Catholic visitors. **How much time to allow** 1 hour.

DESCRIPTION AND COMMENTS This is the only surviving example of pure French Creole construction, begun in 1745, and most people believe it's the oldest surviving building in New Orleans of any sort; it was saved from the fire of 1788 by Père Antoine and his bucket brigade. The Sisters were the guiding social hand of the city's young people for centuries, educating not only the children of aristocrats but blacks, Native Americans, and orphans as well. They served as religious guides, chaperones (it was they who brought over the "casket girls" as brides to the early settlers), nurses, housekeeping instructors, and welfare workers, braving epidemics and massacres alike. Andrew Jackson sent word to the Sisters to ask them to pray for his forces on the eve of the Battle of New Orleans; they responded by spending the entire night in prayer at the chapel here before a statue of the Virgin Mary, and were still there when the messenger brought word of victory. Jackson came in person to thank them, and to this day a celebratory Mass is said on January 8 at the Ursulines' other chapel, the National Shrine of Our Lady of Prompt Succor at State Street and South Claiborne. The lovely old cypress spiral staircase, antique furniture and relics, medicinal garden, and restored chapel are very pretty. Incidentally, in the early years of U.S. government, the convent seemed threatened by anti-Catholic educational reforms; the Mother Superior wrote first to President Jefferson and again to President Madison, asking that the school be allowed to continue, and both wrote back assuringly. The Shrine of Our Lady has not only her petitions, but both presidential responses.

TOURING TIPS This is pleasant, but rather a lot of walking for the effect.

Our Lady of Guadalupe–Shrine of St. Jude ★★½

APPEAL BY AGE PRESCHOOL – GRADE SCHOOL ½ TEENS ½ YOUNG ADULTS ★★ OVER 30 ★★ SENIORS ★★

411 North Rampart Street, at Conti Street; ☎ 504-525-1551; www.saintjudeshrine.com French Quarter

Type of attraction Simple but quirky little chapel built to serve St. Louis Cemetery, but with a couple of not-so-strict saints in charge. **Admission** Free (donations welcome). **Hours** 9 a.m.–5 p.m. **When to go** Anytime. **Special comments** An eccentric but lively side trip. **How much time to allow** 15 minutes.

DESCRIPTION AND COMMENTS This little chapel, built in 1826 as the Chapel of the Dead and originally opening directly onto St. Louis Cemetery No. 1 (there's a street between now) is intriguing for several reasons. First, because in the days of continual epidemic, it operated at tragic speed: bodies were brought in, a swift service was said, and they were shipped right into the waiting graves. (The victims were brought here instead of St. Louis Cathedral in a vain effort to limit contagion.) The second intriguing aspect, for those who take saintly intercession with a grain of salt, is that the shrine is now dedicated to St. Jude, he of the lost causes, who might be considered a sort of lost cause himself: despite his connections—he may have been the brother of either Jesus or James—he has lost a little status, although the petitions and published notices of thanks continue to flow in. Step to the right into his grotto, and see for yourself how active he is. Third, this is also the shrine of the one and only (as far as anyone knows) St. Expedite, whose statue arrived at the chapel without its papers or even an address. Look to the right just as you enter the chapel. He had no identifying attributes, and no other church in New Orleans claimed to be expecting a new saint, so the only thing written on the packing crate—"Expedite!"—was carved into the base by the confused workers, who didn't speak much English. Gradually petitioners began taking him at his word. The legend goes that if you have a request, you go out toward St. Louis Cemetery and say five rosaries; if your prayer is answered (it will be within 36 hours, or probably not at all), you return to the chapel and leave him a teaspoon of salt and a slice of pound cake.

TOURING TIPS This is the official chapel of the city's fire and police departments, so don't be surprised to see visitors in uniform.

Pitot House ★★★

APPEAL BY AGE PRESCHOOL – GRADE SCHOOL ½ TEENS ★ YOUNG ADULTS ★★ OVER 30 ★★ SENIORS ★★

1440 Moss Street; ☎ 504-482-0312; www.louisianalandmarks.org
Mid-City–Esplanade

Type of attraction Historic early-19th-century home. **Admission** $7 adults, $5 seniors, students, and children, free for children under age 6. **Hours** Wednesday–Saturday, 10 a.m.–3 p.m. and by appointment; closed major holidays. **When to go** Anytime. **How much time to allow** ½–1 hour, depending on your interest.

DESCRIPTION AND COMMENTS When it was built in 1799 for Edgar Degas's great-grandmother (it's named for James Pitot, first mayor of the city, who bought it soon after), this West Indies–style home—encircled by porches, protected by full shutters—was 200 yards away from where it now stands (where the girls' Catholic school is). It was used in this century as a convent by Mother Frances Xavier Cabrini, the first American to be declared a saint by the Catholic Church. It has been beautifully restored to its original condition and furnished with period antiques. It is charming but probably not on the top of the touring itinerary except for history or architecture buffs.

TOURING TIPS Under the aegis of the Louisiana Landmarks Society, who moved it in the 1960s, this house has been made wheelchair accessible on the ground floor.

The Presbytere ★★★

APPEAL BY AGE PRESCHOOL – GRADE SCHOOL ★ TEENS ★ YOUNG ADULTS ★★★ OVER 30 ★★★ SENIORS ★★

751 Chartres Street, facing Jackson Square; ☎ 504-568-6968 or 800-568-6968; lsm.crt.state.la.us French Quarter

Type of attraction Of the Louisiana State Museum properties in the French Quarter, the most traditional one, with both permanent and rotating exhibits.

Admission $6 adults; $5 seniors, students, and active military; kids age 12 and under free. **Hours** Friday–Sunday, 10 a.m.–4 p.m. **When to go** Anytime. **Special comments** Like the Cabildo, you have to follow your nose to what interests you, but the rotating exhibits can be very intriguing. **How much time to allow** 45 minutes–1.5 hours.

DESCRIPTION AND COMMENTS Architecturally speaking, this is a somewhat-mongrelized building. Though not unattractive, it has been renovated and expanded several times, and most recently its really fine plank floors have been reconditioned to fine advantage. Intended to be used as an ecclesiastical residence, it wound up as a courthouse; the mansard roof and hurricane-demolished cupola were supposed to mirror the Cabildo. Aside from a fairly elaborate exhibit on Carnival and Mardi Gras, recently transplanted from the U.S. Mint, the exhibits are a bit haphazard but cheerful mishmash: portraits of influential Creoles, such as Don Almonester and his formidable daughter, Baroness Almonester; fine decorative arts, from an 18th-century gold- and silver-embroidered velvet altar cloth and local art glass to wrought iron from the staircase of the great domed (and doomed) St. Charles Hotel; crosses, cameos, and earrings; hand-tinted Audubon plates; silver table settings; etc. Among the busts are two faces of Beauregard, one young and confident, the other older and wiser.

TOURING TIPS Although the age rating shows low for children, it does depend somewhat on the subject of the rotating exhibits. Among fairly recent examples, the collection of very elaborate to-scale builders' ship models, haute couture (à la the Metropolitan Museum in New York), or antique maps might interest certain youngsters, and the rather weird *Tales from the Crypt* effect of the bust-lined second-floor arcade gallery might tickle others' fancies.

Rivertown ★★★★

APPEAL BY AGE PRESCHOOL ★★ GRADE SCHOOL ★★★★★ TEENS ★★★
YOUNG ADULTS ★★★★ OVER 30 ★★★★ SENIORS ★★★

Welcome center at 405 Williams Boulevard off I-10; ☎ 504-468-7231; www.rivertownkenner.com Kenner

Type of attraction Family amusement–education complex, with small museums and activity centers on 16 blocks in suburban Kenner. **Admission** $15 adults, $10 seniors 60 and older and kids age 14 and under; single venues vary. **Hours** Tuesday–Saturday, 9 a.m.–5 p.m. (last admission at 4 p.m.). **When to go** Anytime. **Special comments** Business travelers bringing the family along may find this a good reason to stay in an airport-area hotel. It's a mixed bag, but there's definitely something for everyone. **How much time to allow** 2–4 hours. Note At press time, the Toy Train Museum, the Space Station, and the Kenner Heritage Village were still closed for repairs.

DESCRIPTION AND COMMENTS Families with children can duck the Bourbon Street barrage for at least a half day by heading toward this Victorian village–style complex a half mile from the airport. The Louisiana Toy Train Museum is one of the all-ages attractions, with a half-dozen large dioramas crisscrossed with tracks for the vintage Lionel, American Flyer, and other small-gauge collections (most dating to the 1950s). The Mardi Gras Museum conveys the trashy, flashy fever of Carnival at safe and PG-rated distance, with costumes, beads, a simulated costume shop, and lots of live-action video. The Science Complex, a hands-on if lightweight introduction to car engines, weather, dental hygiene, commercial laundries, and other strange and sundry aspects of everyday life leads into a full-size NASA space station, complete with weightlessness chamber. It also has a planetarium and an observatory, which are open Tuesday through Saturday (# 504-468-7231). On the other hand, the Louisiana Wildlife Museum and Aquarium is well organized and attractive, with more than 700 preserved specimens of indigenous mammals and reptiles and a 15,000-gallon tank holding marine life. Literally in the backyard of the Wildlife Museum is the Cannes Brulee Native American Center of the Gulf South, a living-history installation that re-creates a Native American village, complete with live hogs, poultry, rabbits, and crayfish, and is staffed by serious and well-spoken native craftsmen and "residents." There is also a 300-seat Repertory Theater, and the Children's Castle offers puppet shows, magic displays, and storytelling

TOURING TIPS Like many children's museums, this tends to be busier before lunch than after. Walk across to La Salle's Landing for a good view of the mighty Mississippi.

PART EIGHT

DINING *in* NEW ORLEANS

by Tom Fitzmorris

A RAPID RETURN *to* DISTINCTION

IT'S HARD TO BELIEVE, but less than two years after Katrina devoured New Orleans, the city had more restaurants than before the storm. This surprised nobody who lives here, where eating well is assumed as part of everyday life.

The return of great Creole and Cajun food was rapid and gratifying. Restaurants opened as fast as the strained food supply and lack of employees allowed. But there was never a shortage of customers. It was essential to reconnect with friends in the most important meeting place in town: the dining room.

Fears of long-lasting damage to essential seafood resources proved groundless. All local fish and shellfish—including oysters, whose beds were wiped out by the storm—are back and as good as ever.

These days all of America is food crazy. But that passion wells up through six or seven generations in New Orleans. A complex regional cuisine existed here 150 years ago—long before the rest of the country got the gourmet bug.

That's the essence of New Orleans cooking: it's intensely regional. In the same way that food in Europe is unique to the small area where you find it, so too is Southeast Louisiana obsessed with Creole and Cajun cooking.

That brings up a question that is less important than many will try to make it seem: "What's the distinction between Creole and Cajun flavors?" After noting that Creole is city and Cajun is country, and that Creole cooks like to use tomatoes more than Cajun chefs do, just abandon the matter. Creole and Cajun have influenced each other so much in recent years that you find the same menus and flavors throughout Southeast Louisiana.

Creole and Cajun chefs cook with the same raw materials. Which is a big reason why they're both so good. For starters, this is a land of superb seafood, starting with the Big Four: oysters, shrimp, crabs, and crawfish. Supporting them (or vice versa) is a large cast of finfish from local waters, including pompano, redfish, speckled trout, lemonfish, sheepshead, flounder, red snapper, and grouper. To name the best of them.

Those of us who grew up in New Orleans have a hard time saying what makes our cuisine special. It's our normal, everyday, ubiquitous food. The only time we become keenly aware of its uniqueness is when we travel. Its high seasoning levels, richness, and general intensity of flavor are something we miss when we don't have it.

Many writers trying to nail down Louisiana food mention its rife use of roux, the starting point for a lot of New Orleans dishes. Roux is a blend of flour and oil, butter, or other fat, cooked to various shades of color. It's not universal in Creole cooking, but it certainly is an important flavor.

Over the past couple of decades, there has been a revolution in Creole cooking, spurred by intense competition among the hundreds of new restaurants that have opened. Diners expect new dishes, ingredients, and flavors, and the young, hip chefs trying to establish a high profile for themselves are happy to provide. The new Creole cuisine is lighter than its predecessor. Even roux is becoming rarer. Occasionally it's even left out of gumbo (a state of affairs that an old-time Creole cook would consider heresy).

However, that trend reversed direction after the hurricane. Even the most innovative local chefs traded in their one-big-world-of-taste fusion dishes for revivals of comforting, traditional, local ideas. The dishes don't taste or look like they did 20 years ago—the ingredients, for one thing, are a lot better now. But you can see a lot of familiar old friends under the new guises.

During the 1990s, ethnic restaurants greatly increased in number around town. Local diners welcomed the diversity, and the exotic cuisines are now getting their due in terms of quality foodstuffs, skilled chefs, and pleasant restaurants. I've included a good assortment of them among the restaurants recommended in this book.

If that last fact causes you to wonder whether our gustatory island will lose its distinctiveness, rest easy. No matter how enthusiastically even the most sophisticated New Orleans diners wax about some new Vietnamese-Mexican fusion bistro, you can be sure that in their most relaxed moments, they're still munching poor-boy sandwiches, boiled crawfish, jambalaya, and bread pudding. As will all other aficionados of Creole food from near or far. Because we all know that, like all the world's other great ethnic cuisines, great Creole and Cajun cooking are only found in the land of their birth.

A New Orleans Culinary Calendar

Because the cuisine of New Orleans is so intimately tied to indigenous ingredients, it's important to pay attention to the seasons. Although many restaurants serve, say, crawfish year-round, there's no question that crawfish are incomparably better at the peak of their natural cycle. Here's the schedule:

CRABS, SOFT-SHELL AND OTHERWISE April through October. There's a dip in quality in July, then they get good again. Usually the warmer it is, the better the crabmeat.

CRAWFISH Christmas through the Fourth of July, with peak quality in April and May.

CREOLE TOMATOES These meaty, sweet, gigantic, sensual tomatoes have a short season, in April and May, but they are worth waiting for. Lately we've seen a second crop of Creoles in the fall.

OYSTERS Good year-round, but a little off during the spawn in July and August. (In other words, forget that months-with-an-R myth.) The best months are November and December, especially if a convincing cold front has passed through.

POMPANO Erratic, but early spring and late summer usually see an increase in the population of this best of all Gulf fish.

SHRIMP The several species each have a season, but shrimp are always available. The best times are late spring, late summer, and most of the fall. The only poor month for shrimp is March.

SPECKLED TROUT October through January.

TUNA May through September.

The calendar also predicts when restaurants will be at their best. The best times for gourmets here are spring and fall. The weather is beautiful for patio dining, food supplies are at their best, and conventions aren't overwhelming. Also good are the summer months, especially August and September. The heat and humidity convince tourists and conventions to stay away (despite the fact that there may be no better air-conditioned city on Earth), and the restaurants are eager to please.

Spring also brings superb food festivals. The New Orleans Jazz and Heritage Festival takes place during the last week of April and the first week of May, with an outdoor surfeit of music and indigenous food. In the days before and including Memorial Day weekend, the New Orleans Wine and Food Experience brings you indoors for an extended weekend of special feasting with the city's best chefs and drinking with the world's best winemakers.

HYPE *and* GLORY

IN THE RESTAURANT PROFILES that make up most of this book, you may notice that a few well-known or highly visible restaurants are missing. This is not an oversight. The following restaurants may come to your attention, but in my opinion they're not as worthwhile as other comparable options.

- **Central Grocery** 923 Decatur Street, French Quarter; ☎ 504-523-1620.
  As this old emporium of imported food allowed its floor space to become more taken over for the vending of muffulettas to tourists, both the store and the muffulettas have declined.
- **Court of Two Sisters** 613 Royal Street, French Quarter; ☎ 504-522-7273.
  There's no question that tourists dominate this beautiful restaurant and its lush courtyard tables. Most locals will tell you to stay away. In fact, dinner here is better than decent, with old-style Creole dishes done reasonably well. The daily breakfast-lunch buffet has less-appealing food but does sport a live jazz trio.
- **Deanie's Seafood** 1713 Lake Avenue, Bucktown; ☎ 504-831-4141.
  Deanie's is immensely popular, but the reason is the eye-popping size of its just-okay seafood platters.
- **House of Blues** 225 Decatur Street, French Quarter; ☎ 504-529-2583.
  The place has great music almost every night, including name acts. And sometimes the food is good, but not predictably. The Foundation Room, a private club within the club, has a very ambitious kitchen, but first you have to get in—and I have no advice for you there.
- **Jimmy Buffet's Margaritaville Café** 1104 Decatur Street, French Quarter; ☎ 504-592-2565.
  A must for Parrotheads—but only after eating somewhere else.
- **Landry's Seafood House** 400 North Peters Street, French Quarter; ☎ 504-558-0038.
  A regional chain, Landry's has the look of a great old middle-of-nowhere Louisiana roadhouse, but the food is strictly formulaic and not very good.
- **Mulate's** 201 Julia Street, Warehouse District; ☎ 504-522-1492.
  A mammoth place copied from the original Cajun dance restaurant in Breaux Bridge, Mulate's does indeed have good Cajun music, but the food is only occasionally interesting.

The BEST . . .

Best Sunday Brunch

- **Arnaud's** 813 Bienville Street; ☎ 504-523-5433
- **Begue's** 300 Bourbon Street (Royal Sonesta Hotel); ☎ 504-553-2278
- **Bourbon House** 144 Bourbon Street; ☎ 504-522-0111
- **Brennan's** 417 Royal Street; ☎ 504-525-9711
- **Café Adelaide** 300 Poydras Street; ☎ 504-595-3305

- **Commander's Palace** 1403 Washington Avenue; ☎ 504-899-8221
- **Marigny Brasserie** 640 Frenchmen Street; ☎ 504-945-4472
- **Mr. B's** 201 Royal Street; ☎ 504-523-2078
- **Palace Cafe** 605 Canal Street; ☎ 504-523-1661
- **Ralph's on the Park** 900 City Park Avenue; ☎ 504-488-1000
- **Rib Room** 621 St. Louis Street; ☎ 504-529-7045
- **Veranda** 444 St. Charles Avenue; ☎ 504-525-5566

Best Breakfasts

- **Begue's** 300 Bourbon Street (Royal Sonesta Hotel); ☎ 504-553-2278
- **Bluebird Cafe** 3625 Prytania Street; ☎ 504-895-7166
- **Brennan's** 417 Royal Street; ☎ 504-525-9711
- **Café Adelaide** 300 Poydras Street; ☎ 504-595-3305
- **Cafe du Monde** 800 Decatur Street; ☎ 504-525-4544
- **Cafe Reconcile** 1631 Oretha Castle Haley Boulevard; ☎ 504-568-1157
- **Camellia Grill** 626 South Carrollton Avenue; ☎ 504-866-9573
- **Coffee Pot** 714 St. Peter Street; ☎ 504-524-3500
- **Morning Call Coffee Stand** 3325 Severn Avenue, Metairie; ☎ 504-885-4068
- **Mother's** 401 Poydras Street; ☎ 504-523-9656
- **Peppermill** 3524 Severn Avenue, Metairie; ☎ 504-455-2266
- **Riccobono's Panola Street Cafe** 7801 Panola Street; ☎ 504-314-1810
- **Windsor Court Grill Room** 300 Gravier Street; ☎ 504-522-1992

Best Atmosphere

- **Antoine's** 713 St. Louis Street; ☎ 504-581-4422
- **Arnaud's** 813 Bienville Street; ☎ 504-523-5433
- **Bourbon House** 144 Bourbon Street; ☎ 504-522-0111
- **Brennan's** 417 Royal Street; ☎ 504-525-9711
- **Broussard's** 819 Conti Street; ☎ 504-581-3866
- **Commander's Palace** 1403 Washington Avenue; ☎ 504-899-8221
- **Delmonico** 1300 St. Charles Avenue; ☎ 504-525-4937
- **Emeril's** 800 Tchoupitoulas Street; ☎ 504-528-9393
- **Galatoire's** 209 Bourbon Street; ☎ 504-525-2021
- **GW Fins** 808 Bienville Street; ☎ 504-581-3467
- **Palace Cafe** 605 Canal Street; ☎ 504-523-1661
- **Ralph's on the Park** 900 City Park Avenue; ☎ 504-488-1000
- **Sake Cafe** 2830 Magazine Street; ☎ 504-894-0033

Best for Dining with Children

- **Andrea's** 3100 19th Street, Metairie; ☎ 504-834-8583
- **Bozo's** 3117 21st Street, Metairie; ☎ 504-831-8666
- **Drago's** 3232 North Arnoult Road, Metairie; ☎ 504-888-9254
- **Peppermill** 3524 Severn Avenue, Metairie; ☎ 504-455-2266
- **R&O's** 216 Old Hammond Highway, Metairie; ☎ 504-831-1248
- **Red Fish Grill** 115 Bourbon Street; ☎ 504-598-1200

Best for Dining with Children *(continued)*

- **Sun Ray Cafe** 1051 Annunciation Street; ☎ 504-566-0021
- **Vincent's** 7839 St. Charles Avenue; ☎ 504-866-9313
- **Ye Olde College Inn** 3016 South Carrollton Avenue; ☎ 504-866-3683
- **Zea Rotisserie** 1525 St. Charles Avenue; ☎ 504-520-8100

Best for Local Color

- **Antoine's** 713 St. Louis Street; ☎ 504-581-4422
- **Arnaud's** 813 Bienville Street; ☎ 504-523-5433
- **Brennan's** 417 Royal Street; ☎ 504-525-9711
- **Brigtsen's** 723 Dante Street; ☎ 504-861-7610
- **Broussard's** 819 Conti Street; ☎ 504-581-3866
- **Cafe du Monde** 800 Decatur Street; ☎ 504-525-4544
- **Commander's Palace** 1403 Washington Avenue; ☎ 504-899-8221
- **Court of Two Sisters** 613 Royal Street; ☎ 504-522-7273
- **Feelings** 2600 Chartres Street; ☎ 504-945-2222
- **Galatoire's** 209 Bourbon Street; ☎ 504-525-2021
- **Jacques-Imo's** 8324 Oak Street; ☎ 504-861-0886
- **Liuzza's by the Track** 1518 North Lopez; ☎ 504-218-7888
- **Mandina's** 3800 Canal Street; ☎ 504-482-9179
- **Marigny Brasserie** 640 Frenchmen Street; ☎ 504-945-4472
- **Mother's** 401 Poydras Street; ☎ 504-523-9656
- **Muriel's** 801 Chartres Street; ☎ 504-568-1885
- **Napoleon House** 500 Chartres Street; ☎ 504-524-9752
- **Ralph's on the Park** 900 City Park Avenue; ☎ 504-488-1000
- **Tujague's** 823 Decatur Street; ☎ 504-525-8676

Best Hamburgers

- **Beachcorner** 4905 Canal Street; ☎ 504-488-7357
- **Camellia Grill** 626 South Carrollton Avenue; ☎ 504-866-9573
- **Dickie Brennan's Steakhouse** 716 Iberville Street; ☎ 504-522-2467
- **Port of Call** 838 Esplanade Avenue; ☎ 504-523-0120
- **Snug Harbor** 626 Frenchmen Street; ☎ 504-949-0696
- **Trolley Stop Cafe** 1923 St. Charles Avenue; ☎ 504-523-0090
- **Zea Rotisserie** 1525 St. Charles Avenue; ☎ 504-520-8100

Best Muffulettas

- **Central Grocery** 923 Decatur Street; ☎ 504-523-1620
- **Come Back Inn** 8016 West Metairie Avenue, Metairie; ☎ 504-467-9316
- **Johnny's Po-Boys** 511 St. Louis Street; ☎ 504-524-8129
- **Mr. Ed's** 1001 Live Oak, Metairie; ☎ 504-838-0022
- **Napoleon House** 500 Chartres Street; ☎ 504-524-9752
- **Remoulade** 309 Bourbon Street; ☎ 504-523-0377
- **Two Tonys** 105 Metairie-Hammond Highway, Metairie; ☎ 504-831-0999

Best Barbecue

- **Bywater Bar-B-Que** 3162 Dauphine Street; ☎ 504-944-4445
- **Corky's** 4243 Veterans Boulevard; ☎ 504-887-5000
- **Hillbilly Barbecue** 208 Tallulah Street; ☎ 504-738-1508
- **The Joint** 801 Poland Avenue; ☎ 504-949-3232
- **Ugly Dog Saloon** 401 Howard Avenue; ☎ 504-569-8459

Best Oyster Bars

- **Acme Oyster House** 724 Iberville; ☎ 504-522-5973
- **Bourbon House** 144 Bourbon Street; ☎ 504-522-0111
- **Bozo's** 3117 21st Street, Metairie; ☎ 504-831-8666
- **Casamento's** 4330 Magazine Street; ☎ 504-895-9761
- **Crescent City Brewhouse** 527 Decatur Street; ☎ 504-522-0571
- **Drago's** 3232 North Arnoult Road, Metairie; ☎ 504-888-9254
- **Felix's** 4938 Prytania Street; ☎ 504-895-1330
- **Grand Isle** 575 Convention Center Boulevard; ☎ 504-520-8530
- **Pascal's Manale** 1838 Napoleon Avenue; ☎ 504-895-4877
- **Red Fish Grill** 115 Bourbon Street; ☎ 504-598-1200
- **Remoulade** 309 Bourbon Street; ☎ 504-523-0377

Best Outdoor Dining

- **Bayona** 430 Dauphine Street; ☎ 504-525-4455
- **Broussard's** 819 Conti Street; ☎ 504-581-3866
- **Cafe Rani** 2917 Magazine Street; ☎ 504-895-2500
- **Commander's Palace** 1403 Washington Avenue; ☎ 504-899-8221
- **Court of Two Sisters** 613 Royal Street; ☎ 504-522-7273
- **Dante's Kitchen** 736 Dante Street; ☎ 504-861-3121
- **Martinique** 5908 Magazine Street; ☎ 504-891-8495
- **Mat & Naddie's** 937 Leonidas Street; ☎ 504-861-9600

Best Pizza

- **Brick Oven Cafe** 2805 Williams Boulevard, Kenner; ☎ 504-466-2097
- **Brooklyn Pizza** 4301 Veterans Boulevard; ☎ 504-833-1288
- **Cafe Nino** 1519 South Carrollton Avenue; ☎ 504-865-9200
- **Louisiana Pizza Kitchen** 615 South Carrollton Avenue; ☎ 504-866-5900
- **Mark Twain's Pizza Landing** 2035 Metairie Road; ☎ 504-832-8032
- **Mo's Pizza** 1112 Avenue H, Westwego; ☎ 504-341-9650
- **New York Pizza** 5201 Magazine Street; ☎ 504-891-2376
- **R&O's** 216 Old Hammond Highway, Metairie; ☎ 504-831-1248
- **Reginelli's Pizzeria** 741 State Street; ☎ 504-899-1414
- **Tower of Pizza** 2104 Veterans Boulevard, Metairie; ☎ 504-833-9373

The RESTAURANTS

OUR FAVORITE NEW ORLEANS RESTAURANTS: EXPLAINING THE RATINGS

WE'VE DEVELOPED DETAILED PROFILES for what we consider the best restaurants in town. Each profile features an easy-to-scan heading that allows you to check out the restaurant's name, star rating, cuisine, cost, quality rating, and value rating very quickly.

OVERALL RATING The overall rating encompasses the entire dining experience, including style, service, and ambience in addition to the taste, presentation, and quality of the food. Five stars is the highest rating possible and connotes the best of everything. Four-star restaurants are exceptional, and three-star restaurants are well above average. Two-star restaurants are good. One star is used to connote an average restaurant that demonstrates an unusual capability in some area of specialization—for example, an otherwise unmemorable place that has great barbecued chicken.

COST To the right of the cuisine is an expense description, which provides a comparative sense of how much a complete meal will cost. A complete meal for our purposes consists of an entree with vegetable or side dish and choice of soup or salad. Appetizers, desserts, drinks, and tips are excluded.

Inexpensive	$14 and less per person
Moderate	$15–$25 per person
Expensive	$26–$40 per person
Very Expensive	More than $40 per person

QUALITY RATING The food quality rating is rated on a scale of one to five stars, with five stars being the best rating attainable. It is based expressly on the taste, freshness of ingredients, preparation, presentation, and creativity of food served. There is no consideration of price. If you are a person who wants the best food available and cost is not an issue, you need look no further than the quality ratings.

VALUE RATING If, on the other hand, you are looking for both quality and value, then you should check the value rating. Value ratings, expressed as stars, are defined as follows:

★★★★★	Exceptional value, a real bargain
★★★★	Good value
★★★	Fair value, you get exactly what you pay for
★★	Somewhat overpriced
★	Significantly overpriced

HOURS Most restaurants have returned to predictable hours of operation. However, it's more true than usual that you should check with the restaurants before you head over. Hours were accurate at press time, but it's a certainty that some have changed, perhaps dramatically. Call before you go.

WHO'S INCLUDED This list is highly selective. Exclusion of a particular place does not necessarily indicate that the restaurant is not good, but that it was not ranked among the best or most consistent in its genre. Detailed profiles of each restaurant follow in alphabetical order at the end of this chapter.

RESTAURANT PROFILES

Andrea's ★★★

ITALIAN EXPENSIVE QUALITY ★★★ VALUE ★★★

3100 19th Street, Metairie; ☎504-834-8583; www.andreasrestaurant.com

Reservations Recommended. **When to go** Anytime except holidays, when they have a bad habit of overbooking the room. **Entree range** $14–$36. **Payment** All major credit cards. **Service rating** ★★★. **Friendliness rating** ★★★★. **Parking** Free lot adjacent. **Bar** Full bar. **Wine selection** Substantial list, mostly Italian and French; a bit overpriced. **Dress** Nice casual. **Disabled access** Full. **Customers** Businessmen at lunch, many regulars, daters. **Hours** Monday–Saturday, 11:30 a.m.–10 p.m.; Sunday, 11 a.m.–8 p.m.

SETTING AND ATMOSPHERE The restaurant feels distinctly suburban, but 25 years of bringing in Italian furnishings has given it personality. Lots of private dining rooms. An impressive new bar.

HOUSE SPECIALTIES Antipasto; fish with cream pesto sauce; fish basilico; pannéed veal Tanet; duck with green peppercorns; filet mignon with three-pepper sauce; tiramisu.

OTHER RECOMMENDATIONS Angel-hair pasta Andrea; mussels marinara; *stracciatella di Medici* (spinach and chicken soup); veal chop Valdostana; strawberry cake.

ENTERTAINMENT AND AMENITIES Live singers and pianists in the bar Wednesday through Saturday. Strolling accordionist at Sunday brunch.

SUMMARY AND COMMENTS Capri native Andrea Apuzzo operates the city's most ambitious Italian restaurant, with an enormous menu and an offer from the chef to cook anything else you might want on top of that. The quality of the ingredients (especially seafood and vegetables) is unimpeachable. What began as a pure Northern Italian kitchen has acquired a lot of New Orleans flavor over the years. The food is always beautiful and generous, but the cooking veers unpredictably from brilliant to just okay. Seafood is the best bet, followed by poultry. At its best, Andrea's puts out an unforgettable dinner, with the chef constantly in the room flattering his customers and making people laugh.

french quarter dining

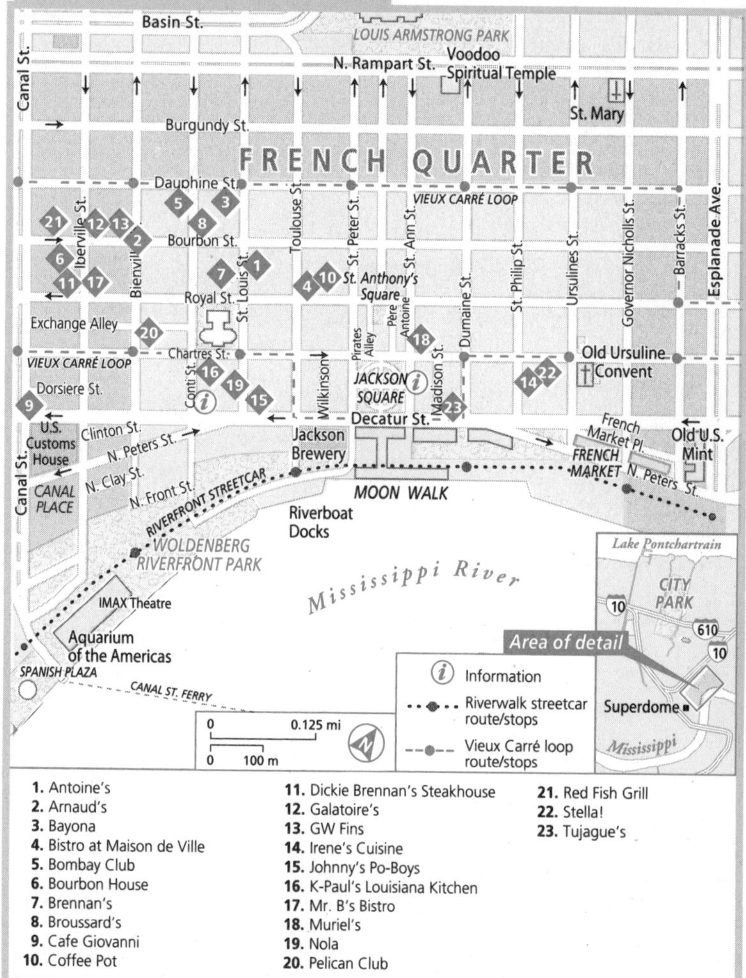

Antoine's ★★★★

CLASSIC CREOLE **VERY EXPENSIVE** **QUALITY ★★★★** **VALUE ★★**

713 St. Louis Street, French Quarter; ☎504-581-4422; www.antoines.com

Reservations Recommended. **When to go** Dinner. **Entree range** $22–$48. **Payment** All major credit cards. **Service rating** ★★★. **Friendliness rating** ★★★. **Parking** Pay garages nearby. **Bar** Full bar. **Wine selection** Distinguished cellar with tremendous inventory, French dominated, many older vintages; the wine

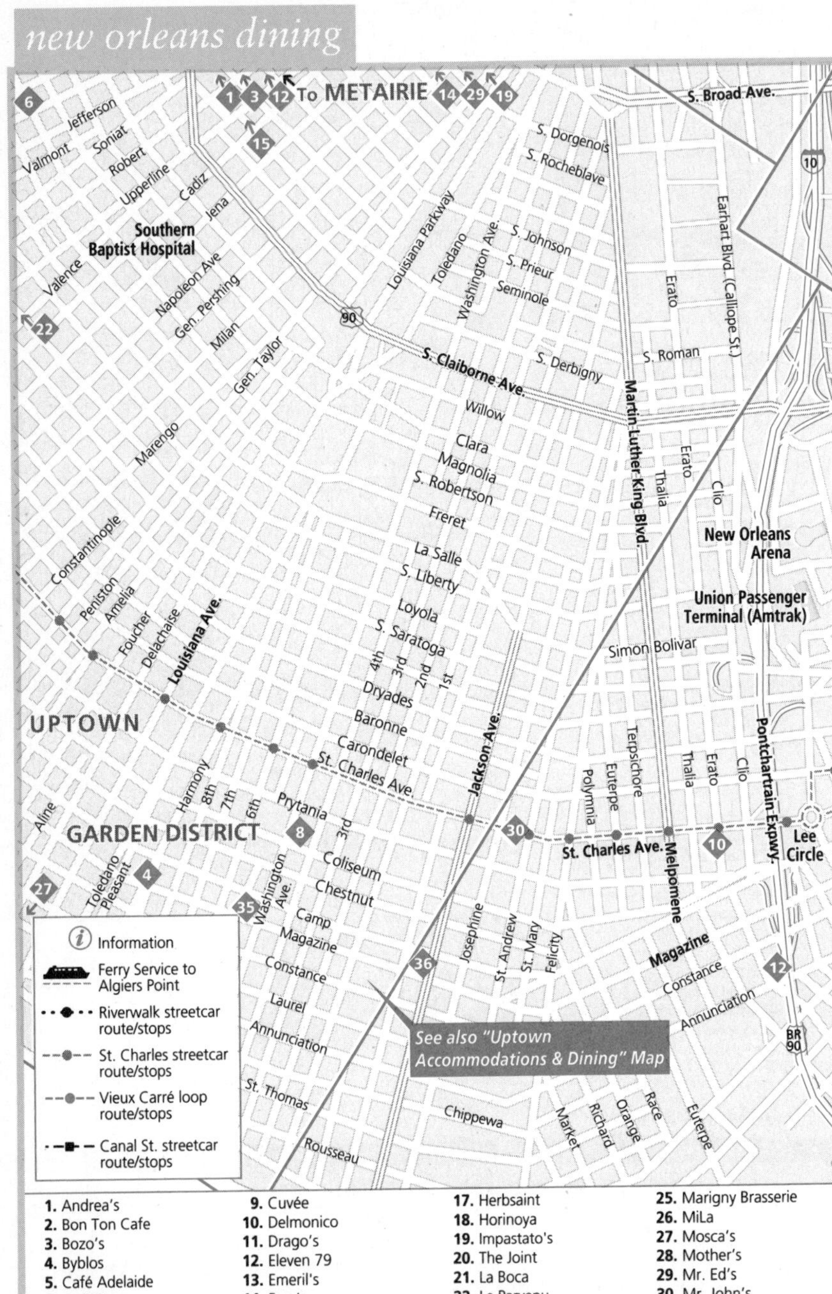
new orleans dining
To METAIRIE
S. Broad Ave.
S. Dorgenois
S. Rocheblave
Earhart Blvd. (Calliope St.)
Valmont
Jefferson
Soniat
Robert
Upperline
Cadiz
Jena
Southern Baptist Hospital
Valence
Napoleon Ave
Gen. Pershing
Milan
Gen. Taylor
Louisiana Parkway
Toledano
Washington Ave.
S. Johnson
S. Prieur
Seminole
Erato
S. Roman
S. Claiborne Ave.
S. Derbigny
Martin Luther King Blvd.
Willow
Clara
Magnolia
S. Robertson
Freret
La Salle
S. Liberty
Loyola
S. Saratoga
Marengo
Constantinople
Peniston
Amelia
Foucher
Delachaise
Louisiana Ave.
Thalia
Erato
Clio
New Orleans Arena
Union Passenger Terminal (Amtrak)
Simon Bolivar
4th
3rd
2nd
1st
Dryades
Baronne
Carondelet
St. Charles Ave.
Jackson Ave.
UPTOWN
Harmony
8th
7th
6th
Prytania
3rd
Aline
GARDEN DISTRICT
Coliseum
Chestnut
Toledano
Pleasant
Washington Ave.
Camp
Magazine
Constance
Laurel
Annunciation
St. Thomas
Rousseau
Chippewa
Terpsichore
Euterpe
Polymnia
Thalia
Erato
Clio
Pontchartrain Expwy.
Lee Circle
St. Charles Ave.
Melpomene
Josephine
St. Andrew
St. Mary
Felicity
Magazine
Constance
Annunciation
See also "Uptown Accommodations & Dining" Map
Market
Richard
Orange
Race
Euterpe
Information
Ferry Service to Algiers Point
Riverwalk streetcar route/stops
St. Charles streetcar route/stops
Vieux Carré loop route/stops
Canal St. streetcar route/stops
1. Andrea's
2. Bon Ton Cafe
3. Bozo's
4. Byblos
5. Café Adelaide
6. Café East
7. Cochon
8. Commander's Palace
9. Cuvée
10. Delmonico
11. Drago's
12. Eleven 79
13. Emeril's
14. Fury's
15. Galley Seafood
16. Grand Isle
17. Herbsaint
18. Horinoya
19. Impastato's
20. The Joint
21. La Boca
22. Le Parvenu
23. Li'l Dizzy's Cafe
24. Lüke
25. Marigny Brasserie
26. MiLa
27. Mosca's
28. Mother's
29. Mr. Ed's
30. Mr. John's Steakhouse
31. Palace Café

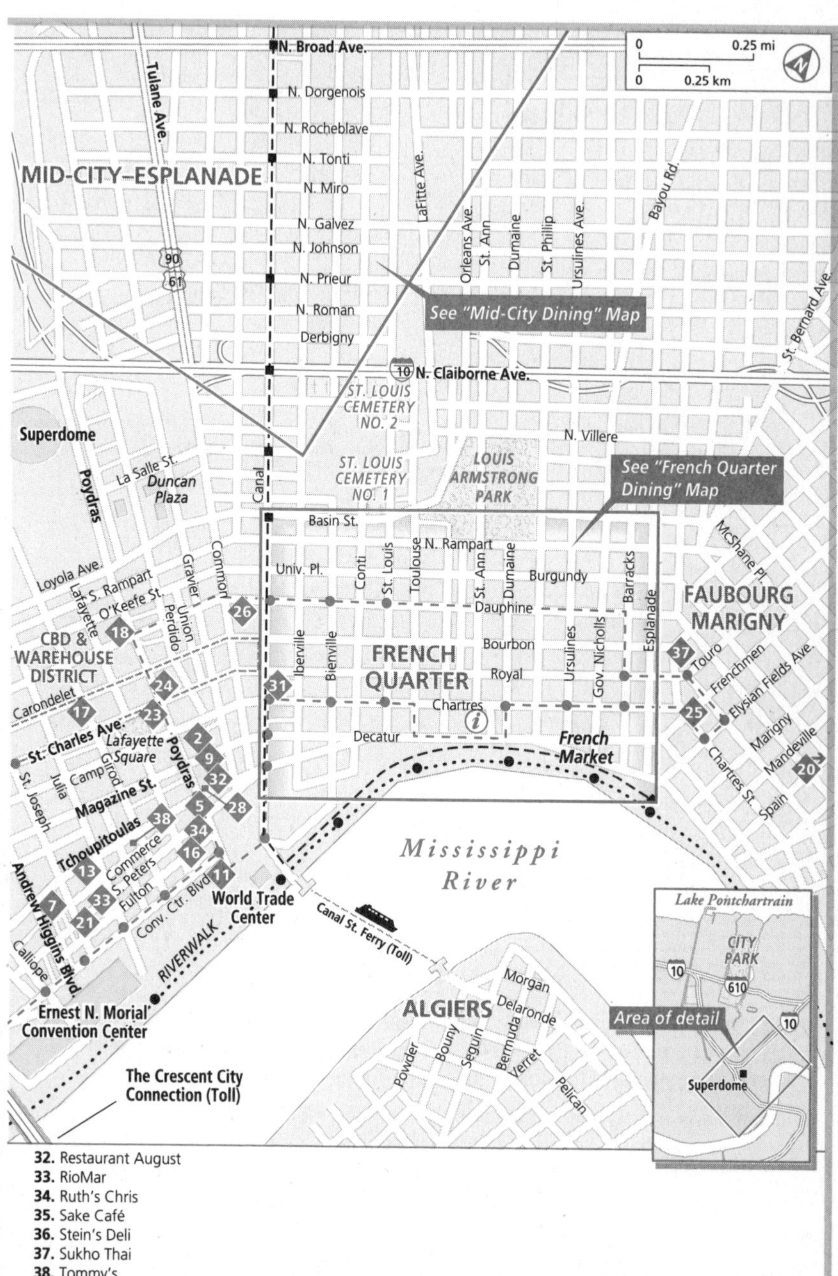

N. Broad Ave.
N. Dorgenois
N. Rocheblave
N. Tonti
N. Miro
N. Galvez
N. Johnson
N. Prieur
N. Roman
Derbigny
Tulane Ave.
MID-CITY–ESPLANADE
LaFitte Ave.
Orleans Ave.
St. Ann
Dumaine
St. Phillip
Ursulines Ave.
Bayou Rd.
St. Bernard Ave.
See "Mid-City Dining" Map
N. Claiborne Ave.
ST. LOUIS CEMETERY NO. 2
ST. LOUIS CEMETERY NO. 1
LOUIS ARMSTRONG PARK
N. Villere
See "French Quarter Dining" Map
Superdome
Poydras
La Salle St.
Duncan Plaza
Canal
Basin St.
N. Rampart
Burgundy
Dauphine
Bourbon
Royal
Chartres
Decatur
Iberville
Bienville
Conti
St. Louis
Toulouse
Ursulines
Gov. Nicholls
Barracks
Esplanade
FRENCH QUARTER
French Market
McShane Pl.
FAUBOURG MARIGNY
Touro
Frenchmen
Elysian Fields Ave.
Marigny
Mandeville
Chartres St.
Spain
Loyola Ave.
S. Rampart
O'Keefe St.
Lafayette
Gravier
Common
Union
Perdido
CBD & WAREHOUSE DISTRICT
Carondelet
St. Charles Ave.
Lafayette Square
Poydras
Julia
Camp
Girod
St. Joseph
Magazine St.
Tchoupitoulas
Commerce
S. Peters
Fulton
Conv. Ctr. Blvd
Andrew Higgins Blvd.
Calliope
World Trade Center
RIVERWALK
Ernest N. Morial Convention Center
The Crescent City Connection (Toll)
Mississippi River
Canal St. Ferry (Toll)
ALGIERS
Morgan
Delaronde
Bermuda
Verret
Seguin
Bouny
Powder
Pelican
0 0.25 mi
0 0.25 km
Lake Pontchartrain
CITY PARK
Area of detail
Superdome

32. Restaurant August
33. RioMar
34. Ruth's Chris
35. Sake Café
36. Stein's Deli
37. Sukho Thai
38. Tommy's

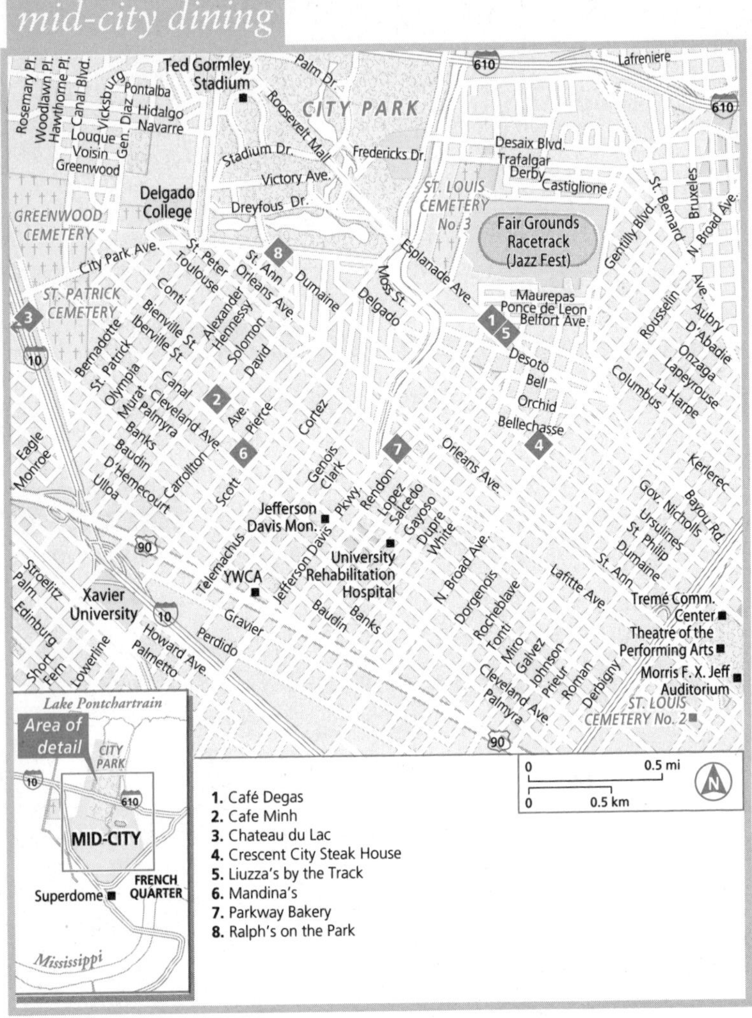

cellar presents a great visual. **Dress** Dressy. **Disabled access** Full in dining rooms; one step in restrooms. **Customers** Local regulars, high society, and tourists. **Hours** Monday–Saturday, 11:30 a.m.–2 p.m. and 5–9 p.m.; Sunday, 11 a.m.–2 p.m.

SETTING AND ATMOSPHERE Antoine's rambling antique premises recall many eras and flavors of the city's social life. The front dining room is charming at lunch; for dinner, get a table in the red-walled (well, we think it's red—most of the surface is covered by framed memorabilia) Annex.

HOUSE SPECIALTIES Oysters Rockefeller; oysters Foch; escargots Bordelaise; shrimp rémoulade; soft-shell crabs Colbert; *tournedos marchand de vin;* baked Alaska.

OTHER RECOMMENDATIONS Crawfish cardinale; grilled pompano; trout amandine; chicken Rochambeau; lamb chops béarnaise.

ENTERTAINMENT AND AMENITIES Strolling jazz trio at Sunday brunch.

SUMMARY AND COMMENTS Antoine's is a living museum of New Orleans dining. Founded in 1840, it's the oldest restaurant in America under continuous operation by one family. If you're fascinated by culinary history, you'll love it. If you require that all current service and food trends are followed, this is not the place for you. The best time to figure Antoine's out is lunch, which is rarely busy and offers the same menu as dinner (plus a short lunch menu with lower prices). Antoine's best dishes, once common elsewhere, are now unique to the restaurant. The beef, chicken, and uncomplicated seafood dishes are most likely to please you. An even better strategy is to make an entire meal of appetizers. The best food here is served to regulars, so either be one or go with one. After a very slack period in the last decade, Antoine's new management (they're still family) has embarked on a program of restoring the premises. They've also made significant improvements to the food.

Arnaud's ★★★★

CLASSIC CREOLE | VERY EXPENSIVE | QUALITY ★★★★ | VALUE ★★★

813 Bienville Street, French Quarter; ☎504-523-5433; www.arnauds.com

Reservations Recommended. **When to go** Dinner, Sunday brunch. **Entree range** $22–$40. **Payment** All major credit cards. **Service rating** ★★★★. **Friendliness rating** ★★★★. **Parking** Pay parking lots nearby. **Bar** Full bar. **Wine selection** Distinguished cellar, good international balance; a bit pricey. There are also exceptional collections of ports, Cognacs, and cigars. **Dress** Jacket recommended but not required. **Disabled access** Full. **Customers** Tourists, some locals. **Hours** Daily, 6–10 p.m.; Sunday 11:30 a.m.–3 p.m.

SETTING AND ATMOSPHERE Nobody ever gave a moribund old restaurant a better rebirth than did Arnaud's owner, Archie Casbarian. An atmospheric exemplar of the old-style New Orleans Creole restaurant, its tiled floors, tin ceilings, beveled-glass windows, and ancient overhead fans are trademarks. If you have time, tour the huge restaurant's many private dining rooms and its Mardi Gras museum.

HOUSE SPECIALTIES Shrimp Arnaud (rémoulade); oysters Arnaud (five different); pompano David; bananas Foster; bread pudding; café brûlot.

OTHER RECOMMENDATIONS Shrimp Bellaire; oysters stewed in cream; pompano en croute; veal tournedos Chantal; crème brûlée.

ENTERTAINMENT AND AMENITIES A small jazz band plays at dinner in Richelieu Room for a small cover charge. Strolling jazz trio at Sunday brunch.

SUMMARY AND COMMENTS In its first heyday, Arnaud's was the leading restaurant of New Orleans, reinventing the way people dined out. It slipped into obscurity in the 1970s but was brought back to life in 1979. The modern Arnaud's blends dishes created eons ago by Count Arnaud with spiffy new food—all with an unmistakable New Orleans flavor. The menu in recent years has become shorter and more manageable than it had been, and the cooking has become more polished.

New Orleans Restaurants by Cuisine

CUISINE/NAME	OVERALL RATING	PRICE	QUALITY RATING	VALUE RATING
AMERICAN				
Gautreau's	★★★★	Expensive	★★★★	★★★★
BARBECUE				
The Joint	★★★	Inexpensive	★★★	★★★★
CAJUN				
K-Paul's Louisiana Kitchen	★★★★	Very Exp.	★★★★	★★★
Cochon	★★★	Expensive	★★★★	★★★
Bon Ton Cafe	★★★	Moderate	★★★	★★★★
Jacques-Imo's	★★★	Moderate	★★★	★★★★
CARIBBEAN				
Baru Bistro & Tapas	★★★	Inexpensive	★★★	★★★★
CHINESE				
Café East	★★★★	Moderate	★★★★	★★★★
Five Happiness	★★★	Inexpensive	★★★	★★★★
CLASSIC CREOLE				
Antoine's	★★★★	Very Exp.	★★★★	★★
Arnaud's	★★★★	Very Exp.	★★★★	★★★
Austin's	★★★★	Expensive	★★★★	★★★★
Brennan's	★★★★	Very Exp.	★★★★	★★
Broussard's	★★★★	Very Exp.	★★★★	★★★★
Galatoire's	★★★★	Very Exp.	★★★★	★★★
Tujague's	★★★	Moderate	★★★	★★★
CONTEMPORARY CREOLE				
Commander's Palace	★★★★★	Very Exp.	★★★★★	★★★★
Emeril's	★★★★★	Very Exp.	★★★★★	★★★
Pelican Club	★★★★★	Expensive	★★★★★	★★★★
Delmonico	★★★★	Very Exp.	★★★★★	★★
Bourbon House	★★★★	Moderate	★★★★	★★★
Brigtsen's	★★★★	Expensive	★★★★	★★★★
Café Adelaide	★★★★	Expensive	★★★★	★★★
Dante's Kitchen	★★★★	Moderate	★★★★	★★★★
Dick & Jenny's	★★★★	Expensive	★★★★	★★★★★

CUISINE/NAME	OVERALL RATING	PRICE	QUALITY RATING	VALUE RATING
CONTEMPORARY CREOLE (CONTINUED)				
Le Parvenu	★★★★	Expensive	★★★★	★★★★
Marigny Brasserie	★★★★	Expensive	★★★★	★★★
Muriel's	★★★★	Expensive	★★★★	★★★★
Nola	★★★★	Expensive	★★★★	★★★
One	★★★★	Expensive	★★★★	★★★★★
Palace Cafe	★★★★	Expensive	★★★★	★★★
Ralph's on the Park	★★★★	Expensive	★★★★	★★★★
Tommy's	★★★★	Expensive	★★★★	★★★★
Upperline	★★★★	Moderate	★★★★	★★★★
Vizard's	★★★★	Expensive	★★★★	★★★★
Bombay Club	★★★	Expensive	★★★	★★★
CREOLE				
Clancy's	★★★★	Expensive	★★★★	★★★★
Mr. B's Bistro	★★★★	Expensive	★★★★	★★★★
Li'l Dizzy's Cafe	★★★	Inexpensive	★★★	★★★★
Mandina's	★★★	Moderate	★★★	★★★★★
Pascal's Manale	★★★	Moderate	★★★	★★★★
Coffee Pot	★★	Inexpensive	★★★	★★★★
ECLECTIC				
MiLa	★★★★★	Very Exp.	★★★★★	★★★★
Restaurant August	★★★★★	Very Exp.	★★★★★	★★★★
Stella!	★★★★★	Very Exp.	★★★★★	★★★
Bayona	★★★★	Expensive	★★★★★	★★★★
Bistro at Maison de Ville	★★★★	Expensive	★★★★	★★★
Cuvee	★★★★	Very Exp.	★★★★	★★★★
FRENCH				
Bistro Daisy	★★★★	Expensive	★★★★	★★★
Chateau Du Lac	★★★★	Expensive	★★★★	★★★
Herbsaint	★★★★	Expensive	★★★★	★★★
La Crepe Nanou	★★★★	Moderate	★★★★	★★★★★
Lilette	★★★★	Expensive	★★★★	★★★★
Patois	★★★★	Expensive	★★★★	★★★

Restaurants by Cuisine (continued)

CUISINE/NAME	OVERALL RATING	PRICE	QUALITY RATING	VALUE RATING
FRENCH (CONTINUED)				
Flaming Torch	★★★	Expensive	★★★★	★★★
Café Degas	★★★	Moderate	★★★	★★★★
Lüke	★★★	Moderate	★★★	★★★
INDIAN				
Nirvana	★★★	Inexpensive	★★★	★★★★
ITALIAN				
Cafe Giovanni	★★★★	Expensive	★★★★	★★★★
Eleven 79	★★★	Expensive	★★★★	★★★
Irene's Cuisine	★★★	Moderate	★★★★	★★★★
Mosca's	★★★	Moderate	★★★★	★★★
Vincent's(Uptown)	★★★	Moderate	★★★★	★★★★
Andrea's	★★★	Expensive	★★★	★★★
Impastato's	★★★	Moderate	★★★	★★★★★
Ristorante Da Piero	★★★	Expensive	★★★	★★★
Vincent's(Metairie)	★★★	Moderate	★★★	★★★★
JAPANESE				
Ninja	★★★★	Moderate	★★★★	★★★
Horinoya	★★★	Moderate	★★★★	★★★
Sake Cafe	★★★	Moderate	★★★★	★★★
KOSHER/MEDITERRANEAN				
Casablanca	★★★	Inexpensive	★★★	★★★★
MIDDLE EASTERN				
Byblos(Uptown)	★★★	Inexpensive	★★★	★★★★
Jamila's	★★★	Inexpensive	★★★	★★★★★
Lebanon's Cafe	★★★	Inexpensive	★★★	★★★★★
NEIGHBORHOOD CAFE				
Liuzza's by the Track	★★★	Inexpensive	★★★	★★★★
Mr. Ed's	★★★	Moderate	★★★	★★★★
SANDWICHES				
Johnny's Po-Boys	★★★	Inexpensive	★★★	★★★★★
Mother's	★★★	Inexpensive	★★★	★★★★

CUISINE/NAME	OVERALL RATING	PRICE	QUALITY RATING	VALUE RATING
SANDWICHES (CONTINUED)				
Parkway Bakery	★★★	Inexpensive	★★★	★★★★
Stein's Deli	★★★	Inexpensive	★★★	★★★★
SEAFOOD				
Drago's (CBD)	★★★★	Moderate	★★★★	★★★★
Drago's (Metairie)	★★★★	Moderate	★★★★	★★★
GW Fins	★★★★	Expensive	★★★★	★★★
Galley Seafood	★★★	Inexpensive	★★★★	★★★★
Grand Isle	★★★	Moderate	★★★★	★★★
Bozo's	★★★	Inexpensive	★★★	★★★★
Fury's	★★★	Inexpensive	★★★	★★★★★
Red Fish Grill	★★★	Moderate	★★★	★★★
SPANISH				
RioMar	★★★★	Moderate	★★★★	★★★★
Cafe Granada	★★★	Moderate	★★★	★★★★★
STEAK				
Dickie Brennan's Steakhouse	★★★★	Very Exp.	★★★★	★★★
Ruth's Chris Steak House (CBD)	★★★★	Very Exp.	★★★★	★★
Ruth's Chris Steak House (Metairie)	★★★★	Very Exp.	★★★★	★★
La Boca	★★★	Expensive	★★★★	★★★
Mr. John's Steakhouse	★★★	Very Exp.	★★★★	★★★
Crescent City Steak House	★★★	High Mod.	★★★	★★★
THAI				
Basil Leaf	★★★	Inexpensive	★★★★	★★★★
La Thai Cuisine	★★★	Moderate	★★★★	★★
Sukho Thai	★★★	Inexpensive	★★★★	★★★★
VIETNAMESE				
Cafe Minh	★★★★	Expensive	★★★★	★★★★
Hoa Hong 9 Roses	★★★★	Low Mod	★★★★	★★★★★

New Orleans Restaurants by Location

NAME	CUISINE	OVERALL RATING
CENTRAL BUSINESS DISTRICT		
Emeril's	Contemporary Creole	★★★★★
MiLa	Eclectic	★★★★★
Restaurant August	Eclectic	★★★★★
Café Adelaide	Contemporary Creole	★★★★
Cuvee	Eclectic	★★★★
Drago's	Seafood	★★★★
Herbsaint	French	★★★★
Palace Cafe	Contemporary Creole	★★★★
RioMar	Spanish	★★★★
Ruth's Chris Steak House	Steak	★★★★
Tommy's	Contemporary Creole	★★★★
Bon Ton Cafe	Cajun	★★★
Cochon	Cajun	★★★
Eleven 79	Italian	★★★
Grand Isle	Seafood	★★★
Horinoya	Japanese	★★★
La Boca	Steak	★★★
Li'l Dizzy's Cafe	Creole	★★★
Luke	French	★★★
Mother's	Sandwiches	★★★
FAUBOURG MARIGNY		
Marigny Brasserie	Contemporary Creole	★★★★
Sukho Thai	Thai	★★★
The Joint	Barbecue	★★★
FRENCH QUARTER		
Pelican Club	Contemporary Creole	★★★★★
Stella!	Eclectic	★★★★★
Antoine's	Classic Creole	★★★★
Arnaud's	Classic Creole	★★★★
Bayona	Eclectic	★★★★
Bistro at Maison de Ville	French	★★★★
Bourbon House	Contemporary Creole	★★★★

NAME	CUISINE	OVERALL RATING
FRENCH QUARTER (CONTINUED)		
Brennan's	Classic Creole	★★★★
Broussard's	Classic Creole	★★★★
Cafe Giovanni	Italian	★★★★
Dickie Brennan's Steakhouse	Steak	★★★★
Galatoire's	Classic Creole	★★★★
GW Fins	Seafood	★★★★
K-Paul's Louisiana Kitchen	Cajun	★★★★
Mr. B's Bistro	Creole	★★★★
Muriel's	Contemporary Creole	★★★★
Nola	Contemporary Creole	★★★★
Bombay Club	Contemporary Creole	★★★
Irene's Cuisine	Italian	★★★
Johnny's Po-Boys	Sandwiches	★★★
Red Fish Grill	Seafood	★★★
Tujague's	Classic Creole	★★★
Coffee Pot	Creole	★★
GRETNA		
Hoa Hong 9 Roses	Vietnamese	★★★★
KENNER		
Le Parvenu	Contemporary Creole	★★★★
Ristorante Da Piero	Italian	★★★
METAIRIE		
Austin's	Classic Creole	★★★★
Café East	Chinese	★★★★
Chateau Du Lac	French	★★★★
Drago's	Seafood	★★★★
Ruth's Chris Steak House	Steak	★★★★
Andrea's	Italian	★★★
Bozo's	Seafood	★★★
Casablanca	Kosher/Mediterranean	★★★
Fury's	Seafood	★★★
Galley Seafood	Seafood	★★★

Restaurants by Location (continued)

NAME	CUISINE	OVERALL RATING
METAIRIE (CONTINUED)		
Impastato's	Italian	★★★
Sake Cafe	Japanese	★★★
Vincent's	Italian	★★★
MID-CITY–ESPLANADE		
Cafe Minh	Vietnamese	★★★★
Ralph's on the Park	Contemporary Creole	★★★★
Café Degas	French	★★★
Crescent City Steak House	Steak	★★★
Liuzza's by the Track	Neighborhood Cafe	★★★
Mandina's	Creole	★★★
Parkway Bakery	Sandwiches	★★★
UPTOWN AND THE GARDEN DISTRICT		
Commander's Palace	Contemporary Creole	★★★★★
Bistro Daisy	French	★★★★
Brigtsen's	Contemporary Creole	★★★★
Clancy's	Creole	★★★★
Dante's Kitchen	Contemporary Creole	★★★★
Delmonico	Contemporary Creole	★★★★
Dick & Jenny's	Creole	★★★★
Gautreau's	American	★★★★
La Crepe Nanou	French	★★★★
Lilette	French	★★★★
Ninja	Japanese	★★★★

Austin's ★★★★

CLASSIC CREOLE EXPENSIVE QUALITY ★★★★ VALUE ★★★★

5101 West Esplanade Avenue, Metairie; ☎504-888-5533; www.austinsno.com

Reservations Recommended. **When to go** Dinner. **Entree range** $18–$32. **Payment** All major credit cards. **Service rating** ★★★. **Friendliness rating** ★★★. **Parking** Ample parking lot adjacent. **Bar** Full bar. **Wine selection** Modest list of wines matched to the food. **Dress** Nice casual. **Disabled access** Full. **Customers** Locals, many of them regulars. **Hours** Monday–Saturday, 5–10 p.m..

NAME	CUISINE	OVERALL RATING
UPTOWN AND THE GARDEN DISTRICT (CONTINUED)		
One	Contemporary Creole	★★★★
Patois	French	★★★★
Upperline	Contemporary Creole	★★★★
Vizard's	Contemporary Creole	★★★★
Baru Bistro & Tapas	Caribbean	★★★
Basil Leaf	Thai	★★★
Byblos	Middle Eastern	★★★
Cafe Granada	Spanish	★★★
Five Happiness	Chinese	★★★
Flaming Torch	French	★★★
Jacques-Imo's	Cajun	★★★
Jamila's	Middle Eastern	★★★
La Thai Cuisine	Thai	★★★
Lebanon's Cafe	Middle Eastern	★★★
Mr. Ed's	Neighborhood Cafe	★★★
Mr. John's Steakhouse	Steak	★★★
Nirvana	Indian	★★★
Pascal's Manale	Creole	★★★
Sake Cafe	Japanese	★★★
Stein's Deli	Sandwiches	★★★
Vincent's	Italian	★★★
WAGGAMAN		
Mosca's	Italian	★★★

SETTING AND ATMOSPHERE As the restaurant grew, it took over more spaces in a strip mall, doing a decent job of decorating but remaining unmistakably suburban.

HOUSE SPECIALTIES Crabmeat Austin; shrimp rémoulade; pannéed oysters; gumbo ya-ya; pecan-crusted trout; double-cut pork chop.

OTHER RECOMMENDATIONS Bacon-wrapped sea scallops; blue cheese wedge salad; sirloin strip steak; cherry or orange duck.

SUMMARY AND COMMENTS Austin's is an upscale version of Mr. Ed's, one of the city's best neighborhood-style cafes. The menu here is a blend of familiar Creole and Italian dishes, using good raw materials in finely tuned renditions of the food the hip places were serving 20 years ago.

That was a great time for New Orleans food, however, and the presence of those dishes here has made Austin's one of Metairie's most popular restaurants. A good place to dine well while avoiding both the cutting edge and the classic New Orleans dishes.

Baru Bistro & Tapas ★★★

CARIBBEAN | INEXPENSIVE | QUALITY ★★★ | VALUE ★★★★

3700 Magazine Street, Uptown; ☎504-895-2225

Reservations Recommended. **When to go** Dinner. **Entree range** $13–$29. **Payment** All major credit cards. **Service rating** ★★★. **Friendliness rating** ★★★. **Parking** Curbside parking only. **Bar** No alcohol. **Wine selection** Bring your own. **Dress** Casual. **Disabled access** None. **Customers** Uptowners, on the young side. **Hours** Tuesday–Saturday, 11:30 a.m.–2 p.m. and 5:30–10 p.m.

SETTING AND ATMOSPHERE An old corner grocery, converted into a tiny restaurant with rows of tables rather close together. When the weather is good, most diners migrate to the tables on the sidewalk, where they come close to being blinded by the bright lavender paint job outside.

HOUSE SPECIALTIES *Mazorca* (corn with cheese and herbs); *parrillada* (grilled meats and chicken); ceviche; red snapper tamal; skirt steak; passionfruit sorbet.

SUMMARY AND COMMENTS The owner and chef are from Cartagena, Colombia, where the cuisine is a fascinating blend of Caribbean, South American, and Central American flavors. Seafood forms the majority of all departments of the menu, but not by much. Grilled, marinated meats and poultry are rendered with more excitement than they sound. The kitchen's entire output is different enough from what you'll find elsewhere to make this place of interest.

Basil Leaf ★★★

THAI | INEXPENSIVE | QUALITY ★★★★ | VALUE ★★★★

1438 South Carrollton Avenue, Riverbend (Uptown); ☎504-862-9001

Reservations Accepted. **When to go** Anytime. **Entree range** $9–$24. **Payment** All major credit cards. **Service rating** ★★. **Friendliness rating** ★★★. **Parking** Curbside parking only. **Bar** Full bar. **Wine selection** Much better selection of wines than is typically found in Asian restaurants. **Dress** Casual. **Disabled access** Limited. **Customers** Uptowners, mostly on the young side. **Hours** Daily, 4–10 p.m.

SETTING AND ATMOSPHERE A single room decorated simply but tastefully, with windows so large that people driving by may well be able to see the faces of the diners.

HOUSE SPECIALTIES Seared scallop salad; spring roll; sautéed calamari; green curry with chicken; soft-shell crabs with sesame.

OTHER RECOMMENDATIONS All the soups; pad Thai; grilled chicken or beef noodle salads.

SUMMARY AND COMMENTS Basil Leaf pulls away from the standard Thai menu and creates numerous original dishes. Many focus on New Orleans ingredients, occasionally with a hint of Creole flavor. On the other hand, if you come here looking for a good Thai curry or noodle dish, you'll find it. Thai food is usually well presented, but this is notably beautiful. Service and wine are better than what you're used to finding in Asian restaurants.

Bayona ★★★★

ECLECTIC EXPENSIVE QUALITY ★★★★★ VALUE ★★★★

430 Dauphine Street, French Quarter; ☎504-525-4455; www.bayona.com

Reservations Required. **When to go** Anytime. **Entree range** $14–$28. **Payment** All major credit cards. **Service rating** ★★★★★. **Friendliness rating** ★★★. **Parking** Validated at garage across the street. **Bar** Full bar. **Wine selection** Distinguished cellar, with many interesting, offbeat bottles; many by-the-glass selections. **Dress** Jacket recommended but not required. **Disabled access** Limited. **Customers** Mostly locals, a few tourists. **Hours** Monday–Friday, 11:30 a.m.–2:30 p.m.; Monday–Saturday, 6–10 p.m.

SETTING AND ATMOSPHERE All dining rooms other than the main one are small and can get a bit noisy. In decent weather you may also dine under the banana trees in the courtyard—very pleasant. Avoid the cramped upstairs rooms.

HOUSE SPECIALTIES Grilled shrimp with coriander; sweetbreads any style; salmon with choucroute and Gewurztraminer sauce; duck with pepper jelly.

OTHER RECOMMENDATIONS The seasonal specials are half the menu offerings, and are worthy of perusal. Roasted garlic soup; pork, lamb, or veal chops; quail dish of the day; apple-almond gratin; orange-scented crepes with gelato.

SUMMARY AND COMMENTS The understated, meticulous personal cuisine of Susan Spicer makes for unexciting menu reading, but her brilliant sense of taste and culinary curiosity come through where it counts—on the plate. This is particularly impressive given the wide range of flavors you encounter here. The menu has two pages: a list of the restaurant's longtime favorites, and a page of market-driven items that changes daily. Either card will serve you well. Both wine and food are sold here at prices a bit below what you'd find in comparable restaurants, and lunch is an excellent bargain.

Bistro at Maison de Ville ★★★★

ECLECTIC EXPENSIVE QUALITY ★★★★ VALUE ★★★

733 Toulouse Street, French Quarter; ☎504-528-9206; www.maisondeville.com/dining/index.html

Reservations Recommended. **When to go** Anytime. **Entree range** $26–$38. **Payment** All major credit cards. **Service rating** ★★★. **Friendliness rating** ★★★★. **Parking** Several pay lots within two blocks. **Bar** Full bar. Many single-malt Scotches, Cognacs, Armagnacs, etc. **Wine selection** Very interesting list, full of offbeat bottles. Every wine on it is available by the glass. **Dress** Jacket recommended but not required. **Disabled access** Limited. **Customers** Mostly locals, a few tourists. **Hours** Tuesday–Saturday, 11 a.m.–3 p.m.; Monday–Saturday, 6–10 p.m.; Sunday brunch, 10 a.m.–2 p.m.

SETTING AND ATMOSPHERE The dining room and kitchen are teeny and the tables are small. Large-format bottles of wine fill every available display space. More elbow room can be had in the small courtyard, if the weather's tolerable for outdoor dining.

HOUSE SPECIALTIES Steamed mussels with warm potato salad or pommes frites; frog legs grillades style; sweetbreads-and-portobello sandwich; roast chicken grandmère style; bouillabaisse; crème brûlée.

OTHER RECOMMENDATIONS Smoked trout with scallops; foie gras with pain perdu; lamb osso buco; duck cassoulet.

SUMMARY AND COMMENTS Claustrophobic but chic, the Bistro (as it's simply called by its regulars) has a history of hiring hot young chefs on their way up. Nowadays, it's hard to imagine the Bistro without chef Greg Picolo, who's been on the job longer than all his predecessors combined. It's a Bistro tradition for the menu to be unpredictable, but there's a certain hard-to-nail-down style that's consistent. Ingredients and techniques tend to the unusual, and a certain Mediterranean aspect seems always to be present.

Bistro Daisy ★★★★

FRENCH EXPENSIVE QUALITY ★★★★ VALUE ★★★

5831 Magazine Street, Uptown; ☎504-899-6987

Reservations Required. **When to go** Dinner. **Entree range** $24–$38. **Payment** All major credit cards. **Service rating** ★★★★. **Friendliness rating** ★★★★. **Parking** Curbside parking only. **Bar** Full bar. **Wine selection** Good wine list. **Dress** Nice casual. **Disabled access** Limited. **Customers** Gourmets, mostly from the Uptown section. **Hours** Tuesday–Saturday, 6–10 p.m.

SETTING AND ATMOSPHERE A century-old cottage converted into a restaurant. The two largest rooms have tall ceilings decorated with imaginative, hand-painted art. Big double-hung windows lend spaciousness even when it's dark outside. When the place is full, it can be a bit noisy.

HOUSE SPECIALTIES Oysters poached in Herbsaint; mussels marinière; crabmeat with roasted beets; pork chop with choucroute; crème brûlée.

OTHER RECOMMENDATIONS Ravioli stuffed with pancetta and wild mushrooms; roast chicken with porcini dust; filet mignon with demi-glace.

SUMMARY AND COMMENTS Bistro Daisy is the product of a young married couple whose previous postings created more than a few fans. Anton and Diane Schulte are both chefs, but she runs the dining room while he presides over the kitchen. The cooking is primarily French in flavor, but the ingredients are local, and some of the flavors are, too. Quite a bit of what they serve is locally grown, and the chef seems to increase that percentage with each visit. It results in a menu that rings familiar notes with local gourmets, even when the finished dishes clearly bear the careful, personal touch of the chef.

Bombay Club ★★★

CONTEMPORARY CREOLE EXPENSIVE QUALITY ★★★ VALUE ★★★

830 Conti Street, French Quarter; ☎504-586-0972; www.thebombayclub.com

Reservations Recommended. **When to go** Late nights. **Entree range** $22–$34. **Payment** All major credit cards. **Service rating** ★★★★. **Friendliness rating** ★★★★. **Parking** Valet ($5); it's better to park in one of the nearby garages. **Bar** Full bar. **Wine selection** Modest wine collection. **Dress** Dressy. **Disabled access** Full. **Customers** Hip, social crowd on their way to or from other events. **Hours** Sunday–Wednesday, 6–10:30 p.m.; Thursday–Saturday, 6 p.m.–1:30 a.m.

SETTING AND ATMOSPHERE It started as a bar and still is dominated by one. The best tables are in small private rooms around the perimeter.

HOUSE SPECIALTIES Oysters Rockefeller; mussels with frites; barbecue shrimp; pancetta-wrapped sea scallops; filet mignon with Stilton; duck duet.

OTHER RECOMMENDATIONS Asian-style calamari; shrimp three ways; five-spice salmon; orange and sage pork chop.

ENTERTAINMENT AND AMENITIES Mixed bag of live music most nights.

SUMMARY AND COMMENTS Before the renaissance of the martini, the Bombay Club was making a big deal of them, and became one of the classiest watering holes around. It's evolved over the years into a hangout and a chic cafe keeping late hours. The food is hip Creole, a blend of classic dishes in new dress with some utterly new ideas. The menu is abbreviated but varied enough to hold one's interest.

Bon Ton Cafe ★★★

CAJUN MODERATE QUALITY ★★★ VALUE ★★★★

401 Magazine Street, Central Business District; ☎504-524-3386; www.thebontoncafe.com

Reservations Recommended. **When to go** Anytime. **Entree range** $15–$22. **Payment** All major credit cards. **Service rating** ★★★. **Friendliness rating** ★★★★. **Parking** Pay lot and curbside (metered). **Bar** Full bar. **Wine selection** A few house wines. **Dress** Dressy. **Disabled access** Limited. **Customers** Mostly locals at lunch, mostly tourists at dinner. **Hours** Monday–Friday, 11:30 a.m.–2:30 p.m. and 5:30–9 p.m.

SETTING AND ATMOSPHERE One big brick-walled room, its tables covered with red-checkered tablecloths; full of regulars.

HOUSE SPECIALTIES Turtle soup; crabmeat au gratin, redfish Bon Ton; oysters or soft-shell crab Alvin; bread pudding.

OTHER RECOMMENDATIONS Fried catfish fingers; shrimp rémoulade; Cajun Caesar salad; crawfish dinner (crawfish four ways: étouffée, bisque, fried, and omelette); pan-broiled oysters; bayou étouffée; filet mignon with burgundy sauce.

SUMMARY AND COMMENTS The Bon Ton has specialized in crawfish longer than anyone else in New Orleans, and can claim to be the town's oldest Cajun (as opposed to Creole) restaurant. Cajun cooking is itself regional;

the Bon Ton's style comes from the Bayou Lafourche area. Its pepper levels are restrained, and the style in general is a bit old-fashioned. The service is straight out of the 1960s. It's a charming, unaffected place delivering good food and value.

Bourbon House ★★★★

CONTEMPORARY CREOLE MODERATE QUALITY ★★★★ VALUE ★★★

144 Bourbon Street, French Quarter; ☎504-522-0111; www.bourbonhouse.com

Reservations Recommended. **When to go** Anytime. **Entree range** $19–$32. **Payment** All major credit cards. **Service rating** ★★★. **Friendliness rating** ★★★★. **Parking** Pay parking lots nearby. **Bar** Full bar. **Wine selection** Good wine list, including many selections by the glass. **Dress** Nice casual. **Disabled access** Full. **Customers** Mostly locals at lunch, a mix of locals and visitors at dinner. **Hours** Daily, 11:30 a.m.–10 p.m.

SETTING AND ATMOSPHERE An expansive room with large windows and interior balconies, the Bourbon House stands at what's considered the gateway to Bourbon Street. Just inside the door is a lavish display of the current seafoods, with an inviting, polished raw oyster bar.

HOUSE SPECIALTIES Oysters on the half shell, with or without caviar; baked oyster trio; redfish "on the half shell" (grilled with the skin on).

OTHER RECOMMENDATIONS Gulf fish with pecans; baked fish Grieg; fried seafood platter; pannéed veal with crabmeat; bread pudding; pecan pie.

SUMMARY AND COMMENTS Dickie Brennan does with seafood here what he did with steak at his restaurant a half-block away—which is to say simple service of top-class foodstuffs in a pleasant but informal environment. But the most pleasant part of the menu is the revival of some of the best dishes from Commander's Palace (that's family) about 20 years ago, when Paul Prudhomme and Emeril Lagasse ruled that kitchen. The kitchen also has its share of original tricks, but even those have a more traditional ring than restaurants this young tend to pursue.

Bozo's ★★★

SEAFOOD INEXPENSIVE QUALITY ★★★ VALUE ★★★★

3117 21st Street, Metairie; ☎504-831-8666

Reservations Not accepted. **When to go** Anytime except the very busy Fridays. **Entree range** $10–$18. **Payment** All major credit cards. **Service rating** ★★★. **Friendliness rating** ★★★. **Parking** Free lot adjacent. **Bar** Full bar. **Wine selection** A few house wines. **Dress** Casual. **Disabled access** Full. **Customers** Mostly locals, a few tourists. **Hours** Tuesday–Saturday, 11 a.m.–3 p.m.; Tuesday–Thursday, 6–10 p.m.; Friday–Saturday, 6–11 p.m.

SETTING AND ATMOSPHERE Two casual dining rooms connected by the oyster bar and an open kitchen.

HOUSE SPECIALTIES Oysters on the half shell; chicken andouille gumbo; fried oysters; hot sausage poorboy.

OTHER RECOMMENDATIONS Boiled crawfish or shrimp in season; fried catfish; broiled shrimp; stuffed shrimp; stuffed crab; bread pudding.

SUMMARY AND COMMENTS Bozo's demonstrates how great simple fried seafood can be when it's meticulously selected and prepared. The catfish, for example, are small, wild Des Allemandes cats (as opposed to the inferior farm-raised fish). They're fried to order, and served while still crackly hot. Each seafood is fried separately, which keeps everything from tasting the same. They also have great boiled seafood here, especially crawfish in season. The portions are not piled as high as elsewhere, but the quality is consistently satisfying. The gumbo, raw oysters, and broiled shrimp are the major specialties on a menu full of good food.

Brennan's ★★★★

CLASSIC CREOLE VERY EXPENSIVE QUALITY ★★★★ VALUE ★★

417 Royal Street, French Quarter; ☎504-525-9711; www.brennansrestaurant.com

Reservations Required. **When to go** Anytime. **Entree range** $28–$45. **Payment** All major credit cards. **Service rating** ★★★★. **Friendliness rating** ★★★★. **Parking** Validated free at Omni Royal Orleans Garage, Chartres at St. Louis. **Bar** Full bar. **Wine selection** The finest restaurant wine cellar in New Orleans. Tremendous inventory, variety, and depth. Lots of unusual, rare, and older wines, very well stored, attractively priced. **Dress** Dressy casual. **Disabled access** Full. **Customers** Tourists at breakfast; a mix of visitors and locals at dinner; wine buffs. **Hours** Daily, 9 a.m.–2 p.m. and 6–9 p.m.

SETTING AND ATMOSPHERE The historic building has dining rooms surrounding a lushly planted, slate-paved courtyard. The best dining rooms are the one just past the bar and the long gallery along the courtyard. The upstairs dining rooms are beautiful—one has a working gasolier—but they tend to be reserved for tourists.

HOUSE SPECIALTIES Eggs Sardou; grillades and grits; turtle soup; buster crabs with pecans; filet mignon Stanley; bananas Foster.

OTHER RECOMMENDATIONS Breakfast: oyster soup; eggs hussarde; eggs St. Charles; crepes Fitzgerald. Dinner: oysters Rockefeller; oysters casino; seafood crepes Barbara; filet mignon Diane; veal Kottwitz; chocolate suicide cake.

SUMMARY AND COMMENTS Breakfast at Brennan's is one of the most original and enjoyable meals you'll ever have—if you can break out of the crowd of tourists who come for it. (Tell them at every contact that you're local and that you don't want to sit upstairs.) Paying upwards of $40 for breakfast is a splurge, of course, but it becomes worth it. At dinner, Brennan's menu is made up almost entirely of the dishes we ate in New Orleans in the 1950s. But nobody seems to get tired of them. They cook with first-class raw materials, served generously. Be sure to ask for the list of specials, which for some reason doesn't always get included in the larger (and more expensive) menu.

Brigtsen's ★★★★

CONTEMPORARY CREOLE EXPENSIVE QUALITY ★★★★ VALUE ★★★★

723 Dante Street, Riverbend (Uptown); ☎504-861-7610; www.brigtsens.com

Reservations Required. **When to go** Dinner. **Entree range** $28–$36. **Payment** All major credit cards. **Service rating** ★★★★. **Friendliness rating** ★★★★. **Parking** Curbside. **Bar** Full bar. **Wine selection** Modest list, but wines well chosen for the food. **Dress** Nice casual. **Disabled access** Limited. **Customers** Mostly locals, a few tourists. **Hours** Tuesday–Saturday, 5:30–10 p.m.

SETTING AND ATMOSPHERE It's a 100-year-old cottage, lightly remodeled to provide three small dining rooms. The best tables are in the windows up front. The conviviality among customers keeps the walls from closing in.

HOUSE SPECIALTIES Grilled rabbit tenderloin; shrimp rémoulade; seafood platter (none of it is fried); slow-roasted duck; double chocolate cake.

OTHER RECOMMENDATIONS Menu changes daily.

SUMMARY AND COMMENTS Unless you have a problem with small dining rooms, you'll find Brigtsen's hospitable and easy to love. Marna Brigtsen acts more like the hostess of a guesthouse than of a restaurant. The familiarity and informality are perfect for husband/chef Frank's original but very Creole cooking style. Because the menu changes daily and because the chef loves to experiment, you'll find fish and vegetables here you have never heard of before, as well as more familiar eats. The problem will be that too much of it will sound irresistible, and ordering may be traumatic. The wine list is short but right for the food and attractively priced.

Broussard's ★★★★

CLASSIC CREOLE VERY EXPENSIVE QUALITY ★★★★ VALUE ★★★★

819 Conti Street, French Quarter; ☎504-581-3866; www.broussards.com

Reservations Recommended. **When to go** Anytime. **Entree range** $21–$38. **Payment** All major credit cards. **Service rating** ★★★. **Friendliness rating** ★★★★. **Parking** Pay parking lots nearby. **Bar** Full bar. **Wine selection** Decent list, good international balance, with more German wines than most local lists offer. **Dress** Dressy. **Disabled access** Full. **Customers** Mostly visitors, but a growing number of locals. **Hours** Tuesday–Saturday, 6–10 p.m.

SETTING AND ATMOSPHERE Three plush, well-kept, romantic dining rooms surround one of the French Quarter's largest and handsomest courtyards.

HOUSE SPECIALTIES Baked oyster trio; crabmeat Marcus; bouillabaisse; pompano with crabmeat and scallops; crepes Broussard.

OTHER RECOMMENDATIONS Trio of cold seafood appetizers; sweet potato, corn, and shrimp bisque; chicken Rochambeau; veal filet on braised leeks; wild-game grill; chocolate pava; bananas Foster.

SUMMARY AND COMMENTS Broussard's, founded in 1920, is one of the Creole restaurant grandes dames. It went through more changes than Galatoire's, Arnaud's, and other members of its generation, but it's at its all-time best right now. Chef Gunter Preuss—an old hand in continental restaurants locally—is the current owner and, with his wife and son, he runs Broussard's as a dynastic restaurant. The menu is dominated by Creole classics, but the chef keeps the flavor palate up to date, and sprinkles the menu with many of his polished originals. The three-course table d'hôte menu for $41.50 (plus tax and gratuity) is a bargain.

Byblos ★★★

MIDDLE EASTERN INEXPENSIVE QUALITY ★★★ VALUE ★★★★

3218 Magazine Street, Uptown; ☎504-894-1233

Reservations Accepted. **When to go** Anytime. **Entree range** $8–$22. **Payment** All major credit cards. **Service rating** ★★★. **Friendliness rating** ★★★★. **Parking** Curbside parking only. **Bar** Full bar. **Wine selection** Modest list of wines matched to the food. **Dress** Casual. **Disabled access** Full. **Customers** Locals. **Hours** Daily, 11:30 a.m.–10 p.m.

SETTING AND ATMOSPHERE A fine restoration of a 150-year-old building, Byblos contains modern furnishings inside an expansive, lofty space.

HOUSE SPECIALTIES Hummus; cheese pie; kafta kabob; lamb chops; chicken shawarma; *ashta* (flaky dessert pastry).

OTHER RECOMMENDATIONS Baba ghanoojh; stuffed kibbe; falafel; stuffed cabbage rolls; tabbouleh salad; beef shawarma; kabobs.

SUMMARY AND COMMENTS Byblos (named for an ancient city in Lebanon) is the best Middle Eastern restaurant this area has ever had. The ingredients are first-class (filet mignon is used for the beef kabob), and the cooking is careful and light. Much care is given to plate presentation, but everything comes out hot anyway. The appetizer meze (an assortment of some 15 appetizers for four to six people) is a great way to eat.

Café Adelaide ★★★★

CONTEMPORARY CREOLE EXPENSIVE QUALITY ★★★★ VALUE ★★★

300 Poydras Street, Central Business District; ☎504-595-3305; www.cafeadelaide.com

Reservations Recommended. **When to go** Anytime. **Entree range** $26–$34. **Payment** All major credit cards. **Service rating** ★★★★. **Friendliness rating** ★★★★. **Parking** Free valet parking. **Bar** Full bar. **Wine selection** Good wine list, including many selections by the glass. **Dress** Dressy. **Disabled access** Full. **Customers** Local businessmen at lunch, a mix of locals and hotel guests at dinner. **Hours** Daily, 7–10:30 a.m., 11:30 a.m.–2:30 p.m., 6–9:30 p.m.

SETTING AND ATMOSPHERE Three spacious rooms with big windows, arranged shotgun-house style. The first is an unusually comfortable and excellent lounge. The dining rooms, with their curious faux-wood columns, follow suit.

HOUSE SPECIALTIES Gumbo; turtle soup; Louisiana boucherie platter; barbecue shrimp; shrimp and grits; herb-roasted fish with crabmeat; café au lait mousse.

OTHER RECOMMENDATIONS Redfish and crab court-bouillon; duck with pepper jelly; grillades and grits (breakfast).

SUMMARY AND COMMENTS Named for the late Adelaide Brennan, the most avid party-goer among the founding generation of the Brennan restaurant family, Café Adelaide is the downtown branch of Commander's Palace. The cooking style is unambiguously Creole, with more emphasis on the rustic touches than at Commander's. Its dining rooms are chock-full of lawyers and businessmen at lunch, and a few too many visitors to keep the local momentum going at dinner. The bar is the best in town, its original cocktails (conceived by a "cocktail chef") made with freshly squeezed juices and other fine ingredients. Also here: the best hotel breakfast in town. Order off the menu for that, and ignore the buffet.

Café Degas ★★★

FRENCH | MODERATE | QUALITY ★★★ | VALUE ★★★★

3127 Esplanade Avenue, Mid-City; ☎504-945-5635; www.cafedegas.com

Reservations Accepted. **When to go** Anytime. **Entree range** $15–$24. **Payment** All major credit cards. **Service rating** ★★★. **Friendliness rating** ★★★★. **Parking** Curbside parking only. **Bar** Full bar. **Wine selection** Limited list of basic wines, mostly French. **Dress** Casual. **Disabled access** Limited. **Customers** Neighborhood people. **Hours** Wednesday–Saturday, 11:30 a.m.–2:30 p.m.; Sunday, 10:30 a.m.–3 p.m.; Wednesday–Thursday and Sunday, 6–9:30 p.m.; Friday–Saturday 6–10:30 p.m.

SETTING AND ATMOSPHERE The tables are on a covered deck surrounded by a junglelike growth of plants and the sidewalk of Esplanade Avenue—very inviting, especially considering the rarity of alfresco dining in New Orleans.

HOUSE SPECIALTIES Onion soup gratinee; salad with goat cheese; filet mignon au poivre with frites; veal cheeks with pappardelle pasta.

OTHER RECOMMENDATIONS Assiette de pâtés; escargots bourguignonne; mussels with fennel broth; omelettes (lunch); crème brûlée.

SUMMARY AND COMMENTS Café Degas (named for the French artist who once lived a few blocks away) used to get by strictly on its open-air charm, but no more. The food gets better with each visit. Like in the French bistros after which the place is patterned, you find simple ingredients cooked simply and in familiar ways—but very well. The service staff is either overly enthusiastic or missing in action, but it's that kind of place and nobody cares. This is the sort of pleasant place where you come to linger with friends (or without them), and where the food is always a lovely surprise. The Sunday brunch is less expensive and more casual than most.

Café East ★★★★

CHINESE | MODERATE | QUALITY ★★★★ | VALUE ★★★★

4628 Rye Street, Metairie; ☎504-888-0078; www.cafeeastnola.com

Reservations Accepted. **When to go** Anytime. **Entree range** $9–$28. **Payment** All major credit cards. **Service rating** ★★. **Friendliness rating** ★★★. **Parking**

Ample parking lot adjacent. **Bar** Full bar. **Wine selection** Good wine list, including many selections by the glass. **Dress** Casual. **Disabled access** Full. **Customers** Suburbanites, plus younger diners digging the more adventuresome fare. **Hours** Daily, 11:30 a.m.–10 p.m.

SETTING AND ATMOSPHERE A striking, almost futuristic cube of a building in which every element makes a statement interesting enough to dwell on. The lighting sconces and their changing colors hold your attention.

HOUSE SPECIALTIES Seared scallops with pepper sauce; Singapore noodles; whole braised fish; veal chop with massaman curry; Szechuan beef "ma la."

OTHER RECOMMENDATIONS Kimchee; mussels with XO sauce; escargots with peppers and garlic; hot and sour soup; red snapper with green curry; chocolate truffle cake.

SUMMARY AND COMMENTS Café East is the most avant-garde Chinese restaurant to open in the New Orleans area in decades. And it's easily the best place for Chinese food, too. After the menu dispenses with the basic dishes mainstream diners expect, it starts breaking rules and dreaming up some really interesting food, holding nothing back. If you like very peppery food, for example, here it is. Not all the food is Chinese; Thai flavors in particular show up in many dishes. And dishes like the veal chop come out whole, not cut up as traditional Chinese places feel compelled to do. The complimentary appetizer is kimchee. The service staff is less deft than the kitchen is.

Cafe Giovanni ★★★★

ITALIAN | EXPENSIVE | QUALITY ★★★★ | VALUE ★★★★

117 Decatur Street, French Quarter; ☎504-529-2154; www.cafegiovanni.com

Reservations Recommended. **When to go** Wednesdays, Fridays, and Saturdays, when the opera singers are there. **Entree range** $18–$35. **Payment** All major credit cards. **Service rating** ★★★. **Friendliness rating** ★★★★. **Parking** Valet parking, $5. **Bar** Full bar. **Wine selection** Reasonable list, mostly Italian; many by-the-glass selections. **Dress** Nice casual. **Disabled access** Full. **Customers** Mostly locals, many of whom come regularly for the singers. **Hours** Every night, 5:30–10 p.m.

SETTING AND ATMOSPHERE The dining room combines the ground floors of two old French Quarter town houses, plus their shared courtyard, with a noisy, uniquely New Orleans environment.

HOUSE SPECIALTIES Antipasto; crab cakes; oysters Giovanni; crabmeat salad Caprese; pasta Gambino; pine-nut butter cheesecake.

OTHER RECOMMENDATIONS Grilled scallops and shrimp with sake soy sauce; eggplant LoCicero (shrimp and crabmeat); Sicilian wedding soup; Italian herbed roast chicken; tiramisu.

ENTERTAINMENT AND AMENITIES Most nights, talented singers stroll about performing opera and Broadway songs, accompanied by a pianist (and occasionally more musicians).

SUMMARY AND COMMENTS Chef Duke LoCicero mixes conventional and very unconventional ideas about the Italian flavor palate, and what he gets is so good that the overwhelming size of the platters he puts out seems way over the top. But that's what happens when New Orleans and Sicilian food enthusiasm comes together. The best strategy is to let the chef feed you an assortment of small portions of the day's specials, plus a few mainstays, for about $50. That meal will swing back and forth from the very familiar (an extraordinary ravioli Bolognese) to the completely original (pannéed asparagus with prosciutto). The place is a little inconsistent (Chef Duke works too hard), but especially on the nights when the singers work the dining room, eating here is an event.

Cafe Granada ★★★

SPANISH MODERATE QUALITY ★★★ VALUE ★★★★★

1506 South Carrollton Avenue, Carrollton; ☎504-865-1612

Reservations Accepted. **When to go** Anytime. **Entree range** $12–$17. **Payment** All major credit cards. **Service rating** ★★★. **Friendliness rating** ★★★★. **Parking** Curbside parking only. **Bar** Full bar. **Wine selection** Modest list of wines matched to the food. **Dress** Casual. **Disabled access** Limited. **Customers** Locals, many college students, and Spanish people. **Hours** Daily, 11:30 a.m.–10 p.m.

SETTING AND ATMOSPHERE This old storefront could use a renovation, but the raffish environment seems to add something to the bohemian atmosphere. It's comfortable enough.

HOUSE SPECIALTIES Mussels; sautéed calamari; paella in any style; lamb chops with aioli; tamarind flan.

OTHER RECOMMENDATIONS Croquetas; Basque chicken roulade.

ENTERTAINMENT AND AMENITIES Live guitarists play Spanish music most nights.

SUMMARY AND COMMENTS Cafe Granada started out serving a mixed menu of Mexican and Spanish food, but the latter was so good that they changed the name of the place and went entirely to a menu of tapas, gazpacho, paella, and other dishes from Spain. That made the restaurant even better, and now it's in the top rank locally for that kind of food. The paella is especially distinguished. And if you come here without getting mussels in the mildly peppery red sauce, you've really missed something.

Cafe Minh ★★★★

VIETNAMESE EXPENSIVE QUALITY ★★★★ VALUE ★★★★

4139 Canal Street, Mid-City; ☎504-482-6266

Reservations Recommended. **When to go** Dinner. **Entree range** $18–$36. **Payment** All major credit cards. **Service rating** ★★★★. **Friendliness rating** ★★★★. **Parking** Curbside. **Bar** Full bar. **Wine selection** Good wine list. **Dress** Nice casual. **Disabled access** Full. **Customers** Local residents, Asians, gourmets. Most are on the young side. **Hours** Tuesday–Saturday, 11:30 a.m.–9 p.m.

SETTING AND ATMOSPHERE This was a corner cafe that operated under many names for almost a century before eight feet of water filled it up after

Hurricane Katrina. The renovation turned the dark, old place into a sparkling, airy restaurant in one long dining room.

HOUSE SPECIALTIES Pecan-crusted oysters; shrimp and lemongrass; crab cake coated with crushed wontons; bouillabaisse; chicken roti; banana crème brûlée.

OTHER RECOMMENDATIONS Rack of lamb; seared sea scallops with Japanese eggplant; flounder "basket."

SUMMARY AND COMMENTS Minh Bui escaped from Vietnam (quite a story) and wound up in New Orleans, where he worked for the likes of Commander's Palace before opening the first in a series of his own, increasingly more ambitious restaurants. This is his best, a sleek cafe where Vietnamese and other Asian flavors show up in cameo roles. For the most part, this food is Chef Minh's original ideas, making the most of local ingredients on the way to thrilling even palates that thought they'd tasted it all.

Casablanca ★★★

MEDITERRANEAN INEXPENSIVE QUALITY ★★★ VALUE ★★★★

3030 Severn Avenue, Metairie; ☎504-888-2209

Reservations Not Accepted. **When to go** Not Fridays and Saturdays. **Entree range** $6–$18. **Payment** All major credit cards. **Service rating** ★★★. **Friendliness rating** ★★★. **Parking** Ample parking lot adjacent. **Bar** Full bar. **Wine selection** A few house wines. **Dress** Casual. **Disabled access** Full. **Customers** Observant Jews, plus an equal number of Gentiles. **Hours** Sunday–Thursday, 11:30 a.m.–9 p.m.; Friday, 11:30 a.m.–3 p.m.

SETTING AND ATMOSPHERE The room has a lofty ceiling, a dramatic mural, and an ambience grander than you'd expect from the look of the exterior.

HOUSE SPECIALTIES Spinach pie; soups; chicken *meshwi;* lamb brochette; couscous; deli sandwiches; kosher (pareve) cheesecake.

SUMMARY AND COMMENTS Casablanca serves Middle Eastern and Moroccan food—and it's all strictly kosher (supervised by a Chabad rabbi). The first courses are better constructed than the entrees, for some reason; the baba ghanoojh and hummus are particularly fine. The soups are simple but extraordinarily good. Then it's on to the couscous variations, tagines, and beguilingly flavored Northern African dishes. They also have a limited selection of kosher deli sandwiches.

Chateau du Lac ★★★★

FRENCH EXPENSIVE QUALITY ★★★★ VALUE ★★★

2037 Metairie Road, Old Metairie; ☎504-831-3773; www.chateaudulacbistro.com

Reservations Recommended. **When to go** Dinner. **Entree range** $19–$45. **Payment** All major credit cards. **Service rating** ★★★★. **Friendliness rating** ★★★★. **Parking** Small parking lot adjacent. **Bar** Full bar. **Wine selection** Excellent wine list—all French!—including many selections by the glass. **Dress** Nice casual. **Disabled access** Full. **Customers** A mixed-age crowd, at least half of whom come from the surrounding Old Metairie neighborhood. **Hours** Tuesday–Friday, 11:30 a.m.–2:30 p.m.; Tuesday–Saturday, 5:30–10 p.m.

SETTING AND ATMOSPHERE The first room of the well-worn but recently renovated space includes a large bar and an open kitchen, as well as a row of tables. To the left is a bigger dining room, with large windows opening onto Metairie Road.

HOUSE SPECIALTIES Escargots any of five ways; mussels in either of two styles; mushroom strudel; onion soup; dry-aged sirloin strip steak; floating island.

OTHER RECOMMENDATIONS Filet mignon with peppercorns; rack of lamb; duck with honey and lavender.

SUMMARY AND COMMENTS In a time when French bistros are all around New Orleans, Chateau du Lac is one of the few that actually has a French chef-owner cooking classical French dishes, many of them not often seen hereabouts. Owner-chef Jacques Saleun moved here in 2007 after a couple of years in a smaller restaurant in Kenner. He's originally from Brittany, in northwestern France, which informs many of his dishes. Meats and birds are more of a specialty than seafood, even in the appetizer courses.

Clancy's ★★★★

CREOLE | EXPENSIVE | QUALITY ★★★★ | VALUE ★★★★

6100 Annunciation Street, Uptown; ☎504-895-1111

Reservations Recommended. **When to go** Anytime. **Entree range** $18–$32. **Payment** All major credit cards. **Service rating** ★★★★. **Friendliness rating** ★★★★. **Parking** Curbside parking only. **Bar** Full bar. **Wine selection** Substantial list, full of oddities. The owner is an oenophile, and buys many short-lot wines he's interested in. Many by-the-glass selections. The bar's stock of spirits is unusually broad. **Dress** Dressy casual. **Disabled access** Limited. **Customers** Locals, gourmets. **Hours** Friday, 11:30 a.m.–2:30 p.m.; Monday–Saturday, 6–10 p.m.

SETTING AND ATMOSPHERE An old neighborhood bar, gentrified over 25 years ago, that still has a neighborhood feeling. The long downstairs dining room is convivial and bright. Upstairs tables are in a sort of maze. Many people dine at the bar.

HOUSE SPECIALTIES Oysters with Brie and spinach; soft-shell crab meunière; lamb chops; veal liver Lyonnaise; lemon icebox pie.

OTHER RECOMMENDATIONS Crabmeat ravigote; shrimp rémoulade; soups (any of them); smoked shrimp; seafood pasta specials; smoked duck; filet mignon with port and Stilton; crème caramel.

SUMMARY AND COMMENTS Clancy's was one of the crop of bistros that redefined Creole cooking in the early 1980s. It's matured into an Uptown answer to Galatoire's, with a passionate local following. Its kitchen leans largely on traditional Creole restaurant dishes that most hip places are afraid to serve. It blends these with adventuresome specials and a few unique signature dishes. It was the first local restaurant with an in-house capability of smoking food, and those dishes form a good part of the menu. The service staff jokes around and takes certain unusual informalities with the mostly regular clientele. The restaurant's owner is a committed wine buff, and so Clancy's has an astounding wine list for a restaurant its size.

Cochon ★★★

CAJUN | EXPENSIVE | QUALITY ★★★★ | VALUE ★★★

930 Tchoupitoulas Street, Warehouse District (CBD); ☎504-588-2123; www.cochonrestaurant.com

Reservations Recommended. **When to go** Anytime. **Entree range** $14–$24. **Payment** All major credit cards. **Service rating** ★★★★. **Friendliness rating** ★★★. **Parking** Curbside parking only. **Bar** Beer and wine. **Wine selection** Good wine list, including many selections by the glass. **Dress** Casual. **Disabled access** Full. **Customers** A mix of Warehouse District residents and visitors. **Hours** Monday–Friday, 11 a.m.–10 p.m.; Saturday, 5:30–10 p.m.

SETTING AND ATMOSPHERE Carved out of an old factory in the Warehouse District, and made to house a country Cajun-style cafe, this place's interior design is unusual. Its simplicity, right angles, and heavy use of wood make it look Scandinavian. Airy, spacious, and comfortable.

HOUSE SPECIALTIES Wood-roasted oysters; fried rabbit livers with pepper jelly; fried boudin; boucherie plate; grilled pork ribs.

OTHER RECOMMENDATIONS Grilled shrimp with chow-chow; hogshead cheese; oven-roasted fish.

SUMMARY AND COMMENTS Cochon is Chef Donald Link's laudable attempt to capture the exciting boucherie in the meat markets and smokehouses of Cajun country. Despite its nearness and relationship to New Orleans, this aspect of Cajun cuisine has only rarely penetrated the city. Here they smoke and cure meats (mostly pork), make sausages, and grill meats and seafood. The small courses and boucherie platters are by far the best food in the house—don't miss the boudin and the rabbit livers, if they have the latter. Although it has similarities, this is not barbecue. It's more expensive, for one thing. And it's made with commensurate care.

Coffee Pot ★★

CREOLE | INEXPENSIVE | QUALITY ★★★ | VALUE ★★★★

714 St. Peter Street, French Quarter; ☎504-524-3500

Reservations Not accepted. **When to go** Anytime. **Entree range** $8–$21. **Payment** All major credit cards. **Service rating** ★★★. **Friendliness rating** ★★★. **Parking** Pay garages nearby. **Bar** Full bar. **Wine selection** A few house wines. **Dress** Casual. **Disabled access** None. **Customers** Tourists, a few Quarterites. **Hours** Daily, 8 a.m.–midnight.

SETTING AND ATMOSPHERE The dining room is the parlor of an old Quarter residence, with windows onto that heavily visited block of St. Peter Street. Alfresco tables are in the carriageway.

HOUSE SPECIALTIES Breakfast: calas; omelettes; lost bread. Shrimp rémoulade; seafood gumbo; red beans and rice; fried seafood platters.

SUMMARY AND COMMENTS Although the Coffee Pot is largely given over to the tourist trade these days, it's a historic restaurant. For over 60 years, it has served home-style Creole classics with pizzazz. This is, for example, the last stand for calas, the nearly extinct but delicious Creole breakfast rice cake. A few Quarterites still use the Coffee Pot as their neighborhood restaurant, coming mainly for the good breakfasts, served all day long. The menu goes on to include the full range of casual Creole food, from gumbo to red beans to ribs. Oddly, the coffee is consistently forgettable.

Commander's Palace ★★★★★

CONTEMPORARY CREOLE VERY EXPENSIVE QUALITY ★★★★★ VALUE ★★★★

1403 Washington Avenue, Garden District; ☎504-899-8221; www.commanderspalace.com

Reservations Required. **When to go** Lunch and weekday dinner. **Entree range** $22–$39. **Payment** All major credit cards. **Service rating** ★★★★★. **Friendliness rating** ★★★★. **Parking** Valet (free). **Bar** Full bar. **Wine selection** Distinguished cellar, good international balance. Many rare wines (although not many older ones) from France and California. **Dress** Dressy. **Disabled access** Full. **Customers** Half tourists, half socializing locals; couples. **Hours** Daily, 11:30 a.m.–2:30 p.m. and 6–10 p.m.

SETTING AND ATMOSPHERE The Victorian mansion and adjacent courtyard were built in the mid-1800s and are part of the fabric of the surrounding Garden District. The upstairs Garden Room is most popular with locals, but every part of the restaurant has its own distinctive, antique charm.

HOUSE SPECIALTIES Commander's is an inventive restaurant, and the best dishes on any given night are likely to be the specials. Here are a few standards of note: tasso shrimp Henican; turtle soup; sautéed fish with pecans; rack of lamb; bread pudding soufflé.

OTHER RECOMMENDATIONS Shrimp rémoulade; oysters and caviar; cast-iron-seared fish; bananas Foster; strawberry shortcake.

ENTERTAINMENT AND AMENITIES Strolling jazz trio at Sunday brunch.

SUMMARY AND COMMENTS Commander's Palace, the flagship of the Brennan family's restaurant empire and one of the two or three most popular restaurants in New Orleans, was hit hard by Hurricane Katrina. It took over a year and millions of dollars of reconstruction to get it back open. Every part of the restaurant was rebuilt almost from scratch, including the kitchen. Chef Tory McPhail kept his staff together and came back with gusto. The restaurant has never been better. And that's saying something. This is where Paul Prudhomme and Emeril Lagasse, among others, rose to prominence. The menu combines both old and new styles of Creole cooking, using first-class, interesting foodstuffs. Commander's has always been a good deal: a three-course dinner can be had for under $50, and lunch for under $20. Service is tightly orchestrated and can seem mechanical; be sure to tell the waiter you're in no hurry.

Crescent City Steak House ★★★

STEAK HIGH MODERATE QUALITY ★★★ VALUE ★★★

1001 North Broad Street, Mid-City; ☎504-821-3271; www.crescentcitysteaks.com

Reservations Accepted. **When to go** Anytime. **Entree range** $18–$28. **Payment** All major credit cards. **Service rating** ★★. **Friendliness rating** ★★★. **Parking** Free lot adjacent. **Bar** Full bar. **Wine selection** A handful of mostly French bottles, distributed on the tables as helpful suggestions. **Dress** Casual. **Disabled access** Full. **Customers** Almost entirely local. **Hours** Wednesday–Sunday, 11:30 a.m.–9 p.m.

SETTING AND ATMOSPHERE Pressed tin above, ceramic tile below, windows all around, in one big room that looks as if it were built as a movie set in the 1940s. Private booths are along one wall.

HOUSE SPECIALTIES Steaks: sirloin strip, porterhouse, or T-bone; Lyonnaise potatoes; bread pudding; café au lait.

SUMMARY AND COMMENTS This is the original high-end New Orleans steak house, founded in 1934 and widely copied so long that few imitators even know they're doing it. The restaurant is more inviting than it once was—the second generation of the family has modernized here and there. But not in the food department. The steaks are all USDA Prime, dry-aged on the premises, served in sizzling butter—a touch that started here. The side dishes are much less interesting. You come here to eat a steak.

Cuvée ★★★★

ECLECTIC VERY EXPENSIVE QUALITY ★★★★ VALUE ★★★★

322 Magazine Street, Central Business District; ☎504-587-9001; www.restaurantcuvee.com

Reservations Recommended. **When to go** Dinner. **Entree range** $23–$35. **Payment** All major credit cards. **Service rating** ★★★★. **Friendliness rating** ★★★★. **Parking** Free valet parking. **Bar** Full bar. **Wine selection** Distinguished wine cellar, with exceptional variety and many wines available by the glass. **Dress** Dressy. **Disabled access** Full. **Customers** Gourmets and wine buffs. **Hours** Wednesday–Thursday, 11:30 a.m.–2 p.m.; Monday–Thursday, 6–9:30 p.m.; Friday–Saturday, 6–10 p.m.

SETTING AND ATMOSPHERE A well-renovated old space, with tall ceilings and exposed brick walls. Wine dominates the decor. Chandeliers, for example, are made out of large-format Champagne bottles.

HOUSE SPECIALTIES Mirliton and shrimp Napoleon; sweetbreads; butter-poached sea scallops; fish with crawfish and limas; sugarcane-smoked duck breast, crisp confit leg, and foie gras; crème brûlée.

OTHER RECOMMENDATIONS The tasting menu is the best possible dinner strategy, especially if paired with wines.

SUMMARY AND COMMENTS Cuvée is the second restaurant of the guys who own the excellent Dakota on the North Shore. They started here with a wine list and built a menu around it. The potential pretentiousness of that idea is kept under control; if you're interested in an unusual bottle, they have one for you, and they'll tell you all you want to know about it. If you just want a good glass of wine, the waiters back off the winespeak and pour. The menu blends ambition with a little playfulness. Many of the dishes will make you smile twice: first, when you read about and imagine them, and again when you taste them. A contemporary version of the local flavor predominates, with admixtures from other traditions here and there. The tasting menu—which can be devised in any number of courses you please, with or without matched wines—is one of the best and most affordable such schemes in New Orleans.

Dante's Kitchen ★★★★

CONTEMPORARY CREOLE MODERATE QUALITY ★★★★ VALUE ★★★★

736 Dante Street, Riverbend (Uptown); ☎504-861-3121; www.danteskitchen.com

Reservations Recommended. **When to go** Anytime. **Entree range** $18–$28. **Payment** All major credit cards. **Service rating** ★★★★. **Friendliness rating** ★★★★. **Parking** Curbside parking only. **Bar** Full bar. **Wine selection** Good wine list, including many selections by the glass. **Dress** Nice casual. **Disabled access** Full. **Customers** Neighborhood people and curious gourmets from the rest of the city. **Hours** Wednesday–Monday, 5–10 p.m.; Saturday–Sunday, 10:30 a.m.–2 p.m.; closed Tuesday.

SETTING AND ATMOSPHERE An old cottage with haphazard add-ons gives a motley assortment of dining areas, including a small alfresco dining space.

HOUSE SPECIALTIES Shrimp and grits with redeye gravy; mussels with chorizo; corn and crab soup; New Orleans barbecue shrimp; redfish "on the half-shell"; chicken under a brick; orange-glazed duck.

SUMMARY AND COMMENTS Chef-owner Emanual Loubier was one of the stalwarts in the kitchen at Commander's Palace during the 1990s before he opened this bistro. His cooking is imaginative, but with a convincing Louisiana flavor. The ingredients are mostly of local origin and well selected. However, E-man (that's what everybody calls him) has a bent for the rustic side of cooking, which keeps the prices down and the presentations simple. Always a surprise or two on the menu. Service, like the place itself, is unceremonious.

Delmonico ★★★★

CONTEMPORARY CREOLE VERY EXPENSIVE QUALITY ★★★★★ VALUE ★★

1300 St. Charles Avenue, Lee Circle Area; ☎504-525-4937; www.emerils.com/restaurant/3/emerils-delmonico/

Reservations Recommended. **When to go** Anytime. **Entree range** $24–$40. **Payment** All major credit cards. **Service rating** ★★★★★. **Friendliness rating** ★★★★★. **Parking** Free valet parking. **Bar** Full bar. **Wine selection** Emeril's restaurants draw from the city's largest and most varied wine cellar. Lots of famous names, as well as offbeat wines, managed by a well-informed sommelier. **Dress** Very dressy. **Disabled access** Full. **Customers** A lot of overflow from

Emeril's winds up here (read "tourists"); locals dominate at lunchtime. **Hours** Daily, 6–10 p.m.

SETTING AND ATMOSPHERE Delmonico was 100 years old when Chef Emeril Lagasse bought it in 1998. He put several million dollars into its renovation—then had to do it all over again after Katrina. It retains an authentic antiquity that makes it very different from Emeril's other, trendier local establishments. It's extremely comfortable and maintains a quiet elegance.

HOUSE SPECIALTIES Charcuterie platter; barbecue shrimp; sirloin strip steak; lamb chops and *merguez* sausage; bananas Foster; café brûlot.

OTHER RECOMMENDATIONS Crab cake; chicken with ham and butterbeans; double-cut pork chop; coconut cream pie.

ENTERTAINMENT AND AMENITIES Live pianist in the second dining room nightly.

SUMMARY AND COMMENTS Those with a taste for more traditional New Orleans cooking will find Delmonico the best of Emeril Lagasse's restaurants in New Orleans. While the dishes have a familiar ring, they're prepared with the innovative touches, ingredients, and excitement for which the chef is known. Here is one of the best chef's tasting menus in town—a great way to experience the best the restaurant has to offer. Although this is not a steak house, steak is a good order. It's Prime beef, dry-aged on the premises and cooked with enough bravado that they're probably the best steaks in a very good steak town.

Dick and Jenny's ★★★★

CONTEMPORARY CREOLE EXPENSIVE QUALITY ★★★★ VALUE ★★★★★

4501 Tchoupitoulas Street, Uptown; ☎504-894-9880; www.dickandjennys.com

Reservations Not accepted. **When to go** Early dinner. **Entree range** $14–$27. **Payment** All major credit cards. **Service rating** ★★★. **Friendliness rating** ★★★★. **Parking** Curbside parking only. **Bar** Full bar. **Wine selection** Modest list of wines matched to the food. **Dress** Casual. **Disabled access** Limited. **Customers** Clientele tends to the younger side and others who have time to wait in line. **Hours** Tuesday–Saturday, 5–10 p.m.

SETTING AND ATMOSPHERE It was a grubby old neighborhood bar when Dick Benz found it. He left much evidence of that past. The bar dominates the front dining room. The back rooms feel almost like enclosed carports. A screened porch in the back is where you may hang out for a while waiting for a table.

HOUSE SPECIALTIES The menu changes deeply three or four times a year. Most of these remain steady: fried green tomatoes with crab claws; fried oysters rémoulade; sweetbreads with red-eye gravy and quail egg; frog legs Marsala; grilled fish with crawfish dynamite; duck with chorizo and andouille-tarragon sauce; peanut butter bread pudding.

SUMMARY AND COMMENTS Dick and Jenny Benz sold their restaurant after Hurricane Katrina, but the new owners kept their idea intact: to steer away from the really expensive ingredients, cook the rest of it with skill, and keep the prices well below those of the other Creole bistros. That is a magic formula in New Orleans, and from the outset, Dick and Jenny's has been wildly popular, enough so that people still wait over an hour for a table at times. The food really is good; whether it's worth the inconvenience is a personal matter.

Dickie Brennan's Steakhouse ★★★★

STEAK VERY EXPENSIVE QUALITY ★★★★ VALUE ★★★

716 Iberville Street, French Quarter; ☎504-522-2467; www.dickiebrennanssteakhouse.com

Reservations Recommended. **When to go** Anytime. **Entree range** $23–$44. **Payment** All major credit cards. **Service rating** ★★★★. **Friendliness rating** ★★★★. **Parking** Validated parking next door. **Bar** Full bar. **Wine selection** Excellent, with many selections by the glass. **Dress** Nice casual. **Disabled access** Full. **Customers** Businessmen at lunch, couples at dinner; some tourists and conventioneers. **Hours** Wednesday–Friday, 11:30 a.m.–3 p.m.; daily, 5:30–10 p.m.

SETTING AND ATMOSPHERE The only sub-street-level restaurant in New Orleans, this is a handsome place. Tile floors, banquette seating, and unusual displays of antique weapons in the private dining rooms make for a distinctly local and masculine environment.

HOUSE SPECIALTIES Tomato and blue cheese Napoleon; house filet mignon (with oysters); black-iron-skillet sirloin strip; Pontalba potatoes.

OTHER RECOMMENDATIONS Turtle soup; barbecue shrimp; crab cakes; wedge salad; porterhouse steak; grilled fish; bananas Foster bread pudding.

SUMMARY AND COMMENTS Dick Brennan Sr. had an idea back in the 1960s: a steak house with a simple menu of first-class beef and chops, in a comfortable restaurant with great service and a real wine list. But it didn't happen until his son opened this place in the late 1990s. In the meantime, of course, a few national chains ran with the same idea. That doesn't make this any less good. The beef is USDA Prime without exception. Each cut is cooked differently: the filet is broiled, the strip is cooked in a hot black iron skillet, and the ribeye is roasted. The menu is significantly more original than what we're used to finding in steak houses. And the Brennan style honed at Commander's Palace is very much in evidence.

Drago's ★★★★

SEAFOOD MODERATE QUALITY ★★★★ VALUE ★★★

3232 North Arnoult Road, Metairie; ☎504-888-9254
2 Poydras Street, Central Business District; ☎504-584-3911
www.dragosrestaurant.com

Reservations Not accepted. **When to go** *Metairie:* Midafternoon, when you won't have to wait for a table or a spot at the oyster bar; *CBD:* Anytime. **Entree range** $12–$24 (higher for big lobsters). **Payment** All major credit cards. **Service rating** ★★★. **Friendliness rating** ★★★★. **Parking** *Metairie:* Inadequate free parking lot adjacent; *CBD:* Validated parking in Hilton Hotel garage. **Bar** Full bar. **Wine**

selection A few house wines, including a few from Croatia. **Dress** Casual. **Disabled access** Full. **Customers** *Metairie:* locals and families; *CBD:* businesspeople and tourists. **Hours** Monday–Friday, 11:30 a.m.–9 p.m.; Saturday, 4–10 p.m.

SETTING AND ATMOSPHERE The oyster bar (where, oddly, you can't stand and eat 'em) with its flaming grill is the centerpiece of the restaurant, with dining rooms radiating out in all directions. Servers move in and out of these in complicated traffic patterns. A crowd, waiting for tables, almost always fills the bar. All of this is true both for the Metairie original and the new downtown restaurant.

HOUSE SPECIALTIES Raw oysters; charbroiled oysters; shrimp Herradura; seafood pasta; Cajun grilled duck breast; boiled lobster; crème brûlée.

OTHER RECOMMENDATIONS Seafood gumbo; oyster brochette; grilled, stuffed drumfish Tommy; La-Mex (black beans with fried chicken or fried catfish); white chocolate bread pudding.

SUMMARY AND COMMENTS Ambitious as casual seafood restaurants go, Drago's is our premier oyster specialist, both at the raw bar and in the kitchen. The dish that turned the place from a sleepy seafood cafe into one of the busiest restaurants in town is charbroiled oysters. With good reason: they're irresistible, grilled on the shells, and basted with garlic-herb butter. Almost everything else in the way of local seafood is here, often in highly original concoctions. They also sell more Maine lobsters than any place else in town, at attractive prices. Both locations have the same menus, prices, and quality—and are just as tough to get a table, particularly on weekends. But well worth the wait.

Eleven 79 ★★★

ITALIAN | EXPENSIVE | QUALITY ★★★★ | VALUE ★★★

1179 Annunciation Street, Warehouse District (CBD); ☎504-569-0001; www.eleven79.com

Reservations Recommended. **When to go** Late lunch or early dinner. **Entree range** $15–$35. **Payment** All major credit cards. **Service rating** ★★★★. **Friendliness rating** ★★★★. **Parking** Curbside parking only. **Bar** Full bar. **Wine selection** Excellent wine list, particularly among Italian bottles. **Dress** Dressy. **Disabled access** Limited. **Customers** A mix of prominent New Orleans people and the owner's friends, and anybody else who can squeeze in. **Hours** Thursday–Friday, 11:30 a.m.–3 p.m.; Monday–Saturday, 5–10 p.m.

SETTING AND ATMOSPHERE A restored building from the early 1800s, in the shadow of the Mississippi River Bridge. The bar is usually busy; there are tables in there, and more in a narrow room that looks like a library.

HOUSE SPECIALTIES Much of the best food here runs as specials. Oysters panne; fried calamari; tomato and mozzarella; half-orders of pasta as a preliminary course; veal Milanese, piccata, or saltimbocca; filet mignon pizzoiola.

SUMMARY AND COMMENTS Owner Joe Segreto is a veteran of decades in the New Orleans restaurant business, including some very famous ones. This modest restaurant keeps him from retiring, which he doesn't want to do anyway. His friends from all those years keep it busy, and you never know whom you'll encounter here. The menu is a collection of familiar Italian standards, very well prepared with classy ingredients. If you like veal, this is the place for you. A complimentary antipasto table gets things off to a nice start. Service moves at a leisurely pace; the kitchen is small and rarely keeps up. Segreto (who's always there) shrugs his shoulders and tells you about a wine he thinks you should try.

Emeril's ★★★★★

CONTEMPORARY CREOLE VERY EXPENSIVE QUALITY ★★★★★ VALUE ★★★

800 Tchoupitoulas, Warehouse District (CBD); ☎504-528-9393; www.emerils.com/restaurant/1/Emerils-New-Orleans/

Reservations Required. **When to go** Dinner. **Entree range** $24–$39. **Payment** All major credit cards. **Service rating** ★★★★★. **Friendliness rating** ★★★. **Parking** Free valet parking. **Bar** Full bar. **Wine selection** One of the city's most distinguished cellars, with extremely wide range and many rarely seen bottles. Many by-the-glass selections. **Dress** Dressy casual. **Disabled access** Full. **Customers** Mix of tourists looking to see Emeril and locals. Hip, gourmet crowd. **Hours** Monday–Friday, 11:30 a.m.–2 p.m.; daily, 6–10 p.m.

SETTING AND ATMOSPHERE Emeril Lagasse's first and flagship restaurant is in a renovated warehouse, its industrial aspect softened—although it's a little loud—with artfully designed, casual furnishings. Particularly interesting is the food bar, where those most interested in cooking can watch the action while eating atop barstools.

HOUSE SPECIALTIES The best meal at Emeril's is the chef's tasting menu, five courses of the day's specials. A la carte: barbecue shrimp; andouille and boudin with greens; lamb spareribs; double-cut pork chop; banana cream pie; artisanal cheeses.

OTHER RECOMMENDATIONS Gumbo of the day; andouille-crusted redfish; shrimp and grits; rack of lamb with Creole mustard crust; chocolate pecan pie.

SUMMARY AND COMMENTS Emeril Lagasse is America's best-known chef, thanks to his winning personality, his television shows, and his constant flow of cookbooks. His media activities and growing empire of ten restaurants (at latest count; the other two in New Orleans are Nola and Delmonico) mean that your chances of seeing him here are slim. The staff makes up for that by talking about him, a line of conversation encouraged by most customers. Despite that, Emeril's has always been a first-class restaurant. The menu is based on Louisiana flavors and is highly ingredient-driven, in thrall to the vagaries of the fresh food market. The result is big taste and high adventure. A great way to sample it is to get the tasting menu.

Five Happiness ★★★

CHINESE INEXPENSIVE QUALITY ★★★ VALUE ★★★★

3605 S. Carrollton, Uptown; ☎504-482-3935; www.fivehappiness.com

Reservations Accepted. **When to go** Anytime; on Saturday and Sunday there's more dim sum. **Entree range** $7–$12. **Payment** All major credit cards. **Service rating** ★★★. **Friendliness rating** ★★★. **Parking** Free lot adjacent. **Bar** Full bar. **Wine selection** A few house wines. **Dress** Casual. **Disabled access** Full. **Customers** Locals, families. **Hours** Sunday–Thursday, 11 a.m.–10 p.m.; Friday–Saturday, 11 a.m.–11 p.m.

SETTING AND ATMOSPHERE The restaurant was rebuilt from the studs and slab up after Hurricane Katrina, into a handsome, glittery, spacious main dining room with many booths.

HOUSE SPECIALTIES Hot and sour soup; pot stickers; chicken salad with hot sauce; soft-shell crabs with savory sauce; sizzling scallops; Peking duck; moo-shu anything; Hunan beef; minced chicken in lettuce wrap.

SUMMARY AND COMMENTS The longest-running of the city's major Chinese restaurants, Five Happiness is also one of the busiest. Its menu is extensive and more adventuresome than most, with food that always seems a touch better than the time before. The emphasis is on Mandarin classics and Szechuan dishes. Although they are capable of it, they usually stop short of really spectacular food and service, as if these might keep you in your seat a little too long. But you could do a lot worse than to eat here.

Flaming Torch ★★★

FRENCH | EXPENSIVE | QUALITY ★★★★ | VALUE ★★★

737 Octavia Street, Uptown; ☎504-895-0900; www.flamingtorchnola.com

Reservations Recommended. **When to go** Anytime. **Entree range** $17–$33. **Payment** All major credit cards. **Service rating** ★★★. **Friendliness rating** ★★★. **Parking** Curbside parking only. **Bar** Full bar. **Wine selection** Good wine list. **Dress** Nice casual. **Disabled access** Limited. **Customers** Uptowners. **Hours** Daily, 11:30 a.m.–3 p.m. and 5:30–9:30 p.m.

SETTING AND ATMOSPHERE A small dining room, elegant, dim, and borderline romantic at night. Sconces shaped like torches line the walls. Another dining room upstairs is more obviously a converted residential space.

HOUSE SPECIALTIES Escargots bourguignonne; mussels; magret of duck breast with port reduction; coq au vin; rack of lamb with mustard crust; sirloin strip steak au poivre.

OTHER RECOMMENDATIONS Shrimp Sazerac; sweetbreads poulette; onion soup gratinee; grilled salmon beurre blanc; crème brûlée.

SUMMARY AND COMMENTS The lengthy menu is a twist on the classic French bistro menu. Some pure New Orleans dishes show up, as well as a few complete originals. It's worth coming here for the mussels (in a brilliant, creamy, spicy sauce) and the coq au vin (the best in town) alone. Much is made of beefsteak here, including a fine version of New Orleans steak and oysters. The menu at lunch is substantially lighter than the dinner fare, with salade Nicoise and that sort of thing.

Fury's ★★★

SEAFOOD | INEXPENSIVE | QUALITY ★★★ | VALUE ★★★★★

724 Martin Behrman Avenue, Metairie; ☎504-834-5646

Reservations Not accepted. **When to go** Anytime. **Entree range** $10–$18. **Payment** All major credit cards. **Service rating** ★★. **Friendliness rating** ★★★. **Parking** Ample parking lot adjacent. **Bar** Full bar. **Wine selection** A few house wines. **Dress** Casual. **Disabled access** Limited. **Customers** Neighborhood people. **Hours** Monday–Friday, 11 a.m.–9 p.m.

SETTING AND ATMOSPHERE A tight, well-worn, L-shaped room, with a small bar in the back.

HOUSE SPECIALTIES Seafood gumbo; trout amandine; fried or broiled seafood platters; fried or broiled chicken; fried onion rings.

OTHER RECOMMENDATIONS Crabmeat au gratin; barbecue shrimp; crawfish étouffée; chicken or veal Parmesan; bread pudding.

SUMMARY AND COMMENTS A neighborhood seafood cafe in the old style, with all that implies both in the way of honest, cooked-to-order food as well as a few outmoded (but also honest) atrocities (the salads, for example). These shortcomings are forgivable, in view of the low prices and goodness of the basic specialties. Seafood dominates, with every imaginable combination platter, fried or broiled. The daily specials are pure backstreet New Orleans cuisine, and even the smattering of Italian food is good.

Galatoire's ★★★★

CLASSIC CREOLE | VERY EXPENSIVE | QUALITY ★★★★ | VALUE ★★★

209 Bourbon Street, French Quarter; ☎504-525-2021; www.galatoires.com

Reservations Accepted only for upstairs rooms. **When to go** Late lunch or early dinner. Locals completely take over at Friday lunch and Sunday dinner. **Entree range** $15–$32. **Payment** All major credit cards. **Service rating** ★★★. **Friendliness rating** ★★★. **Parking** Pay parking lots nearby. **Bar** Full bar. Drinks are very generously poured and modestly priced. **Wine selection** Peculiar list of French and California wines with the absolute minimum identification of maker and vintage; very attractive prices. **Dress** Very dressy. **Disabled access** Full. **Customers** Both tourists and locals; the latter tend to be regulars who know all the other regulars. **Hours** Tuesday–Sunday, 11:30 a.m.–9 p.m.

SETTING AND ATMOSPHERE A cornerstone of fine Creole dining for over a century, Galatoire's is to many people the image of the traditional New Orleans white-tablecloth restaurant. The main dining room downstairs has tiled floors, mirrored walls, motionless ceiling fans, and bright, naked light bulbs. At peak times, it seems chaotic and can be very noisy. The second-floor dining areas are less distinctive, but the newly added bar up there is a welcome relief from the uncomfortable waits in line on the sidewalk that used to be almost unavoidable.

HOUSE SPECIALTIES Crabmeat maison; oysters Rockefeller; trout meunière or amandine; grilled pompano; lamb chops béarnaise; crème caramel.

OTHER RECOMMENDATIONS Shrimp rémoulade; canapé Lorenzo; oysters en brochette; green salad with garlic; poached salmon or drum hollandaise; shrimp Marguery; crabmeat Yvonne; chicken Clemenceau.

SUMMARY AND COMMENTS Even though its menu and style are a century old, for most avid local diners, all other restaurants are measured against it. The restaurant underwent changes of management and a renovation a few years ago, upsetting many customers. But everybody's used to all the changes now, and the party that is dining here has resumed. The definitive French-Creole menu remains, as does the loose, generous operating style of the cooks and waiters. Galatoire's has the style of a bistro, and its best food is made from great fresh ingredients cooked in a simple, sometimes even homely way. Seafood is the main draw, but they cook everything deftly. Regular diners can recommend their own favorite mystery dishes from the catalog-like menu.

Galley Seafood ★★★

SEAFOOD INEXPENSIVE QUALITY ★★★★ VALUE ★★★★

2535 Metairie Road, Old Metairie; ☎504-832-0955

Reservations Not accepted. **When to go** It's busy all the time Friday and Saturday, and a wait for a table is to be expected at peak hours. **Entree range** \$10–\$18. **Payment** All major credit cards. **Service rating** ★★. **Friendliness rating** ★★★★. **Parking** Free lot adjacent. **Bar** Beer and wine. **Wine selection** A few house wines. **Dress** Casual. **Disabled access** Full. **Customers** Neighborhood people. **Hours** Tuesday–Saturday, 11:30 a.m.–9:30 p.m.

SETTING AND ATMOSPHERE A converted convenience store with a few tables in a covered area outside makes for a pleasant neighborhood cafe.

HOUSE SPECIALTIES Boiled shrimp, crabs, or crawfish; spicy meat pies; fried seafood platters or sandwiches.

OTHER RECOMMENDATIONS Seafood gumbo; any other soup; daily specials; pecan catfish.

SUMMARY AND COMMENTS The proprietors are famous for the soft-shell crab poorboy at the Jazz Festival. The Galley serves that year-round here, as well as a menu of small and large seafood platters, usually fried lightly to order. The blackboard shows off a passel of home cooking daily; the soups here are always especially good. They also boil the usual crustaceans for eating in or removing to home. Good news: the boiled seafood is served hot, instead of refrigerated.

Gautreau's ★★★★

AMERICAN EXPENSIVE QUALITY ★★★★ VALUE ★★★★

1728 Soniat Street, Uptown; ☎504-899-7397; www.gautreausrestaurant.com

Reservations Recommended. **When to go** Anytime. **Entree range** \$18–\$26. **Payment** All major credit cards. **Service rating** ★★★★. **Friendliness rating** ★★★★. **Parking** Free valet parking. **Bar** Full bar. **Wine selection** Modest list, but wines well chosen for the food. **Dress** Jacket recommended but not required.

Disabled access Limited. **Customers** Locals, couples, gourmets. **Hours** Tuesday–Saturday, 6–10 p.m.

SETTING AND ATMOSPHERE The small dining room was once an antique pharmacy, from which some relics remain. There's more room upstairs, but they don't use it every night. The dining room can get noisy when full.

HOUSE SPECIALTIES Duck confit; seared sea scallops; filet mignon; crème brûlée.

OTHER RECOMMENDATIONS Crab cake; roasted chicken; roasted lamb loin; fish specials.

SUMMARY AND COMMENTS Deep in an Uptown residential neighborhood, Gautreau's many regulars (they're the only ones who can find the place) have come to expect a certain hard-to-define but polished style of contemporary Creole cooking. The abbreviated menu has one of just about everything, in understated compositions that change from week to week. The best are the least exotic—the filet mignon and roast chicken, to name two. Service has a chummy style; the servers give frank opinions about everything. It's difficult to get a table here on short notice, and there's no comfortable place to wait.

Grand Isle ★★★

SEAFOOD MODERATE QUALITY ★★★★ VALUE ★★★

575 Convention Center Boulevard, Warehouse District (CBD); ☎504-520-8530; www.grandislerestaurant.com

Reservations Accepted. **When to go** Anytime. **Entree range** $16–$29. **Payment** All major credit cards. **Service rating** ★★★. **Friendliness rating** ★★★. **Parking** Validated parking at Harrah's parking. **Bar** Full bar. **Wine selection** Modest list of wines matched to the food. **Dress** Casual. **Disabled access** Full. **Customers** A mix of people who live and work downtown with convention visitors. **Hours** Sunday–Thursday, 11 a.m.–11 p.m.; Friday–Saturday, 11 a.m.–midnight.

SETTING AND ATMOSPHERE The design recalls, in much larger and cleaner form, the eateries found in the fishing towns along the Louisiana coast—of which Grand Isle is among the most famous. Tiled everything.

HOUSE SPECIALTIES Raw oysters; baked oysters Rockefeller, Bienville, and Grand; grilled fish with Creole meunière sauce; fried seafood platter.

OTHER RECOMMENDATIONS Potted crab; seafood gumbo; seafood poorboy sandwiches.

SUMMARY AND COMMENTS The restaurants one finds at "the end of the world"—the last signs of civilization on the roads leading to the water that surrounds everything in Southeast Louisiana—are as much about subsistence as going out to dinner. This restaurant attempts to recapture that feeling, but don't you try to. Things like turtle stew and pot roast are authentic, but not very good. Instead, emphasize seafood. The oyster bar has good raw ones, and Grand Isle bakes oysters with the classic sauces on the shells as well as anybody. Fish is prepared many ways, all with fresh local species. Fried seafood platters and poorboy sandwiches round out the menu.

GW Fins ★★★★

SEAFOOD | EXPENSIVE | QUALITY ★★★★ | VALUE ★★★

808 Bienville Street, French Quarter; ☎504-581-3467; www.gwfins.com

Reservations Recommended. **When to go** Anytime. **Entree range** $18–$32. **Payment** All major credit cards. **Service rating** ★★★. **Friendliness rating** ★★★★. **Parking** Pay parking lots nearby. **Bar** Full bar. **Wine selection** Excellent wine list, with plenty of offbeat bottles and dozens of wines by the glass. **Dress** Nice casual. **Disabled access** Full. **Customers** A mix of locals and visitors, tending toward the younger side. **Hours** Daily, 5–10 p.m.

SETTING AND ATMOSPHERE A big, modern room with the best tables arrayed in an arc around the main seating area. The wall of windows in front allows a great view of Arnaud's, across the street.

HOUSE SPECIALTIES The whole menu changes daily. Crab cake; tuna tartare; wood-grilled fish; short-smoked salmon; bouillabaisse; grilled scallops; baked-to-order apple pie.

OTHER RECOMMENDATIONS Seafood gumbo; whole roasted fish; blackened redfish.

SUMMARY AND COMMENTS GW Fins does with seafood what the prime steak houses do with beef. The kitchen's main task is finding top-quality finfish and shellfish wherever it is to be found. Half of the menu is locally sourced; the rest comes from all over the world. Because the seafood market is so variable, the menu is written daily—although a few steady dishes appear on it. The intrinsic merits of the fish make it all happen, with the chef's tricks kept in the background. GW Fins often runs theme specials—an around-the-world crab platter, for example. Appetizers and side dishes are just okay; service varies. You might like the little sweet biscuits they serve all night long.

Herbsaint ★★★★

FRENCH | EXPENSIVE | QUALITY ★★★★ | VALUE ★★★

701 St. Charles Avenue, Central Business District; ☎504-524-4114; www.herbsaint.com

Reservations Recommended. **When to go** Anytime. **Entree range** $16–$31. **Payment** All major credit cards. **Service rating** ★★★. **Friendliness rating** ★★★★. **Parking** Free valet parking. **Bar** Full bar. **Wine selection** Good wine list with an emphasis on French bottles. **Dress** Nice casual. **Disabled access** Full. **Customers** Couples by night, long-lunch-hour types by day. **Hours** Monday–Friday, 11:30 a.m.–1:30 p.m.; Monday–Saturday, 5:30–10 p.m.

SETTING AND ATMOSPHERE The L-shaped dining room, with its big windows onto the increasingly green urban streetscape, is sharply furnished and comfortable.

HOUSE SPECIALTIES Tomato and shrimp bisque; fried frog legs with fines herbes; confit of duck leg; pan-roasted chicken; grilled hanger steak.

OTHER RECOMMENDATIONS Shrimp and grits with tasso; seared scallops with risotto; lamb shoulder with white beans; coconut cream pie.

SUMMARY AND COMMENTS Herbsaint is named for a New Orleans–born, anise-flavored liqueur, famous for its use in oysters Rockefeller. Chef Donald Link uses it in other dishes as well, but stops short of turning it into a motif. The real theme here is a contemporary Cajun interpretation of French country cooking, made with local ingredients. Both the prices and ambitions of the kitchen are kept in the moderate range, but the food's goodness excels in all dishes that avoid trendiness. Best reason to come here: the frog legs, sautéed in butter with herbs and a good shot of pepper, are the best around.

Hoa Hong 9 Roses ★★★★

VIETNAMESE LOW MODERATE QUALITY ★★★★ VALUE ★★★★★

1100 Stephens Street, Gretna; ☎504-366-7665; www.nomenu.com/restaurants/hoahong9roses.html

Reservations Accepted. **When to go** Anytime. **Entree range** $5–$14. **Payment** All major credit cards. **Service rating** ★★. **Friendliness rating** ★★★. **Parking** Ample parking lot adjacent. **Bar** Full bar. **Wine selection** A few house wines; beer is better with this food. **Dress** Casual. **Disabled access** Full. **Customers** Asians and aficionados of Asian cuisine. **Hours** Sunday–Tuesday and Thursday, 10:30 a.m.–9:30 p.m.; Friday and Saturday, 10:30 a.m.–10 p.m.; closed Wednesday.

SETTING AND ATMOSPHERE Set back from the highway on a side street, the comfort and richness of the dining room surprise you. Don't let the West Bank location deter you; it's really just over the river from downtown.

HOUSE SPECIALTIES Vietnamese spring rolls; Vietnamese crepe; hot and sour fish soup for two; *pho; bo tai chanh* (beef salad with mint); black pepper crab; lemongrass chicken; curry and coconut shrimp or chicken; fish in clay pot; "bun" dishes (grilled meats over cool noodles).

SUMMARY AND COMMENTS This is the best—and with a menu of 300 dishes, the most ambitious—of the many local Vietnamese restaurants. They make it all, from the famous beef-noodle soup called *pho* through the exotic "fondue" (no cheese; the word is an imperfect translation) dishes prepared atop the table before you. The servers will almost certainly wave you away from something or other if you wade too far into the highly ethnic dishes, but if something sounds interesting, persist. They cook well with good ingredients. The owners are very friendly and will go out of their way to make you feel comfortable.

Horinoya ★★★

JAPANESE MODERATE QUALITY ★★★★ VALUE ★★★

920 Poydras Street, Central Business District; ☎504-561-8914

Reservations Accepted. **When to go** Anytime. **Entree range** $9–$21. **Payment** All major credit cards. **Service rating** ★★★. **Friendliness rating** ★★★. **Parking** Curbside parking only. **Bar** Full bar. **Wine selection** A few house wines. **Dress** Casual. **Disabled access** Limited. **Customers** People who work downtown, visitors from the nearby hotels, many Asians. **Hours** Monday–Saturday, 11:30 a.m.–3 p.m. and 5:30–9:30 p.m.

SETTING AND ATMOSPHERE A single long, narrow room gets extra dimension through the use of mirrors. There's a small private dining room behind it for the special feasts the restaurant is capable of holding.

HOUSE SPECIALTIES Sushi and sashimi; multicourse *kaiseki* dinners.

OTHER RECOMMENDATIONS—Chirashi sushi combination; grilled black cod; beef negimaki; sukiyaki; *shabu-shabu.*

SUMMARY AND COMMENTS Horinoya is one of the best Japanese and sushi restaurants in New Orleans, and one of the most convenient to those who work, live, or stay downtown. It's also one of the few decent restaurants near the Superdome. The bar is well stocked with a wide variety of fresh fish, and the chef—who is also the owner—gets the details right. The nonsushi menu includes many dishes not available in other Japanese restaurants. Horinoya also offers to perform a *kaiseki* dinner of a dozen or more courses, and pulls it off with aplomb.

Impastato's ★★★

ITALIAN | MODERATE | QUALITY ★★★ | VALUE ★★★★★

3400 16th Street, Metairie; ☎504-455-1545; www.impastatos.com

Reservations Recommended. **When to go** Early evenings. **Entree range** $13–$32. **Payment** All major credit cards. **Service rating** ★★★★. **Friendliness rating** ★★★. **Parking** Ample parking lot adjacent. **Bar** Full bar. **Wine selection** Decent list, mostly Italian. **Dress** Nice casual. **Disabled access** Full. **Customers** Local regulars, sports types (the Saints eat here a lot). **Hours** Tuesday–Saturday, 6–11 p.m.

SETTING AND ATMOSPHERE Two rooms: a busy, convivial main room with walls and ceilings covered with stained glass; and a smaller room off the bar, its walls covered with a staggering collection of sports memorabilia.

HOUSE SPECIALTIES Sautéed crab fingers; fettuccine Alfredo; pasta asciutta (in a light, spicy red sauce); veal or trout Marianna (artichokes and mushrooms).

OTHER RECOMMENDATIONS Fried calamari; crabmeat cannelloni; shrimp scampi; crabmeat au gratin; osso buco; rack of lamb; blueberry-banana pie; torroncino ice cream.

ENTERTAINMENT AND AMENITIES Live karaoke-style singer most nights.

SUMMARY AND COMMENTS Joe Impastato is one of two Sicilian brothers (the other operates Sal & Judy's across the lake) who got a feel for the New Orleans palate after stints at the legendary Moran's. The menu is straightforward, but everything is cooked with élan from great ingredients. That's particularly true of the seafood. The famous dish, however, is fettuccine Alfredo, the pasta manufactured on site and prepared in the dining room by Joe personally. The menu's table d'hôte section is quite a bargain; a five-course dinner can be had for $30. Regular customers, of which there are many, get preference for tables. Be sure to get a reservation and show up early. The bar makes great drinks.

Irene's Cuisine ★★★

ITALIAN | MODERATE | QUALITY ★★★★ | VALUE ★★★★

539 St. Philip Street, French Quarter; ☎504-529-8811

Reservations Accepted. **When to go** Early evenings. **Entree range** $11–$22. **Payment** All major credit cards. **Service rating** ★★★. **Friendliness rating** ★★★. **Parking** Pay parking at French Market lot, a block away. **Bar** Full bar. **Wine selection** Decent list, mostly Italian. **Dress** Casual. **Disabled access** Full. **Customers** Mostly locals, a few tourists, many Quarterites. **Hours** Thursday–Friday, 11:30 a.m.–3 p.m.; Monday–Saturday, 6–10 p.m.

SETTING AND ATMOSPHERE The dark main dining room of this great Creole-Italian trattoria is in an old warehouse, and pleasantly informal. It's always busy, and reservations won't save you from a wait for a table. A big part of the experience of dining here involves who you'll socialize with in the meantime.

HOUSE SPECIALTIES Oysters Vittorio (Italian style, plus artichokes); veal Sorrentino; roast duck with spinach and mustard; roasted chicken with rosemary and garlic.

OTHER RECOMMENDATIONS Mussels marinara; oysters Irene (pancetta and Romano); grilled shrimp and pannéed oysters; sautéed soft-shell crab and pasta; lamb rack à la Provence; tiramisu; Italian ice creams.

SUMMARY AND COMMENTS Irene DiPietro cooks up lusty, robust, generally simple food with a country Italian flavor—meaning lots of fresh herbs, garlic, and olive oil. It's a style you don't run into much around here (Mosca's is about the only other place), which may explain the crowds. The bustle can reach chaos at times. A recent addition has loosened things up a bit, fortunately. This is one of the few restaurants deep in the French Quarter that has a substantial local clientele.

Jacques-Imo's ★★★

CAJUN MODERATE QUALITY ★★★ VALUE ★★★★

8324 Oak Street, Riverbend (Uptown); ☎504-861-0886; www.jacquesimoscafe.com

Reservations Accepted for parties of five or more. **When to go** Avoid Friday and Saturday. **Entree range** $9–$18. **Payment** All major credit cards. **Service rating** ★★. **Friendliness rating** ★★★. **Parking** Curbside parking only. **Bar** Full bar. **Wine selection** Modest list of wines matched to the food. **Dress** Casual. **Disabled access** Limited. **Customers** Younger crowd, plus hip visitors with a taste for New Orleans funk. **Hours** Tuesday–Saturday, 5:30–10:30 p.m. Stays open later during Jazz Festival. Closed for a week to a month in later summer.

SETTING AND ATMOSPHERE A study in self-conscious New Orleans funkiness, which many people erroneously interpret as essential to dining here. But it works: the place is always packed. The kitchen is in the middle of the well-worn building. You walk through it to the larger of the two dining rooms, a sort of hut built into what was once a backyard. A few tables are scattered here and there in the rest of the building.

HOUSE SPECIALTIES Fried green tomatoes meet Godzilla (a soft-shell crab); fried chicken; Cajun bouillabaisse; blackened tuna.

OTHER RECOMMENDATIONS Eggplant with oyster dressing; fried oysters with spicy garlic sauce; gumbo; broiled escolar with shrimp; stuffed pork chop; pannéed rabbit with oyster-tasso pasta; banana cream pie; white chocolate bread pudding.

SUMMARY AND COMMENTS Jacques-Imo's is a cult restaurant, so popular that dinner here necessarily includes time spent on the sidewalk talking with others waiting for tables. Owner Jack Leonardi, a former K-Paul's chef, at first set out with a menu that recalled the food of K-Paul's and other restaurants around town. These days the place has a flavor of its own. Portions are large, seasoning levels are convincing, and everything is unapologetically lusty, fresh, and local. Always interesting, sometimes amazingly good, but rarely as fabulous as the local lore may have you believe.

Jamila's ★★★

MIDDLE EASTERN INEXPENSIVE QUALITY ★★★ VALUE ★★★★★

7806 Maple Street, Uptown; ☎504-866-4366

Reservations Accepted. **When to go** Anytime. **Entree range** $8–$16. **Payment** All major credit cards. **Service rating** ★★. **Friendliness rating** ★★★★. **Parking** Curbside parking only. **Bar** Full bar. **Wine selection** Limited list of wines well suited to the food. **Dress** Casual. **Disabled access** Limited. **Customers** Locals. **Hours** Tuesday–Sunday, 11:30 a.m.–2:30 p.m. and 6–10 p.m.

SETTING AND ATMOSPHERE A small dining room with fanciful murals painted on the ceiling. A few more tables in a carriageway.

HOUSE SPECIALTIES Homemade *merguez* (herbal lamb sausage); grilled fish with roasted garlic tomato sauce; couscous royale (lamb, chicken, *merguez*, and vegetables).

OTHER RECOMMENDATIONS *Brik* (shrimp or tuna baked in phyllo pastry); *chorba* (whole-wheat fish soup); soups; salade tunisienne (apples, peppers, tuna, cucumbers); stuffed calamari with shrimp and bulgur wheat; *makroud* (semolina cake with dates and orange blossom syrup); Turkish coffee.

SUMMARY AND COMMENTS Jamila's serves the food of Tunisia—an interesting cuisine that blends French and Middle Eastern flavors. Appetizers and soups tend toward the French side of the equation, with the flaky pastries of the Middle East filled with rather rich fillings. The dominant entree is couscous, steamed over the boiling broth in which the meat part of the dish is cooking. The menu covers a great deal more ground, including food familiar enough for the timid eater. This is a total family operation: Mom is the chef, Dad waits on all the tables, and the two sons help out.

Johnny's Po-Boys ★★★

SANDWICHES INEXPENSIVE QUALITY ★★★ VALUE ★★★★★

511 St. Louis Street, French Quarter; ☎504-524-8129; www.johnnyspoboy.com

Reservations Not accepted. **When to go** Anytime. **Entree range** $4–$6. **Payment** No credit cards accepted. **Service rating** ★★. **Friendliness rating** ★★★. **Parking** Pay parking lots nearby. **Bar** No alcohol. **Wine selection** No wine. **Dress** Very casual. **Disabled access** Limited. **Customers** Locals and visitors. **Hours** Monday–Friday, 9 a.m.–3 p.m.; Saturday–Sunday, 9 a.m.–4 p.m.

SETTING AND ATMOSPHERE More pleasant and spacious than it appears from the outside, the dining room is dominated by the setup for ordering and making sandwiches, and the accompanying bustle.

HOUSE SPECIALTIES Roast beef poorboy; red beans and rice with hot sausage.

OTHER RECOMMENDATIONS Broiled ham and cheese poorboy; fried seafood poorboys; muffuletta.

SUMMARY AND COMMENTS The best poorboy stand in the French Quarter and one of the best in town, Johnny's starts with a terrific roast beef (freshly cooked and juicy, with a classic poorboy gravy) and ends with things like salami and liver cheese that hardly anybody puts on a poorboy anymore. A handful of daily platters completes the picture. The place gets the prize for its motto: "Even our failures are edible!"

K-Paul's Louisiana Kitchen ★★★★

CAJUN VERY EXPENSIVE QUALITY ★★★★ VALUE ★★★

416 Chartres Street, French Quarter; ☎504-524-7394; www.kpauls.com

Reservations Accepted. **When to go** Early dinner. **Entree range** $26–$38. **Payment** All major credit cards. **Service rating** ★★★. **Friendliness rating** ★★★★. **Parking** Pay parking lots nearby. **Bar** Full bar. **Wine selection** Good wine list, including many selections by the glass. **Dress** Casual. **Disabled access** Full. **Customers** Mostly tourists, but in recent years locals have been returning in larger numbers. **Hours** Monday–Saturday, 5:30–9:30 p.m.

SETTING AND ATMOSPHERE K-Paul's has come a long way from its raffish early days. The dining rooms are still casual, but you can now get reservations, your own table, tablecloths, and atmosphere. The upstairs dining room is a bit more formal than the downstairs, where table-sharing is still the rule. Chef Paul himself is on hand more often than in past years, sometimes chatting on the sidewalks with passersby, while a jazz trio plays.

HOUSE SPECIALTIES The menu changes daily, but these dishes show up often: chicken-andouille gumbo; blackened tuna; blackened beef tenders in debris sauce; sweet potato pecan pie.

OTHER RECOMMENDATIONS Cajun popcorn with sherry sauce; shrimp or crawfish étouffée; stuffed soft-shell crab; fried mirliton and oysters with tasso hollandaise; roast duck with pecan gravy; pan-fried veal with roasted stuffed peppers.

SUMMARY AND COMMENTS Chef Paul Prudhomme's seminal restaurant—and its methods, dishes, and former employees—changed the flavors of restaurant food in New Orleans and beyond in the 1980s. Although they compose a new menu daily, if you dined here 10 or even 20 years ago, you're likely to find the dishes you remember. Blackened fish, very spicy étouffées and bisques, thick slices of beef and other meats with intense sauces, and hyper-rich desserts still rule. The ingredients are of the best quality, turned out in a rustic style. Appropriately so—Cajun food is country food. The prices may strike you as a touch high given the informality of the place, but they're justified by the goodness of the groceries.

La Boca ★★★

STEAK | EXPENSIVE | QUALITY ★★★★ | VALUE ★★★

857 Fulton Street, Warehouse District (CBD); ☎504-525-8205; www.labocasteaks.com

Reservations Recommended. **When to go** Anytime. **Entree range** $16–$36. **Payment** All major credit cards. **Service rating** ★★★. **Friendliness rating** ★★★★. **Parking** Pay valet parking. **Bar** Full bar. **Wine selection** Good wine list, especially of Argentine wines. **Dress** Casual. **Disabled access** Limited. **Customers** Warehouse District residents and other locals, on the younger side; a few savvy visitors. **Hours** Monday–Wednesday, 6–10 p.m.; Thursday–Saturday, 6 p.m.–midnight.

SETTING AND ATMOSPHERE A lightly converted warehouse with a distinctly rough-hewn style, the dining rooms have the comfort of your favorite well-worn shoes.

HOUSE SPECIALTIES Grilled sweetbreads; chorizo; sirloin strip; skirt steak; hanger steak; "bistro tenderloin" (a Kobe chuck filet); dulce de leche pancakes.

SUMMARY AND COMMENTS Co-owners Adolfo Garcia (he's the chef) and Nick Bazan (he's the Argentine) wanted a beef restaurant to balance RioMar, their seafood place up the street. And here it is. There's a grill, and there are many cuts of beef, some of which are offbeat. All are prepared in the spirit of the steak houses in Argentina, a country that makes American steak consumption look anemic. The steaks come out with a variety of chimichurri sauces, fresh-cut fries, and big grilled asparagus, but are essentially left to speak for themselves.

La Crepe Nanou ★★★★

FRENCH | MODERATE | QUALITY ★★★★ | VALUE ★★★★★

1410 Robert Street, Uptown; ☎504-899-2670; www.lacrepenanou.com

Reservations Not accepted. **When to go** Early evenings. **Entree range** $9–$24. **Payment** All major credit cards. **Service rating** ★★. **Friendliness rating** ★★★. **Parking** Curbside parking only. **Bar** Full bar. **Wine selection** Substantial list, French-dominated; many by-the-glass selections; attractive prices. **Dress** Casual. **Disabled access** Limited. **Customers** Uptowners and Francophiles. **Hours** Sunday–Thursday, 6–10:30 p.m.; Friday–Saturday, 6–11 p.m.

SETTING AND ATMOSPHERE It looks as if it had been transported here from a Parisian backstreet. The premises are a collage of mismatched decors and furnishings. Always busy, with a happy crowd of locals waiting for tables.

HOUSE SPECIALTIES Mussels marinière; crepes, especially crab, crawfish, florentine, and Provençal; roast chicken; lamb chops with Cognac sauce.

OTHER RECOMMENDATIONS Pâté maison; escargots de bourguignonne; onion soup au gratin; salad tropicale; filet mignon with green peppercorn sauce; sweetbreads with lemon and capers; dessert crepes, especially Antillaise, Belle Helene, and Calvados.

SUMMARY AND COMMENTS Evolved far beyond its origins as a crepe shop, Nanou is a fix for Francophiles. Understandably popular, meals here usually include at least a short wait for a table. The social scene during the delay is a subspecies of the Uptown cocktail party. The food is classic bistro fare: fresh, French, inexpensive, and more delicious than you anticipate. Crepes—savory and sweet—remain a specialty not much available around town, let alone this well made. But the menu goes on to include whole fish, great roast chicken, extraordinary mussels, and much more.

La Thai Cuisine ★★★

THAI MODERATE QUALITY ★★★★ VALUE ★★★

4938 Prytania Street, Uptown; ☎504-899-8886; www.lathaiuptown.com

Reservations Recommended. **When to go** Anytime. **Entree range** $9–$18. **Payment** All major credit cards. **Service rating** ★★. **Friendliness rating** ★★★. **Parking** Ample parking lot adjacent. **Bar** Full bar. **Wine selection** Good wine list. **Dress** Casual. **Disabled access** Full. **Customers** A youngish clientele of Uptowners. **Hours** Monday–Saturday, 11:30 a.m.–3 p.m. and 5–10 p.m.

SETTING AND ATMOSPHERE A spacious dining room with just enough Thai decoration to make it feel right.

HOUSE SPECIALTIES Pecan-crusted oysters with wasabi artichoke sauce; duck with orange-tamarind sauce; sesame-crusted soft-shell crab with green Thai curry.

OTHER RECOMMENDATIONS Spicy red curry shrimp soup; Thai crawfish rolls; tuna tataki; pad Thai; panang curry with chicken or shrimp; chicken roti with lemongrass.

SUMMARY AND COMMENTS New Orleans's first reverse-fusion restaurant, La Thai is owned by the family that opened the first Thai restaurant here in the 1980s. By blending Creole and Thai flavors and ingredients, the kitchen arrives at a fascinating, unique style of cookery. Some dishes are straight Asian, some are pure Creole, but most are a combination of the two. Surprisingly, La Thai almost never trips up on this adventure, and the eating is terrific and light. Since the restaurant moved Uptown in 2008, the menu has grown even more interesting.

Le Parvenu ★★★★

CONTEMPORARY CREOLE EXPENSIVE QUALITY ★★★★ VALUE ★★★★

509 Williams Boulevard, Kenner; ☎504-471-0534; www.leparvenu.com

Reservations Recommended. **When to go** Anytime. **Entree range** $13–$24. **Payment** All major credit cards. **Service rating** ★★★★. **Friendliness rating** ★★★★. **Parking** Small parking lot adjacent. Lots of curbside parking nearby. **Bar** Full bar. **Wine selection** Excellent wine list, including many selections by the glass. **Dress** Nice casual. **Disabled access** Limited. **Customers** People from the suburbs along the river, and people with a need to eat well near the airport. **Hours** Tuesday–Saturday, 5:30–9:30 p.m. Lunch will likely be added as the recovery continues.

SETTING AND ATMOSPHERE A porch-surrounded cottage in the historic Rivertown part of Kenner, Le Parvenu's dining spaces are small but kept from being claustrophobic by its many windows. They also have a few tables on their wraparound porch.

HOUSE SPECIALTIES Crabmeat and artichoke with pink mayonnaise; mirliton, shrimp, and crab bisque; smoked salmon and fried green tomato; roast duck with smoked orange sauce; filet mignon with mushrooms and Chateaubriand sauce.

OTHER RECOMMENDATIONS Warm spinach salad, prepared tableside; lobster Le Parvenu; veal liver Lyonnaise; lemon crepes; crème brûlée.

SUMMARY AND COMMENTS Le Parvenu is the best restaurant in the vicinity of the airport, as well as a star by any other standard. The name means "the newcomer," but chef-owner Dennis Hutley is hardly that. His tour of duty in classy restaurant kitchens lasted decades before he opened this fine little bistro. He's a local guy and cooks New Orleans food, but a touch of Europe shows in the polish he applies. A good strategy for dining here is the tasting menu, which varies dramatically from day to day. Service is more casual than the dramatically overdressed maître d' (Mike Juan, another old hand in fine restaurants hereabouts) might suggest.

Lebanon's Cafe ★★★

MIDDLE EASTERN INEXPENSIVE QUALITY ★★★ VALUE ★★★★★

1500 South Carrollton Avenue, Riverbend (Uptown); ☎504-862-6200; www.lebanonscafe.com

Reservations Not Accepted. **When to go** Anytime. **Entree range** $6–$18. **Payment** All major credit cards. **Service rating** ★★★. **Friendliness rating** ★★★. **Parking** Curbside parking only. **Bar** Full bar. **Wine selection** A few house wines. **Dress** Casual. **Disabled access** Full. **Customers** Uptowners, college students. **Hours** Daily, 11 a.m.–10:30 p.m.

SETTING AND ATMOSPHERE A big, stark, dimly lit room with large windows looking into the big live oaks and the turning streetcars. The main atmosphere is the aroma of grilling food wafting in from the kitchen.

HOUSE SPECIALTIES Hummus; baba ghanoojh; *lebna;* zaatar bread; tabbouleh; *musaha* (a cold, spicy eggplant salad); chicken shawarma; lamb chops; chicken, beef, lamb, or shrimp kebabs; baklava.

OTHER RECOMMENDATIONS Greek salad; spinach pie; cheese pie; kafta kebabs; lamb with hummus; steak specials.

SUMMARY AND COMMENTS Lebanon's Cafe has one of the most extensive and inexpensive collections of Middle Eastern food in the city. Its cooking is among the best in that style locally. The kitchen boasts a charcoal grill, and the plate of lamb chops that issues forth from above the coals is extraordinary, especially at the price. Even those who eat here often are always finding something new to try.

Li'l Dizzy's Cafe ★★★

CREOLE INEXPENSIVE QUALITY ★★★ VALUE ★★★★

610 Poydras Street, Central Business District; ☎504-212-5656; www.nomenu.com/restaurants/lildizzys.html

Reservations Accepted. **When to go** Anytime. **Entree range** $9–$26. **Payment** All major credit cards. **Service rating** ★★. **Friendliness rating** ★★★. **Parking** Curbside parking only. **Bar** No alcohol. **Wine selection** None. **Dress** Casual. **Disabled access** Limited. **Customers** A mix of locals of every background, plus people from the many nearby hotels. **Hours** Monday–Saturday, 7 a.m.–2 p.m.; Wednesday–Saturday, 6–9 p.m.

SETTING AND ATMOSPHERE I once made up a restaurant like this as an April fool joke. Now somebody has opened it. The dining room occupies half of an enormous Greek-columned, marble-and-brass bank lobby. (The other half is still a bank.) An improbably grandiose space for a down-home cafe, but it sure is comfortable.

HOUSE SPECIALTIES Creole gumbo; fried chicken; red beans and rice; jambalaya omelette; trout Baquet; Seventh-Ward pork chop; bread pudding.

OTHER RECOMMENDATIONS Breakfasts; fried seafood; poorboy sandwiches.

SUMMARY AND COMMENTS Li'l Dizzy's (a tribute to jazz trumpeter Dizzy Gillespie) is the successor to one of the most famous of all New Orleans soul-food restaurants. The old Eddie's filled up with fans of Creole home cooking for decades. Eddie Baquet's son Wayne took the baton a decade ago, and he's still cooking his father's Creole gumbo, red beans and rice, fried chicken, and fried seafood, without any gap in the goodness. To that he's added a popular breakfast and a Sunday brunch buffet. It all draws the most mixed crowd imaginable. All of this is very inexpensive.

Lilette ★★★★

FRENCH | EXPENSIVE | QUALITY ★★★★ | VALUE ★★★★

3637 Magazine Street, Uptown; ☎504-895-1636; www.liletterestaurant.com

Reservations Recommended. **When to go** Dinner. **Entree range** $9–$20. **Payment** AE, DS, MC, V. **Service rating** ★★★. **Friendliness rating** ★★★. **Parking** Curbside parking only. **Bar** Full bar. **Wine selection** About a hundred different wines, with a significant number in half bottles. **Dress** Nice casual. **Disabled access** Full. **Customers** A youthful crowd of Uptown gourmets. **Hours** Tuesday–Saturday, 11:30 a.m.–2 p.m.; Tuesday–Thursday, 5:30–9:30 p.m.; Friday–Saturday, 5:30–10 p.m.

SETTING AND ATMOSPHERE Tall ceilings and many windows lend a spacious feeling to a deceptively small dining room. It looks as if they filled the room with furnishings before the first table was put in.

HOUSE SPECIALTIES Boudin noir; braised veal-cheek salad; hanger steak with Bordelaise sauce; roasted duck breast with chorizo; potato-crusted black drumfish.

OTHER RECOMMENDATIONS Grilled beets with goat cheese; escargots with mushrooms and Calvados; white gazpacho; goat cheese quenelles with poached pears; almond financier with apples.

SUMMARY AND COMMENTS Lilette serves the personal cuisine of owner John Harris, a local chef with a history in and a taste for the country flavors of France. Harris arrived with enough of a reputation that he could offer the likes of veal cheeks, boudin noir, and whatever other rarity strikes his fancy, and find eager diners. With good reason. All of his food is delicious, cooked with a component of herbs and garlic that suggest the South of France. A large board of daily specials may offer the most interesting food. It's important to study the large board of specials on the back wall before studying the menu too closely.

Liuzza's by the Track ★★★

NEIGHBORHOOD CAFE | INEXPENSIVE | QUALITY ★★★ | VALUE ★★★★

1518 North Lopez, Esplanade Ridge; ☎504-218-7888; www.nola.com/sites/liuzzas

Reservations Not Accepted. **When to go** Anytime. **Entree range** $5–$11. **Payment** All major credit cards. **Service rating** ★★. **Friendliness rating** ★★★. **Parking** Curbside parking only. **Bar** Full bar. **Wine selection** A few house wines. **Dress** Very casual. **Disabled access** None. **Customers** A younger crowd, plus Esplanade Ridge people. **Hours** Monday–Saturday, 11 a.m.–7 p.m.

SETTING AND ATMOSPHERE A joint even by New Orleans standards, this place is more bar than restaurant, although there are usually more people eating than drinking. It explodes with customers at Jazz Festival time; the event is right outside its doors, at the Fair Grounds Race Course.

HOUSE SPECIALTIES Creole gumbo; poorboy sandwiches, especially the breathtaking roast beef and the garlic oyster poorboys; fried seafood platters; daily specials.

SUMMARY AND COMMENTS Liuzza's by the Track combines a menu of the familiar New Orleans sandwiches and blue plate platters with some surprisingly ambitious specials. And even the sandwiches take unexpected flights of fancy. The breathtaking roast beef poorboy, for example, adds a sharp horseradish mayonnaise to the classic, scrumptious roast beef flavor profile. The seafood gumbo is one of the city's best. There's no connection with the Liuzza's on Bienville Street.

Lüke ★★★

FRENCH | MODERATE | QUALITY ★★★ | VALUE ★★★

333 St. Charles Avenue, Central Business District; ☎504-378-2840; www.lukeneworleans.com

Reservations Recommended. **When to go** Anytime. **Entree range** $16–$29. **Payment** All major credit cards. **Service rating** ★★★. **Friendliness rating** ★★★. **Parking** Pay parking lots nearby. **Bar** Full bar. **Wine selection** Good wine list, tilted toward France, with many selections by the glass. **Dress** Nice casual. **Disabled access** Full. **Customers** Downtown office people at lunch, a mix of locals and visitors at night. **Hours** Daily, 7 a.m.–11 p.m.

SETTING AND ATMOSPHERE Lüke is Chef John Besh's most casual restaurant, a reminiscence of the many European-style restaurants that once were common in downtown New Orleans. It's in the delightfully eccentric former Masonic Temple building, now a hotel. Two dining rooms: one dominated by the antique bar, the other by the open kitchen. Tile below, tin ceilings with belt-driven fans above. The umlaut over the "u" in the logo is just an affectation; the place has only a suggestion of Germanic food.

HOUSE SPECIALTIES Assortment of chilled seafood; pâtés; charcuterie; mussels with fries; shrimp and grits; steak au poivre; choucroute with pork loin.

OTHER RECOMMENDATIONS Daily lunch and dinner specials; pressed cochon de lait poorboy; poulet grand mere.

SUMMARY AND COMMENTS Many New Orleans restaurants went comfortably retro after Hurricane Katrina, but nobody's gone as far back as John Besh did here. This has much of the food we used to eat in the 1950s and earlier—including a few items we're glad we forgot. The opener is an icy display of oysters, ready for the shucking, along with many other chilled seafoods. The menu goes on to a large array of pâtés and charcuterie. The entrees are straightforward: steaks, fish, mussels, chops, roast chicken, and sandwiches. One can eat grandly or simply, from breakfast all the way through dinner. And start with anise-flavored drinks to make you think you're in Lyon or Strasbourg, or at the long-closed Kolb's.

Mandina's ★★★

CREOLE MODERATE QUALITY ★★★ VALUE ★★★★★

3800 Canal Street, Mid-City; ☎504-482-9179; www.mandinasrestaurant.com

Reservations Not accepted. **When to go** Off-peak lunch and dinner hours to avoid waiting. **Entree range** \$11–\$21. **Payment** No credit cards accepted. **Service rating** ★★. **Friendliness rating** ★★★. **Parking** Ample parking lot adjacent. **Bar** Full bar. **Wine selection** A few house wines. **Dress** Casual. **Disabled access** Limited. **Customers** Locals, families, businessmen at lunch. **Hours** Monday–Saturday, 11 a.m.–10 p.m.; Sunday, noon–9 p.m.

SETTING AND ATMOSPHERE Mandina's stood in six feet of water for two weeks after Hurricane Katrina, and there was brief talk of tearing the old place down and building a new restaurant. No dice, said the customers, who were a little suspicious even of the necessarily new look and layout of the dining room. It's one big casual room with a busy bar at one end and windows partially blocked by neon signs on the other.

HOUSE SPECIALTIES Oyster and artichoke soup; turtle soup; fried soft-shell crab; trout amandine; daily specials, especially red beans with Italian sausage (Monday), beef stew (Tuesday), crabmeat au gratin (Sunday).

OTHER RECOMMENDATIONS Shrimp rémoulade; crab fingers in wine sauce; bread pudding.

SUMMARY AND COMMENTS Mandina's comes to most Orleanians' minds when they try to conjure up the cherished image of the old-time neighborhood cafe. The food is simple, inexpensive, and generally good. The range of the kitchen goes from first-class poorboy sandwiches to a few saucy, fancy dishes. In the middle of all that is some forgettable Italian food and an array of homely daily specials of varying goodness.

Nobody does better red beans and rice on Mondays. The best of it all is seafood—from basic fried to more complex arrangements.

Marigny Brasserie ★★★★

CONTEMPORARY CREOLE EXPENSIVE QUALITY ★★★★ VALUE ★★★

640 Frenchmen Street, Faubourg Marigny; ☎504-945-4472; www.cafemarigny.com

Reservations Recommended. **When to go** Anytime. **Entree range** $15–$30. **Payment** All major credit cards. **Service rating** ★★★. **Friendliness rating** ★★★. **Parking** Curbside parking only. **Bar** Full bar. **Wine selection** Good wine list, including many selections by the glass. **Dress** Casual. **Disabled access** Full. **Customers** Marigny residents; couples and singles. **Hours** Monday–Friday, 11:30 a.m.–2:30 p.m.; Sunday, 11 a.m.–3 p.m.; Sunday–Thursday, 5:30–10 p.m.; Friday–Saturday, 5:30 p.m.–midnight.

SETTING AND ATMOSPHERE In the center of the Faubourg Marigny club-and-cafe strip, this angular, sharp dining room has big windows all around for viewing the always-interesting passing parade. The main dining room is an airy, open space with two rows of banquettes.

HOUSE SPECIALTIES Mussels marinière; gumbo of the day; redfish ceviche; duck confit with beets and arugula; pistachio-crusted lamb loin.

OTHER RECOMMENDATIONS Braised rabbit with pasta; sea scallops any style; New York strip steak with marsala and sun-dried tomatoes.

SUMMARY AND COMMENTS Marigny Brasserie gets more sophisticated and serves more interesting food with each passing year, as a parade of good young chefs come in and spend a year or two before moving on to bigger things. All leave something delicious in their wakes, creating a very appealing, varied menu. Beyond that, there's a large specials board. This is one of surprisingly few New Orleans restaurants that always have wild-caught Pacific salmon. The Brasserie is often busier (and more entertaining) late in the evening.

MiLa ★★★★★

ECLECTIC VERY EXPENSIVE QUALITY ★★★★★ VALUE ★★★★

817 Common Street, Central Business District; ☎504-412-2580; www.milaneworleans.com

Reservations Recommended. **When to go** Anytime. **Entree range** $19–$36. **Payment** All major credit cards. **Service rating** ★★★★. **Friendliness rating** ★★★★. **Parking** Free valet parking in Renaissance Hotel. **Bar** Full bar. **Wine selection** Modest wine list, sprinkled with enough unusual wines by the glass that it's entertaining. **Dress** Nice casual. **Disabled access** Full. **Customers** Businesspeople at lunch; locals and a few hotel guests at dinner. **Hours**Monday–Friday, 11:30 a.m.–2:30 p.m.; daily, 5:30–10 p.m.

SETTING AND ATMOSPHERE The tiles and rectangularity suggest the modernism of the 1950s. The dining room is separated into several small areas, with much of the seating on banquettes—unusual in New Orleans.

HOUSE SPECIALTIES Sweetbreads with black truffle grits; New Orleans–style barbecue lobster; tian of crabmeat; tournedos of veal; hickory-smoked rack of lamb; warm Italian almond cake.

OTHER RECOMMENDATIONS Deconstructed oysters Rockefeller; porcini-dusted grouper; poussin with peas and onions.

SUMMARY AND COMMENTS A married couple of locally born chefs—Slade Rushing and Allison Vines-Rushing—went to New York, had a hit there, then came back to Louisiana. They took over a hotel restaurant that was badly messed up by Katrina, and installed a menu based on the country food of Mississippi and Louisiana. It gets sophisticated quickly, though, and a tasting menu here provides as polished, unique, and fine a meal as can be found hereabouts. The price and volume of the tasting menu are tolerable enough that it's hard to pass up, unless you're in a hurry. And this is a restaurant that's good for the whole evening. The three-course daily lunches are rightly popular.

Mosca's ★★★

ITALIAN | MODERATE | QUALITY ★★★★ | VALUE ★★★

4137 U.S. 90, Waggaman (West Bank); ☎504-436-9942

Reservations Accepted but rarely honored promptly. **When to go** Weeknights. **Entree range** $18–$26. **Payment** No credit cards accepted. **Service rating** ★★. **Friendliness rating** ★★. **Parking** Ample parking lot adjacent. **Bar** Full bar. **Wine selection** Decent list, almost entirely Italian; several Amarones. **Dress** Casual. **Disabled access** Limited. **Customers** Mostly locals (many of them regular customers); a few tourists; families of adults. **Hours** Tuesday–Saturday, 5–10 p.m.

SETTING AND ATMOSPHERE A two-room roadhouse, stark and noisy, way out on the old westbound highway out of town through the marshland. From the outside, it doesn't look very inviting. Inside, it's modest but clearly very lively, as the many regular customers create their own parties over surfeits of family-style Italian food every night.

HOUSE SPECIALTIES Crab salad; oysters Italian style; shrimp Italian style; chicken grandee; spaghetti bordelaise.

OTHER RECOMMENDATIONS Chef's bean soup; roast chicken; roast quail or squab; Italian sausage; filet mignon; pineapple fluff.

SUMMARY AND COMMENTS Mosca's has hardly changed, except in price, since it opened in the 1940s. Finally, here is all the olive oil, garlic, and rosemary you always wanted, scattered around roasted chickens, sausage, shrimp, and oysters. All this is delivered with a startling lack of ceremony—big platters of food accompanied by stacks of plates and utensils for you to distribute among yourselves. Come with at least four people to best enjoy it; six is even better.

Mother's ★★★

SANDWICHES | INEXPENSIVE | QUALITY ★★★ | VALUE ★★★★

401 Poydras Street, Central Business District; ☎504-523-9656; www.mothersrestaurant.net

Reservations Not accepted. **When to go** Anytime except around noon and during large conventions. **Entree range** $9–$15. **Payment** No credit cards accepted. **Service rating** ★★. **Friendliness rating** ★★★. **Parking** Curbside; pay lot nearby. **Bar** Beer and wine. **Wine selection** A few house wines. **Dress** Very casual. **Disabled access** Full. **Customers** Tourists, some locals, businessmen at lunch. **Hours** Daily, 6 a.m.–10 p.m.

SETTING AND ATMOSPHERE The main room has a cafeteria-style line, concrete floors, tables jammed together, and some counters. The new back room is a bit more spacious, but even more spartan, with an immense fire door giving off a strange vibe.

HOUSE SPECIALTIES Gumbo; ham poorboy; Ferdi (ham and roast beef debris); red beans and rice; corned beef and cabbage; bread pudding; café au lait.

OTHER RECOMMENDATIONS Mae's omelette; biscuits; pancakes; fried seafood poorboys; gumbo of the day; jambalaya.

SUMMARY AND COMMENTS The world's most famous vendor of poorboy sandwiches, Mother's is also among the city's busiest restaurants on a volume-per-square-foot basis. There's almost always a line. While standing in it, you may have cooks break through with their buckets of hot gravy or beans or whatever from the kitchen. Everything is cooked on site—exceptional for a poorboy shop. Portions on the plate specials are absurdly large, and the food tends to the heavy side. Lunch and supper are the main meals, but breakfast is terrific, too. Don't come here when there's a large convention in town, or when you have less than $15 cash in your pocket.

Mr. B's Bistro ★★★★

CREOLE | EXPENSIVE | QUALITY ★★★★ | VALUE ★★★★

201 Royal Street, French Quarter; ☎504-523-2078; www.mrbsbistro.com

Reservations Accepted. **When to go** Early evenings. **Entree range** $20–$31. **Payment** All major credit cards. **Service rating** ★★★★★. **Friendliness rating** ★★★★★. **Parking** Validated ($2) at Dixie Parking, behind restaurant on Iberville Street. **Bar** Full bar. **Wine selection** Substantial list, almost entirely West Coast. **Dress** Nice casual. **Disabled access** Limited. **Customers** Mostly locals, some tourists, couples. **Hours** Monday–Saturday, 11:30 a.m.–2:30 p.m.; Sunday, 11 a.m.–3 p.m.; daily, 6–10 p.m.

SETTING AND ATMOSPHERE The wide, deep, dark, moderately noisy room with its semi-open kitchen hosts a party of local diners matched by few other restaurants. The extra-long bar is usually full at dinner with people waiting for tables, a product of a reservation system that favors locals and walk-ins.

HOUSE SPECIALTIES Gumbo ya-ya; crab cake; grilled scallops; hickory-grilled fish; barbecue shrimp; bread pudding; Mr. B's chocolate cake.

OTHER RECOMMENDATIONS Skillet shrimp with garlic; fried oysters with bacon and horseradish hollandaise; hickory-roasted chicken with garlic glaze.

ENTERTAINMENT AND AMENITIES Pianist at dinner nightly and at Sunday brunch.

SUMMARY AND COMMENTS In 1979 Brennans transformed the New Orleans dining scene by opening this, the archetype of the casual, contemporary Creole bistro. Its kitchen creates innovative and excellent Creole dishes from top-rung fresh ingredients, but serves them in an easy, informal way. Hickory-grilled fish, now common, was pioneered here; so was using pasta as the basis for new Creole concoctions. The chicken-andouille gumbo and barbecue shrimp are definitive. The service staff and the wine list are both better than they need to be. This is a sleeper venue for Sunday brunch; the food is great and the music fun.

Mr. Ed's ★★★

NEIGHBORHOOD CAFE MODERATE QUALITY ★★★ VALUE ★★★★

1001 Live Oak Street, Uptown; ☎504-838-0022; www.austinsno.com

Reservations Not Accepted. **When to go** Anytime. **Entree range** $9–$16. **Payment** All major credit cards. **Service rating** ★★★. **Friendliness rating** ★★★★. **Parking** Ample parking lot adjacent. **Bar** Full bar. **Wine selection** A few house wines. **Dress** Casual. **Disabled access** Full. **Customers** Local people, tending to the older side. **Hours** Monday–Saturday, 11 a.m.–9 p.m.

SETTING AND ATMOSPHERE A large, long restaurant with a series of dining rooms kept bright by day by big windows.

HOUSE SPECIALTIES Oyster-artichoke soup; fried calamari; fried eggplant; shrimp rémoulade salad; fried chicken; seafood platters; poorboy sandwiches; muffuletta.

SUMMARY AND COMMENTS Ed McIntyre created this unpretentious revival of the good old New Orleans neighborhood cafe in the early 1990s. After several expansions it still purveys that little-of-everything menu. There's a tilt toward seafood platters and poorboys, with the rest of the day's specials being in the red-beans category. They also put out reasonably decent Italian food of the home-style, very cheesy variety, and very good fried chicken. The soups are reliably delicious. Always busy.

Mr. John's Steakhouse ★★★

STEAK VERY EXPENSIVE QUALITY ★★★★ VALUE ★★★

2111 St. Charles Avenue, Garden District; ☎504-679-7697; www.mrjohnssteakhouse.com

Reservations Recommended. **When to go** Dinner. **Entree range** $14–$40. **Payment** All major credit cards. **Service rating** ★★★. **Friendliness rating** ★★★. **Parking** Free valet parking. **Bar** Full bar. **Wine selection** Modest list of wines matched to the food, with particular strength among the Italian wines. **Dress** Nice casual. **Disabled access** Limited (the restaurant is in a hotel that is not yet fully recovered from the storm). **Customers** Uptowners and steak lovers. **Hours** Tuesday–Saturday, 5:30–10 p.m.

SETTING AND ATMOSPHERE The tiled dining room and the tables on the sidewalk offer a pleasant view of the passing streetcars. The style of the place is loose and easy.

HOUSE SPECIALTIES Barbecue shrimp; fried calamari; wedge salad; cuts of steak, particularly the sirloin strip; crème brûlée.

OTHER RECOMMENDATIONS Filet mignon Christian; garlic-rubbed chicken; spinach or broccoli au gratin.

SUMMARY AND COMMENTS The restaurant doesn't have the atmosphere or the service of the premium national steak house chains. But the steaks are better. All of the cuts are USDA Prime (even the filets, which usually are not elsewhere), broiled in a superheated broiler until crusty, and then sent out with the New Orleans–style sizzling butter. Also here is a substantial menu of Italian food. That's a terrific match to the steaks, particularly if you share one of the bigger cuts along with one of the pastas.

Muriel's ★★★★

CONTEMPORARY CREOLE EXPENSIVE QUALITY ★★★★ VALUE ★★★★

801 Chartres Street, French Quarter; ☎504-568-1885; www.muriels.com

Reservations Recommended. **When to go** Anytime. **Entree range** $15–$35. **Payment** All major credit cards. **Service rating** ★★★. **Friendliness rating** ★★★★. **Parking** Validated parking at a number of nearby garages; ask when you reserve. **Bar** Full bar. **Wine selection** Excellent wine list, including many selections by the glass. **Dress** Nice casual. **Disabled access** Full. **Customers** A mix of visitors and locals. **Hours** Daily, 11:30 a.m.–2:30 p.m. and 5:30–10 p.m.

SETTING AND ATMOSPHERE If your idea of New Orleans atmosphere includes an ancient building with quirky, rumpled furnishings, hints of voodoo and the bordello, and crumbling brick walls, this is the place for you. Even Orleanians find this place interesting, particularly the upstairs rooms, which are illuminated almost entirely by candles in chandeliers. All this is on Jackson Square, the spiritual center of New Orleans since its earliest years.

HOUSE SPECIALTIES Turtle soup; shrimp rémoulade; shrimp and goat-cheese crepe; wood-grilled fish or chicken; slow-roasted duck; pain perdu bread pudding.

OTHER RECOMMENDATIONS Seafood gumbo; shrimp Herbsaint; sautéed crab cake; pecan-crusted drumfish; filet mignon with fried oysters.

SUMMARY AND COMMENTS The food at Muriel's blends with the old Creole environment. It's not as traditional as in the places that really are as old as Muriel's looks, but it is unambiguously Louisiana in its ingredients and flavors. Seafood dominates the menu, and the wood-burning grill in the kitchen adds a special touch of flavor. The dining room staff is young and sometimes unpolished—the only significant hitch here. The place is fun and unique, and the pricing of the menu is a surprising value, given the prime location. Watch for seasonal table d'hôte menus that occur from time to time—the fall oyster menu, for example.

Ninja ★★★★

JAPANESE MODERATE QUALITY ★★★★ VALUE ★★★

8433 Oak Street, Uptown; ☎504-866-1119

Reservations Accepted. **When to go** Anytime. **Entree range** $7–$18. **Payment** All major credit cards. **Service rating** ★★★. **Friendliness rating** ★★★★. **Parking** Small parking lot adjacent. **Bar** Full bar. **Wine selection** Modest list of wines matched to the food. **Dress** Casual. **Disabled access** Limited. **Customers** Neighborhood people; some college students. **Hours** Daily, 11:30 a.m.–2:30 p.m. and 5–10 p.m.

SETTING AND ATMOSPHERE Downstairs is a dark bar with a low ceiling where you might have to wait for a table. It gives no suggestion of the brighter, sleeker dining room upstairs.

HOUSE SPECIALTIES Sushi specials; Ninja dinner (a bit of all their specialties); barbecued eel.

OTHER RECOMMENDATIONS Mixed seafood platter; *chirashizushi* (like sashimi, scattered over a bed of rice); beef tataki; gyoza; teriyaki beef or chicken; edamame; tempura shrimp.

SUMMARY AND COMMENTS Ninja is one of the best, most creative sushi bars around. It's a place where they always get the fine points right—such as the temperature of the fish, the moistness of the rice, and the relative quantities of the ingredients. The menu includes the usual array of fried and grilled dishes, but sashimi, sushi, and the like are clearly the specialties. The regular clientele is particularly vociferous in its opinion that there's no better place than this. However, newbies are treated to the same fine food and service as the regulars.

Nirvana ★★★

INDIAN | INEXPENSIVE | QUALITY ★★★ | VALUE ★★★★

4308 Magazine Street, Uptown; ☎504-894-9797; www.insidenirvana.com

Reservations Accepted. **When to go** Dinner. **Entree range** $9–$17. **Payment** All major credit cards. **Service rating** ★★. **Friendliness rating** ★★. **Parking** Curbside parking only. **Bar** Full bar. **Wine selection** A few house wines; a good selection of Indian beers. **Dress** Casual. **Disabled access** Full. **Customers** Uptowners, bohemians, Indians. **Hours** Tuesday–Sunday, 11:30 a.m.–2:30 p.m. and 5:30–9:30 p.m.

SETTING AND ATMOSPHERE A Woolworth's from a century ago, with a beautiful pressed-tin ceiling high above a large dining room. A few tables are on a small patio in the front of the restaurant.

HOUSE SPECIALTIES *Seenkh kebab; saag paneer* (creamed spinach with homemade cheese); mint-encrusted lamb; chicken, lamb, or vegetarian *biryani.*

OTHER RECOMMENDATIONS Soups, particularly those made with beans; tandoori chicken; *malai kebab* (chicken marinated in yogurt and cream cheese); *macchi tikka* (marinated, roasted fish); lamb Goa (spicy coconut-milk curry).

SUMMARY AND COMMENTS Nirvana is the most ambitious restaurant yet from the Keswani family, who introduced Indian food to New Orleans in 1982. The kitchen dispatches tandoori dishes, some 30 isotopes of curry, dishes with sauces ranging from mild and buttery to flamethrowing, a vast array of vegetarian offerings, and more than a few complete inventions and fusions. Like every other Indian restaurant in the world (it seems), they serve from a buffet here, but that's for beginners and chowhounds. Ask for Anjay Keswani, tell him what you like, and he'll make something real happen.

Nola ★★★★

CONTEMPORARY CREOLE EXPENSIVE QUALITY ★★★★ VALUE ★★★

534 St. Louis Street, French Quarter; ☎504-522-6652; www.emerils.com/restaurant/2/nola-restaurant/

Reservations Recommended. **When to go** Anytime. **Entree range** $15–$28. **Payment** All major credit cards. **Service rating** ★★★★. **Friendliness rating** ★★★★. **Parking** Validated at Omni Royal Orleans Hotel. **Bar** Full bar. **Wine selection** Substantial list, emphasis on California; many by-the-glass selections. **Dress** Nice casual. **Disabled access** Full. **Customers** A mix of tourists and locals, with a hip, young tilt. **Hours** Saturday–Sunday, 11:30 a.m.–2 p.m.; daily, 6–10 p.m.

SETTING AND ATMOSPHERE An old French Quarter building is done up in a swell, high-tech way. The whole place is a sort of modern sculpture. The second-floor dining room gives an interesting view of the French Quarter parade, and a look into the kitchen.

HOUSE SPECIALTIES Vietnamese stuffed chicken wings; wood-oven-baked oysters and crabmeat; pizza; pork porterhouse with sweet potatoes; shrimp and grits; Nola buzz bomb (a chocolate overkill).

OTHER RECOMMENDATIONS Crab cake; barbecue shrimp; filet mignon with garlic mashed potatoes; hickory-roasted duck; banana pudding layer cake.

SUMMARY AND COMMENTS Emeril Lagasse's second and most casual restaurant, Nola is where new ideas, chefs, and managers in the organization are tried out. It holds to the same standards as the flagship in using well-selected fresh ingredients in innovative ways, while keeping a distinctly Louisiana flavor. Many come here looking for a glimpse of the superstar chef; they probably won't get one, but the waitstaff is happy to tell visitors all about him. The open kitchen sports a wood-burning oven and grill. Full advantage is taken of that resource. They like devising twists on familiar local standards, as well as totally innovative concoctions, with equally good results. The pastry department makes an exceptional assortment of desserts.

One ★★★★

CONTEMPORARY CREOLE EXPENSIVE QUALITY ★★★★ VALUE ★★★★★

8132 Hampson Street, Riverbend (Uptown); ☎504-301-9061; www.one-sl.com

Reservations Recommended. **When to go** Anytime. **Entree range** $16–$24. **Payment** All major credit cards. **Service rating** ★★★★. **Friendliness rating** ★★★★. **Parking** Curbside parking only. **Bar** Full bar. **Wine selection** Good wine list, including many selections by the glass. **Dress** Nice casual. **Disabled access** Limited. **Customers** Uptowners, on the young side. **Hours** Monday–Saturday, 5–10 p.m. (or later).

SETTING AND ATMOSPHERE One uses every square centimeter of its scant space for all it's worth. The most interesting place to dine is the food bar, which fronts the main action of the kitchen so closely that you can almost reach out and touch the food being assembled before you.

HOUSE SPECIALTIES Spicy tuna and smelt roe with avocado; seared sea scallops with orange; roasted rabbit with lentils and grits; beef tenderloin with braised beef shoulder.

OTHER RECOMMENDATIONS Grilled oysters with blue cheese; crab and corn bisque; grouper with pesto.

SUMMARY AND COMMENTS The regulars here consider themselves lucky when they score a table in the teeny, wood-floored dining room. The partners (the chef and the dining room boss) give them much to be glad about. This is lusty, original food with a decided Creole tilt, fresh and uncomplicated, but with unique twists in the seasoning and saucing. The chef's dishes come out looking irresistible and tasting better. Despite the cramped quarters, everything is made in house. And underpriced.

Palace Café ★★★★

CONTEMPORARY CREOLE EXPENSIVE QUALITY ★★★★ VALUE ★★★

605 Canal Street, Central Business District; ☎504-523-1661; www.palacecafe.com

Reservations Recommended. **When to go** Anytime. **Entree range** $15–$31. **Payment** All major credit cards. **Service rating** ★★★★. **Friendliness rating** ★★★★★. **Parking** Validated (free) at Marriott Hotel, across the street. **Bar** Full bar. **Wine selection** Substantial list, almost entirely from the West Coast. **Dress** Dressy casual. **Disabled access** Full. **Customers** A mix of locals and tourists; businessmen at lunch; families. **Hours** Daily, 11:30 a.m.–2:30 p.m. and 5:30–10 p.m.

SETTING AND ATMOSPHERE The Palace Café's redesign of the historic Werlein Music Building created a marvelous two-story restaurant with a striking old New Orleans look. The best tables are situated along the large windows opening onto Canal Street. When full, the tile floors and large windows conspire to create high sound levels.

HOUSE SPECIALTIES Crabmeat cheesecake with pecan crust; chicken gumbo; seafood au gratin; andouille-crusted fish; honey-roast duck any way; white chocolate bread pudding.

OTHER RECOMMENDATIONS Oyster pan roast with rosemary cream; shrimp rémoulade; turtle soup; Werlein salad; catfish pecan; bananas Foster.

SUMMARY AND COMMENTS The flagship of Dickie Brennan's group of restaurants, the Palace Café started as a casual sister restaurant to Commander's Palace. Over the years it's developed its own style, reminiscent of the flavors of 20 or so years ago. However, along the way this kitchen has launched a few dishes that have become classics around town: white chocolate bread pudding and crabmeat cheesecake among them. Duck has become a specialty: every night, they feature it in at least three different entrees. Service appears to be casual, but suddenly they roll up a gueridon and start flaming or carving something. A great favorite with the local lunch crowd.

Parkway Bakery ★★★

SANDWICHES INEXPENSIVE QUALITY ★★★ VALUE ★★★★

538 Hagan Avenue, Mid-City; ☎504-482-3047; www.parkwaybakeryandtavernnola.com

Reservations Not Accepted. **When to go** Anytime. **Entree range** $6–$12. **Payment** All major credit cards. **Service rating** ★★. **Friendliness rating** ★★★★. **Parking** Curbside only. **Bar** No alcohol. **Wine selection** None. **Dress** Very casual. **Disabled access** Limited. **Customers** Locals of every stripe. **Hours** Wednesday–Monday, 11 a.m.–8 p.m.; closed Tuesday.

SETTING AND ATMOSPHERE An old frame building with tables and counters scattered throughout the corridors, plus more tables on a patio outside.

HOUSE SPECIALTIES Poorboy sandwiches: roast beef, ham, hot sausage, or fried shrimp or oyster.

SUMMARY AND COMMENTS The Parkway made poorboy sandwiches with the bread it baked on the premises for decades before closing in the 1990s, after a long decline. Enough people recall the glory days (or wanted to) that when Jay Nix reopened it in 2003, it became a phenomenon. This time, however, the food was actually good. Everything (except the bread) is cooked on the premises and served generously, with the classic New Orleans poorboy flavor.

Pascal's Manale ★★★

CREOLE MODERATE QUALITY ★★★ VALUE ★★★★

1838 Napoleon Avenue, Uptown; ☎504-895-4877; www.neworleansrestaurants.com/pascalsmanale

Reservations Recommended. **When to go** Anytime. **Entree range** $11–$32. **Payment** All major credit cards. **Service rating** ★★★. **Friendliness rating** ★★★. **Parking** Ample parking lot adjacent. **Bar** Full bar. **Wine selection** Modest list of wines, mostly Italian and California. **Dress** Casual. **Disabled access** Limited. **Customers** A mix of Uptown locals and tourists. **Hours** Monday–Friday, 11:30 a.m.–2:30 p.m.; Monday–Saturday, 5–9:30 p.m.

SETTING AND ATMOSPHERE The Katrina flood brought the most sweeping renovations to this 95-year-old neighborhood cafe that anyone remembers. The main dining room is brighter and airier with the big window uncovered. The bar, however, retains that scruffiness that many Orleanians like in their venerable local eateries.

HOUSE SPECIALTIES Raw oysters; oysters Bienville or Rockefeller; crab and oyster pan roast; barbecue shrimp; sirloin strip steak or filet mignon; bread pudding.

OTHER RECOMMENDATIONS Stuffed mushrooms; shrimp and crabmeat rémoulade; turtle soup; veal liver and grits; veal Puccini; filet mignon; key lime pie.

SUMMARY AND COMMENTS New Orleans's oldest Italian restaurant serves the epitome of Creole-Italian cuisine—a hybrid so well blended now that no Italian would recognize it as being from the homeland. Manale's is not a one-dish restaurant, but the fame of that one dish is tremendous. It's barbecue shrimp: gigantic heads-on shrimp cooked in a distinctive pepper-butter sauce. It's a misnomer, since the shrimp are neither grilled nor smoked, and there's no barbecue sauce. Other restaurants now do the dish better, but here they're very good. A better specialty here is oysters, from the freshly shucked raw jobs at the bar to the many cooked oyster dishes at the table. You'll find surprisingly good steaks and veal dishes. Avoid red-sauce dishes and you'll eat well.

Patois ★★★★

FRENCH EXPENSIVE QUALITY ★★★★ VALUE ★★★

6078 Laurel Street, Uptown; ☎504-895-9441; www.patoisnola.com

Reservations Recommended. **When to go** Dinner. **Entree range** $21–$27. **Payment** All major credit cards. **Service rating** ★★★★. **Friendliness rating** ★★★★. **Parking** Curbside parking only. **Bar** Full bar. **Wine selection** Excellent wine list, including many selections by the glass. **Dress** Nice casual. **Disabled access** Limited. **Customers** Uptown gourmets. **Hours** Friday, 11:30 a.m.–2 p.m.; Sunday, 10:30 a.m.–2:30 p.m.; Wednesday–Saturday, 5:30–10 p.m.

SETTING AND ATMOSPHERE The building has been a neighborhood cafe and bar for decades, and still shows signs of that. The bar sports a row of booths along the windowed wall. Most of the tables are up a few steps in a long room behind the bar.

HOUSE SPECIALTIES Gnocchi with crabmeat; rabbit terrine; mussels with smoked tomato broth; duck and andouille gumbo; roasted whole poussin; hanger steak.

OTHER RECOMMENDATIONS Duck confit salad; pannéed rabbit; almond-crusted fish.

SUMMARY AND COMMENTS When a just-okay Italian restaurant here closed in 2008, Chef Aaron Burgau found himself on the loose from another closed restaurant. And he wound up here. His cooking is a fine example of a new kind of French-Creole cuisine that's taken hold in New Orleans in the past few years. The ingredients are local, but the techniques are French bistro in style. It works brilliantly, and Patois (that's the word for a language spoken by Creoles) has become one of the most difficult dining rooms to penetrate. The tariff helps: nothing here hits the $30 mark (yet).

Pelican Club ★★★★★

CONTEMPORARY CREOLE EXPENSIVE QUALITY ★★★★★ VALUE ★★★★

312 Exchange Place, French Quarter; ☎504-523-1504; www.pelicanclub.com

Reservations Recommended. **When to go** Anytime. **Entree range** $26–$32. **Payment** All major credit cards. **Service rating** ★★★★. **Friendliness rating** ★★★★. **Parking** Validated (free) at Monteleone Hotel garage, across the street. **Bar** Full bar. **Wine selection** Substantial list, good international balance; many by-the-glass selections. **Dress** Dressy. **Disabled access** Limited. **Customers** A mix of locals and tourists; couples, gourmets. **Hours** Daily, 5:30–9:30 p.m.

SETTING AND ATMOSPHERE The three dining rooms line up into a long hall, with enough marble flooring and wood panels to give both elegance and lively acoustics. The front room, where the bar is, offers a quieter and, somehow, more intimate setting.

HOUSE SPECIALTIES Shrimp rémoulade; baked oysters with bacon, red peppers, and herb butter; seafood martini; scallop-stuffed artichoke; Louisiana cioppino; seafood fricassee.

OTHER RECOMMENDATIONS Escargots with mushrooms and tequila; clay pot barbecue shrimp; Creole Caesar salad; pannéed fish with crabmeat; jambalaya; dessert specials.

ENTERTAINMENT AND AMENITIES Live piano in the bar most nights.

SUMMARY AND COMMENTS Keeping a low profile on mysterious Exchange Alley, the Pelican Club can wine and dine you with the best of them. Chef-owner Richard Hughes fuses Creole, Italian, Asian, Southwestern, and other influences with ingredients of impressive pedigree. The food nevertheless has a familiar flavor profile for all its innovation. Here you find the most polished jambalaya ever served in a restaurant, for example. Hughes buys beautiful local seafood–his shrimp and crabmeat are particularly stunning–and serves it generously. All the pieces of a grand dinner are here except the pretension.

Ralph's on the Park ★★★★

CONTEMPORARY CREOLE EXPENSIVE QUALITY ★★★★ VALUE ★★★★

900 City Park Avenue, Mid-City; ☎504-488-1000; www.ralphsonthepark.com

Reservations Recommended. **When to go** Anytime. **Entree range** $25–$40. **Payment** All major credit cards. **Service rating** ★★★★. **Friendliness rating** ★★★★. **Parking** Free valet parking. **Bar** Full bar. **Wine selection** Decent list, good international balance. **Dress** Dressy. **Disabled access** Full. **Customers** Locals. **Hours** Friday, 11:30 a.m.–2 p.m.; Sunday–Thursday, 6–9 p.m.; Friday–Saturday, 5:30–9:30 p.m.

SETTING AND ATMOSPHERE The structure has been a restaurant since just after the Civil War. That's when City Park–right across the street–began to be developed. Ralph's takes advantage of the atmospheric possibilities with big windows and balconies for the best view. A generally antique style prevails in the dining room decor. The bar is particularly pleasant, although all the rooms, upstairs and down, have great style.

HOUSE SPECIALTIES Oysters Ralph; crabmeat gratinee; wild mushroom ravioli; prosciutto-wrapped sea scallops; turtle soup; shrimp rémoulade; grilled skin-on redfish; barbecue shrimp; double pork chop; creamsicle bread pudding; chocolate chip pecan pie.

SUMMARY AND COMMENTS This is the most atmospheric of Ralph Brennan's three local restaurants, and the best, too. The cooking is a fresh, light version of New Orleans food, with just a touch of innovation and an overall layer of polish. The restaurant's early-evening menu and other specials allow three courses for between $25 and $30, and are much better than the price might suggest. The regular menu seems too short (that's how it is at Ralph's other restaurants, too), but there are specials.

Red Fish Grill ★★★

SEAFOOD MODERATE QUALITY ★★★ VALUE ★★★

115 Bourbon Street, French Quarter; ☎504-598-1200; www.redfishgrill.com

Reservations Accepted. **When to go** Anytime. **Entree range** $20–$36. **Payment** AE, DC, MC, V. **Service rating** ★★★★. **Friendliness rating** ★★★★. **Parking** Pay parking garages nearby. **Bar** Full bar. **Wine selection** Good wine list, mostly California. **Dress** Casual. **Disabled access** Full. **Customers** A mix of locals and visitors, with a sizable local lunch crowd. **Hours** Daily, 11 a.m.–3 p.m. and 5–10 p.m.

SETTING AND ATMOSPHERE What once was the menswear section of a department store looks as if it was hit by a bomb, then painted over. Walls, floors, and tabletops are fancifully decorated by artist Luis Colmenares in a way that almost suggests a slick chain restaurant, but this is the one and only.

HOUSE SPECIALTIES Coconut shrimp; barbecue oysters; alligator sausage gumbo; hickory-grilled fish; chocolate bread pudding.

OTHER RECOMMENDATIONS Shrimp rémoulade with fried green tomatoes; pasta jambalaya; red bean soup; bananas Foster "up" (in a martini glass).

SUMMARY AND COMMENTS The seafood specialty is obvious, but Red Fish differs from other casual seafood places in emphasizing grilling and sautéing instead of universal frying. The namesake dish—grilled redfish—is seared over a wood fire, and that's unusual enough to make it a specialty. So are oysters, available at the bar raw or in an irresistible appetizer called barbecue oysters. The menu is decidedly New Orleans in taste and, the kicky surroundings notwithstanding, represents a talented kitchen. One only wishes the offerings were a bit more extensive.

Restaurant August ★★★★★

ECLECTIC VERY EXPENSIVE QUALITY ★★★★★ VALUE ★★★★

301 Tchoupitoulas Street, Central Business District; ☎504-299-9777; www.rest-august.com

Reservations Required. **When to go** Anytime. **Entree range** $22–$40. **Payment** All major credit cards. **Service rating** ★★★★★. **Friendliness rating** ★★★★★. **Parking** Free valet parking. **Bar** Full bar. **Wine selection** Excellent with many selections by the glass. **Dress** Dressy. **Disabled access** Full. **Customers** Gourmets. **Hours** Daily, 6–10 p.m.

SETTING AND ATMOSPHERE In an early-1800s building, the restaurant has towering ceilings, antique-wood walls and columns, large windows, and a general feeling of antebellum grandeur. The wine room and bar look a bit more modern but are equally comfortable.

HOUSE SPECIALTIES Gnocchi with crabmeat and truffles; foie gras three ways; soft-shell crab BLT; herb- or almond-crusted fish; whole roasted chicken with black trumpet mushrooms for two; banana rum cake; terrine of blueberries.

OTHER RECOMMENDATIONS There are two tasting menus: one of five courses, another that must be planned with the chef in advance and takes the entire evening.

SUMMARY AND COMMENTS Chef John Besh now owns the restaurant that was built for him, and his impressive career marches on. Besh is a local guy, but he spent a lot of time in kitchens in France (and he returns annually). That informs his cooking, in a rustic way. Look for dishes involving homely items like rabbit, chicken, and variety meats. August is a restaurant for those who get a kick out of eating offbeat items prepared in highly original combinations. Everything changes with the seasons, which sometimes brings dishes from far-flung origins. The tasting menu in three to five courses, all composed of the day's specials, is the best approach to dinner.

RioMar ★★★★

SPANISH | MODERATE | QUALITY ★★★★ | VALUE ★★★★

800 South Peters Street, Warehouse District (CBD); ☎504-525-3474; www.riomarseafood.com

Reservations Recommended. **When to go** Anytime. At lunch, the tapas menu is fun and widely varied. **Entree range** $19–$22. **Payment** All major credit cards. **Service rating** ★★★. **Friendliness rating** ★★★. **Parking** Validated ($6) at Embassy Suites across the street. **Bar** Full bar. **Wine selection** Excellent wine list, with Spanish wines a specialty, many by the glass. **Dress** Casual. **Disabled access** Full. **Customers** A mix of locals and people attending events at the nearby Convention Center. **Hours** Monday–Friday, 11:30 a.m.–2 p.m.; Monday–Saturday, 6–10 p.m.

SETTING AND ATMOSPHERE In a converted warehouse, the floors are concrete, the walls are stucco decorated with wrought ironwork art, and the open kitchen creates a buzz. The bar offers tapas and wine tastings.

HOUSE SPECIALTIES Ceviche assortment; oysters *al ajillo;* mussels with chorizo; *zarzuela* (Spanish fish stew); *tres leches de coco* cake.

OTHER RECOMMENDATIONS Empanadas of tuna; grilled giant squid; grilled fish with romesco; "unilateral" salmon; drumfish with salpicon and squid chorizo; hanger steak with chimichurri; arroz con anything.

SUMMARY AND COMMENTS Chef-owner Adolfo Garcia is an Orleanian with Panamanian roots. RioMar's main theme is seafood, but with a twist: almost nothing is fried, and the flavors are those of Central America and Spain. So we get four or more distinct preparations of ceviche daily, for example. The chef also likes to find and experiment with little-seen species. Razor clams show up when the chef can get them. There's a little beef and sausage and chicken, but you should come here with an appetite for fish. All of the lunch menu and much of the dinner menu are structured as tapas, at $4–$6 per item.

Ristorante Da Piero ★★★

ITALIAN | **EXPENSIVE** | **QUALITY ★★★** | **VALUE ★★★**

401 Williams Boulevard, Kenner; ☎504-469-8585; www.ristorantedapiero.net

Reservations Recommended. **When to go** Dinner. **Entree range** $16–$30. **Payment** All major credit cards. **Service rating** ★★★. **Friendliness rating** ★★★. **Parking** Curbside parking only. **Bar** Full bar. **Wine selection** Good wine list, including many selections by the glass. **Dress** Nice casual. **Disabled access** Limited. **Customers** People from the suburbs along the river, and those needing to go to the airport. **Hours** Tuesday–Friday, 11:30 a.m.–2 p.m.; Tuesday–Saturday, 5–9 p.m.

SETTING AND ATMOSPHERE A century-old house, brought here from elsewhere in the old railroad town of Kenner, is an ideal setting for the kind of restaurant run by Piero Cenni. One big room with many large windows, a wood-plank floor, and tall ceilings.

HOUSE SPECIALTIES Crostini misti; steamed mussels with pancetta and cippolini onions; salad Caprese; strozzapreti pasta with speck, arugula, and cream; *filetto di manzo ai pepe verde;* rabbit with Madeira sage sauce; tiramisu.

SUMMARY AND COMMENTS Piero Cenni is from the Romagna region of Italy. The food there is distinctive, and Piero doesn't hesitate to serve it all—even dishes that might not be fully understood by Americans. (The mixed grill is a good example.) Meanwhile, the chef—Piero's son—creates some utterly new dishes that seem to be from a different restaurant. It all contributes to a unique evening of dining, with unusual wines. It's worth the trip, but if you have to be near the airport, this is a good place to take a meal.

Ruth's Chris Steak House ★★★★

STEAK | **VERY EXPENSIVE** | **QUALITY ★★★★** | **VALUE ★★**

3633 Veterans Boulevard, Metairie; ☎504-888-3600
525 Fulton Street, Central Business District; ☎504-587-7099
www.ruthschris.com

Reservations Accepted. **When to go** Anytime. **Entree range** $18–$40. **Payment** All major credit cards. **Service rating** ★★★★. **Friendliness rating** ★★★★. **Parking** Valet (free). **Bar** Full bar. **Wine selection** Substantial list, heavily tilted toward the red end of the spectrum, from all over the world. Nothing extraordinary, though, which is just as well because they don't handle wine well here. **Dress** Dressy casual. **Disabled access** Full. **Customers** Politicians, media figures, businesspeople, couples at dinner. **Hours** Daily, 5–10 p.m.

SETTING AND ATMOSPHERE In Metairie, the dining rooms have a masculine, clubby feel, with well-padded tables either out in the middle of things or secluded, as customers' needs be. The newer downtown location is a striking, Italianate parlor with marble tile floors and tall draperies. It also has tables on the mall outside.

HOUSE SPECIALTIES Shrimp rémoulade; crab-tini; sizzling crab cakes; New York strip; porterhouse for two; Lyonnaise potatoes; bread pudding.

OTHER RECOMMENDATIONS Barbecue shrimp; stuffed mushrooms; filet mignon; lamb chops; veal chops; French fries; cheesecakes.

SUMMARY AND COMMENTS Several decades before it became one of the leading chains of prime steak houses in America, Ruth's Chris was the dominant steak house here in its hometown. It still is. Since the 1940s, they've served Prime aged beef from rigorously selective sources, brought to something like the temperature you ordered in a superheated broiler. It is rendered sinful and irresistibly aromatic by the addition of bubbling butter, the traditional New Orleans gilding to a steak. Also here are big lobsters, great lamb and veal chops, and thick flanks of salmon. Side dishes are prosaic but prepared well. Service is effective but unceremonious. While the menu is the same at both locations, the predominance of local diners in Metairie—now Ruth's Chris's oldest restaurant—keeps it closer to standards.

Sake Café ★★★

JAPANESE | MODERATE | QUALITY ★★★★ | VALUE ★★★

4201 Veterans Boulevard, Metairie; ☎504-779-7253
2830 Magazine Street, Garden District; ☎504-894-0033

Reservations Accepted. **When to go** Anytime. **Entree range** $7–$23. **Payment** All major credit cards. **Service rating** ★★★. **Friendliness rating** ★★★. **Parking** Ample parking lot adjacent. **Bar** Full bar. **Wine selection** Modest list of wines matched to the food. **Dress** Casual. **Disabled access** Full. **Customers** *Metairie:* Suburban Gen-X-ers and other sushi buffs; *Uptown:* A younger crowd (mostly from Uptown); also popular with preteens, for some reason. **Hours** Daily, 11:30 a.m.–10 p.m.

SETTING AND ATMOSPHERE The two best locations of the five-unit Sake Café are the original in Metairie and the large Uptown restaurant. The former is unusually handsome, with a sleek, dim dining room with great lighting. The Uptown Sake Café is a conversion of a large drugstore into a striking, unusual work of interior design, with paneling you'll want to take a close gander at.

HOUSE SPECIALTIES Torched tuna with chili sauce; baby mackerel sashimi, plus fried head and tail; seaweed salad; salmon skin salad; *shu-mai; oshitashi* (steamed spinach with bonito flakes); sushi and sashimi; *negimaki* (grilled beef rolls); bento box dinners.

SUMMARY AND COMMENTS The Metairie and Uptown Sake Cafés are among the best Japanese restaurants in the city. Both pull a few pages from the Western restaurant playbook. You're greeted at the sushi bar by a complimentary appetizer—often the most unusual tidbit you'll have all night. Both places have extensive menus not only of sushi, but also of noodles, grilled dishes, barbecue eel, teriyaki (on sizzling platters), tempura, and much else. All of this starts with good raw materials and ends with an appetizing presentation. The sushi chefs cut their fish generously—almost too much so—and serve it artfully.

Stein's Deli ★★★

SANDWICHES | INEXPENSIVE | QUALITY ★★★ | VALUE ★★★★

2207 Magazine Street, Uptown; ☎504-527-0771; www.steinsdeli.net

Reservations Not Accepted. **When to go** Anytime. **Entree range** Under $10. **Payment** All major credit cards. **Service rating** ★★. **Friendliness rating** ★★★★. **Parking** Curbside parking only. **Bar** No alcohol. **Wine selection** None. **Dress** Very casual. **Disabled access** None. **Customers** Uptowners. **Hours** Tuesday–Thursday, 7 a.m.–7 p.m.; Friday–Sunday, 9 a.m.–5 p.m.

SETTING AND ATMOSPHERE A cramped, battered old retail space, with little done to renovate. Sausages, hams, and cheeses hang about.

HOUSE SPECIALTIES Muffuletta; beef tongue sandwich; Tuscan panini; Fernando sandwich (prosciutto, fresh mozzarella, pesto on ciabatta); bagels and bialys.

SUMMARY AND COMMENTS The best ideas of the Jewish delicatessen and the Italian salume vendor come together in one place. It would be difficult to find a better source of sliced meats. The sandwiches are imaginative and well made. Although you can't drink it here, beer is available in amazing variety, including some real rarities. Also here: a smattering of gourmet groceries.

Stella! ★★★★★

ECLECTIC | VERY EXPENSIVE | QUALITY ★★★★★ | VALUE ★★★

1032 Chartres Street, French Quarter; ☎504-587-0091; www.restaurantstella.com

Reservations Recommended. **When to go** Dinner. **Entree range** $29–$45. **Payment** All major credit cards. **Service rating** ★★★★★. **Friendliness rating** ★★★★. **Parking** Free valet parking. **Bar** Full bar. **Wine selection** Excellent wine list, including many selections by the glass. **Dress** Dressy. **Disabled access** Full. **Customers** A blend of local gourmets and visitors who happen to stumble onto the place. **Hours** Wednesday–Monday, 5:30–10 p.m.

SETTING AND ATMOSPHERE Enclosed by—but not part of—the Provincial Hotel, Stella! has two dining rooms flanking the carriageway of a very old French Quarter mansion. The dining room nearer the street is smaller and isolated, but overlooks the street and a row of town houses. Missing: a guy yelling "Stella!"

HOUSE SPECIALTIES The menu changes daily and is unpredictable. The few regular items include a trio of oysters with three caviars, granitas, and vodkas; shrimp and scallops with truffled potato hash; moulard duck breast with foie gras wontons; bouillabaisse; bananas Foster French toast.

SUMMARY AND COMMENTS Chef-owner Scott Boswell is one of a brilliant group of chefs who worked together at the Windsor Court a decade ago, then went on to run their own personal kitchens in other restaurants. Boswell's style blends local ingredients, flavors, and techniques with those of nearly all the rest of the world, with particular attention to

Italy, France, and Japan. He spends what must be a lot of time locating offbeat, wonderful ingredients. Some of these are a little too interesting and verge on silly (e.g., a single drop of 100-year-old balsamic vinegar on a plate). But for the most part, everything comes together in brilliantly original food. The chef's tasting menu (paired with wines) at around $180 per person may be the finest dinner it's possible to order without advance notice anywhere in New Orleans.

Sukho Thai ★★★

THAI | INEXPENSIVE | QUALITY ★★★★ | VALUE ★★★★

1913 Royal Street, Faubourg Marigny; ☎504-948-9309; www.sukhothai-nola.com

Reservations Accepted. **When to go** Anytime. **Entree range** $9–$18. **Payment** All major credit cards. **Service rating** ★★★. **Friendliness rating** ★★★. **Parking** Curbside parking only. **Bar** No alcohol. **Wine selection** You're welcome to bring your own wine. **Dress** Casual. **Disabled access** None. **Customers** Marigny and French Quarter residents, and a younger clientele from elsewhere in town. **Hours** Tuesday–Friday, 11:30 a.m.–2:30 p.m.; Tuesday–Sunday, 5:30–10 p.m.

SETTING AND ATMOSPHERE This used to be an old grocery store, with large windows looking up several Marigny streets.

HOUSE SPECIALTIES Shrimp in pouches; Thai spring rolls; soft-shell crab salad; shrimp or chicken satays; green curry with seafood combination; whole fried fish; pad Thai.

SUMMARY AND COMMENTS Thai food is always exciting, but these guys have a real gift for it. Particularly in the seafood dishes, the vivid freshness of everything triggers slams and waves of flavor. The menu includes all the familiar Thai noodle dishes and colors of curries, plus a few things you may never have had before. This is the place to break away from pad Thai and try something new. The kitchen is very adept.

The Joint ★★★

BARBECUE | INEXPENSIVE | QUALITY ★★★ | VALUE ★★★★

801 Poland Avenue, Bywater; ☎504-949-3232; www.alwayssmokin.com

Reservations Not Accepted. **When to go** Anytime. **Entree range** $7–$16. **Payment** All major credit cards. **Service rating** ★★. **Friendliness rating** ★★★★. **Parking** Small parking lot adjacent. **Bar** No alcohol. **Wine selection** None. **Dress** Very casual. **Disabled access** None. **Customers** Barbecue fanatics and Bywater residents. **Hours** Monday–Tuesday, 11:30 a.m.–2:30 p.m.; Wednesday–Saturday, 11:30 a.m.–9 p.m.

SETTING AND ATMOSPHERE Minimal dining accommodations.

HOUSE SPECIALTIES St. Louis ribs; pulled pork; brisket; smoked *chaurice* (Creole hot sausage); pies.

SUMMARY AND COMMENTS New Orleans is not historically a barbecue town. But if this place was your only exposure to 'cue here, you'd think it a major specialty. In a historic part of town that got badly beat up by

Hurricane Katrina (it's coming back slowly but surely), this place does barbecue well enough to convince a Kansas Citian or a Memphian. Smoke is king here, the rubs are applied generously, and time is an investment in deliciousness.

Tommy's ★★★★

CONTEMPORARY CREOLE EXPENSIVE QUALITY ★★★★ VALUE ★★★★

746 Tchoupitoulas Street, Warehouse District (CBD); ☎504-581-1103; www.tommyscuisine.com

Reservations Recommended. **When to go** Dinner. **Entree range** $16–$26. **Payment** All major credit cards. **Service rating** ★★★★. **Friendliness rating** ★★★★. **Parking** Pay valet parking. **Bar** Full bar; the lounge next door, separated from but part of the restaurant, is among the most comfortable and well stocked in town. **Wine selection** Good wine list, including many selections by the glass. **Dress** Dressy. **Disabled access** Limited. **Customers** All local. **Hours** Daily, 6–10 p.m.

SETTING AND ATMOSPHERE What was once an industrial space has been crammed with so many plates, pictures, and gewgaws that the two dining rooms appear to have been here for a hundred years, instead of having been built this way in 2003. Convivial and noisy.

HOUSE SPECIALTIES Baked oyster trio; grilled shrimp; roast duck Tchoupitoulas; sautéed fish with brown butter and crabmeat.

OTHER RECOMMENDATIONS Crabmeat canapé; escargots with vermouth and garlic; veal Sorrentino; filet mignon; rack of lamb; caramel custard.

ENTERTAINMENT AND AMENITIES Live piano in the lounge.

SUMMARY AND COMMENTS Tommy Andrade has a long history in the upscale dining rooms of New Orleans, and he knows every waiter in town. His restaurant opened with a staff of old pros who made everyone feel at home. And a menu of the kind of food well known to be favored by local customers—namely, local classics along traditional lines, with some goosing up here and there. Half the menu is Italian, half is classic Creole of the kind you'd find at, say, Galatoire's. The formula works perfectly: dinner here is just delicious, and the prices are below standard.

Tujague's ★★★

CLASSIC CREOLE MODERATE QUALITY ★★★ VALUE ★★★

823 Decatur Street, French Quarter; ☎504-525-8676; www.tujagues.com

Reservations Recommended. **When to go** Anytime. **Entree range** Table d'hôte: $20–$32. **Payment** All major credit cards. **Service rating** ★★. **Friendliness rating** ★★. **Parking** French Market pay lot, one block. **Bar** Full bar. **Wine selection** Limited list of inexpensive wines. **Dress** Casual. **Disabled access** Limited. **Customers** Tourists, some locals. **Hours** Daily, 5–10 p.m.

SETTING AND ATMOSPHERE It looks like a restaurant founded in 1856—which it was. The unreconstructed, minimal dining room is flanked by a great antique bar. The upstairs dining rooms have a view of the river. Filling the walls is an amazing collection of several thousand little bottles of booze.

HOUSE SPECIALTIES Table d'hôte dinner: shrimp rémoulade; crabmeat and spinach soup; boiled brisket of beef; chicken *bonne femme;* cranberry bread pudding.

SUMMARY AND COMMENTS Tujague's began as a lunchroom for workers in the French Market and on the nearby docks, serving a table d'hôte meal of the day. Today, Tujague's antique dining rooms serve a very traditional five-course home-style Creole meal, with five or so choices for the entree. One of the courses is always the restaurant's famous boiled brisket of beef, good enough to inspire a desire for seconds. This is a great place to come on the major holidays; they're open for all of them.

Upperline ★★★★

CONTEMPORARY CREOLE MODERATE QUALITY ★★★★ VALUE ★★★★

1413 Upperline Street, Uptown; ☎504-891-9822; www.upperline.com

Reservations Recommended. **When to go** Anytime. The garlic festival in summer is always interesting. **Entree range** $16–$28. **Payment** All major credit cards. **Service rating** ★★★★. **Friendliness rating** ★★★★. **Parking** Small parking lot adjacent. **Bar** Full bar. **Wine selection** Excellent wine list, with many delightful surprises. **Dress** Nice casual. **Disabled access** Limited. **Customers** A mix of locals and tourists. Lots of the arts crowd, gourmets, and oenophiles. **Hours** Wednesday–Sunday, 5:30–10 p.m.

SETTING AND ATMOSPHERE The original restaurant flows into an adjacent cottage to make a string of small dining rooms. All are filled with artworks, with primitive and folk artists dominating the theme.

HOUSE SPECIALTIES Fried green tomatoes with shrimp rémoulade; Cane River Country shrimp; filet mignon with garlic Port sauce; roast duck with ginger peach sauce.

OTHER RECOMMENDATIONS Trio of soups (turtle, gumbo, oyster stew); seared salmon with crawfish bouillabaisse; rack of lamb with mint and Madeira; beef tournedos with Stilton; pecan pie; chocolate sweet potato cake.

SUMMARY AND COMMENTS This is one of the gourmet Creole bistros that changed the dining scene in the 1980s. From that time to this, the Upperline's greatest asset is the fertile mind of owner JoAnn Clevenger. Eating here is to open oneself to her creative statements about art, drama, literature . . . and, yes, food, too. Her most famous culinary idea is the summer-long garlic menu, but there's almost always a festival of something or other here. Not everything is offbeat: the Upperline's menu is full of classic Creole dishes, including a tasting menu of traditional local dishes. Prices are lower than you'd expect, and the wine list much more impressive.

Vincent's ★★★

ITALIAN MODERATE QUALITY ★★★ VALUE ★★★★

4411 Chastant Street, Metairie; ☎504-885-2984
7813 St. Charles Avenue, Riverbend (Uptown); ☎504-866-9313
www.vincentsitaliancuisine.com

Reservations *Metairie:* required; *Uptown:* not accepted. **When to go** *Metairie:* Weeknights and lunch; *Uptown:* Anytime. **Entree range** $13–$27. **Payment** All major credit cards. **Service rating** ★★★. **Friendliness rating** ★★★★. **Parking** *Metairie:* ample lot adjacent; *Uptown:* curbside parking only. **Bar** Full bar. **Wine selection** *Metairie:* Modest list of wines matched to the food; *Uptown:* minimal, largely Italian. **Dress** Casual. **Disabled access** Limited. **Customers** Locals, couples and foursomes, college students at Uptown. **Hours** *Metairie:* Tuesday–Friday, 11:30 a.m.–2:30 p.m.; Monday–Saturday, 5–10 p.m. *Uptown:* Tuesday–Friday, 11:30 a.m.–2:30 p.m.; Tuesday–Sunday, 5–10 p.m.

SETTING AND ATMOSPHERE The Metairie original is an unpretentious, hidden, side-street cafe, with two dining rooms that are usually a little too crowded. The Uptown restrike took over Compagno's, a beloved old Italian cafe and bar, and kept everything more or less the same. On one side of a short brick dividing wall is the bar; on the other, next to the windows, are the tables. It's a little cramped, a situation not helped by the popularity of the place.

HOUSE SPECIALTIES Eggplant sandwich; artichoke Vincent (with crawfish and shrimp); corn and crab bisque en croute; veal cannelloni with two sauces; soft-shell crab with tomato garlic sauce; pannéed fish, crab cream sauce; garlic chicken; braciolone; osso buco; parmesan-crusted chicken; tiramisu; spumone and torroncino ice creams.

SUMMARY AND COMMENTS Vincent Catalanotto, former waiter, discovered he could cook as well as any of the chefs who shouted at him. So he opened an unpretentious side-street cafe in Metairie and started cooking some of the most impressive food ever sold at prices this low. The style is Creole-Italian, with enough polish that it could be sold in a much more expensive restaurant. Seafood is especially fine, sauced with terrific and original sauces. Salad, vegetable, and dessert courses are less impressive, but hardly grounds for complaining at these prices. The service staff is chummy. Getting a table, particularly on weekends, is a tough deal.

Vizard's ★★★★

CONTEMPORARY CREOLE EXPENSIVE QUALITY ★★★★ VALUE ★★★★

5015 Magazine Street, Uptown; ☎504-895-2246

Reservations Required. **When to go** Dinner. **Entree range** $18–$30. **Payment** All major credit cards. **Service rating** ★★★★. **Friendliness rating** ★★★★. **Parking** Curbside parking only. **Bar** Full bar. **Wine selection** Good wine list; relatively few by the glass. **Dress** Nice casual. **Disabled access** Limited. **Customers** Uptown gourmets. **Hours** Tuesday–Saturday, 5:30–10 p.m.

SETTING AND ATMOSPHERE A very small dining room that formerly served as the office of an architect—so it's a cool space, in a clean, linear way. Not big enough for all Vizard's fans, it's always a full house.

HOUSE SPECIALTIES Crabmeat Nelson; greens, eggs, and ham; soft-shell crab with tomato and okra; roast chicken with roasted garlic; grilled redfish with sweet corn; lamb chops with pepper jelly demi-glace.

SUMMARY AND COMMENTS Kevin Vizard has been frustrating New Orleans diners for over 20 years by serving exciting, innovative cooking for a year or two, and then disappearing from the scene for a while. This is his best restaurant ever, and one of the finest new restaurants since the hurricane. In all his years, Vizard has never hitched himself to a signature dish; the guy seems to have an endless well of new ideas. They're usually close to the cutting edge of Creole cookery, using all the familiar foodstuffs in previously unexplored ways. Sometimes he plays games: chicken and dumplings, for example, was really a roasted chicken half with gnocchi, and his greens, eggs, and ham defies description. Always fun to eat here.

PART NINE

SHOPPING

PROBABLY THE ONLY REASON VISITORS to New Orleans spend any less time shopping than they do eating and drinking is that the stores tend to close earlier—and even at that, you'll find a surprising number of merchants open until 8 or even 10 p.m. After all, trade and conspicuous consumption are at the heart of New Orleans history. In the mid–18th century, it was the third-busiest port in the United States and had the highest per capita income of any city in the country, according to some figures.

So you can easily shop until you drop. Stores and galleries are abundant in the Vieux Carré, making for spectacular window shopping, and that can be the danger as well. Just as there is a tendency to keep eating because you can smell all that food around you, there's a tendency to keep falling in love with jewelry and posters and rings and masks. (And remember, alcohol loosens your inhibitions, including financial ones.) If you have a budget, or if you are looking for something particular, it's best to know in advance where you want to go, or you might get sidetracked.

Also, if you think of shopping by type—high-end antiques or specialty stores, upscale supermalls, or souvenir troves—you can head to the neighborhood with the most options. If you have a couple of days to spare, then you can range a little farther, but even then, if you don't have a background in antiques, a knowledgeable companion, or a friend who lives in town, you're probably not going to stumble onto a hidden treasure.

Among the neighborhoods with good browsing are the most famous shopping strip in New Orleans, **Royal Street;** the entire riverfront strip from the **Farmers Market** to the **Convention Center;** and **Magazine Street,** uptown from Canal over to Audubon Park. You might also enjoy the somewhat-more-relaxed **Riverbend District** in Carrollton, which you can stroll as part of the St. Charles streetcar tour (see Part Seven, Sightseeing, Tours, and Attractions).

Of course, the temptation is to load up on so much stuff that you're hauling a truckload through the streets; and now that airlines routinely charge extra for baggage, you may want to consider shipping your acquisitions, even if they aren't all that large. Not only that, if you ship to another state, it saves you the 9% sales tax, so the handling charge may well be less than the tax. (Here's another tip: some vendors who don't want to bother providing the shipping may "split the difference" by taking another $10 or $15 off the price, so you might want to bargain over something small like jewelry.) If you do want to ship something yourself, check out **Royal Mail Service,** which boxes and/or sells packing supplies and deals with UPS and FedEx (828 Royal Street; ☎504-522-8523) or the **FedEx/Kinko's** at 762 St. Charles Avenue (☎ 504-581-2541).

If you are visiting from another country, you can take advantage of Louisiana's Tax-Free Shopping, although this will mean carrying your passport (or at least a good photocopy) with you instead of putting it in the hotel vault. Here's how it works: If the store posts an LTFS sticker (or ask at the counter), show the passport and ask for the special refund voucher. You'll still pay the tax, but when you get to the airport, stop by the LTFS counter and show them your receipts *and* refund vouchers. Up to $500 will be refunded in cash, anything over $500 by check. There are Refund Centers in the Riverwalk Marketplace near the Julia Street entrance, and in Louis Armstrong Airport across the main lobby from the American Airlines counter. Refunds are also available by mail to Louisiana Tax-Free Shopping, P.O. Box 20125, New Orleans, LA 70141. You will have to pay a handling fee based on the purchase amount; fees begin at $1 for a purchase up to $50 and go up to a maximum fee of $75 for purchases of $8,000 or more. For more information, call ☎ 504-467-0723 or visit **www.louisianataxfree.com.**

The FRENCH QUARTER

AS BOURBON STREET IS TO NIGHTLIFE, so **Royal Street** is to antiques—and if it's not there, it's probably on Chartres. That's an exaggeration, of course, but the Royal antiques row goes back several generations, on both the selling and buying sides. Royal Street makes for the most riveting window-shopping in the city: cases of earrings, necklaces, cufflinks, and enamels; chandeliers and candelabra; gold leaf, crystal, and silver; china dolls; silver-headed walking sticks; and sterling cigarette cases, all glittering with the mystique of Creole culture. Some of these stores advertise all over the country (which is a

unofficial **TIP**
If you're a serious antiquer—or a restaurant or hotel needing decorating help—the best thing to do is to contact shopping maven Macon Riddle for a personalized tour; call ☎ 504-899-3027 or go to **www.neworleans antiquing.com.**

consideration that cuts both ways—somebody has to pay for all that publicity); still others capitalize on Royal Street's reputation to embellish both the value and the actual cost of their goods.

One of the oldest names in the antiques game here is **Keil's Antiques** (325 Royal Street; ☎ 504-522-4552), founded before the turn of the 19th century and still among the best choices for French and English art and furnishings, chandeliers, and decorative arts. It remains a family concern, and other stores in the clan's hands are **Royal Antiques Limited** (309 Royal Street; ☎ 504-524-7035), its annex around the corner (715 Bienville Street), and **Moss Antiques** (411 Royal Street; ☎ 504-522-3981). Another good spot is the **French Antique Shop** (225 Royal Street; ☎ 504-524-9861; **www.gofrenchantiques.com**). Its collection of bronzes, chandeliers, and Baccarat crystal looms out of the dark to draw you in. **Ida Manheim Antiques** (409 Royal Street; ☎ 504-620-4114 or 888-627-5969; **www.idamanheimantiques.com**) deals in 17th-, 18th-, and 19th-century mantels, chandeliers, and bronze and marble statuary.

For Asian art and antiquities, contact **Diane Genre,** a member of the Appraisers Association of America and a specialist in Japanese woodblock prints, temple carvings, lacquer work, and extraordinary Japanese and Chinese textiles, including gold- and silver-embroidered dragons as would bring your fantasies to life. Call for an appointment (☎ 504-595-8945) or visit **www.dianegenreorientalart.com.**

unofficial **TIP**
Royal Street used to be the financial heart of the Vieux Carré, and several of the old financial institutions are into their second lives as antiques stores. The Waldhorn building, for example, served as the Bank of the United States in 1800; the police station at Royal and Conti was the Bank of Louisiana; and the building on the northeast corner of Royal and Conti streets, now Latrobe's special events room, was designed in 1818 by Benjamin Latrobe as the Louisiana State Bank: notice the intertwined "LB" wrought iron on the second-floor balcony—partly his initials and partly the bank's.

If you're interested in fine estate jewelry, check out **Waldhorn & Adler Antiques** (343 Royal Street; ☎ 504-581-6379; **www.waldhornadlers.com**). For an array of vintage wrist, pocket, and locket watches by Rolex, Tiffany, Cartier, Patek Philippe, and other makers—and a fascinating collection of vintage radios and salt-and-pepper sets as well—stop at **Quarter Past Time** (606 Chartres Street; ☎ 504-410-0010). (And if you can tango, owner Julio Canosa may give you a twirl or two.)

For the hostess with the mostest, nothing could be more fun than a lesson in preparing an absinthe cocktail—the sharp-tipped, perforated absinthe spoons range from $65 to $125—from Patrick Dunne, proprietor of **Lucullus Antiques** (610 Chartres Street; ☎ 504-528-9620; **www.lucullusantiques.com**). Lucius Licinius Lucullus was a famous Roman epicure, and Dunne's shop stocks cookware, silver, and culinary objets d'art dating to the 17th century. Now that absinthe is legal again, you might find slightly less antique but more affordable paraphernalia, along with some museum pieces, at **Maison d'Absinthe** (823 Royal Street; ☎ 877-899-7647). At the old **M. S. Rau Antiques, LLC,** store you'll find such items as walking sticks (many of them hiding rapiers), music boxes, and decanters (630 Royal Street; ☎ 504-523-5660 or 800-544-9440; **www.rauantiques.com**). Even if you don't buy anything, take a peek in the window to see the 260-piece, 24-karat-gold–plated silver service of former Dominican Republic dictator Rafael Trujillo in its baroque Messien cabinet—a mere $148,500.

Serious collectors should be aware of the seasonal and special sales at the **New Orleans Auction Galleries** located upstairs at 801 Magazine Street (☎ 504-566-1849 or 800-501-0277; **www.neworleansauction.com**), although it's a few blocks outside the French Quarter.

Kurt E. Schon, Ltd. (510 St. Louis Street; ☎ 504-524-5462) has what he advertises as the largest inventory of 19th-century European paintings in this country, particularly featuring works by Impressionist, Postimpressionist, French Salon, and Royal Academy artists, and the price tags are as breathtaking as the collection. (If your budget only goes up to $100,000 or so, don't even attempt the six floors of private showrooms, open by appointment only.) If you love the styles but can't quite afford the Schon prices, try the **Mann Gallery** (305 Royal Street; ☎ 504-523-2342), which specializes in the second rank, but high second rank, of predominantly French Postimpressionists.

Books, Records, and Prints

Not surprisingly, a literary town like New Orleans is rich in bookstores, particularly those specializing in out-of-print titles, first editions, and rare publications. **Faulkner House Books** is in the building overlooking St. Anthony's garden, where William Faulkner lived while writing *Soldier's Pay* and various short stories set in New Orleans. It naturally features first editions of his works and other titles important to Southern literature (624 Pirates Alley; ☎ 504-524-2940). The house where Tennessee Williams wrote *A Streetcar Named Desire,* coincidentally, is right through Exchange Alley, in the next block, at 632 St. Peter Street.

At the north end of the Quarter is **Kitchen Witch** (631 Toulouse Street; ☎ 504-528-8382), a funky parlor filled with used and vintage cookbooks and some vintage LP's, as well. Hours vary, so it's best to call ahead.

Faubourg Marigny Bookstore, on Frenchmen Street at Chartres (☎ 504-947-3700), specializes in gay, lesbian, and feminist literature. Most of these stores belong to an association of antiquarian and secondhand-book sellers, and any one of them can give you a list and a simple map of the others.

Other good bookshops in the Quarter, especially for those who love to linger among the shelves, include **Beckham's Bookshop** (228 Decatur Street; ☎ 504-522-9875), **Librarie Bookshop** (823 Chartres Street; ☎ 504-525-4837), **Crescent City Books** (204 Chartres Street;

☎ 504-524-4997), **Arcadian Books and Art Prints** (714 Orleans Street; ☎ 504-523-4138), and **Dauphine Street Books** (410 Dauphine Street; ☎ 504-529-2333).

New converts to jazz, zydeco, Cajun, blues, swamp pop, and gospel sounds may want to flip through the 25,000 albums at **Louisiana Music Factory** (210 Decatur Street; ☎ 504-586-1094; **www.louisianamusic factory.com**). For those just as interested in music memorabilia as the recordings themselves, check out the autographed albums—Sinatra to Stevie Ray Vaughan—at **Vintage 429** (429 Royal Street; ☎ 866-846-8429; **www.vintage429.com**). If you're interested in photographs, either vintage or contemporary, **A Gallery for Fine Photography** (241 Chartres Street; ☎ 504-568-1313; **www.agallery.com**) carries works by such artists as Berenice Abbott, Eadweard Muybridge, Edward Weston, Yousuf Karsh, Edward Steichen, Henri Cartier-Bresson, Diane Arbus, Ansel Adams, and Helmut Newton. For fine mezzotints and other vintage prints, try the **Stone and Press Gallery** (238 Chartres Street; ☎ 504-561-8555; **www.stoneandpress.com**).

OTHER FRENCH QUARTER COLLECTIBLES

FOR A HAT YOU CAN WEAR TO THE RITZ or on a Royal Street balcony, consult Tracy Thomson of **Kabuki** at the Dutch Alley Artists Co-op (912 North Peters Street near Dumaine and Decatur; ☎ 504-914-1080) or **Fleur de Paris** (523 Royal Street; ☎ 504-525-1899). It's a couple of blocks away, but men can rely on the venerable **Meyer the Hatter** (120 St. Charles Avenue; ☎ 504-525-1048) for classic Stetson Panamas. For fabulous vintage looks with accessories to match, check out **Trashy Diva** (829 Chartres Street; ☎ 504-581-4555). There are plenty of gewgaws at the French Market, but if you prefer one-of-a-kind and custom jewelry pieces, look for Ken Bowers at the **Quarter Smith** (535 St. Louis Street; ☎ 504-524-9731).

The New Orleans School of Weaving not only has a shop at 616 Chartres called **Loom Works** (☎ 504-566-7788) but also offers would-be artisans two- or four-day teaching sessions at their school at 527 Dumaine Street ($225 and $375; ☎ 504-592-1007). For sterling and otherwise stunning mezuzahs, menorahs, and jewelry, visit **Naghi's Judaica** (633 Royal Street; ☎ 504-586-8373).

Weapons and ammunitions—flintlocks, pistols, muzzle loaders, swords, bayonets, sabers, shot, and even cannonballs—are the signature stock at the fourth-generation **James H. Cohen & Sons** (437 Royal Street; ☎ 504-522-3305), but it also deals in coins and currency. For those who prefer their warfare a little less realistic, **Sword and Pen** (528 Royal Street—or as they continue to put it, 528 Rue Royale—☎ 504-523-7741) carries not only vintage lead and more modern toy soldiers of the familiar Civil War and Napoleonic eras but also figures of Sherlock Holmes and Watson, "Kagemusha"-style samurai, Roman emperors, Winston Churchill, and even Hitler, along with service decorations and pilots' wings.

George Rodrigue's **Blue Dog** paintings, which refer in part to the old *loup-garou* or werewolf legends of the artist's childhood, have become cult items. His gallery, **Rodrigue Studio,** is at 721 Royal Street (☎ 504-581-4244). Another artist whose posters for Jazz Fest and other local institutions have made him a favorite is **Jamie Hayes;** his shop is at 621 Chartres Street (☎ 504-596-2344).

What would a trip to the voodoo capital of the country be without a little mysticism? For charms, potions, mojo dolls, and the most atmospheric palm or tarot readings, head to the **New Orleans Historic Voodoo Museum** (724 Dumaine Street; ☎ 504-680-0128), which is more theater than museum; **Erzulie's** (807 Royal Street; ☎ 504-525-2055); **Voodoo Authentica** (612 Dumaine Street; ☎ 504-522-2111); **Esoterica Occult Goods** (541 Dumaine Street; ☎ 504-581-7711); or **Marie Laveau's House of Voodoo** (739 Bourbon Street; ☎ 504-581-3751). If you prefer to walk on the sunnier side, the **Bottom of the Cup Tea Room** stocks crystals, wrought-iron stands and heavy crystal balls, and scores of tarot decks reproduced from various countries and centuries (327 Chartres Street; ☎ 504-524-1997).

Another New Orleans must is pralines, those brown sugar–pecan sweets; try **Aunt Sally's** (810 Decatur Street; ☎ 504-524-3373), **Leah's Pralines** (714 St. Louis Street; ☎ 504-523-5662), or **Laura's** (331 Chartres Street; ☎ 504-525-3880).

For neo-Creos who can't live without their morning stogie, there's **Cigar Factory of New Orleans** at 415 Decatur Street (☎ 504-568-1003), where you can watch the (Central American, not Cuban) tobacco actually being rolled. The Cigar Factory has a second location at 206 Bourbon Street (☎ 504-568-0168) but without the action, or try **Crescent City Cigar Shop** (730 Orleans Avenue; ☎ 504-522-4427) or **New Orleans Cigar Company** (201 St. Charles Avenue, Suite 125; ☎ 504-524-9631). If those frozen-drink bars on Bourbon Street that resemble laundromats aren't your style, or you're invited to someone's house, the selection at **Vieux Carré Wine and Spirits** (422 Chartres Street, near K-Paul's; ☎ 504-568-9463) is quite good. And they're even open on Sunday. Hey, this *is* New Orleans, after all.

unofficial **TIP**
To check your e-mail over your morning coffee, go wireless at **Royal Blend Tea & Coffee** (621 Royal Street; ☎ 504-523-2716).

Although it's moved, **Bourbon French Perfumes** (805 Royal Street; ☎ 504-522-4480) used to be on the street it's named for—back in 1843, when it opened. You can either get French scents like those preferred by Creole society (for fun, see the super-economy-sized bottles in the Hermann-Grima House) or have a fragrance blended for you. A huge variety of spa goods and services are available at **Spa Aria** located in the Hotel Monteleone at 214 Royal (☎ 504-523-9990; **www.spaaria.com**).

If your boss is the sort of guy who has everything, here are a few leather items that might save you the annual Christmas-list blues: golf bags for $595; roll-on suitcases for $249 and $349; even cell-phone carriers of various sizes. The smartest idea yet is a leather duffel weekender that folds flat into itself so you can pack it inside another suitcase for souvenirs. All, as well as belts, shoes, totes, and purses, are at **Leather Creations** (835 Decatur Street; ☎ 504-527-0033). If you're sticking to the Royal Street Strip, look into the lavish **Royal Masks** at 710 Royal (☎ 504-525-7464).

Finally, for those interested in restoring old homes, **Bevolo Gas and Electric Lights** has been turning out handmade and hand-riveted lamps, including the gaslight-look fixtures around Jackson Square, for half a century (521 Conti Street; ☎ 504-522-9485). And **Fischer-Gambino** specializes in chandeliers—a ceiling full—and garden ornaments and iron (637 Royal Street; ☎ 504-524-9067).

MAGAZINE STREET

EVEN BEFORE KATRINA, rising rents and stiffer competition forced many antiques dealers either to move off the main drag or to leave the French Quarter altogether. A number of stores and galleries have opened up on **Magazine Street** (☎ 866-679-4764; **www.magazinestreet.com**) in the Uptown-University area, and the Magazine Street merchants have been promoting their association with brochures and maps. The area was largely spared major damage, and businesses there are once again open; but again, it might be wise to call ahead if there's a store you're particularly interested in, since some have cut back on business hours.

unofficial **TIP**
Magazine Street begins near the convention center, but don't think the stores are nearby. The convention center is quite a hike from the antiques strip.

Despite the promotional brochures raving about "six miles of antiques shops, art galleries, restaurants, and specialty shops in Historic Uptown New Orleans," the road is still primarily residential; there is a block or two with a lot of stores, and then it may be several blocks before another cluster. Without a car, it's difficult to see more than a few stores at a time.

Also, alongside many of the nicer stores are still lower-scale salvage shops, more like flea market or "granny's attic" affairs. So if you don't already know something about antiques, and if you aren't willing to spend a couple of hours sorting through showrooms and comparing prices, you may be disappointed.

One possibility is to hire a professional antiquing companion, such as Macon Riddle (see tip on page 271), who has made a career of custom-designing half- or full-day shopping tours geared to your interests. Another possibility is to drive about 45 minutes to Ponchatoula, on the other side of Lake Pontchartrain, which has more than 30 antiques shops at non-Royal prices. If you do go to Magazine, here are a few clusters of specialty shops of particular interest, so you can make at least some sort of park-and-walk visit or walk over from the streetcar without exhausting yourself. Or consult with the Regional Transit Authority about bus routes and VisiTour passes, as described under "Public Transportation" in Part Six.

Start off near St. Mary Street at **Jim Russell Records** (1837 Magazine Street; ☎ 504-522-2602) for eight-tracks and semiprecious vinyl. The **Thomas Mann Gallery** is a Royal Street émigré that showcases local as well as national jewelers and artisans (1802 Magazine Street; ☎ 504-581-2113), as does the **Perrin Benham Gallery** at 1914 Magazine (☎ 504-565-7699). There are numerous antiques and "collectibles" if you're the patient browser type: **Estate Treasures** has 3,800 square feet of good and good-willed stuff (2014 Magazine Street; ☎ 504-679-6600), but a little farther on, the **Magazine Antique Mall** (3017 Magazine Street; ☎ 504-896-9994) is even larger.

Bush Antiques has an amazing assortment of ecclesiastical remnants, so to speak: gilded high altars; heavy bishops' chairs; old chapel statuary, including the Virgin Mary and various saints; iron crucifixes from cemeteries; stained glass; and even vestments (2109–2111 Magazine Street; ☎ 504-581-3518). **La Belle Nouvelle Orleans** (2112 Magazine Street; ☎ 504-581-3733) specializes in architectural antiques. Then head to **Antiques on Jackson** (around the corner at 1028 Jackson Avenue; ☎ 504-524-8201), where the similarly flamboyant creations might seem especially tasty (owner Simon Hardeveld used to be a chef).

This area is also home to several popular spas, including **Aidan Gill for Men** (2026 Magazine Street; ☎ 504-587-9090); and **Belladonna Day Spa** (2900 Magazine Street; ☎ 504-891-4393); so you can shop, drop—then get a massage and start over.

Among the other interesting stops are the **New Orleans Music Exchange** for new or used instruments (3342 Magazine; ☎ 504-891-7670); **Ele Shoes,** a designer shoe store for the inner Imelda (3316 Magazine; ☎ 504-309-8674); and **Angelique,** chic baby and mom-to-be wear (3719 Magazine; ☎ 504-301-2583). Funky 1950s (and '60s, and even '70s) interior designs inspire **Neophobia** (2855 Magazine; ☎ 504-899-2444). Missing that sterling-silver fork? **As You Like It** (3033 Magazine Street; ☎ 504-897-6915) has rounded up an array of silver julep cups, antique flatware, candelabras, and the like. And if you've got the money, honey, they've got the time: **Kohlmaier and Kohlmaier** (1018 Harmony Street, just off the 3200 block of Magazine Street; ☎ 504-895-6394) specializes in standing and cabinet clocks, mantel clocks, and personal timepieces.

Another few blocks out is a cluster for decorators with an eye for decorative accessories and

unofficial **TIP**
Ranging from tables to standing screens, the custom-etched and -carved architectural glass at **Whiteglass** (☎ 504-522-3544; by appointment only) is not to be missed. Artist Gerry White won his wife with the panels in the studio's windows, which were etched to look like venetian blinds.

ethnic and folk arts. **Katy Beh** represents over 20 fine jewelry designers (3708 Magazine Street; ☎ 504-896-9600). **Mignon Faget** (3801 Magazine Street; ☎ 504-891-2005), and **Anne Pratt** (3937 Magazine Street; ☎ 504-891-6532) are local artists developing national reputations. **Julie Neill** (3908 Magazine Street; ☎ 504-899-4201) designs lighting fixtures from wall sconces to stand-ups. And **Neal Auction Co.** at 4038 Magazine Street (☎ 504-899-5329) specializes in estate jewelry as well as art. Pottery fans will be drawn to the studio showroom of **Potsalot** (3818 Magazine Street; ☎ 504-899-1705) at **Shadyside Pottery** (3823 Magazine Street; ☎ 504-897-1710). Charlie Bohn served his apprenticeship in Japan but also loves classical Greco-Roman styles. **Cole Pratt Gallery** (3800 Magazine Street; ☎ 504-891-6789) handles several local artists' works.

Finally, hop to the wonderful **Miss Claudia's Vintage Clothing** at 4204 Magazine (☎ 504-897-6310) and **Lili Vintage Boutique** (4514 Magazine; ☎ 504-931-6848)—even if it isn't Halloween.

The WAREHOUSE DISTRICT

ANOTHER NEIGHBORHOOD EMERGING as a shopping center is the old Warehouse District, a loosely defined area roughly squared off by the convention center, Lafayette Street to Lafayette Square, St. Charles Avenue between Lafayette and Lee Circle, and Howard Avenue from Lee Circle back to the convention center. A number of former mills, machinery suppliers, and storehouses have been gutted and refurbished as art spaces and condominiums, although there are still pockets of industry all over. Taking most of its impetus from the 1984 World's Fair (which was a succès d'estime if not an economic one), this neighborhood is an intriguing combination of retail and residential. It is home to the Contemporary Arts Center, the National World War II Museum (formerly known as the D-Day Museum), the Ogden Museum of Southern Art, the Civil War Museum, and the Louisiana Children's Museum, as well as such historic landmarks as St. Patrick's Cathedral. (See the walking tour of the Warehouse District and the museum profiles in Part Seven, Sightseeing, Tours, and Attractions.)

The main strip, nicknamed **Gallery Row,** is along Julia Street between St. Charles and the convention center. Since art is definitely a matter of taste, you'll just have to wander around the galleries and check them out.

Some of the best-known galleries in this district include **LeMieux Galleries** (332 Julia Street; ☎ 504-522-5988) which showcases regional art; **Heriard-Cimino Gallery** (440 Julia Street; ☎ 504-525-7300); **d.o.c.s.** (709 Camp Street;

unofficial **TIP**
You can get to the Warehouse District from the French Quarter by riding the Riverfront streetcar to the Julia Street stop. And if you're not tired afterwards, you can wind up at St. Charles and take that streetcar for a spin out to the Garden District.

☎ 504-524-3936); **Arthur Roger Gallery** (432 Julia Street; ☎ 504-522-1999); and the **New Orleans Auction Galleries** (801 Magazine Street at Julia; ☎ 504-566-1849), which innovatively employs only women auctioneers.

At the corner of Julia and Camp, in one of the "Thirteen Sisters" row houses, is the **Jean Bragg Gallery of Southern Art,** which is not only worth a visit in itself but is also the starting point for monthly gallery walks (600 Julia Street; ☎ 504-895-7375).

This is also a great neighborhood in which to find one-of-a-kind handmade furniture. **Ariodante Gallery** (535 Julia Street; ☎ 504-524-3233) displays contemporary art glass, ceramics, jewelry, decorative accessories, and furniture by regional and national artisans.

Aside from the art galleries and studios, there are a couple of particularly noteworthy addresses along Magazine Street. **New Orleans ArtWorks at the New Orleans School of GlassWorks and Printmaking Studio** (727 Magazine Street between Girod and Julia; ☎ 504-529-7279) is the largest contemporary glass-arts studio in the South, and it offers glassblowing classes to the public—not only six-week courses but two-day intensive introductions to the art, two-hour hands-on demos, and even private tutoring. Exhibitions go on constantly, and the studio shares space with fine bookmakers and print- and papermakers, who also offer exhibitions and workshops. This is a first-class family attraction as well as an art gallery.

And although it may be a little fine for beginners, good amateur and even professional musicians should make a special trip to **International Vintage Guitars** (646 Tchoupitoulas Street; ☎ 504-524-4557), which has used and vintage Martin, Rickenbacher, Fender, and Gibson instruments, along with accessories, amplifiers, and such.

MALLS *of the* AMERICAS

NEW ORLEANS HAS DEVELOPED AN ALMOST CONTINUOUS line of those prepackaged, upscale-label shopping malls stretching along the waterfront from Jackson Square to the convention center, or commercially speaking, from the French Market to the Riverwalk Marketplace. This baby-boomer boomtown also houses that most notorious of souvenir franchises, the Hard Rock Cafe (and was home to the now-defunct Planet Hollywood); across Decatur Street is the Crescent City Brewhouse. The whole area is bookended by two other theme-sales centers: the Jimmy Buffett shop at Margaritaville, at the corner of Decatur and Ursulines, filled with Parrothead paraphernalia; and the House of Blues souvenir store on Decatur past Bienville.

This Great Wall o' Malls winds in and out among the various riverside promenades, cruise-ship landings, and the Aquarium of the Americas, and in good weather kite fliers and inline skaters wind in and

unofficial **TIP**
Take a break from dodging tourists on riverside promenades by getting a 15-minute neck massage or a hair wrap.

out of tourists hefting huge shopping bags and wielding baby strollers.

Starting at the east end of the French Quarter and stretching along North Peters Street to the Café du Monde at Jackson Square is the **French Market,** (☎ 504-522-2621; **www.frenchmarket.org**), which legend says was a trading post for American Indians long before the Europeans arrived. Nowadays the complex comprises a half-dozen nicely restored pink stucco buildings housing everything from high-priced souvenirs to jazz bars to orange-juice stands. The building closest to Barracks Street is the **Old Farmers Market**—or, rather, what is now called the Old Farmers Market. The crates of live poultry, rabbits, turtle, and squid that locals used to buy right off the dock have pretty much been replaced by stands of pepper sauce and braided ropes of garlic being sold at inflated prices to credulous tourists as "Cajun hot garlic."

The next stretch of the market, which spills out into the street on weekends, is the **Community Flea Market** (☎ 504-596-3420), a grab bag of tie-dyed dresses, carved masks, old chairs, and mass-produced "stained glass" that for most people provides all the cheap souvenirs their officemates can stand. Inside these buildings are scores of vendors offering voodoo dolls, T-shirts, earrings, cheap ties (including Jimi Hendrix patterns and copies of Nicole Miller designs for $5), rock posters, sunglasses, blackface pecan-shell magnets, reproduction grocery labels, fabric pins, mobcaps, novelty ballpoint pens (including some that resemble syringes), rubber-band guns, and sports caps. Hot-sauce and Cajun-spice fans can find stalls selling hundreds of gumbo mixes and seasonings bearing both old names (Zatarain's, McIlhenny) and new celebrity imprints (Paul Prudhomme's and Emeril's).

As you work your way toward Jackson Square, you'll find some clothing boutiques, indoor-outdoor bars (there are usually at least two jazz trios playing at any given time), and gift shops with pralines and pepper sauce and cutesy statuettes of Louis Armstrong. (Note that the similarly styled building a little behind the French Market at about St. Philip Street is the Jean Lafitte National Park Visitors Center; see Part Seven, Sightseeing, Tours, and Attractions.) Beyond the legendary **Café du Monde** (800 Decatur Street; ☎ 504-525-4544 or 800-772-2927; **www.cafedumonde.com**), where you can buy chicory coffee and beignet mix right from the source, the commercial strip briefly gives way to Washington Artillery Park and the wooden Moonwalk promenade along the river. Of course, down along the Square, the sidewalks will be full of mule carriages, caricaturists, and clowns; and Artillery Park will probably have some street theater or music going on, but that's just for fun.

Then the shopping picks up again at the old **Jackson Brewery** (600 Decatur Street; ☎ 504-566-7245; **www.jacksonbrewery.com**), one-time house of Jax beer (as it's familiarly known). There is now a river-view branch of Pat O'Brien's (called **Pat O's on the River**) at the top of the building, but it's only available for private parties. The **Hard Rock Cafe, Peaches Records,** and several generic clothing stores follow the sidewalk.

Another pretty stretch—Woldenberg Park—meanders over to the Aquarium of the Americas; just west of the Aquarium, the Spanish Plaza segues into the huge **Riverwalk Marketplace** (☎ 504-522-1555) **www.riverwalkmarketplace.com**) complex, an upscale development of about 150 boutiques and eateries (one with seven-pound live lobsters and another with pizza slices almost as big) that connects to the Hilton Hotel and the convention center. Most of these stores seem to come as a package deal now, and even in duplicate: **Gap, Chico's, Ann Taylor Loft,** and **Brookstone,** and . . . well, you get the idea. On the other hand, there are also a half-dozen shoe stores, including several specializing in comfortable walking shoes that might come in handy if you're facing the agony of da feet.

From the river, you can see where the facade of Riverwalk was torn away by the runaway barge (it looks a little like an intentional architectural model, actually), but you'd never know from strolling through the glossy mall inside that anything had ever happened. And there's a cute little magic shop, where the free demonstrations keep the kids cool.

At the foot of Canal Street, across the streetcar tracks from the Aquarium, is **Canal Place** (☎ 504-522-9200; **www.theshopsatcanalplace.com**), a lushly appointed and label-conscious mall that blazons the logos of its **Gucci, Saks Fifth Avenue, Kenneth Cole, BCBG Max Azria, Coach,** and **Brooks Brothers** tenants. If you're really into fine ties (hand-painted, not cutesy), try the **New Orleans Knots** vendor on the first floor. Be sure to browse through **RHINO** (☎ 504-523-7945), which is an acronym for "Right Here in New Orleans," describing where the store's one-of-a-kind crafts were made. It's a nonprofit shop, and the clothing and art are extremely attractive. Canal Place is also the home of jewelry designer **Mignon Faget** (☎ 504-524-2973), whose creations in silver, 14-karat gold, and bronze d'or for both men and women are highly prized.

PART TEN

EXERCISE *and* RECREATION

WORKING OUT *and* PLAYING HARD

A FEW YEARS AGO, it would have seemed silly to put a chapter on exercise in a vacation guide—particularly a guide to a city as famed for self-indulgence as New Orleans. But most of us at the *Unofficial Guides* are into some form of exercise, if only as a matter of self-preservation: it reduces stress, helps offset those expense-account and diet-holiday meals (no, it's not true that food eaten on vacation has no calories), and even ameliorates some of the effects of jet lag. Even more remarkably, we have discovered that jogging, biking, and just plain walking are among the nicest ways to experience a city on its own turf, so to speak, and we're happy to see that more and more travelers feel as we do.

However, remember what we said in the beginning about the climate of New Orleans—hot and humid, cool and damp. In the summer months, it's a good idea to schedule exercise early in the day or in the first cool of the evening; those late-afternoon showers can make a nice difference. (On the other hand, insects prefer the cooler hours, too, so pack some bug spray. Better yet, double up and get sunscreen with repellent built in.) It's rarely too cold for a run, even in January, but again it may be damp, so pack a weather-resistant layer as well as a first-aid kit: we go nowhere without sports-style adhesive strips, ibuprofen or some other analgesic, petroleum jelly, and a small tube of antiseptic. Blisters can ruin the most perfect vacation. We know.

WALKING

CONSIDERING HOW STRONGLY WE'VE URGED YOU TO WALK at least the French Quarter, you may have already guessed that we find not agony but ecstasy in the feet. And in addition to the neighborhood walks, New Orleans has several picturesque options, starting with the roughly two miles of **Riverwalk** from Esplanade Avenue to the Spanish Plaza, which takes you past Jackson Square, the various cruise ships, and a wonderful assortment of vendors and relaxing natives. (Keep an ear out; this is also popular among inline skaters.) If you take the St. Charles Avenue streetcar to where St. Charles ends, you'll discover the tracks take a sharp right turn onto Carrollton Avenue; that's because the Mississippi River takes a hard right as well, and you can get off and walk the levee there, too, before exploring the shops and cafes of the **Riverbend** neighborhood.

unofficial **TIP**
City Park (**www.neworleanscitypark.com**) covers 1,500 acres, twice the size of New York's sweeping Central Park, and you can wander pretty much as long as you like. It's not only a beautiful spot for nature, family fun, and art, but has a vast variety of sporting options: tennis, golf, horseback riding, running, team sports, even fishing

If you like those walking trails with built-in exercise stations equipped with chin-up bars and stretching posts and the like, go to **Audubon Park** (☎ 504-895-1042); part of the macadam bike trail over by the duck pond has 18 mild challenges.

RUNNING AND JOGGING

AGAIN, THE RIVERFRONT AREA IS A COMMON DRAW for runners who deal in limited distance, and the long, lovely stretch of **St. Charles Avenue** down through the Garden District is a great possibility—the annual Crescent City 10K starts in Jackson Square and ends at the zoo—or even go half-marathon distance by running to Audubon Park, circling the two-mile path around the golf course, and returning. If you'd like to participate in the Crescent City Classic and its sports and fitness expo, go to **www.ccc10k.com.** The race is usually run in mid-April, which is a great time to be in the city.

Along with its pleasure paths, **City Park** has two 400-meter polyurethane tracks built for the 1992 Olympic trials and 1993 NCAA championships, one inside **Tad Gormley Stadium** (☎ 504-482-4888). At **Chalmette Battlefield and National Cemetery,** there is a dirt track that is ideal for runners of the contemplative sort; although the car gate is locked at dusk, there is a smaller pedestrian gate next to the national cemetery that will give you access (☎ 504-589-2133 or **www.nps.gov/jela**). And if you're used to running with a club, contact the **New Orleans Track Club** at **www.runnotc.org** for event schedules.

BIKING

WE ALREADY MENTIONED that it's a good idea to rent a bike. **Bicycle Michael's** on Frenchmen Street (☎ 504-945-9505; **www.bicyclemichaels.com**) is a good place to start. They offer a large selection of bikes for rent by the hour, day, or week. They're open Monday, Tuesday, and Thursday through Saturday, 10 a.m. to 7 p.m.; Sunday, 10 a.m. to 5 p.m.; and closed on Wednesday. A new riverfront path now extends all the way from Jefferson Parish through Orleans Parish and St. Charles as well. And that two-mile track in Audubon Park is very popular with inline skaters and bikers, particularly on weekends. You can also contact the **Crescent City Cyclists** (☎ 888-901-9581; **www.crescentcitycyclists.org**) for group-ride information.

TENNIS

PERHAPS ONE OF THE FEW UPSIDES to the hurricane damage that local recreational facilities suffered is the fact that most now have new and better ones. **City Park** now has 11 hard-surface tennis courts ($7 an hour) and ten clay courts ($10; ☎ 504-483-9383). **Audubon Park's** ten clay courts ($10 an hour; ☎ 504-895-1042) are nice but not lighted; reservations are accepted but not required.

There are six indoor tennis courts (two other tennis courts are used for volleyball and basketball), three racquetball courts, and three squash courts at the **Health Club by Hilton** in the Hilton Riverside at 2 Poydras Street (☎ 504-556-3742). It also offers lessons, a stringing service, and a match-a-partner service, so if you can make arrangements in advance, it's a good place to go.

unofficial **TIP**
The Health Club at the Hilton Riverside is open to the public for $15 a day.

GOLF

LIKE MUCH OF THE SOUTH, this is popular golf territory, and as usual, you can start at City Park; though only one of three courses (the par-67 North Course) was open at press time, repairs to the other two were well under way (☎ 504-483-9397 or 800-504-0677). **Audubon Park** (☎ 504-212-5290) has a very picturesque 18-hole, par-62 course at 6500 Magazine Street; look for the live oaks canopy over the fairway at 4. Just across the river on the Westbank is **Brechtel Park** course (☎ 504-362-4761).

There are other municipal courses in the area as well, but if you're a serious golfer, spring for a round at **English Turn** (pro shop, ☎ 504-391-8018), which is on a curve of the Mississippi River on the Westbank, a pretty drive down St. Bernard Highway. The Jack Nicklaus–designed club is private, but if you're willing to shell out more than $150—and a nice tip for the concierge—you may be able to tee up. It formerly hosted the Zurich Classic, and the 471-yard, par-4 18th hole was then considered among the three hardest on the PGA tour.

GYMS AND HEALTH CLUBS

IN ADDITION TO ITS TENNIS AND RACQUETBALL COURTS, the **Health Club by Hilton** at the Hilton Riverside (☎ 504-556-3742) has massage therapists, a whole list of name-brand machines, salon treatments, a whirlpool, and a sauna. A one-day pass is $15, with additional days (up to five days) for $10 per day.

The **Elmwood Fitness Center,** at Poydras and Carondelet streets in the Warehouse District (☎ 504-588-1600), keeps up with the trends in its classes; a one-day pass is $21, but a weekly pass is only $45—and if you have a friend who's a member, it will cost you only $13.

unofficial **TIP**
Using the fitness center at the **Ritz-Carlton** (☎ 504-670-2929) costs non-guests $75, but indulge in any service at the hotel's exquisite spa and use of the gym is free.

The New Orleans Athletic Club, in the 200 block of Rampart Street backing up to the French Quarter, is in a great old university club–style building complete with chandeliers, ballroom, library, pub, cafe and salon. It's a private club but is open to hotel and B&B guests for $20 (☎ 504-525-2375).

The **Downtown Fitness Center** in the Canal Place complex has aerobics, treadmills, bikes, stair machines, free weights and leveraged machines, saunas, and even personal trainers. You can get a daily pass for $12, a three-day pass that is good for five days for $30, and a five-day pass that is good for seven days for $45 (☎ 504-525-2956). There is also a branch on the eighth floor of the Sheraton Hotel on Canal Street (☎ 504-592-5631), and you can use the passes at either.

OTHER RECREATIONAL ACTIVITIES

IF YOU WANT TO SWIM and are not staying in a hotel with a pool (which only a few in the French Quarter or Garden District have), check with the Y or the health and fitness clubs. There is a public swimming pool at **Audubon Park** as well.

If you like a little outdoor entertainment, but don't go for regimented exercise, you have a couple of other choices. You can ride at a few stables including, of course, City Park's **Equest Farm** (☎ 504-483-9398; **www.equestfarm.com**), which has only a ring, but offers one-hour group lessons and 30-minute individual lessons in English-style riding. **Audubon Park's stables** (☎ 504-891-2246) allow riders to go out into the park a bit.

City Park also offers docks for a little light **catfish and bass fishing** (you must get a state fishing license before you come); **soccer and rugby** fields (three with lights); **softball** diamonds (not yet open); and a **batting cage** is in the works at the four-field softball center.

unofficial **TIP**
Fishing permits are available from most sporting-goods stores, marinas, and guide companies. You can get a basic one-day license for $5, plus $15 for bigger game such as deer and wild turkey; and there are additional requirements for hunting with bows or muzzle loaders. You will need to bring your driver's license.

And if you're interested in serious fishing and hunting a little farther outside the city, perhaps for your second New Orleans visit, there are dozens of guides and charters to choose from. There are two famous names, or at least faces, in the fishing biz. One is former TV weatherman Nash Roberts, of **Fishunter Guide Service,** which will not only supply you with everything you need but come and get you at your hotel

(☎ 504-837-0703 or 800-887-1385; **www.fishunterguideservice.com**). The other is television sportfishing-series character Phil Robichaux of **Captain Phil's Saltwater Guide Services** (☎ 504-689-2006), whose charters leave from the Lafitte Marina near the Barataria unit of the Jean Lafitte National Historic Park and Preserve, about an hour's drive from the French Quarter. You can probably get several other names and numbers out of promotional brochures or by calling marinas and fishing stores, but we suggest you contact the New Orleans Visitors Bureau for a list of reliable guides. Remember, you *do* need a permit from the **Department of Wildlife and Fisheries** (☎ 888-765-2602; **www.wlf.louisiana.gov**).

SPECTATOR SPORTS

TIME WAS, NEW ORLEANS WAS NOT A GREAT Pro-football town—which meant that it was a great football town for tourists, because you could get tickets—until the reopening of the Superdome and the return of the **New Orleans Saints** (☎ 504-731-1700; **www.neworleans saints.com**) became symbols of the city's revival. But while attendance is way up, it's not impossible to find seats (call **Ticketmaster** at ☎ 504-522-5555 for information). **Tulane University** plays some home games at the Superdome, and every other year, there's an old-fashioned, rah-rah LSU–Tulane grudge match there; call the Dome offices at ☎ 504-861-WAVE or visit **www.tulane.edu** for schedules and ticket information. You can also inquire about ticket availability for the **Sugar Bowl** collegiate duel, but you'll need to do so well in advance of the match.

There are times when New Orleans is a *super* football town—as in the **Super Bowl.** When it's played here, getting in is a long shot, but you can try to get in on the ticket lottery not by besieging the Superdome itself but by sending a certified letter to the National Football League offices at 410 Park Avenue, New York, NY 10022. (However, the Super Bowl is not scheduled to return to New Orleans for several years at least.)

The **New Orleans VooDoo** of the indoor Arena Football League play at the 18,500-seat New Orleans Arena behind the Superdome; the season begins in February. Like the Saints (with whom it shares ownership), this team draws big crowds; go to **www.govoodoo.com** for information. New Orleans even has a women's football team: the **New Orleans Blaze**, who play at Muss Bertolino Stadium in Kenner (**www.neworleansblaze.com**). For those to whom "football" means a round ball, the **Shell Shockers** soccer team has finally returned to its hurricane-damaged home at Pan American Stadium in City Park. In 2009 the Shockers will move to minor league status. With this change will come a new name for the team, but they were still undecided at press time (**www.noshellshockers.com**).

Speaking of roundball, the **New Orleans** (formerly Charlotte) **Hornets** basketball team moved to Oklahoma City in the wake of Katrina but is back at the Arena. Call ☎ 504-525-HOOP for information, or consult **www.hornets.com.** They are likely to be sold out, but if you don't mind either the nosebleed section or premium prices, you can probably score a seat.

unofficial **TIP**
For Zephyrs game schedules and ticket information, call the team office at ☎ 504-734-5155 or log on to www.zephyrsbaseball.com.

New Orleans does pretty well by baseball, with the **New Orleans Zephyrs** (now the AAA affiliate of the New York Mets), winners of the 1998 AAA World Series. Zephyr Stadium in Metairie, which opened for the 1997 season, cost $23 million and seats 12,000 in the height of retro-stadium style.

New Orleans also does well by the blue-blooded sport of horse racing (as you might expect from a former French and Spanish royal colony). The **Fair Grounds** (☎ 504-944-5515; **www.fairgroundsracecourse.com**) near City Park, is the oldest operating racing site in America, having been laid out in 1852 as Union Race Course—but even at that, it was the third thoroughbred racetrack in the neighborhood (one of those is now the Metairie Cemetery). It was briefly operated as a standardbred-trotters' course, and the great Ethan Allen raced there in 1859, but it became a general fairground, hosting bull and bear fights as well as races, during the Union occupation of New Orleans. Frank James was once a betting commissioner, Diamond Jim Brady gambled here, and Edgar Degas made the track and horses the subjects of scores of paintings. Just as famously, it was here that Black Gold, the great champion, broke his leg but refused to stop, finishing the race on three legs. He is buried in the infield—as is one of the finest mares to race, Pan Zareta. The course, which is now owned by the same company as Churchill Downs, hosts thoroughbred racing on turf and dirt courses from Thanksgiving to mid-April, when it gives way to the Jazz and Heritage Festival.

Finally, although perhaps it's not so aristocratic a pastime, New Orleans has a women's flat-track roller derby squad, the **Big Easy Rollergirls,** who skate in a rink at Blaine Kern's Mardi Gras World in Algiers. You might not care for the sport itself, but the team's annual "run with the Bulls" through the French Quarter in July is a hoot. Check them out at **www.bigeasyrollergirls.com.**

PART ELEVEN

ENTERTAINMENT *and* NIGHTLIFE

by Will Coviello

THE NICKNAME "BIG EASY"—coined by early jazz musicians while on the road—has stuck to New Orleans because that sums up its spirit. For some it means the less-than-spiritual romp on Bourbon Street. For others it's the laissez-faire attitude—or, rather, the laissez les bons temps rouler attitude—or just the simple truth that New Orleans isn't like other places. New Orleans is come-as-you-are and unpretentious. But whatever it is about spring break, bachelor/bachelorette parties, and major sports championships that causes otherwise-normal people to discard their inhibitions, New Orleans seems to automatically trigger the same response.

For better or worse, exaggeration or outright lie, New Orleans has a reputation as the Babylon of the South. The reason has changed over the years. Once it was the nation's first legal prostitution district: Storyville. Then it was the burlesque houses. Now it's Bourbon Street. The glitzy-seedy strip is neither as good nor as bad as it seems. But if New Orleans is an oasis of tolerance, then Bourbon is its highest concentration of indulgence. For every truth Bourbon Street reflects about New Orleans, there's an only-on-Bourbon application. You can carry a cocktail on the street anywhere in New Orleans as long as it's not in a glass container, but you won't find many people off the strip toting around bucket-sized drinks in plastic fishbowls or yard-long fluorescent tubes. There are good musicians in the house bands on Bourbon, but they spend most of their time covering "Mustang Sally" for tourists. Locals do let it all hang out when they're having a good time, but not with the hell-bent abandon stirred up on the strip. Bourbon Street may be the first thing that comes to mind when newcomers set out to explore the city at night, but it's hardly the best or last.

With balmy temperatures, bars that don't close, and funky, sultry music, New Orleans nights are easy to get lost in, but the city has more than French Quarter saloons. Refined lounges and wine bars offer more-graceful settings. The arcing curve of the Mississippi cradles the quieter uptown areas, also full of bars and music clubs. And there are more bohemian hangouts downriver in the Marigny and Bywater neighborhoods. Mid-City's graying hippie crowd and younger set have a few notable bars, and the Lakefront is again teeming with restaurants that have active bars. Performing-arts organizations such as the symphony and opera are also woven into the city's musical nature. There's a comedy scene that seems to be always growing but never all the way established.

BOURBON STREET

BOURBON IS A SURREAL MIX OF ROWDY BARS and T-shirt shops, strip clubs and tourist traps, gawking conventioneers and college kids, strippers and proselytizers, barkers and buskers, neon lights and feather boas, chintzy beads and big drinks. It's a nine-block scratch-and-sniff circus of bright lights, cheap thrills, quick hustles, and spilled beer.

The mystique of Bourbon Street comes from the heyday of the burlesque theaters from the 1940s forward. Some of the dancers graced the covers of national magazines and mingled with the likes of Frank Sinatra, comedian Shecky Green, and the clique of entertainers that later became associated with Babylon West, Las Vegas. But mostly the street had a little bit of glamour and a lot of plain old bumps and grinds. Over the years it evolved or devolved such that clubs replaced live bands with records. Exotic dancers were replaced by go-go dancers, who were replaced by strippers, who were replaced by lap dancers.

Now Bourbon Street has a handful of good restaurants; a slew of mediocre-fare-at-gouge-price eateries; an expansive row of indistinguishable strip clubs, many of which moved in after Katrina; clubs with DJs; clubs with house bands; and souvenir shops selling everything from rude T-shirts to crawfish-shaped oven mitts. The strip has come to look like a nonstop spring-break venue with a few oddly historic Greek Revival and Southern Gothic details peeking through the shadows as one walks from Canal Street into the eye of the storm. Just past the center of the Quarter, a cluster of gay bars and clubs adds a little extra diversity, and the last few blocks are even residential.

The vibe for many on Bourbon is to find their drink of choice and stroll the strip. Daiquiris, with their neon colors and icy sweetness, are popular throughout most of the year; local chains specializing in the slushtails include **Mango Mango, Jester Daiquiris,** and **Original New Orleans Daiquiri.** Other signature drinks of note are **Pat O'Brien**'s Hurricane and **Tropical Isle**'s Hand Grenade, identifiable by its grenade-shaped plastic cup. Pat O's is happy to sell Hurricanes in its signature hourglass-shaped glass, but be forewarned that if you want to sip on the street, you'll have to pour your drink into a nonglass cup.

unofficial **TIP**
It's legal to walk the streets of New Orleans with a drink in hand as long as it's not in a glass container. Many bars have plastic go-cups right at the door in case you decide to finish your drink elsewhere

One of the industry leaders in novelty-shaped plastic drink containers is the local **Giacona Corporation.** Its founder, Corrado Giacona II, is known in the beverage-container industry as "The Graduate" for his work with plastics. Chances are that if you see someone walking down Bourbon drinking out of a fishbowl, a chemistry beaker, or another totemic shape, it's his work.

There is music on the strip, but it's generally not the music of New Orleans. Some clubs have traditional jazz, and you'll hear "When the Saints Go Marching In" just about every hour on the hour for a one-drink-per-set minimum. **Maison Bourbon** (641 Bourbon Street; ☎ 504-522-8818) still features endless sets of Dixieland jazz by a credible band. The rest of the clubs offer house bands playing a mix of funk, rock, soul, and blues, or DJs spinning whatever is popular in top-40 rock and hip-hop. **Bourbon Cowboy** and **Bourbon Cowboy Saloon** (135 Bourbon Street; ☎ 504-586-9022; **www.bourbonsbest.com**) mix in a little country music and have the French Quarter's only mechanical bull. **Bourbon Rocks** (227 Bourbon Street; ☎ 504-523-4404) is a large complex with a flaming fountain in its courtyard and five bars. Many revelers like to skip the ground floor and find their way up to balconies overlooking the street. **Bourbon Street Blues Company** (441 Bourbon Street; ☎ 504-566-1507; **www.thebestofbourbonstreet.com**) has a throbbing house band downstairs and a wraparound corner balcony. The Old Absinthe House (240 Bourbon Street; ☎ 504-523-3181; **www.oldabsinthehouse.com**) looks like a tourist trap but is actually historic—it created the Absinthe House frappé cocktail in the 1870s—and is a longtime locals' favorite after Saints games and on certain days (like the Friday before Mardi Gras). There's no opera at the Old Opera House (601 Bourbon Street; ☎ 504-522-3265; **www.oldoperahouse.com**), but there are three-for-one happy-hour specials. **Famous Door** (339 Bourbon Street; ☎ 504-598-4334; **www.thebestofbourbonstreet.com**) hasn't had jazz in a while, but it is one of the oldest continually operating clubs. **Tropical Isle** (600 Bourbon Street; ☎ 504-529-1720; **www.tropicalisle.com**) has a couple of locations; the one farther down (721 Bourbon Street; ☎ 504-529-4109; **www.tropicalisle.com**) has a Parrothead/country rock vibe and a large balcony. As the street has become more generic, a few marquees sound like the old Burlesque theaters, like the **Coco Club** (241 Bourbon Street; ☎ 504-587-7172), but many bars have shed the facades of local identity and catered to the crowds with names like Fat Catz and Razoo.

Just off the strip, the once-legendary den of late-night head-banging music, S&M chic, and freak antics, **Ye Olde Original Dungeon** (738 Toulouse Street; ☎ 504-523-5530; **www.originaldungeon.com**) has put on a more tourist-friendly face. The ground-floor bar has TV sports, pool tables, and easy access to the street. The Original

Dungeon downstairs retains the house-of-horrors decor and a few cheesy themed drinks like the Witch's Brew and Dragon's Blood, and occasionally resurrects its haunted spirits.

One of the busiest bars in the city is **Cats Meow** (701 Bourbon Street; ☎ 504-523-2788; **www.catsmeow-neworleans.com**), a karaoke bar in the middle of the strip where you can sing anything from classic rock to sitcom themes. Get your cell phones ready, because its Webcast allows your friends back home to enjoy your vocal stylings. The bar also has a balcony with a great vantage point.

If you like live music, Big Al Carson and his blues band are usually at the helm of the **Funky Pirate** (727 Bourbon Street; ☎ 504-523-1960; **www.tropicalisle.com**). He specializes in nursery rhymes that would make your parents blush. **Fritzel's** (733 Bourbon Street; ☎ 504-586-4800) bills itself as a European-style jazz club and sometimes features famous older musicians and singers.

One of the most popular music spots on Bourbon is the request-driven dueling-grand-piano room at **Pat O'Brien's** (718 St. Peter Street; ☎ 504-525-4823; **www.patobriens.com**). The well-known home of the Hurricane is now a sprawling complex that stretches from a carriageway on St. Peter Street to Bourbon Street. In between, there are multiple barrooms and the French Quarter's original flaming fountain. The green-tuxedoed staff hustle about, and it remains one of the historic district's institutions.

Several historic entities have weathered all sorts of change. **Chris Owens'** club is one of the strip's immovable objects. A long-reigning queen of the strip at her namesake club (500 Bourbon Street; ☎ 504-523-6400), Owens performs only so often but is entertaining when she does. Her stage show is sort of a Latin-infused Vegas-on-a-cruise-ship–style revue of popular tunes. The club is a disco when she's not performing.

The dancers at **Temptations** (327 Bourbon Street; ☎ 504-525-4470) take it off in the former residence of Judah P. Benjamin, treasurer of the Confederacy. The Greek Revival town house now features a collection of smaller individual stages over three flours and VIP rooms in the former slave quarters in back.

Bourbon's strip clubs range from plush, corporate-expense-account–friendly gentlemen's clubs to shadier joints with more-ambiguous offerings. **Rick's Cabaret** (315 Bourbon Street; ☎ 504-524-4222; **www.ricks.com**) was the first strip-club franchise ever to issue stock and be publicly traded. **Barely Legal** (423 Bourbon Street; ☎ 504-571-6340; **www.hustlerclubs.com**) is one of Larry Flynt's licensed brands and has all sorts of weekly special promotions. Among the post-Katrina glut of new strip clubs are places with names like Little Darlings, LipstiXX, Stilettos, Déjà Vu Showgirls, and many more.

If you make it all the way down the strip to **Lafitte's Blacksmith Shop** (941 Bourbon Street; no phone), the good news is that it's an

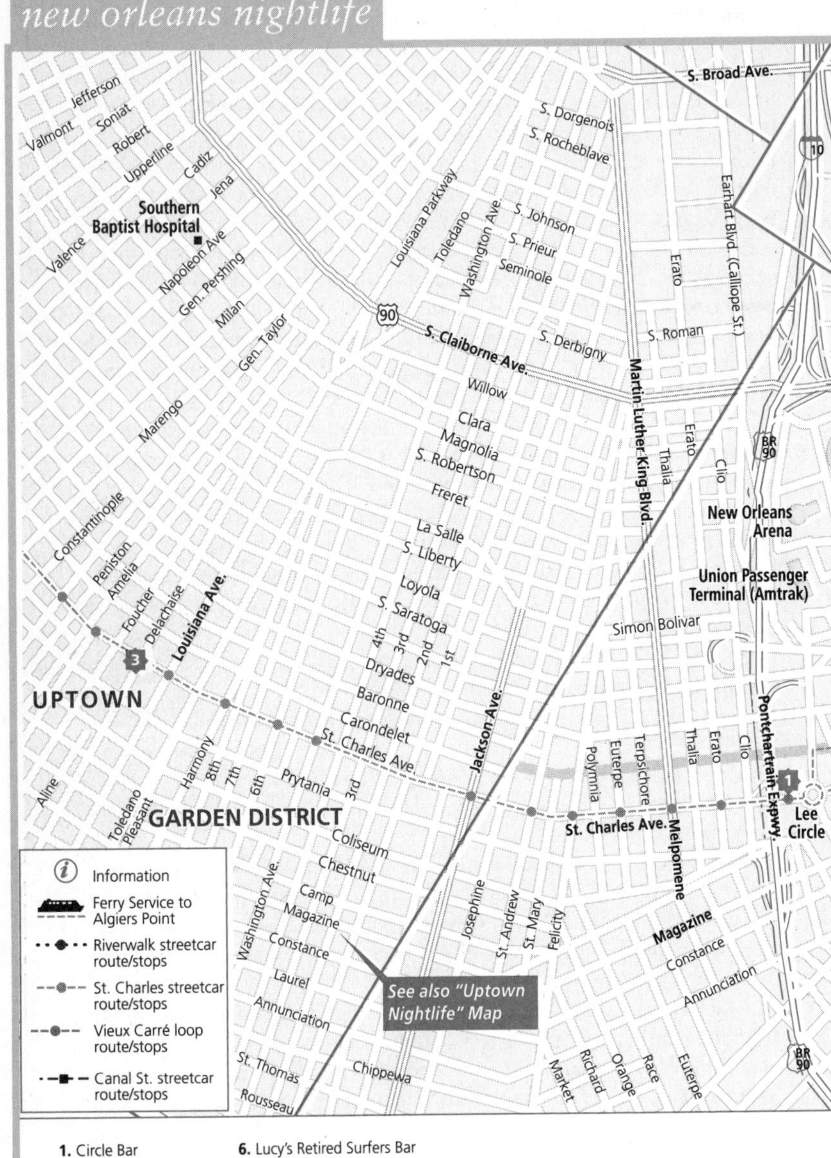
new orleans nightlife
S. Broad Ave.
Jefferson
Valmont
Soniat
Robert
Upperline
Cadiz
Jena
Southern Baptist Hospital
Valence
Napoleon Ave
Gen. Pershing
Milan
Gen. Taylor
Marengo
Constantinople
Peniston
Amelia
Foucher
Delachaise
Louisiana Ave.
UPTOWN
Louisiana Parkway
Toledano
Washington Ave.
S. Johnson
S. Prieur
Seminole
S. Dorgenois
S. Rocheblave
S. Derbigny
S. Claiborne Ave.
S. Roman
Erato
Earhart Blvd. (Calliope St.)
Martin Luther King Blvd.
Willow
Clara
Magnolia
S. Robertson
Freret
La Salle
S. Liberty
Loyola
S. Saratoga
4th
3rd
2nd
1st
Dryades
Baronne
Carondelet
St. Charles Ave.
Thalia
Clio
New Orleans Arena
Union Passenger Terminal (Amtrak)
Simon Bolivar
Jackson Ave.
Harmony
8th
7th
6th
Prytania
3rd
Aline
Toledano
Pleasant
GARDEN DISTRICT
Coliseum
Chestnut
Camp
Magazine
Constance
Laurel
Annunciation
St. Thomas
Rousseau
Chippewa
Washington Ave.
Josephine
St. Andrew
St. Mary
Felicity
Polymnia
Euterpe
Terpsichore
Melpomene
Pontchartrain Expwy.
Lee Circle
Magazine
Constance
Annunciation
Market
Richard
Orange
Race
Euterpe
See also "Uptown Nightlife" Map
Information
Ferry Service to Algiers Point
Riverwalk streetcar route/stops
St. Charles streetcar route/stops
Vieux Carré loop route/stops
Canal St. streetcar route/stops
1. Circle Bar
2. d.b.a.
3. The Delachaise
4. Howlin' Wolf
5. Loa
6. Lucy's Retired Surfers Bar
7. Mimi's in the Marigny
8. Mulate's
9. Saturn Bar
10. Whiskey Blue

0 0.25 mi
0 0.25 km
N. Broad Ave.
N. Dorgenois
N. Rocheblave
N. Tonti
N. Miro
N. Galvez
N. Johnson
N. Prieur
N. Roman
Derbigny
Tulane Ave.
MID-CITY–ESPLANADE
LaFitte Ave.
Orleans Ave.
St. Ann
Dumaine
St. Phillip
Ursulines Ave.
Bayou Rd.
St. Bernard Ave.
See "Mid-City Attractions & Nightlife" Map, page 161
N. Claiborne Ave.
ST. LOUIS CEMETERY NO. 2
N. Villere
Superdome
ST. LOUIS CEMETERY NO. 1
LOUIS ARMSTRONG PARK
See "French Quarter Nightlife" Map
La Salle St.
Duncan Plaza
Poydras St.
Canal
Basin St.
N. Rampart
Common
Gravier
Univ. Pl.
Conti
St. Louis
Toulouse
St. Ann
Dumaine
Burgundy
Barracks
Esplanade
St Claude Ave.
FAUBOURG MARIGNY
Loyola Ave.
Lafayette
S. Rampart
O'Keefe St.
Union
Perdido
Dauphine
Iberville
Bienville
FRENCH QUARTER
Bourbon
Royal
Ursulines
Gov. Nicholls
Touro
Frenchmen
Elysian Fields Ave.
Poydras
Carondelet
St. Charles Ave.
Lafayette Square
CENTRAL BUSINESS DISTRICT
Chartres
Decatur
French Market
Marigny
Mandeville
Spain
Chartres St.
Camp
Julia
Girod
Magazine St.
Tchoupitoulas
Commerce
S. Peters
Fulton
Conv. Ctr. Blvd.
WAREHOUSE DISTRICT
St. Joseph
Howard Ave.
Calliope
Mississippi River
World Trade Center
Canal St. Ferry (Toll)
RIVERWALK
Ernest N. Morial Convention Center
The Crescent City Connection (Toll)
Morgan
Delaronde
ALGIERS
Powder
Bouny
Seguin
Bermuda
Verret
Pelican
Lake Pontchartrain
CITY PARK
Area of detail
Superdome

Information
Riverwalk streetcar route/stops
Vieux Carré loop route/stops

1. The Bombay Club
2. Café Brasil
3. Carousel Lounge
4. Cats Meow
5. Donna's Bar and Grill
6. House of Blues
7. Jimmy Buffett's Margaritaville Cafe
8. Molly's at the Market
9. Napoleon House
10. One Eyed Jacks
11. Oz
12. Palm Court Jazz Cafe
13. Pat O'Brien's
14. Preservation Hall
15. Snug Harbor

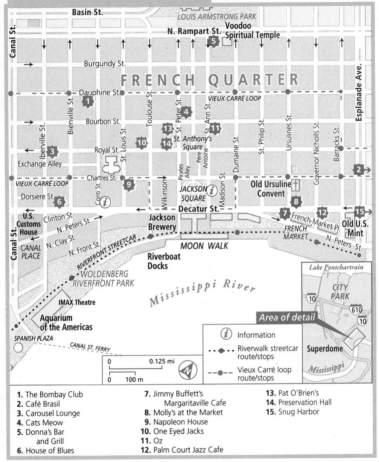

exceedingly quaint little bar occupying a sagging Creole cottage with a gas fireplace in the center and piano bar in the back. As for the rest of what tourists are told, it's not the oldest building in the French Quarter, there is no evidence that the pirate Jean Lafitte owned the property, and he certainly never kept his fortune hidden there. But it's an easy place to catch your breath and not have to shout above the clamor.

JAZZ, FUNK, *and* SOUL

MUSIC—ESPECIALLY JAZZ—IS THE REAL DEAL in the Big Easy. With the exception of **Preservation Hall** (726 St. Peter Street; ☎ 504-

uptown nightlife

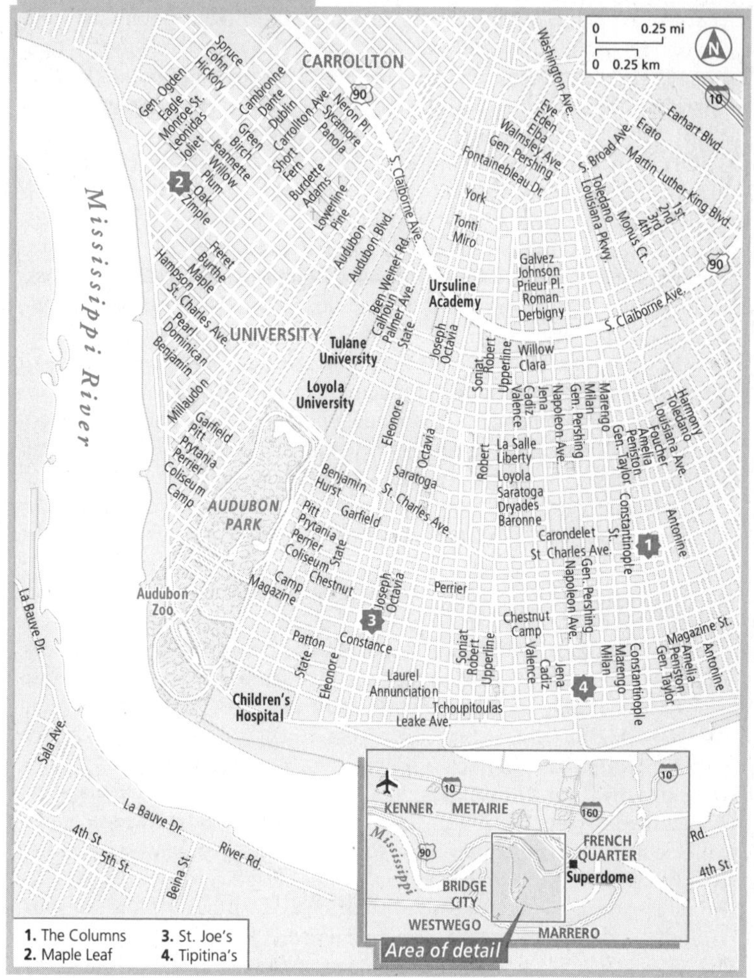

522-2841 or 888-946-JAZZ; **www.preservationhall.com**), jazz doesn't sound like it did when it was born in the downtown blocks of Perdido and North Rampart streets more than a century ago. But it's mostly played like it was then, as a hot music danced to in clubs and in the streets. There is also modern jazz, as one would hear at **Snug Harbor** (626 Frenchmen Street; ☎ 504-949-0696; **www.snugjazz.com**) in the Marigny neighborhood, but much of the rest is somewhere in between, and easier to find in bars than in concert halls. Some Bourbon Street saloons may have house bands that play Dixieland tunes, but the strip was a workplace for musicians primarily because it offered paying gigs (usually in the burlesque houses) and not because anyone wanted to hear the art form develop. At the height of the street's popularity and cleanliness in the 1960s and 1970s, both Al Hirt and Pete Fountain had clubs there. But those days are gone and Fountain's former address is now **Oz** (800 Bourbon Street; ☎ 504-593-9491; **www.ozneworleans.com**), the Quarter's biggest gay bar and dance club.

Off Bourbon Street, there are plenty of places to hear jazz and brass band music without leaving the French Quarter. For both traditional and the funky new form of brass-band music, which is infused with funk, soul, and hip-hop, head to **Donna's Bar and Grill** (800 North Rampart Street; ☎ 504-596-6914; **www.donnasbarandgrill.com**) across from Congo Square, where jazz traces its roots. **Preservation Hall** has been the city's best-known revival house for jazz, with musicians playing the ensemble style of early New Orleans jazz. But since Katrina, Preservation Hall has enjoyed a renaissance and dedicated itself to becoming a home to many genres of indigenous music. It has hosted both gospel and New Orleans–style (of the 1950s) R&B. During festival times, it has even expanded its offerings and featured modern New Orleans jazz musicians. One can also hear the traditional style at the supper club **Palm Court Jazz Cafe** (1204 Decatur Street; ☎ 504-525-0200). Proprietor Nina Buck is a British émigré who used to book European tours for New Orleans jazz musicians. Now she leads the second line in her club to the old style of strutting parade music.

For newer jazz sounds, one can head in almost any direction. Just outside the French Quarter in the Marigny, there is a range of options. Across from **Snug Harbor** is the **Spotted Cat** (623 Frenchmen Street; ☎ 504-943-3887), a rickety joint that features acoustic and gypsy jazz by groups like the New Orleans Jazz Vipers, Washboard Chaz's trio, and the Treme Brass Band. The upscale watering hole **d.b.a.** (618 Frenchmen Street; ☎ 504-942-3731; **www.drinkgoodstuff.com**) hosts an eclectic array of bands from Rob Wagner's progressive jazz trio to Linnzi Zaorski or Ingrid Lucia's Billie Holiday–esque stylings to blues by younger Burnsides like Cedric (R. L. Burnside's grandson) to indie-styled local rock. **Sweet Lorraine's** (1931 St. Claude Avenue; ☎ 504-945-9654; **www.sweetlorrainesjazzclub.com**) hosts jazz and New Orleans–style funk and R&B.

Uptown, one could head to **Dos Jefes Uptown Cigar Bar** (5535 Tchoupitoulas Street; ☎ 504-891-8500), a smoky environment that hosts a mix of small jazz setups playing Latin rhythms or the melodic old-school style of trumpeter Wendell Brunious, and sometimes piano crooners perform as well.

The Superdome (1500 Sugar Bowl Drive; ☎ 504-587-3663; **www.superdome.com**), the adjacent 18,000-seat **New Orleans Arena** (1501 Girod Street; ☎ 504-587-3663; **www.neworleansarena.com**), or "Baby Dome," and the UNO Lakefront Arena (6801 Franklin Avenue, ☎ 504-280-7222; **www.arena.uno.edu**) are the city's biggest concert venues.

The Sugar Mill (1021 Convention Center Boulevard, ☎ 504-586-0004; **www.sugarmillevents.com**) is a midsized venue open for special events like concerts, boxing, and awards galas. But most touring shows pass through larger music clubs like the **House of Blues** (225 Decatur Street; ☎ 504-310-4999; **www.hob.com**). With headphone-clad staff patrolling the club and shows starting on time, the "House of Rules" has more of a corporate approach than clubs in the rest of the city. But it consistently books a top lineup of touring acts in a huge variety of genres that stretch from classic-rock icons to new country to hip-hop to New Orleans funk. The two-story, 1,000-capacity club room has good sound and the balconies offer plenty of great views. The House of Blues complex also features a restaurant, a backyard, open-air Voodoo Garden, a smaller venue called the Parish, and a luxurious members-only penthouse club called the Foundation Room.

Also in the French Quarter, **One Eyed Jacks** (615 Toulouse Street; ☎ 504-569-8361; **www.oneeyedjacks.net**) is a good venue for touring indie-rock bands. The entrance is a tattoo-friendly hipster bar decorated in Victorian-goth splendor, with red walls and a chandelier. The club room has an obtrusively large horseshoe-shaped bar that looks like it crashed into place like a UFO. The tiered club room is cozy and also suitable for theater and fairly regular retro-burlesque shows.

New Orleans has its own variety of hippie: the jazzbo. This Big Easy denizen lives for the city's music, especially anything played under the big-tent collection of jazz, New Orleans R&B, funk, and swamp rock. That includes everything from swinging jazz standards to brass bands to steamy rock by the Radiators to thick funk by the original Meters and Neville Brothers. Jazzbos don't wait for the weekend to go out, and they always know which bars put out free red beans and rice. They're loyal to everything New Orleans and have been since the renaissance of indigenous folk culture boomed in the early 1970s, when the New Orleans Jazz & Heritage Festival was founded, the community radio station WWOZ hit the air, and a new age of brass-band music was forged by groups like the Dirty Dozen and Chosen Few (and later the Rebirth).

Around the same time, many older music legends also came out of retirement to the adoration of enthusiastic crowds of budding jazzbos. One such legend, pianist Henry Roeland Byrd, better known as Professor Longhair, became the patron saint of **Tipitina's** (501 Napoleon Avenue; ☎ 504-895-TIPS; **www.tipitinas.com**), an Uptown warehouse that was converted into a music hall in the early '70s. Just inside the door, there's a bust of Professor Longhair, and his visage hangs on a massive banner over the stage. For more than three decades, rock bands like the Radiators, the Neville Brothers, and various reconfigurations of the Meters have immortalized the club with steamy all-night marathons. The place was an incubator for jazzbos.

Two other large venues are longtime jazzbo haunts. In a short row of businesses in the Riverbend, the **Maple Leaf Bar** (8316 Oak Street;

NEW ORLEANS JAZZ CLUBS

- **Café Beignet** 311 Bourbon Street; no phone; **www.cafebeignet.com**
- **Crescent City Brewhouse** 527 Decatur Street; ☎ 504-522-0571; **www.crescentcitybrewhouse.com**
- **Donna's Bar and Grill** 800 North Rampart Street; ☎ 504-596-6914; **www.donnasbarandgrill.com**
- **Dos Jefes Cigar Bar** 5535 Tchoupitoulas Street; ☎ 504-891-8500
- **Fritzel's** 733 Bourbon Street; ☎ 504-561-0432
- **Maison Bourbon** 641 Bourbon Street; ☎ 504-522-8818
- **Palm Court Jazz Café** 1204 Decatur Street; ☎ 504-525-0200
- **Preservation Hall** 726 St. Peter Street; ☎ 504-522-2841 or 888-946-JAZZ; **www.preservationhall.com**
- **Royal Sonesta Hotel**(lobby) 300 Bourbon Street; ☎ 504-586-0300
- **Snug Harbor** 626 Frenchmen Street; ☎ 504-949-0696; **www.snugjazz.com**
- **Spotted Cat** 623 Frenchmen Street; ☎ 504-943-3887
- ***Steamboat Natchez*** Toulouse Street Wharf, ☎ 504-586-8777; **wwwsteamboatnatchez.com**
- **Sweet Lorraine's** 1931 St. Claude Avenue; ☎ 504-945-9654
- **Vaughan's Lounge** 800 Lesseps Street; ☎ 504-947-5562

☎ 504-866-9359) looks like an unremarkable double-barreled storefront from the outside. But it packs in college students and jazzbos like clowns in a Volkswagen for shows by the Rebirth on Tuesday nights, a 14-year standing gig. The eccentric James Booker used to be the patron saint of the club, and it tends to stick to booking established New Orleans acts. During crowded shows, press through the long, narrow dance hall with ornamental pressed-tin ceiling tiles, and you'll find a less-crowded back bar and a pleasant open-air patio.

Even over the crash of pins, **Mid City Lanes Rock 'N' Bowl** (4133 South Carrollton Avenue; ☎ 504-482-3133; **www.rocknbowl.com**) is a popular music spot with a large bandstand and plenty of room on the dance floor. The weekly schedule includes the city's most regular zydeco showcase on Thursday nights, with the best bands coming in from Acadiana. Zydeco is perfect for a Cajun two-step ramped up with better rhythms and a faster tempo. Rock 'N' Bowl hosts all sorts of local music, and at festival time, it puts on great showcases of roots music in jazz, brass bands, Cajun, zydeco and swamp pop.

For barroom music, the best place to head is the Marigny, where there typically is a surprising range of choices in just three short blocks. Besides the jazz-heavy offerings at **Snug Harbor** and **Spotted Cat,** a handful of clubs offer local hybrid jazz-funk-rock. **Café Brasil** (2100 Chartres Street; no phone) is wildly eclectic, with everything from Latin and world-beat sounds to local brass bands. It's also temperamental and not always open. But it helped build the scene on Frenchmen and is an epicenter of activity on Fat Tuesday. Across the street, **Blue Nile** (532 Frenchmen Street, ☎ 504-948-2583; **www.bluenilelive.com**) offers a mix of jazz, funk, and steamy New Orleans rock. Around the corner, **Checkpoint Charlie** (501 Esplanade Avenue; ☎ 504-281-4847) features gritty folk, punk, and harder-edged rock. **The Dragon's Den** (435 Esplanade Avenue; no phone) is a two-story establishment that offers unconventional vibes, from experimental alternative rock sounds and psychedelia to DJs and electronica. Across the street on the edge of the French Quarter is the **Balcony Bar** (1331 Decatur Street, no phone), which doesn't have a balcony but does host brass bands as well as jazz, funk, and rock.

Downriver from the Marigny, the Bywater has a handful of notable music stops. On the edge of the neighborhood, **Mimi's in the Marigny** (2601 Royal Street; ☎ 504-872-9868) offers a boho refuge with a barroom and pool table downstairs and a lounge upstairs that features mellower jazz and acoustic gypsy jazz, as well as funky and soulful DJ shows. There's even a kitchen that offers Spanish tapas past midnight most nights. **Saturn Bar** (3067 St. Claude Avenue, ☎ 504-949-7532) has been reborn as a hipster bar, and weekend nights frequently feature bands or DJ parties. **Hi-Ho Lounge** (2239 St. Claude Avenue, ☎ 504-945-4446, **www.thehiho.com**) presents an eclectic mix of music from experimental jazz to bluegrass to punk/metal. At the edge of the Bywater, **Vaughan's Lounge** (800 Lesseps Street; ☎ 504-947-5562) has Thursday nights locked down with a jazz jam. Kermit Ruffins started the gig more than a decade ago and if he's not playing, a brass band will fill in. The show starts late, but the bar usually sets out free red beans and rice during the set break to keep you going.

On the Uptown side of the French Quarter, the Warehouse District has a few clubs, as well. **Howlin' Wolf** (907 South Peters Street; ☎ 504-522-WOLF; **www.howlin-wolf.com**), is a large venue for local and up-and-coming rock bands. The booking vibe ranges from cooler-than-thou to eclectic, such as Brazilian samba nights. Outside murals of New Orleans musicians and street scenes make the club easy to find. **Republic New Orleans** (828 South Peters Street; ☎ 504-528-8282; **www.republicnola.com**) mixes it up with quality touring indie band bookings and throwback DJ nights.

OTHER BEATS

DOWNTOWN AND THE LOWER GARDEN DISTRICT have also seen a sudden blossoming of the types of clubs one finds in major urban scenes, the kinds of places with DJs pulsing techno, disco, and electronica through the sound system. With so many bars and great live music, few such velvet-rope clubs have lasted in New Orleans. Before Katrina, two had established themselves in the dress-to-impress vein. **Metropolitan** in **Generations Hall** (310 Andrew Higgins Avenue; ☎ 504-568-1702) is a cavernous club with two large dance areas spinning different music. One features popular dance tunes, disco, and some Latin sounds, while the other leans toward hip-hop. It's only a disco on Saturday nights and for special events, but it's been a draw, especially among suburbanites, for more than a decade. By itself in the Central Business District, **Ampersand** (1100 Tulane Avenue; ☎ 504-587-3737; **www.clubampersand.com**) exudes celebrity-chic attitude but seems to cater to emigrés from other cities who prefer sleek club environments. It opens late, and gets going very late. Its sleek decor is windowless and plush, and the bar pushes premium tastes in spirits. It's the best place to abuse your trust fund and put off sleep for another decade. The **Cricket Club** (2040 St. Charles Avenue; ☎ 504-304-9467; **www.cricketclubevents.com**) occupies a former piece of the Eiffel Tower now sitting on St. Charles Avenue on the edge of the Garden District. Primarily it functions as an event and reception hall, but it also hosts weekly hip-hop DJ nights and occasional concerts, particularly at festival times. Unique barroom music joints are spread around the city. R&B singer Ernie K-Doe and his wife, Antoinette K-Doe, opened the **Mother-in-Law Lounge** (1500 North Claiborne Avenue; ☎ 504-947-1078; **www.k-doe.com**) as both a home and a shrine to his 1961 number-one hit. It's become even more of a shrine since K-Doe passed away and he was replaced by a wax effigy, but it's still a music venue occasionally hosting local rock or R&B shows. The **Circle Bar** (1032 St. Charles Avenue; ☎ 504-588-2616) on Lee Circle looks like a hangout for Edward Gorey's Gashlycrumb characters, but the eclectic little club has plenty of its own character. Shows feature everything from DJ parties to back-from-the-crypt blues and swamp-pop legends to electronica and more. Per square foot, it has the most ambitious bookings in town, but it takes only 75 people to pack the place, which limits the kinds of bands that can play the venue—but also can lead to some as-yet-undiscovered gems on tour. Uptown, **Le Bon Temps Roule** (4801 Magazine Street; ☎ 504-895-8117) is popular with students, the waiter-and-cook side of the restaurant industry, and black-T-shirted rocker-biker sorts. The back room features brass and rock bands several nights a week, generally Wednesday through Saturday. In the Riverbend, **Carrollton Station** (8140 Willow Street; ☎ 504-865-9190) offers mellower local-rock and singer/songwriter showcases. Just beyond the city limits in Jefferson Parish, along River Road and the Mississippi River levee, lie a couple of good biker roadhouse–style spots for rock and blues. **Southport Hall** (200 Monticello Street, Jefferson; ☎ 504-835-2903; **www.newsouthport.com**) is a large music club in what was once an illegal gambling hall complete with an escape tunnel stretching under the parish line and into New Orleans. **The Rivershack Tavern** (3449 River Road, Jefferson; ☎ 504-834-4938) is a smaller barroom with plenty of draft beer and decor marked by old tin soda and beer signs nailed to the walls. It features music on weekend nights.

For music in an all-ages or alcohol-free environment, the **Neutral Ground Coffee House** (5110 Danneel Street; ☎ 504-891-3381) offers a full lineup of acoustic and folk music as well as mellow sets of other genres, including jazz and rock. The alternative art gallery **The Big Top** (1638 Clio Street; ☎ 504-569-2700; **www.3rcp.com**) is a frequent venue for music and is often kid-friendly. The **Ogden Museum of Southern Art** (925 Camp Street; ☎ 504-539-9600; **www.ogdenmuseum.org**) hosts an excellent Thursday evening music series called Ogden After Hours (6–8 p.m.) featuring everything from obscure blues and roots music legends to jazz and Afro-Caribbean percussion groups. There's also a kids' arts and crafts table well within earshot of the music.

Some clubs offer occasional all-ages shows and 18-and-up shows, including the **House of Blues** and **Dragon's Den.** Another family-friendly music option is to enjoy the Cajun bands that play at **Mulate's** (201 Julia Street; ☎ 504-522-1492) during dinner. The dance floor is open, and it's easy to pick up the steps. Dinner jazz cruises also offer entertaining packages with Creole cuisine and traditional jazz bands. The steamboat ***Natchez*** (Toulouse Street Wharf; ☎ 504-586-8777; **www.steamboatnatchez.com**) is a steam-powered paddle wheeler that churns its way downriver past the French Quarter and Algiers Point and back.

I'LL DRINK *to* THAT

IT'S NOT HARD TO FIND A BAR IN NEW ORLEANS. Including restaurant and hotel lounges, there are literally hundreds of them in the French Quarter alone. **Pat O'Brien's** is easily the best-known tourist beacon, but there are bars of all stripes to check out.

To start at the top and work your way down, choose one of the following nightspots. Big gin drinks never went out of style at **The Bombay Club** (830 Conti Street; ☎ 504-586-0972; **www.thebombayclub.com**) in the Prince Conti Hotel, and its martini menu offers esoteric options like blue cheese–stuffed olives and grapefruit martinis. The upscale and old-fashioned scene makes it the perfect place to wear a seersucker suit and mix with a more seasoned generation of locals. In spite of the English-manor decor, there's a little dance floor that gets put to use on weekend nights, when jazz trios or pianists play. Another old favorite with many New Orleanians, the **Carousel Lounge** at the distinguished Monteleone Hotel (214 Royal Street; ☎ 504-523-3341; **www.hotelmonteleone.com**), is ever-so-slightly more casual, and being closer to downtown, has more of an after-work happy-hour crowd of downtown professionals. Just like an old-fashioned merry-go-round, the central carousel features bar seats that rotate around the canopied center. A baby grand piano is also manned Wednesday through Saturday nights, and there are cozy and stationary booths. On the more stately and elegant side is the **Polo Lounge** at Windsor Court Hotel (300 Gravier Street; ☎ 504-523-6000; **www.windsorcourthotel.com**), an Anglophile luxury hotel. The spacious lounge is furnished with comfortable armchairs and sofas and offers a top-shelf list of spirits, cognacs, wines, and all the amenities.

Sleek and modern upscale lounges have proliferated in the Central Business District, particularly in boutique hotels. Lounge impresario Rande Gerber created **Whiskey Blue** (333 Poydras Street; ☎ 504-525-9444) in the mod W Hotel. A fashionably late crowd likes the lounge's dark decor, lit mostly by the midnight-blue bar backdrop. There's a steady pulse of club music, and if everything seems a little too perfectly designed, the clientele can be similarly enhanced. **Loa** (221 Camp Street; ☎ 504-553-9550; **www.ihhotel.com**) is a much brighter lounge with a voodoo vibe. Off the lobby of the International House Hotel, it's named for voodoo spirits but is set in almost-pristine white with plush couches and banquettes. The long, U-shaped copper-top bar is a popular meeting place after work and late at night. The Asian-styled **Ohm Lounge** (135 St. Charles Avenue; ☎ 504-587-1330; **www.ohm-lounge.com**) is another slick downtown lounge. The upscale **Swizzle Stick** lounge in the lobby of the Loews Hotel (300 Poydras Street; ☎ 504-595-3305; **www.cafeadelaide.com**) has staked out a cocktail connoisseur reputation (and you may hear the bartenders referred to as "bar chefs"). **Masquerade,** in the core of the Harrah's Casino (Canal Street at the Riverfront; ☎ 504-533-6000; **www.harrahs.com**), features a video tower rising like a cone from the central, frosted ice–top bar. Blackjack tables are spread out like satellites around the flashing tower, but an ultra–lounge area with wide, low couches and cabaret tables offers a more intimate setting.

A couple of somewhat-less-formal downtown bars include **Dino's** (1128 Tchoupitoulas Street; ☎ 504-558-0900) in the Warehouse District and the **Bridge Lounge** (1201 Magazine Street; ☎ 504-299-1888; **www.bridgeloungeneworleans.com**), which is canine friendly. The **Rusty Nail** (1100 Constance Street; ☎ 504-525-5515; **www.therustynail.org**) is a locals' bar for the Warehouse District's condo dwellers.

Back in the French Quarter, the **Napoleon House** (500 Chartres Street; ☎ 504-524-9752; **www.napoleonhouse.com**) has a distinguished yet very casual air. Once the home of an early mayor of the city, it was to have been offered to Napoleon as a residence if he could escape imprisonment at St. Helena. The emperor never arrived, and the place has been a charming bar and restaurant for most of the last century. In nice weather, double-shutter doors are opened, and tables offer great views of the surrounding blocks of the Quarter. A central open-air slate courtyard is also a cool place to enjoy one of the bar's specialties, a Pimm's Cup: a mix of Pimm's (an English gin-based liqueur) and 7UP garnished with a cucumber.

Many locals prefer some of the Quarter's ultracasual corner bars. The **Chart Room** (300 Chartres Street; ☎ 504-522-1708) offers rock-bottom prices, vaguely nautical themes, and captains' chairs on the open-air face of the bar. **Harry's Corner Bar** (900 Chartres Street; ☎ 504-524-1107) is also a low-frills locals' hangout off the more-traveled blocks. A couple of Irish-style pubs also draw locals with draft Guinness and other amenities. The **Kerry Irish Pub** (331 Decatur Street; ☎ 504-527-5954; **www.kerryirishpub.com**) sits on a heavily traveled thoroughfare, but is a locals' nook offering live folk and Irish music many nights of the week. A couple of blocks away, **Ryan's Irish Pub** (241 Decatur Street; ☎ 504-523-3500) isn't so consciously Irish, but it has big comfortable booths, a busy pool table, and wide-screen TVs for sports. At the far corner of the Quarter, where it is mostly residential, Cosimo's (1201 Burgundy Street; ☎ 504-522-9715) is an unassuming refuge for locals.

Molly's at the Market (1107 Decatur Street; ☎ 504-525-5169; **www.mollysatthemarket.net**) draws a wide and boozy mix of tattooed kids, disgruntled intelligentsia types, news reporters not pretty enough for television, and "y'atty" New Orleanians, meaning the natives who speak in what sounds like a Brooklyn accent (as in "Where y'at?") and know everything they need to know about fellow locals by the neighborhood they grew up in and the high school they attended. Molly's is a super-late-night hangout that almost never closes, in the sense that it reopened roughly 36 hours after Katrina.

The rest of upper Decatur Street features **Jimmy Buffett's Margaritaville Cafe** (1104 Decatur Street; ☎ 504-592-2565; **www.margaritavilleneworleans.com**) and a string of hole-in-the-wall joints, which range from shabby-chic to just plain shabby. Jimmy Buffett actually does own Margaritaville and even has roots in the city, where he got his start playing on Bourbon Street. But the club has more of a blues vibe in the Tavern, which never charges a cover for live music. The rest of the two-floor tropical getaway has little nests, including an upstairs bar with tire swings for seats, to cluster around some blender drinks with fellow Parrotheads. The gritty string of bars between there and Esplanade Avenue includes the **Abbey** (1123 Decatur Street; ☎ 504-523-7177) and **Tiki's** (1207 Decatur Street; ☎ 504-680-8454), where even the men's restroom is legendary. **Pravda** (1113 Decatur Street; ☎ 504-525-1818) brings some style to the block with its communist-kitsch decor. It offers a good selection of high-quality absinthes, which are legal again in the United States.

The French Quarter's gay nightlife is highly concentrated in the blocks between Bourbon and Dauphine streets, from St. Ann to St. Philip. The balconied, two-story **Oz** is the biggest dance club and the busiest in terms of weekly entertainment and promotions. Drop by for bingo after work on Friday or late in the afternoon on Sunday for a little razzing from some of the campy hosts. Across the street, **Bourbon**

Pub and Parade (801 Bourbon Street; ☎ 504-529-2107; **www.bourbonpub.com**) has a downstairs lounge with soul divas on the video screen, plus a dance floor upstairs. **Café Lafitte in Exile** (901 Bourbon Street; ☎ 504-522-8397; **www.woodenterprises.com**), **Good Friends** (740 Dauphine Street; ☎ 504-566-7191; **www.goodfriendsbar.com**), and **Rawhide** (740 Burgundy Street; ☎ 504-525-8106; **www.rawhide2010.com**), home of the "Bring Your Own Meat" barbecue night, are also busy bars. **Tubby's Golden Lantern** (1239 Royal Street; ☎ 504-529-2860) is not in the cluster but is one of the more senior gay establishments. Recently, **Napoleon's Itch** (734 Bourbon Street; ☎ 504-371-5450) in the Bourbon Orleans hotel has taken on a lesbian-friendly ambience. A few blocks away in the Marigny, there is a more solidly local gay scene at places like the **Friendly Bar** (2301 Chartres Street; ☎ 504-943-8929) and **Cowpokes** (2240 St. Claude Avenue; ☎ 504-947-0505; **www.cowpokesno.biz**). In warm weather, there's nothing terribly exclusive about **The Country Club** (634 Louisa Street; ☎ 504-945-0742), an old Creole mansion with a huge pool and several bars that is gay owned, run, and populated.

Farther downriver from the French Quarter, the Bywater neighborhood is home to a couple of oddities. **Bud Rip's** (900 Piety Street; ☎ 504-945-5762) has been a bar almost since the Civil War, and some of the regulars seem to have been there as long. With its strange mix of wild neon fixtures and sci-fi art of the 1970s, the **Saturn Bar** (3067 St. Claude Avenue; ☎ 504-949-7532) is a cool hangout in a tough neighborhood. It was used as a set in *The Pelican Brief,* and snapshots on the wall prove that Nicolas Cage and John Goodman hung out there at least a couple of times (well before that movie was shot).

As you head toward the lake from the French Quarter, Mid-City has several popular watering holes. **Liuzza's by the Track** (1518 North Lopez Street; ☎ 504-218-7888) mixes a killer Bloody Mary and is particularly popular during Jazz Fest. **Pal's Lounge** (949 North Rendon Street; ☎ 504-488-7257) is a hangout for people who like to bring their dogs out drinking with them. The drinks are cheap, and air hockey and vintage pinball machines clinch the retro crowd's loyalty. **Finn McCool's** (3701 Banks Street; ☎ 504-486-9080; **www.finnmccools.com**) is the best place to hang out with ex-pats and watch international soccer matches, which sometimes means drinking early in the morning to catch European competition.

Remarkable bars Uptown range from the grand to the grubby. While locals like the spacious, if a little musty, lounge area inside, the veranda of **The Columns** (3811 St. Charles Avenue; ☎ 504-899-9308; **www.thecolumns.com**) is perfect in nice weather. **Monkey Hill** (6100 Magazine Street; ☎ 504-899-4800) is a comfortable spot for finer spirits Uptown. It's full of plush couches, a free pool table, and a who's-who Uptown clientele. **St. Joe's** (5535 Magazine Street; ☎ 504-899-3744) has a peculiarly religious decor, a relaxed ambience, and a mix of college students and yuppie hangers-on. Other popular neighborhood bars Uptown include **Parasol's** (2533 Constance Street;

☎ 504-897-5413; **www.parasols.com**) in the Irish Channel, **Kingpin** (1307 Lyons Street; ☎ 504-891-2373; **www.kingpinbar.com**), the **Mayfair Lounge** (1505 Amelia Street; ☎ 504-895-9163), and **45 Tchoup** (4529 Tchoupitoulas Street; ☎ 504-891-9066), a good place to drink before or after catching a show at Tipitina's, which is a block down.

Uptown collegiate favorites include **Cooter Brown's** (509 South Carrollton Avenue; ☎ 504-866-9104; **www.cooterbrowns.com**), which features hundreds of bottled beers, an oyster bar, and plasma screens everywhere. Tulane students gather and watch their hometown pro teams at Cooter's, while grad students gather and watch undergraduates. Many LSU grads favor the **Bulldog** (3236 Magazine Street; ☎ 504-891-1516; **www.draftfreak.com**), which also has hundreds of beers on tap and in bottles. **Fat Harry's** (4330 St. Charles Avenue; ☎ 504-895-9582) is rowdy and young, and it has a grill that's open late. Folks who want to keep living the collegiate lifestyle flock to the **F&M Patio Bar** (4841 Tchoupitoulas Street; ☎ 504-895-6784) late at night. The front room's leopard-print pool table is covered nightly because people inevitably dance on it.

Uptown also has some of the city's most hardcore dive bars. The windowless **Saint** (961 St. Mary Street; ☎ 504-523-0050) has a doom-rocker vibe and a photo booth in case you need help remembering where you ended up last night or who you were with. If your idea of going home early is when the sun rises, then head to **Snake and Jake's Christmas Club Lounge** (7612 Oak Street; ☎ 504-861-2802), a dark and dank cavern where cheap suds flow freely.

In a city that is so devoted to finely crafted cuisine, two underrepresented venues include wine bars and brewpubs. Locals have an affinity for Abita beers, brewed on the north shore of Lake Pontchartrain, but there are also a couple of downtown brewpubs. **Crescent City Brewhouse** (527 Decatur Street; ☎ 504-522-0571; **www.crescentcitybrewhouse.com**) always features several German-style offerings and a seasonal option. The American brewpub chain **Gordon Biersch** (200 Poydras Street; ☎ 504-552-2739) moved into the Central Business District near the casino and convention center. And **Zea Rotisserie & Grill** (1525 St. Charles Avenue; ☎ 504-520-8100), a local dressy-casual dining concept, serves beers crafted for it by a Northshore microbrewer.

Wine bars have become more popular in recent years. One of the top wine lists is at the bar at **Emeril's** (800 Tchoupitoulas Street; ☎ 504-528-9393; **www.emerils.com**), which is a good place to launch an evening downtown. Across the street, **Tommy's Wine Bar** (752 Tchoupitoulas Street; ☎ 504-525-4790) is elegant and clubby. Down the street, **W.I.N.O.** (610 Tchoupitoulas Street; ☎ 504-324-8000; **www.winoschool.com**) is a wine-taster's delight. Automated dispensers activated by debit cards allow guests to sample a wide array and many expensive wines in one-, three-, and six-ounce pours. Uptown, **The Delachaise** (3442 St. Charles Avenue; ☎ 504-895-0858) is popular late at night with the yuppie crowd and restaurant-industry people. In the heart of the French Quarter, **Grapevine** (720 Orleans Avenue; ☎ 504-523-1930) offers a deep wine list and a gourmet menu as well.

FINE ARTS

THE PERFORMING ARTS ARE BY NO MEANS AN ALSO-RAN in New Orleans. In fact, the opera *Sylvain* was performed there in 1796. The early colony even had problems concerning preferences for waltzes versus French quadrilles at public dances. The governor had to intercede. But things have calmed down, and New Orleans currently has an opera association, a dance association, the nation's largest musician-run symphony orchestra, and an active theater community.

Unfortunately, Katrina severely damaged the city's three main large-scale theaters. The city-owned **Mahalia Jackson Theatre for the Performing Arts** is the only one to return. The privately run **Saenger Theatre** and **Orpheum** remain shuttered due to severe flooding of basement electrical systems. In the meantime, fine-arts organizations have patched together other venues for full seasons of performances. The **Louisiana Philharmonic Orchestra** (LPO; ☎ 504-523-6530; **www.lpomusic.com**) performs at the following venues: First Baptist in Kenner, Pontchartrain Center, Mahalia Jackson Theatre, Roussel Center at Loyola, and Dixon Hall at Tulane. The LPO's season runs from September through May with classics, casual-dress nights, pops concerts, and occasional free outdoor concerts.

The **New Orleans Ballet Association** (NOBA; ☎ 504-522-0996; **www.nobadance.com**) hosts major ballet companies from across the nation and abroad. In recent years, it has scheduled Chicago's Joffrey Ballet, the Alvin Ailey Dance American Theater, the Virsky Ukrainian National Dance Company, and modern-dance companies such as Momix. The **New Orleans Opera Association** (NOOA; ☎ 504-529-2278 or 800-881-4459; **www.neworleansopera.org**) has shoot-for-the-star showcases with Placido Domingo at the Mahalia Jackson Theatre.

For theater, New Orleans is home to many production companies and a handful of theaters. The city's three mainstays had been musicals, campy gay comedies, and Southern-fried dramas, which could be delightful and wicked on the Tennessee Williams end and perhaps a bit more stuffy at the *Steel Magnolias* end. But in recent years, a younger generation of actors and artistic directors has livened up all offerings. **Southern Rep** (The Shops at Canal Place, third floor, 333 Canal Street; ☎ 504-522-6545; **www.southernrep.com**) has revitalized its mission, staging a mix of works by local playwrights and fresh-off off-Broadway pieces. On Jackson Square, **Le Petit Théâtre du Vieux Carré** (616 St. Peter Street; ☎ 504-522-2081; **www.lepetittheatre.com**) is one of the oldest community theaters in the country. It tends to focus on popular musical productions. **Le Chat Noir** (715 St. Charles Avenue; ☎ 504-581-5812;

www.cabaretlechatnoir.com) is one of the city's more popular theater venues, offering smaller-scale productions in its modern performance space. Seating is cabaret-style, and there is drink service during performances. On nights when Le Chat is open for productions, the theater crowd often gathers in the front bar later in the evening. On the other side of the French Quarter, the **Marigny Theatre** (1030 Marigny Street; ☎ 504-218-8559; **www.marignytheatre.org**) hosts a mix of musicals, from nostalgia pieces to Broadway to farces and gay-themed plays. Uptown, the **Anthony Bean Community Theater and Acting School** (1333 South Carrollton Avenue; ☎ 504-862-PLAY; **www.anthonybeantheater.com**) has added high-quality productions, generally with African-American themes. Several independent production companies stage quality smaller-scale shows in alternative venues in an off-off-Broadway kind of way. Check local listings for groups like the NOLA Project (**www.nolaproject.com**), Cripple Creek Theatre Company (**www.seeaplay.org**), and Running with Scissors (**www.norunningwithscissors.com**).

unofficial **TIP**
During Mardi Gras and Jazz Fest, cover charges rise or appear where they weren't before. In some cases, it's because clubs book showcases with multiple big names and have to charge accordingly. Many clubs will accept credit cards inside but expect cash at the door. Also during Carnival, French Quarter bars can get tight about making you buy something before you can use their restrooms. But given that hundreds of people are arrested each year during Mardi Gras for urinating in public, it's money well spent if you've just gotta go.

Anchoring the more avant-garde end of local performances, the **Contemporary Arts Center** (900 Camp Street; ☎ 504-528-3800; **www.cacno.org**) sometimes has theater performers as artists in residence but is always a good venue to check for fine-arts events, from dance to jazz-masters concerts. **Tulane** (**www.tulane.edu**) and **Loyola** (**www.loyno.edu**) universities host many student productions. The **Shakespeare Festival at Tulane** (☎ 504-865-5105; **www.neworleansshakespeare.com**) is a professional summer-stage operation that usually performs at Tulane's Dixon Hall.

As much as New Orleanians like to laugh, the city's comedy scene always seems to be on the cusp of establishing itself. While the city has no dedicated comedy clubs, a few venues host regular stand-up and some improv. **La Nuit Theater** (5039 Freret Street; ☎ 504-899-0336; **www.lanuittheater.com**) holds regular stand-up and improv as well as theatrical comedies. **Harrah's New Orleans Casino** (Canal Street at the Riverfront; ☎ 504-533-6000; **www.harrahs.com**) sometimes hosts touring national comedians.

EXPECT *the* UNEXPECTED

THE FRENCH QUARTER AND DOWNTOWN are generally walkable, but it's best to take a cab when traveling to unknown destinations.

While the Quarter is laid out on a simple grid, all other streets bend with the river, and it is easy to lose your way. Trying to stumble to your hotel tipsy can be asking for trouble. Play it safe when wandering outside of the historic district, and don't hesitate to cross the street or reverse course to avoid anyone you'd rather not talk to. Petty scams are common but usually no more harmful than someone telling you that he or she "knows where you got your shoes." The obvious answer is that you've "got your shoes" on your feet, or on Bourbon Street, or some such variation. Banter if you like, but you'll probably end up shelling out a few bucks. New Orleans is a very friendly place, but never, ever get in a car with someone you just met on Bourbon Street who suddenly wants to take you "to more of a local's place" or to a party. If curiosity is killing you, get the name and address and take a cab. Do not depend on the kindness of strangers.

All that said, you're ready to hit the streets and let the good times roll.

NIGHTCLUB PROFILES

Bombay Club

GIN-PERFUMED LAIR OF THE SOUTHERN BON VIVANT

830 Conti Street; ☎ 504-586-0972 or 800-699-7711; www.thebombayclub.com French Quarter

Cover Only during major festivals and events. **Minimum** None. **Mixed drinks** \$7–\$8, martinis \$10–\$15. **Wine** \$8–up. **Beer** \$4–up. **Dress** Proper dress required. Fancy in a traditional Southern way preferred. **Specials** Add \$1 to drink prices during live music. **Food available** Gourmet menu available till 10 p.m. or midnight on weekends. **Disabled access** Yes. **Hours** Open daily at 4 p.m. for cocktails; dinner begins at 5 p.m.

WHO GOES THERE In a word, money—this is one of old New Orleans's preferred downtown watering holes.

WHAT GOES ON A bit of boisterous hobnobbing, a little politicking and society gossiping, and even a little dancing on weekends. It's a better-dressed, more well-heeled, and older crowd than the one carousing on Bourbon Street a block away, but their livers are well seasoned, and these folks aren't going home early.

SETTING AND ATMOSPHERE The English-manor decor is a tad stuffy, but the ambience is inviting and country club–ish in its sense of camaraderie. There are draped booths for privacy and tables set about.

IF YOU GO Wear a seersucker suit, sling back martinis, disregard the occasional nip and tuck, settle in, relax, and play the chameleon. Everyone's friendly, even when given to elliptical storytelling patterns full of names regulars would be expected to remember. But take it at a casual pace: old New Orleans is in no hurry, so merge carefully and adjust to the speed of local traffic.

Café Brasil

URBAN AMERICA MEETS THE LATIN SIDE OF THE CARIBBEAN

2100 Chartres Street; no phone Faubourg Marigny

Cover Free–$15. **Minimum** None. **Mixed drinks** $4. **Wine** $4. **Beer** $3. **Dress** Whatever. You're most likely already overdressed. Strip down to sandals, sarongs, linen, tie-dyes, Cuban shirts, and porkpie hats. **Specials** None. **Food available** No. **Disabled access** Yes. **Hours** Brazilian time. Management opens at its own discretion—generally nighttime only—but it's a hub on some weekend afternoons for special events like costume bazaars, community group fairs, the occasional grassroots town hall, and sometimes a spoken-word event.

WHO GOES THERE It all depends on the show. Mostly the urban and hippie world-beat crowds hang out at Brasil. An international flavor is usually part of the scene, and at Mardi Gras, you'll probably hear some Samba beats. Brasil is one of the anchors that made this little stretch of the Marigny a funky locals' spot.

WHAT GOES ON Brasil likes to march to its own drummer, but it often takes on a funky boho feel because the music spills out onto the nearby sidewalk, which is often set with tables and chairs. Brasil is always a good destination at Mardi Gras, festival times, and holidays like Halloween. If an ad hoc tribal-drumming circle is going to break out somewhere in the city, this is where it's likely to be. Its back bar is occupied by a separate business, Yuki Izakaya (525 Frenchmen Street; no phone), a Japanese-style bar offering sake, shochu, a full bar, and Japanese cuisine in snack sizes while Japanese films are projected on the walls.

SETTING AND ATMOSPHERE The vibrant blues, greens, and yellows of Brasil beckon an artsy crowd. Large picture windows make the interior a bright oasis, enhanced by hanging neon art, large modern sculptures placed around the stage, and hanging tapestries. The crowd is generally an open-minded one that likes international airs, urban beats, and cultural exchange.

IF YOU GO Go for a casual good time and dancing, but it is what it is on any given night. If it's not your vibe one night, it might be the next, but there are plenty of good bars and clubs within two blocks if you want to wander in and out.

Carousel Lounge

BOISTEROUS OLD NEW ORLEANS MINGLES WITH LUXURY-HOTEL GUESTS

214 Royal Street; ☎ 504-523-3341; www.hotelmonteleone.com French Quarter

Cover None. **Minimum** None. **Mixed drinks** $5.50–up. **Wine** $6–$9. **Beer** $4–up. **Dress** From "just got off work" to "just got off the plane" to "just about to go to one of the jacket-required old Creole restaurants." **Food available** Free hors d'oeuvres during Monday–Friday happy hours (5–7 p.m.). **Disabled access** Yes. **Hours** Opens 11 a.m. daily.

New Orleans Nightspots by Location

NAME	DESCRIPTION	COVER
FRENCH QUARTER		
Bombay Club	Gin-perfumed lair of the Southern bon vivant	None
Carousel Lounge	Boisterous old New Orleans mingles with hotel guests	None
Cats Meow	Spring break on a karaoke stage	Varies
Donna's Bar and Grill	Brass-band junction	\$5–\$10
House of Blues	Music hub for any decent local or national act	Tickets \$10–\$50
Jimmy Buffett's Margaritaville Cafe	Parrothead beacon with live music	None
Molly's	Got tattoos?	None
Napoleon House	Gracefully aging spot for drinks and conversation	None
One Eyed Jacks	Hipster rock club with '80s flair	\$5–\$20
Oz	The Quarter's largest gay dance club	Varies
Palm Court Jazz Cafe	Supper club with traditional New Orleans jazz	None
Pat O'Brien's	Tourist drinking Mecca	None
Preservation Hall	No-frills music hall for old-time New Orleans jazz	\$10
CENTRAL BUSINESS DISTRICT AND WAREHOUSE DISTRICT		
Circle Bar	Boho hipsters with eclectic musical tastes	Varies for music
Howlin' Wolf	Must be in or have a friend in a band	\$5–\$15
Loa	Sophisticates sip fine cocktails	None

WHO GOES THERE The Carousel is literally and consciously a few steps above the fray. With a picture window overlooking Royal Street, it's classier than the bustle on the street below and just around the corner heading toward Bourbon Street.

WHAT GOES ON It's a well-heeled refuge for the more weathered of New Orleanians who work downtown and congregate after work. The later it gets, the more convivial it is in a gather-round-the-piano kind of way. The baby grand gets a workout most nights, and a chanteuse usually cinches the bar's flair for melodrama.

SETTING AND ATMOSPHERE The center of the bar is, of course, the carnival-esque antique-looking carousel with a rotating bar top and stools. The genteel Southern milieu is more *Cat on a Hot Tin Roof* than *Gone with the Wind,* and the crowd isn't as innocent as it looks. In its heyday, this

NAME	DESCRIPTION	COVER
CBD AND WAREHOUSE DISTRICT (CONTINUED)		
Lucy's Retired Surfers Bar	Surf shack for guys who bought midlife-crisis Harleys	None
Mulate's	Cajun music and dining	None
Whiskey Blue	Martini bar for the image conscious	None
UPTOWN AND THE GARDEN DISTRICT		
The Columns	Ongoing Southern wedding	None
The Delachaise	Wine bar for hip Uptowners and foodies	None
Maple Leaf	Locals' spot for steamy, funky jazz-rock	\$5–\$12
St. Joe's	Uptown spot for cool students and hangers-on	None
Tipitina's	Legendary New Orleans music club	Varies
FAUBOURG MARIGNY		
Café Brasil	Urban America meets the Caribbean	Free–\$15
d.b.a.	Yuppies and hipsters with discriminating booze palates	\$5–\$20
Mimi's in the Marigny	Gritty hipster scene	None
Saturn Bar	Cool for its indifference to change	Varies
Snug Harbor	New Orleans's contemporary-jazz club	Varies
MID-CITY–ESPLANADE		
Mid-City Lanes Rock 'N' Bowl	Local institution for bowling and good-time local bands	\$5–\$10

was a play spot for literary lushes, where distinguished New Orleanians could mingle with the likes of Tennessee Williams or Truman Capote, who were both tickled by the grandeur and not shy about tossing back the cocktails.

IF YOU GO Hop on the carousel and know when it's time to get off. Get to know the regulars, because everyone's got a good story. The guests at the hotel probably come back for the bar alone.

Cats Meow

SPRING BREAK ON A KARAOKE STAGE

701 Bourbon Street; ☎ 504-523-2788; www.catsmeow-neworleans.com
French Quarter

Cover Generally none but sometimes charged for those under 21. **Minimum** None. **Mixed drinks** $5.25–up. **Wine** $5. **Beer** $5.50. **Dress** It's Bourbon Street. Shirt and shoes will do. **Specials** Happy-hour specials till 8 p.m. **Food available** No. **Disabled access** Yes. **Hours** Opens 4 p.m. Monday–Friday, 2 p.m. weekends.

WHO GOES THERE College kids, tourists, *American Idol* contenders and pretenders, life-of-the-party sorts. It's consistently one of Bourbon Street's most crowded bars. During Mardi Gras, its balcony is one of the most desirable perches, but it can be hard to get upstairs.

WHAT GOES ON Booze-fueled karaoke. And it's broadcast on their Web site, so consider it a virtual postcard and ring home on the cell before you take the stage.

SETTING AND ATMOSPHERE The crowd gets revved up whether the singer on stage is crooning, strutting, rocking, or flat-out dying. When it's packed, the bar can be a bit steamy and you can expect a little jostling. Order drinks early and often, because its one of the strip's busiest bars. The karaoke sign-up list can be lengthy as well.

IF YOU GO Down as many drinks as necessary before signing up to belt out AC/DC's "You Shook Me All Night Long" or Madonna's "Like a Virgin" or Neil Diamond's "Heartlight," and then go for it. Or get your friends loaded and sign them up. It's totally cheesy to pick up a stranger by singing directly to that person, but you won't be the first to try. Just pick a song you can handle. A little enthusiasm goes a long way.

Circle Bar

BOHO HIPSTERS SHOWING OFF ECLECTIC MUSICAL TASTES

1032 St. Charles Avenue; ☎ 504-588-2616 **Warehouse District**

Cover Varies depending on musical entertainment: tip jar–$10. **Minimum** None. **Mixed drinks** $3–up. **Wine** $4. **Beer** $2–up. **Dress** Jeans, thrift-store cowboy boots, service-station shirts embroidered with someone else's name, go-go dresses and boots, T-shirts for obscure bands. **Specials** $2 beer and well drinks during happy hour (daily, 4 p.m.–8 p.m.). **Food available** No. **Disabled access** No. **Hours** Opens 4 p.m. daily.

WHO GOES THERE Haven for roots-rock revivalists and connoisseurs of indie rock and Black Sabbath. The early crowd can be rough around the edges and probably didn't need any more drinks when they arrived.

WHAT GOES ON The Circle Bar is for music lovers who have no use for MTV, *Billboard,* or *Rolling Stone.* They revere old regional R&B one-hit wonders and iconoclastic types alike, and sometimes they just like to get their freak on to off-the-wall electronica and organ or accordion music.

SETTING AND ATMOSPHERE Bathed in a red glow, the bar is almost too small to let extra light in, let alone a band's equipment. When the music is playing, it's the friendliest place in the world. But on some nights, it's like a saloon full of cranks and loners, and it's best to let sleeping dogs lie.

IF YOU GO Go late for music or to hang out. The early hours can be slow. Don't try to impress the natives; that will just smell like desperation. The jukebox is full of great old songs, but don't sing along to prove you know them. Don't mention that you were in a band—if your band mattered, they would already know who you are.

The Columns

REGULAR PRACTICE FOR HOW TO MINGLE AT A LARGE SOUTHERN WEDDING

3811 St. Charles Avenue; ☎ 504-899-9308; www.thecolumns.com
Uptown and the Garden District

Cover None. **Minimum** None. **Mixed drinks** \$5–up. **Wine** \$5–up. **Beer** \$3.50–up. **Dress** Sunday-brunchy, business casual, not-too-high heels, khakis and button-downs. **Specials** Half-price beer, well drinks, and house wine during daily happy hour (5–7 p.m.). **Food available** The restaurant serves breakfast, has a bistro dinner menu (5–10 p.m.), and offers Sunday brunch (11 a.m.–3 p.m.). **Disabled access** Yes. **Hours** Opens 3 p.m. weekdays, noon Saturday, 11 a.m. Sunday.

WHO GOES THERE Patrician Southern women with androgynous names like Taylor and Jordan, new partners at the firm, private-school grads, Uptown singles, tourists.

WHAT GOES ON Consider it a socially selective happy-hour spot on the edge of the Garden District. While the scene is fun and freewheeling, everyone is at least a little bit in the know socially.

SETTING AND ATMOSPHERE This mini–Victorian palace was used as a set for the filming of *Pretty Baby,* starring Brooke Shields and Susan Sarandon. The stately elegance of the facade carries throughout most of the building, but the dimly lit barroom and adjoining parlors have a vaguely musty ye-olde-college-pub feel. Across the main hall, the parlors sparkle with chandeliers, ceiling medallions, and beautiful blond floors.

IF YOU GO Grab a table on the veranda and enjoy the view of oak-lined St. Charles Avenue. Or find the niche that suits your mood; it's large and varied enough to suit many purposes, from an engagement announcement to a frat reunion to a breathy tryst.

d.b.a.

YUPPIES AND HIPSTERS WITH DISCRIMINATING BOOZE PALATES

618 Frenchmen Street; ☎ 504-942-3731; www.drinkgoodstuff.com
Faubourg Marigny

Cover With music, \$5–\$20. **Minimum** 1 drink per person per set whenever there is no cover. **Mixed drinks** \$4–up. **Wine** \$5–up. **Beer** \$3–up. **Dress** Casual chic, but don't overdo it—err on the casual side. **Specials** Drinks \$1 off before 7 p.m. daily. **Food available** No. **Disabled access** Yes. **Hours** Opens 5 p.m. Monday–Thursday, 4 p.m. Friday–Sunday.

WHO GOES THERE The work-hard-and-party-hard crowd, young professionals, people who like upscale spirits in hip environments, New Yorkers in for the weekend, college kids with money.

WHAT GOES ON The bar can have a neighborhood vibe in the afternoon and gain a clublike buzz on busy nights. It's a smart scene in any case, and you can get away with expounding on architecture or literary theory without sticking out. A couple of symmetrical storefronts were joined to form the bar; one side hosts music, while the other is more conducive to conversation.

SETTING AND ATMOSPHERE This is a place for people with all-around decent taste—meaning drinks, music, and fashion. There are deep premium selections in all categories, from beer to vodka to Scotch to boutique Caribbean rums. The music is modulated just right, and the range is reasonably eclectic. The stained-wood walls and spare decor are nonetheless stylish. While not overdoing the TV-screen presence, there is a video monitor with a cam on the bar's sister of the same name in New York City.

IF YOU GO Try some of the more exotic American microbrews or Belgian-style beers. It's an easy environment to settle into, so just enjoy it. The music is generally rather competent, from local rock to jazz fusion to occasional ringers like blues legend David "Honeyboy" Edwards. Sometimes the bar's popularity is its downfall, and Saturday nights can get overrun with weekend warriors. But it's a got a good scene on Sunday and Monday nights as well as super-late on weekends.

The Delachaise

WINE BAR FOR HIP UPTOWNERS AND RESTAURANT OWNERS/CHEFS

3442 St. Charles Avenue; ☎ 504-895-0858; www.thedelachaise.com

Uptown and the Garden District

Cover None. **Minimum** None. **Mixed drinks** $5–up. **Wine** $5–up. **Beer** $5–up. **Dress** Casual to fine. **Specials** None. **Food available** Gourmet menu of hot and cold small plates. **Disabled access** Yes. **Hours** Opens 5 p.m. Monday–Saturday, 6 p.m. Sunday.

WHO GOES THERE A smart crowd of Uptowners, professionals, and foodies likes The Delachaise for its ever-so-slightly urbane ambience and its conversation-friendly volume.

WHAT GOES ON The Delachaise opened as a wine bar, and its wine list draws foodie types. No New Orleans bar survives without full service, and this one also has an impressive selection of premium spirits and a wildly eclectic short list of beers from around the world. Fine-dining waiters from across town like to gather here when their kitchens close.

SETTING AND ATMOSPHERE The wedge-shaped railroad car of a building housing the bar used to turn over annually with unsuccessful restaurants before The Delachaise opened and put this odd space on the map. Now it's a solid hot-spot with a hint of French-cafe intimacy and style. There's plenty of seating along the long bar and banquettes, which extend to the fishbowl-like picture windows looking out onto St. Charles Avenue.

IF YOU GO It's a great place for intimate conversation, but bring your own partner. It's also a good spot to grab a small or late-night bite from their bistro-style menu of small plates. Try one of the indulgences, such as French fries cooked in duck fat or one of the cheese plates.

Donna's Bar and Grill

FRENCH QUARTER BRASS-BAND JUNCTION

800 North Rampart Street; ☎ 504-596-6914; www.donnasbarandgrill.com French Quarter

Cover $5–$10. **Minimum** None. **Mixed drinks** $4–$7. **Wine** $4–$6. **Beer** $3–up. **Dress** The same stuff you wore to Jazz Fest. **Specials** Free red beans during certain shows. **Food available**. The back of Donna's harbors a kitchen that turns out its own barbecue. **Disabled access** Yes. **Hours** Generally opens at 6:30 p.m.

WHO GOES THERE Jazzbos, die-hard jazz and brass-band fans, tourists looking for the everyday live jazz of New Orleans.

WHAT GOES ON The music is the draw, and there is precious little in the way of amenities. When it packs in a ten-piece brass band, the dance floor is whatever space is left between the horns and the bar. But the sound is straight-up, freewheeling New Orleans street music that comes from the jazz-funeral and social-aid-and-pleasure-club-parade traditions. Both traditional and newer, younger, funkier brass bands play Donna's. Jazzbos appreciate that this is the only club that primarily features this kind of music. Jazz jams are solid, and sometimes-stellar local talents sit in for a few sets.

SETTING AND ATMOSPHERE Even after ten years, Donna's appears to have never completely removed the remnants of whatever business occupied the building before. That seems to have been some sort of greasy-spoon restaurant, and the kitchen is put to good use with the proprietor's home-cooked barbecue. The bar is low on frills, and there isn't too much seating.

IF YOU GO Before you pay the cover, take a gander across the street at the entrance to Armstrong Park and Congo Square, where New Orleans jazz traces its roots. Donna's works on brass-band time, so don't worry about going late, and don't be shy about asking the doorman how late the band will be playing. Keep in mind that this is a homegrown environment that can't be reproduced elsewhere, no matter what bands go on tour.

House of Blues

MUSIC HUB FOR ANY DECENT LOCAL OR NATIONAL ACT

225 Decatur Street; ☎ 504-310-4999; www.hob.com French Quarter

Cover Tickets $10–$50. **Minimum** None. **Mixed drinks** $3.75–up. **Wine** $4.50–up. **Beer** $2.50–up. **Dress** T-shirt casual to club wear. **Food available** Restaurant offers upscale versions of Southern cooking, New Orleans dishes, and some barbecue. **Disabled access** Yes. **Hours** Restaurant/bar opens for lunch Monday–Saturday (11:30 a.m.–3 p.m.) and Tuesday–Saturday at 4 p.m.; club opens 1 hour before showtime.

WHO GOES THERE Sooner or later everyone goes to the House of Blues for a big show. The club hosts all genres of music and leverages great acts for a venue of its size. There's also a smaller music room, a bar, a restaurant, a backyard Voodoo Garden, and an exclusive and exquisite private penthouse club called the Foundation Room.

WHAT GOES ON The House of Blues is in, but not particularly of, New Orleans. The good news is that it has adopted a highly professional approach to running a music club in a city accustomed to sweaty dance halls with shows starting late and running to all hours. So on the upside, this club books many top acts that for years other clubs didn't have the muscle, finesse, or cash to book. On the other hand, the ambience here could exist anywhere—that is, in the House of Blues Cambridge or Myrtle Beach—as opposed to capturing New Orleans's let-it-all-hang-out spirit.

SETTING AND ATMOSPHERE All the authenticity of a corporate-branded juke joint manned by bouncers wearing headphones make this a Disneyfied version of a local club. That said, even if you're skeptical of the approach, they did a good job, so feast your eyes on the pseudo-homey decor, including the large and authentic collection of Southern folk art spread throughout the club.

IF YOU GO They don't call it the "House of Rules" for nothing: be on time for the show, and be forewarned that they'll remove you if you become a nuisance to anyone else's good time. Bring a credit card.

Howlin' Wolf

MOST PEOPLE THERE ARE IN OR HAVE A FRIEND IN A BAND

907 South Peters Street; ☎ 504-522-wolf; www.howlin-wolf.com
Central Business District

Cover $5–$15. **Minimum** None. **Mixed drinks** $4–up. **Wine** $4. **Beer** $2.50–up. **Dress** Rock T-shirts, jeans with holes, shades. **Food available** No. **Disabled access** Yes. **Hours** Opens 1 hour before showtime.

WHO GOES THERE Rockers with attitudes, easier-going indie-rock lovers, groupies, and up-and-coming-band wannabes.

WHAT GOES ON Howlin' Wolf is open to touring independent-rock bands, local rock and jazz-rock acts, and the occasional jazz show or Brazilian-music night. The club is run with some rock idealism, possessed of the notion that the message in the music can change the world. Maybe even for the better. The owners sincerely love and believe in music and do their best to support local musicians.

SETTING AND ATMOSPHERE Following Katrina, the Howlin' Wolf moved to a bigger, better location, complete with outdoor murals of New Orleans street scenes and jazz musicians. The club's interiors are nicer than its previous not-totally-converted warehouse space.

IF YOU GO The local showcases can be a mixed bag, so go knowing that this can be an incubator for great things to come.

Jimmy Buffett's Margaritaville Cafe

PARROTHEAD BEACON WITH LIVE MUSIC

1104 Decatur Street; ☎ 504-592-2565;
www.margaritavilleneworleans.com French Quarter

Cover None.**Minimum** None.**Mixed drinks** $4.50–up.**Wine** $6.50.**Beer** $3.50–up.**Dress** Hawaiian shirts, tie-dyes, sundresses, shades, deck shoes.**Specials** Half-price margaritas, mojitos, and other select cocktails in the upstairs crow's nest during Monday–Friday happy hour (5 p.m.–7 p.m.).**Food available** Gulf Coast cuisine stretching from Texas to the Keys to the Caribbean.**Disabled access** Yes. **Hours** Daily 11 a.m.–9:30 p.m. for food; bar till 10 p.m.

WHO GOES THERE Parrotheads on a pilgrimage. It shouldn't come as a surprise that Margaritaville is popular with Jimmy Buffett's Southern fan base.

WHAT GOES ON This is much more of a bar and hangout than a music club, but the Tavern has live music most nights from 7 to 10 p.m. Most of the main room is set for dining, though occasionally it is cleared for a larger concert. Upstairs are a few little nests where you can gather and choose from the menu of frozen margaritas and tropical rum and coconut drinks. The second-floor balcony is a large and breezy space for drinking and watching French Quarter traffic go by.

SETTING AND ATMOSPHERE The place is something of a shrine to Buffett and his "it's happy hour somewhere" worldview. While the decor is sort of over the top, it's unique, not the product of a chain restaurant. Tabletops are individually covered with replica paintings of his album covers. Faux palm trees and a seaplane jut out of the walls. An upstairs bar features tire swings for seats. And blended drinks have little compasses in them. It's all supercasual and inviting, even if you can't sing all of Jimmy's hits. Locals don't admit they go here, but what happens at Margaritaville stays at Margaritaville.

IF YOU GO You can't go wrong. Get a top-shelf margarita, turn off your cell phone, and hang out at one of the little faux cabanas. This is a bright and fun respite from picking through the neighboring French Market or wandering the Quarter.

Loa

SOPHISTICATES, PROFESSIONALS, AND METROSEXUALS SIP FINE COCKTAILS

221 Camp Street; ☎ 504-553-9550; www.ihhotel.com
Central Business District

Cover None.**Minimum** None.**Mixed drinks** $7–up.**Wine** $8–up.**Beer** $3–$9. **Dress** Trendy but stylish to finer dress.**Specials** Monthly specials on cocktail menu; drink discounts during happy hour from 5 to 8 p.m.**Food available** Tapas from hotel restaurant, Rambla.**Disabled access** Yes.**Hours** Opens 4 p.m. daily.

WHO GOES THERE This is the more urbane side of New Orleans. Professionals, developers, and business-oriented and fashion-conscious locals mingle here, sometimes hatching deals amid the gentle din of chatter and Champagne corks popping.

WHAT GOES ON This is one of downtown's trendier venues and fills with lawyers from neighboring offices after work. By late evening, a sharply dressed singles scene sets in.

SETTING AND ATMOSPHERE Candlelight flickers over white walls, plush couches, and low banquettes, setting a low-key and sophisticated vibe.

The ambience is conducive to conversation and the tastes are refined, perhaps suited to the ethereal dimensions traveled by the voodoo spirits the lounge is named for.

IF YOU GO Dress up and enjoy the specials on the house-cocktail list. Keep an eye out for the occasional celebrity staying at the hotel.

Lucy's Retired Surfers Bar

SURF SHACK FOR GUYS WHO BOUGHT MIDLIFE-CRISIS HARLEYS

701 Tchoupitoulas Street; ☎ 504-523-8995; www.lucysretiredsurfers.com **Central Business District**

Cover None for the bar; special events upstairs sometimes have a cover, generally $5–up. **Minimum** None. **Mixed drinks** $5–up. **Wine** $5. **Beer** $3–$4. **Dress** Hawaiian shirts, sundresses, jeans, T-shirts. **Specials** Weekday happy hour (4 p.m.–7 p.m.) offers $3 margaritas. **Food available** Burgers, salads, and California-Mexican fare. Kitchen closes at 10 p.m. weeknights and 11 p.m. on Friday and Saturday. Brunch on Saturday and Sunday, 10 a.m.–3 p.m. **Disabled access** Yes. **Hours** 11 a.m.–late.

WHO GOES THERE The lunchtime crowd comes from neighboring law offices and downtown businesses. The after-work scene is for people who like the surf-shack casual atmosphere and classic rock. Friday-night happy hours spill out onto the sidewalk with people who remember college as the best years of their lives and middle-age guys who just bought their first boutique motorcycle.

WHAT GOES ON A loud and slightly rowdy party crowd downs margaritas and Coronas. There's the occasional but not entirely spontaneous bout of dancing on the bar. High tide is right after work and generally ebbs by 10 p.m. Lucy's has a full menu and plenty of seating for dining; food is also served at the bar.

SETTING AND ATMOSPHERE "Surf-shack casual" is the only way to describe the bright, flowery colors, blond wood, and restrained use of bamboo throughout. Pictures of famous surfers cover the walls, though the TVs are typically dominated by SEC sports.

IF YOU GO Order a fruity, beach-friendly cocktail with a little plastic mermaid floating on top, and live it up. It's easy good times with classic tunes and sports on a couple of TVs. An upstairs party room is open for comedy Wednesday nights and occasionally for live music.

Maple Leaf

LOCALS' SPOT FOR STEAMY, FUNKY JAZZ-ROCK

8316 Oak Street; ☎ 504-866-9359 **Uptown and the Garden District**

Cover Varies $5–$12. **Minimum** None. **Mixed drinks** $4. **Wine** Half bottles available starting at $12. **Beer** $3–up. **Dress** University T-shirts and sweatshirts, Hawaiian shirts, Birkenstocks. **Specials** Cheaper drinks before 9 p.m. **Food available** No. **Disabled access** Yes. **Hours** Opens 3 p.m. daily.

WHO GOES THERE College kids and neighborhood folks from the Riverbend and surrounding Uptown neighborhoods; jazzbos and New Orleans–

music lovers. It's a popular neighborhood bar before the music gets started.

WHAT GOES ON An aging James Booker used to tickle the ivories at the Maple Leaf, and early zydeco innovator Rockin' Dopsie used to hold down regular weekend gigs. Both legends are gone now but are irrevocably linked to the club's stature in the local music scene. The Rebirth Brass Band has been carrying on a 14-year residency on Tuesday nights that starts at 11 p.m. and heats up the dance floor for three long, steamy sets. It's a New Orleans institution. The rest of the week features other big local names like Papa Grows Funk, guitarist Walter "Wolfman" Washington, and bluesman John Mooney or funky pianist Jon Cleary when they are in town.

SETTING AND ATMOSPHERE It's an even mix of college kids there to dance and local jazzbos who love the music. The Maple Leaf isn't fancy, but it has the charm of old pressed-tin ceiling tiles and a wooden floor worn from a couple billion miles worth of dancing. At the end of the dance hall, a back room features a second bar, pool table, and access to a breezy brick patio.

IF YOU GO Go late and don't plan to leave early. The Rebirth plays harder after the first set break. Forget your schedule. Just give yourself to the music and burn the midnight oil.

Mid City Lanes Rock 'N' Bowl

LOCAL INSTITUTION FOR BOWLING AND GOOD-TIME LOCAL BANDS

4133 South Carrollton Avenue; ☎ 504-482-3133; www.rocknbowl.com
Mid-City–Esplanade

Cover $5–$10. **Minimum** None. **Mixed drinks** $4.25–$5.75. **Wine** $5.75. **Beer** $1.75–$3.75. **Dress** Jeans, Jazz Fest wear. **Specials** None. **Food available** Bar food (cheese fries, wings). **Disabled access** No. **Hours** Opens 5 p.m. Tuesday–Saturday.

WHO GOES THERE Cajun and zydeco dancing fans, rockers (if you mean 1950s- and 1960s-era rock fans), bowlers, soccer moms and dads.

WHAT GOES ON Bowling and live music coexist here in a one-of-a-kind local institution. The bowling lanes are active even during shows, but music is the club's big draw. Owner John Blancher is a huge local music fan and has made his club a home to New Orleans's best zydeco dance night, a good club for local rock bands, and a great Jazz Fest nighttime venue, when he books showcases with everyone from Cajun country slide-guitar wiz Sonny Landreth to the Rebirth Brass Band.

SETTING AND ATMOSPHERE Located in a strip mall, this isn't where most people would go looking for live music. But climb the stairs to the second-floor club and enter another world. The staff wears retro '50s bowling shirts and skirts and (if you could see their feet behind the bar) probably saddle shoes and bobby socks. Dress as if you were going to a bowling lane and enjoy the genuine and friendly ambience.

IF YOU GO Go early and get some bowling in before the show starts. Then trade in your bowling shoes, because the club books very danceable acts, whether they play Cajun, zydeco, swing, rock, or brass-band music.

Mimi's in the Marigny

GRITTY HIPSTER SCENE

2601 Royal Street; ☎ 504-872-9868 **Faubourg Marigny**

Cover None. **Minimum** None. **Mixed drinks** $4.50–up. **Wine** $5–$7.50. **Beer** $2.50–$6. **Dress** Punk rock to hipster chic. **Specials** None. **Food available** Spanish tapas available from the upstairs kitchen from 6 p.m. until past midnight every night. **Disabled access** No. **Hours** Downstairs opens at 4 p.m., Upstairs at 5 p.m. daily.

WHO GOES THERE Mimi's has an upstairs–downstairs divide. Downstairs is for tattoos, art punks, neighborhood regulars, and pool players. Upstairs is more of a boho lounge scene for people who do yoga by day and swill wine by night.

WHAT GOES ON Downstairs is a low-key spot to hang out, with cheap draft-beer options. Though it's not popular with all of the neighbors, Upstairs features live music, whether it's acoustic gypsy jazz or weekend funk and soul DJ shows.

SETTING AND ATMOSPHERE Downstairs is a casual spot to hop on a barstool at the bar or the ledge lining the windows. Some old New Orleans charm comes from the exposed brick, high ceilings, and tall windows looking out on some quaint blocks of the Marigny neighborhood. Upstairs looks like a 1970s lounge, with old couches and not-so-chic dropped-ceiling tiles. A kitchen serving Spanish and Latin American tapas is part of the point, so it's an easy place to order small dishes, drink inexpensive wine, and talk with friends. There's music several nights a week.

IF YOU GO Even though the city was once a Spanish colony, you don't find many Spanish restaurants here. The kitchen at Mimi's comes to it by way of Latin America, meaning dishes like ceviche are on the menu. It's a nice addition to the dining scene and a comfortable spot to eat light in a fun environment. Go upstairs late for the tapas and live jazz.

Molly's at the Market

GOT TATTOOS?

1107 Decatur Street; ☎ 504-525-5169; www.mollysatthemarket.net
French Quarter

Cover None. **Minimum** None. **Mixed drinks** $4–$8. **Wine** $4.50–up. **Beer** $2.50–$4.50. **Dress** Anything goes. **Specials** Frozen Irish-coffee drinks. **Food available** A separate restaurant in back serves food 2 p.m.–midnight to Molly's customers. **Disabled access** Yes. **Hours** Daily 10 a.m.–6 a.m.

WHO GOES THERE Molly's draws a wide mix of punk rockers, French Quarter cooks, y'atty New Orleanians, print-media types who gather on Thursday nights, and aging hippies.

WHAT GOES ON Molly's is an easy, boozy place to hang out at all hours. The faded clutter of memorabilia that covers the walls—from old signs to newspaper clippings—attest to how long the bar's owners and regulars have been in the thick of French Quarter life. Despite its Decatur Street location, it draws a very loyal local following.

SETTING AND ATMOSPHERE Molly's has a bright pub atmosphere with plenty of high cocktail tables running along the wall. Head for the front window to watch French Quarter traffic go by. Molly's draws all sorts, but often it's the most severely tattooed and pierced folks, including the bar staff, that one notices first. This is the most civil of bars, though, so the bark is far worse than the bite.

IF YOU GO Listen for loose talk about what's really going on locally, from disgruntled intelligentsia offering up conspiracy theories to longtime Quarter residents explaining who knows who and owns what. It's a cheap and friendly place to drink, and genuinely local in all its stripes.

Mulate's

CAJUN MUSIC AND DINING

201 Julia Street; ☎ 504-522-1492 Central Business District

Cover None. **Minimum** None. **Mixed drinks** $6–up. **Wine** $6–$8. **Beer** $3.25–$3.75. **Dress** Convention badges, jeans, and T-shirts. **Specials** None. **Food available** Cajun cuisine from adapted family recipes. **Disabled access** Yes. **Hours** Open 11 a.m.–10 p.m. daily, until 11 p.m. weekends.

WHO GOES THERE Mulate's is a tourists' and conventioneers' spot.

WHAT GOES ON Serving Cajun cuisine is the point of the location near the convention center, downtown hotels, and cruise-ship launch. But the eatery is one of the few venues to feature Cajun bands nightly.

SETTING AND ATMOSPHERE This converted warehouse space has been adapted to look like a rustic Cajun restaurant. Bright tablecloths and blond wood conjure Cajun prairie life. Proprietor Kerry Boutté opened the original Mulate's in Breaux Bridge, but serving Cajun food in Cajun country was unremarkable, so he started bringing in bands. Eventually, with the growing national popularity of Cajun culture, he got the idea that the concept would really stand out where there are not many other Cajuns around.

IF YOU GO Go for the bona fide Cajun bands that drive in from Acadiana. It's a good, family-friendly night of casual dining and upbeat music. But it's also fine for couples who want unpretentious fun.

Napoleon House

GRACEFULLY AGING SPOT FOR DRINKS AND CONVERSATION

500 Chartres Street; ☎ 504-524-9752; www.napoleonhouse.com
French Quarter

Cover None. **Minimum** None. **Mixed drinks** $4. **Wine** $5. **Beer** $2.50. **Dress** Casual, academic, whatever suits the weather. **Specials** Pimm's Cups. **Food available** Daytime bistro offers simple Creole dishes and po' boys. **Disabled access** Yes. **Hours** Cafe is open 11:30 a.m.–5:30 Monday–Saturday; only cocktails served on Fridays and Saturdays from 6 p.m. to midnight.

WHO GOES THERE Given its location and charm, this is a tourist magnet. But plenty of locals are loyal to the spot's casual elegance, with busts of Napoleon set about and classical music on the sound system.

WHAT GOES ON For locals and tourists alike, Napoleon House is a casual spot to get lost daydreaming or chattering while the world passes by. Its credible little kitchen offers Creole fare and muffulettas.

SETTING AND ATMOSPHERE The building was the residence of Mayor Nicholas Girod, who agreed to offer it to Napoleon if the deposed emperor could escape St. Helena and come to New Orleans, but that never came to pass. The house retains its old charm, especially when the double shutters are opened in nice weather and tables sit under the arches right up to the sidewalk. Old photos and paintings of the bar and owners cover the walls, and the building is intriguing throughout, from the slate courtyard to the elegant upstairs rooms. The Impastato family has run Napoleon House for much of the last century and has maintained its understated charm. Grab a quiet table and devise the great American novel, or just listen to French Quarter buggies clop by full of tourists.

IF YOU GO Drop by in the afternoon and get a table on the outer wall under the arches. Try a Pimm's Cup, a strangely British accent to a Francophile establishment.

One Eyed Jacks

HIPSTER ROCK CLUB WITH '80S FLAIR

615 Toulouse Street ☎ 504-569-8361; www.oneeyedjacks.net
French Quarter

Cover \$5–\$20. **Minimum** None. **Mixed drinks** \$4–up. **Wine** \$5–up. **Beer** \$2.50–up. **Dress** Retro-punk, vintage clothes, rock T-shirts. **Specials** None. **Food available** No. **Disabled access** Yes. **Hours** Lobby bar is open nightly; club room opens for shows only.

WHO GOES THERE The more-credentialed crowd of punk rockers, heavily tattooed folks, and an occasional Hollywood Brat Packer.

WHAT GOES ON The club features touring indie bands, weekly '80s dance nights, and a mishmash of retro-burlesque shows, comedy, and theater. Because the club is owned by Rio Hackford, son of director Taylor Hackford and stepson of actress Helen Mirren, there are occasional celebrity interlopers, particularly if a film crew is in town. But don't mistake that possibility for exclusivity; mostly, this is a hangout for the severe crowd suffering the artist's life.

SETTING AND ATMOSPHERE The chandeliers, red velvet, and black vinyl make the lobby a Victorian-goth hybrid that is both lush and sinister, and a lair for the flamboyantly inked, pierced, and hair dyed. The club room looks a bit more glittery and sports a large horseshoe-shaped bar right in the middle. It's actually a relic from another now-closed venue, so go around it and get a place up front for any show.

IF YOU GO The regulars are friendly, if not particularly talkative. The celebs, however, can be moody, so approach them at your own risk. The venue is great for music shows and other performances, but get there early to get a seat.

Oz

THE QUARTER'S LARGEST GAY DANCE CLUB

800 Bourbon Street; ☎ 504-593-9491; www.ozneworleans.com
French Quarter

Cover $5 Friday and Saturday nights. **Minimum** None. **Mixed drinks** $4.50–up. **Wine** $4.25–up. **Beer** $4–up. **Dress** Speedos, cowboy boots, club wear, as sexy as you want to be. **Specials** Happy hour (4–8 p.m.) 2-for-1 specials on well drinks and domestic beers. **Food available** No. **Disabled access** Yes. **Hours** Open 24 hours every day except Monday and Tuesday.

WHO GOES THERE Out, loud, and proud, Oz is friendly to boy toys, drag queens, bears, leather freaks, and people who just want to dance.

WHAT GOES ON Primarily, Oz is a huge dance club with two floors and a massive disco ball. Well into the night, this is one of the Quarter's busiest dance clubs, playing more techno, disco, trance, and bubblegum music than you'll find elsewhere in the Quarter. The club also keeps a regular slate of promos like talent contests, boys dancing on the bar, and bingo games, in which your reward for playing is an onslaught of campy abuse from the host. Catch the drag show on Sundays at no charge.

SETTING AND ATMOSPHERE The core of the building is an open dance space, but upstairs are a lounge area and entrances to a very large wraparound balcony. The crowd tends to comprise younger guys and those who want to date them. The dance floor is open to anyone, but women shouldn't expect too much attention from the guys dancing on the bar.

IF YOU GO When the dance floor is crowded, Oz can get pretty steamy, so dress for a tropical climate. The reigning fashion sense here is that less is more. Bingo is a hoot, and all in good fun. Games typically run on Fridays after work and Sunday afternoons.

Palm Court Jazz Café

SUPPER CLUB WITH TRADITIONAL NEW ORLEANS JAZZ

1204 Decatur Street; ☎ 504-525-0200 **French Quarter**

Cover None; table seating is for dining. **Minimum** None. **Mixed drinks** $4.50. **Wine** $5. **Beer** $3. **Dress** Casual–fancy. **Specials** None. **Food available** Traditional Creole cuisine. **Disabled access** Yes. **Hours** Open 7 p.m. Wednesday–Sunday.

WHO GOES THERE Tourists and European jazz fans.

WHAT GOES ON Featuring some of the most seasoned performers in town, the Palm Court is dedicated to traditional New Orleans jazz. It's also a supper club dedicated to traditional New Orleans cuisine, but not all of it fancy. The music starts at 8 p.m., and guests should expect a second-line jazz parade led by proprietor Nina Buck at some point in the evening.

SETTING AND ATMOSPHERE New Orleans jazz legends such as Danny Barker and Pud Brown played the Palm Court. Barker even authored "The Palm Court Strut" in honor of it. The pictures on the wall document many of the other legends who played the club. With the old tiled floor and picture windows, the atmosphere is a perfect setting for the era the music recalls. Seating is for dining only, but there are always a few barstools where you can come in and catch some of the show.

IF YOU GO Make a night of it and definitely join the second line. The old jazz was meant to dance to, so at least give it a little strut. If you're by yourself, relax at the bar.

Pat O'Brien's

TOURIST DRINKING MECCA

718 St. Peter Street; ☎ 504-525-4823; www.patobriens.com
French Quarter

Cover None. **Minimum** None. **Mixed drinks** $3.50–$6.50. **Wine** $3.75–$5.25. **Beer** $3.50–$5.50. **Dress** Jeans and T-shirts to dressed up. **Specials** Hurricanes, Hurricanes, Hurricanes! **Food available** A Creole restaurant is part of the complex. **Disabled access** Yes. **Hours** Opens noon Monday–Thursday, 10 a.m. Friday–Sunday.

WHO GOES THERE While Pat O's is at the eye of the storm for French Quarter nightlife and lore, it's not only for tourists. Plenty of locals act as tour guides and lead people to the dueling-grand-piano request room, but mostly it's tourists.

WHAT GOES ON No matter who goes, it's the same scene: green-tuxedoed waiters carting around trays of tall, maraschino cherry–red Hurricanes (actually a concoction of rum and passion-fruit juice), though Pat O's has all sorts of specialty drinks and corresponding glassware. When it's busy, there are entrances on both St. Peter and Bourbon streets. In between are several bars and barrooms, and at the center of it all is a slate courtyard with wrought-iron tables and chairs and a flaming fountain. The large courtyard's vine-covered walls and French Quarter–style lampposts supply a pretty setting for any social gathering.

SETTING AND ATMOSPHERE Pat O's was once a Prohibition-era speakeasy and just marked its 75th anniversary, but at a different location a block down. But what solidified its fame was the creation of the Hurricane during World War II, when some spirits were rationed. It was hard to get whiskey and Scotch, and bars had to buy cases of rum as part of the deal. Pat O's made the most of it by creating the Hurricane, which has become New Orleans's most famous drink. Pat O's became the most popular bar on the strip for locals. That's not surprising, given how much rum goes into a Hurricane. It's easy to lose track of an evening after just two, and maybe that accounts for all the loud and lusty chatter.

IF YOU GO Start out with a Hurricane in the piano room and see if you can stump the ladies on the keys. But don't hassle them. They'll play your request when it's your turn, of which they'll inform you like a librarian hushing a class of students. They know just about everything, including your alma mater's fight song. Head out to the courtyard for a round before you go and remember to take the souvenir glass home with you.

Preservation Hall

NO-FRILLS MUSIC HALL FOR OLD-TIME NEW ORLEANS JAZZ

726 St. Peter Street; ☎ 504-522-2841 or 888-946-jazz; www.preservationhall.com French Quarter

Cover $10. **Minimum** None (no bar). **Dress** Wear comfortable clothes because you may be sitting on the floor. **Specials** None. **Food available** No. **Disabled access** No. **Hours** Doors open 8 p.m.

WHO GOES THERE Tourists and European jazz hounds on pilgrimage.

WHAT GOES ON Preservation Hall is the city's premier shrine to the early style of ensemble jazz played in New Orleans. The band may ham up "When the Saints Go Marching In," but also expect a good tour through early classics like "Tiger Rag." You may even see a banjo player or more of a clarinet presence than contemporary jazz features. For whatever reason, little attention has been paid to audience comfort. The music is acoustic, and the audience mostly stands or sits on the floor. Once you pay admission, you can stay as long as you like, but many people cycle in and out through the evening's many sets.

SETTING AND ATMOSPHERE Preservation Hall was created out of an art gallery in the early 1960s, and some of the old art still hangs on the wall. The gallery owner brought in then-senior musicians some nights of the week, both to draw in tourists and because he loved the old music. Ultimately, Allen and Sandra Jaffe took on the mission of preserving the old style of jazz there as Preservation Hall. Many musicians who play at the Hall come from musical families whose members were early jazzmen. But for many young jazz musicians in the city, even if they won't spend most of their careers playing traditional New Orleans jazz, playing here is a rite of passage and a rickety conservatory to master the old tunes.

IF YOU GO Sit up front and enjoy the show. There are fewer of the old legends around—people like Sweet Emma Barrett or Narvin Kimball or the Humphrey Brothers—but the distinguished band leaders are fun, if a little curmudgeonly at times. Since Katrina, Preservation Hall has also opened its doors to some of the city's R&B legends and even hosts the occasional jazz band/gospel hymns set.

Saturn Bar

COOL FOR ITS INDIFFERENCE TO CHANGE

3067 St. Claude Avenue; ☎ 504-949-7532 Faubourg Marigny

Cover Sometimes; ranges $5–$10. **Minimum** None. **Mixed drinks** $4–$6. **Wine** $3. **Beer** $2–$3.50. **Dress** Jeans and T-shirts, work clothes, thrift-store finds. **Specials** None. **Food available** Bags of chips. **Disabled access** Yes. **Hours** Days and hours vary depending on the live music offered.

WHO GOES THERE Neighborhood folks and hipsters.

WHAT GOES ON Saturn Bar endures as a hipster favorite in spite of nearly a decade in which the pool table was covered by air-conditioners under repair as part of the former owner's other job. Unfortunately, O'Neal Broyard passed away, but his family reopened this odd relic of a bar. It's once again a dusty hangout for regulars and devoted hipsters.

SETTING AND ATMOSPHERE The Saturn Bar was dedicated when the surrounding Bywater community was full of engineers who worked on NASA rocket programs, the vestiges of which are now the Michoud plant, which is involved in the space shuttle program. The bar is famous for its wild neon lights, its bizarre and kitschy 1970s sci-fi art, and its leopard-print booths. Pictures on the walls document celebrities such as John Goodman and Nicolas Cage hanging out in the bar, back when the jukebox played Frank Sinatra's "Witchcraft" no matter what buttons you pushed. The long-neglected pool table is open again.

IF YOU GO Go with low expectations and enjoy the cheap drinks. You won't see celebrities, and unless there's live music, you won't see many people period, but you'll get an idea of why the place's charm comes from time passing it by.

Snug Harbor Jazz Bistro

NEW ORLEANS'S CONTEMPORARY-JAZZ CLUB

626 Frenchmen Street; ☎ 504-949-0696; www.snugjazz.com
Faubourg Marigny

Cover Varies; generally $15–$30. **Minimum** 1 drink per set in bar. **Mixed drinks** $4.50–up. **Wine** $5–up. **Beer** $2.75–up. **Dress** Casual to elegant. **Specials** None. **Food available** Not in the club room, but Snug has a full-fledged bistro with steaks, pasta, and Creole dishes. **Disabled access** Yes. **Hours** Restaurant opens 5 p.m.; shows at 8 p.m. and 10 p.m. most nights.

WHO GOES THERE Modern-jazz fans, students from the University of New Orleans's jazz-studies program.

WHAT GOES ON Snug Harbor is New Orleans's premier club for contemporary and modern jazz. Neither of those veins are particularly common in the city, but its top talents and elder statesmen like Ellis Marsalis play here regularly. Touring modern-jazz players also come through Snug, and you'll hear some New Orleans R&B.

SETTING AND ATMOSPHERE Snug has a bit of a nautical theme, though it's very casual, considering what clubs with similar bookings look like in places like New York. And it's quite a bargain in comparison. The club room isn't particularly pretty or comfortable, but you will sit close to the stage either in the cabaret seating in front or on the shallow second floor's balcony-like perches. On busy nights, the music is typically piped into the rest of the club, so sometimes just interloping at the bar can come with pretty good acoustics.

IF YOU GO Jazz is as much an art form as entertainment here. An evening with Ellis Marsalis can even be a short course in the history of jazz. The schedule includes plenty of names only jazz aficionados will recognize, but the lineup is solid, and many of the local talents who have gone on to bigger jazz markets in New York and elsewhere play here when they come home.

St. Joe's

UPTOWN SPOT FOR COOL STUDENTS AND HANGERS-ON

5535 Magazine Street; ☎ 504-899-3744 **Uptown and the Garden District**

Cover None. **Minimum** None. **Mixed drinks** $3.50–up. **Wine** $5. **Beer** $3–up. **Dress** Khakis, jeans, and T-shirts. Loosened ties and work attire. **Specials** Blueberry mojitos. **Food available** No. **Disabled access** No. **Hours** Opens 5 p.m.

WHO GOES THERE When the doorman is reading Beckett and Sartre, it's a pretty good bet you're at a college hangout. But this is no college dive. And the bar is popular with 20- and 30-something Uptowners. People who have to get up and work in the morning often drop by for a last round here.

WHAT GOES ON St. Joe's is a neighborhood bar with a little extra style. It's an easy place to drink and talk or cluster around a game of pool. The back patio is pleasant and shaded by banana palms.

SETTING AND ATMOSPHERE St. Joe's is decorated with a religious theme dominated by crosses. Beyond that, the only devotion is to pouring drinks. The back patio looks like some sort of southeast Asian temple, but with booze.

IF YOU GO Try a blueberry mojito and settle in. The back patio is great in cool weather.

Tipitina's

LEGENDARY NEW ORLEANS MUSIC CLUB

501 Napoleon Avenue; ☎ 504-895-tips; www.tipitinas.com
Uptown and the Garden District

Cover Varies. **Minimum** None. **Mixed drinks** $4–$7. **Wine** $4. **Beer** $3. **Dress** Jeans, T-shirts, casual. **Specials** $2 Abita draft and $3 well drinks one or two times a month on "homegrown night." **Food available** No. **Disabled access** Yes. **Hours** Doors open an hour before showtime; Sunday fais-do-do dance party goes from 5:30 p.m.–9:30 p.m.

WHO GOES THERE Everyone: music lovers, jazzbos, college kids; Cajun dancers for Sunday-evening fais-do-do parties.

WHAT GOES ON New Orleans's best-known bands play "Tip's," from the Radiators to the Dirty Dozen and Rebirth to Galactic to various Neville family bands. The club also features jams led by top musicians, including original Meter George Porter Jr. and drummer Johnny Vidacovich. Indie-rock touring bands are also booked, but Tip's has ceded most of the touring market to newer downtown clubs and focused more on local bands, many of which have had a home there since it opened in the early 1970s. The Tipitina's Foundation raises money year-round and donates musical instruments to the public schools, reflecting the founders' dedication to the local music scene.

SETTING AND ATMOSPHERE A converted warehouse, Tip's is rough around the edges in terms of comfort. It was aggressively indifferent to amenities before the House of Blues provided a little competition. There's still room for improvement, say in the restroom department. The stage is small and the dance floor almost as intimate, but there is extra room on the second floor when the club fills up for big shows. When full, the dance floor can get pretty steamy, but there's nothing like sweating through a marathon show at Tip's.

IF YOU GO The music is all that matters at Tip's, so dress comfortably and be ready to dance or stand, because there is precious little seating. For big shows, definitely buy tickets in advance. When you get there, rub the bust of Professor Longhair for good luck.

Whiskey Blue

MARTINI BAR FOR THE IMAGE CONSCIOUS

W Hotel, 333 Poydras Street; ☎ 504-207-5016; www.gerberbars.com
Central Business District

Cover None. **Minimum** None. **Mixed drinks** $6–up. **Wine** $10–up. **Beer** $4–up. **Dress** Dress to impress—no shorts or baseball caps. Play it safe and wear black. **Specials** None. **Food available** No. **Disabled access** Yes. **Hours** Opens daily at 5 p.m.

WHO GOES THERE Fashionistas, beautiful people, visitors looking for a cosmopolitan club scene, hotel guests.

WHAT GOES ON As sleek, chic, and modern as the ambience at Whiskey Blue is, it's not typical of New Orleans. Created by Rande Gerber, it's an exotic fish in swampy water. The city has never really had a chic celebrity scene, but the decor here is set for one. There's always a bit of primping and fronting, and this is really a singles scene.

SETTING AND ATMOSPHERE Midnight blue radiates from the bar's backdrop and glistens off metallic surfaces. The minimalist decor features a long, tall cocktail island in the middle and some wide, low chaise lounges spread about. Most of the patrons are as buff as they are decked out, but this being New Orleans, the attitude is more friendly and less exclusive than in similar bars in other metropolitan centers. The velvet rope is rarely used, but there's probably one in storage. Piped-in urban beats tend to pulse at a level that isn't conducive to conversation, but window-shopping is more the mode here anyway.

IF YOU GO Dress up and go late. Hobnob a little, and tell everyone you own a mansion and a yacht. Slip into the stylish lobby of the W Hotel for a little change of pace or for easier conversation.

SUBJECT INDEX

Unofficial Guide Reader Survey

If you'd like to express your opinion about traveling in New Orleans or this guidebook, complete the following survey and mail it to:

Unofficial Guide Reader Survey
P.O. Box 43673
Birmingham, AL 35243

Inclusive dates of your visit:______________________________

Members of your party:

	Person 1	Person 2	Person 3	Person 4	Person 5
Gender:	M F	M F	M F	M F	M F

Age:______________________________

How many times have you been to New Orleans?______________
On your most recent trip, where did you stay?______________

Concerning your accommodations, on a scale of 100 as best and 0 as worst, how would you rate:

The quality of your room? The value of your room?
The quietness of your room? Check-in/checkout efficiency?
Shuttle service to the airport? Swimming pool facilities?

Did you rent a car?__________ From whom?______________

Concerning your rental car, on a scale of 100 as best and 0 as worst, how would you rate:

Pickup-processing efficiency?____ Return processing efficiency?___
Condition of the car?____ Cleanliness of the car?____
Airport shuttle efficiency?____

Concerning your dining experiences:

Estimate your meals in restaurants per day? ______________

Approximately how much did your party spend on meals per day?____

Favorite restaurants in New Orleans:______________________
____

Did you buy this guide before leaving? _____ While on your trip?_____

How did you hear about this guide? (check all that apply)

☐ Loaned or recommended by a friend ☐ Radio or TV
☐ Newspaper or magazine ☐ Bookstore salesperson
☐ Just picked it out on my own ☐ Library
☐ Internet

Unofficial Guide Reader Survey (*continued*)

What c

On a s ate them?

Using the same scale, how would you rate the *Unofficial Guide*(s)?

Are *Unofficial Guides* readily available at bookstores in your area?

Have you used other *Unofficial Guides*?

Which one(s)?

Comments about your New Orleans trip or the *Unofficial Guide*(s):